Social History of Africa

MONEY MATTERS

Social History of Africa
Series Editors: Allen Isaacman and Jean Hay

MONEY MATTERS

Instability, Values and Social Payments in the Modern History of West African Communities

edited by

Jane I. Guyer

HEINEMANN
Portsmouth, NH

JAMES CURREY
London

Heinemann   James Currey Ltd.
A division of Reed Elsevier Inc.   54b Thornhill Square,
361 Hanover Street   Islington
Portsmouth, NH 03801–3912   London N1 1BE
Offices and agents throughout the world

ISBN 0-435-08955-2 (Heinemann cloth)
ISBN 0-435-08957-9 (Heinemann paper)
ISBN 0-85255-665-9 (James Currey cloth)
ISBN 0-85255-615-2 (James Currey paper)

Library of Congress Cataloging-in-Publication Data
Guyer, Jane
    Money matters : instability, values and social payments in the modern
history of West African communities / edited by Jane I. Guyer.
        p.   cm. — (Social History of Africa)
    Includes bibliographical references and index.
    ISBN 0-435-08955-2 (cloth : acid-free paper). — ISBN
0-435-08957-9 (paper : acid-free paper)
        1. Money—Africa, West.   2. Africa, West—Economic conditions.
    3. Africa, West—Social conditions.   I. Guyer, Jane I.   II. Series.
    HG1370.M66   1994
    332.4'966—dc20   94–11804
                                                                CIP

British Library Cataloguing-in-Publication Data
Guyer, Jane
    Money Matters: Instability, Values and
    Social Payments in the Modern History of
    West African Communities. — (Social
    History of Africa Series)
        I. Guyer, Jane I.   II. Series
        332.4966

Cover design by Jenny Greenleaf.

About cover photograph: "Headman of Bébai (from the Esseng family) counting iron money. In the background a basket is used as a purse." Photograph circa 1910. Cover photograph and translated caption taken from *Die Pangwe* by Günter Tessman. Published by Ernst Wasmuth A.-G., Berlin 1913 p. 212.

Printed in the United States of America.
99   98   97   96   95   EB   1   2   3   4   5   6   7   8   9

CONTENTS

CONTRIBUTORS

Kwame Arhin, Professor, is Director of the Institute of African Studies, University of Ghana, Legon. A member of over the years of numerous national committees in Ghana and an authority on the history and society in Asante, he is the author of several monographs, including *West African Traders in the Nineteenth and Twentieth Centuries* (1980), the editor of *West African Colonial Civil Servants in the Nineteenth Century* (1985) and co-editor of *Marketing Boards in Tropical Africa* (1985).

Karin Barber is Senior Lecturer at the Center of West African Studies, University of Birmingham (U.K.). She researched and taught in western Nigeria for many years and has published extensively on Yorùbá culture. Her research interests include popular culture, oral literature, and religion. Her book on Yorùbá oral texts, *I Could Speak Until Tomorrow: Oriki Women and the Past in a Yorùbá Town,* was published in 1991. She is currently writing a book on Yorùbá popular theatre.

Sara S. Berry is Professor of History at Johns Hopkins University. She is author of *Cocoa, Custom and Socio-Economic Change in Rural Western Nigeria* (1975), *Fathers Work for their Sons: Accumulation, Mobility and Class Formation in an Extended Yorùbá Community* (1985), and *No Condition is Permanent* (1993). Her current research in Ghana is concerned with the history of land access.

Georges Dupré is Directeur de Recherches at the Institute Français de Recherche Scientifique pour le Developpement en Cooperation (ORSTOM) in Paris. He has published two monographs from research in the Congo, *Un Ordre et sa Destruction* (1992) and *Les Naissances d'une Société, Espace et Historicité chez les Beembe du Congo* (1985). He edited a collection entitled *Savoirs Paysons et Developpement,* and is currently finishing a monograph on agricultural and environmental history in Arabinda, Burkina Faso.

Marie-Claude Dupré is Chargée de Recherches at the Centre National de Recherche Scientifique (CNRS) in Paris. She has published widely on the history, political anthropology, semiology of art and the history of techniques of the Congo, including a Thèse d'Etat entitled "The Births and Rebirths of the Kidumu Mask: Art, Politics and History, University of Paris V.

Felica Ekejiuba, Professor of Anthropology, is UNIFEM Regional Program Advisor in Nigeria. Formerly Professor and Chair of the Department of Sociology, Anthropology and Social Work at the University of Nigeria, Nsukka, she has published widely on the history and culture of the Arochukwu, and on women's studies, and has co-authored a book with K. O. Dike.

Toyin Falola is Professor of African History at the University of Texas at Austin. He has published widely on Nigeria history and political economy, including a history of Ibadan. His current research interest is on Nigeria's political and economic transformations after the Second World War.

Jane I. Guyer is Director, Program of African Studies, Northwestern University. She is author of *Family and Farm in Southern Cameroon* (1984), editor of *Feeding African Cities* (1987), author of papers on change in the social organization of production and valuation in Cameroon and Nigeria. She is currently completing a monograph from a twenty-year re-study of a Nigerian agricultural community in the hinterland of Ibadan.

Robin Law is Professor of African History, University of Stirling, Scotland. He is author of *The Oyo Empire c. 1600–c. 1836* (1977), *The Horse in West African History* (1980) and *The Slave Coast of West Africa 1550–1750* (1991). He is currently working on an edited collection on the transition.

Akin L. Mabogunje is currently Chairman of the National Board of Community Banks in Nigeria. A geographer by training and professor and dean before retiring from academia, he has published widely on developmental issues and been active in development policy in Nigeria. His best known book-length works are *Urbanization in Nigeria* (1968) and *The Development Process: A Spatial Perspective* (1980).

Takyiwaa Manuah is Senior Research Fellow at the Institute of African Studies, Legon, and is currently a Ph.D. Student in Anthropology at Indiana University. A lawyer by training, she has conducted research on socio-legal and developmental issues relating to women in Ghana. Her publications include *Law and the Status of Women in Ghana* UNECA, Addis Ababa 1984; "The Asantehemaa's Court and its Jurisdiction over Women in Asante: A Study in Legal Pluralism," *Research Review* NS vol. 4, No. 2 1989; "Women and their Organizations during the Period of CPP Rule in Ghana" in K. Arhin (Ed.) *The Life and Work of Kwame Nkrumah,* African World Press, 1993; and "Women Traders in Ghana and the Structural Adjustment Program" (with G. Clark) in C. Gladwin (Ed.) *Structural Adjustment and African Women Farmers,* 1991, University of Florida Press.

Gwendolyn Mikell is Professor of Anthropology at Georgetown University. She is author of *Cocoa and Chaos in Ghana* (1989) and editor of *African Women: States of Crisis* (in press). She is currently working on a book entitled *Assault on Matriliny: Ghanaian Social Policy and Development* and will be starting new research on black family and the law in South Africa.

Parker Shipton, a social anthropologist, is a Research Associate at the Harvard Institute for International Development and a Lecturer in the Department of Anthropology, Harvard University. Holding a Ph.D. from Cambridge University, he has carried out intensive field research in Kenya and Sene-Gambia, and has published widely on cultural dimensions of agrarian economics and politics. His next book is *The Golden Pendulum: Culture, Credit and Debt in Western Kenya.*

PREFACE

This topic, and the importance of addressing it through a collective endeavor rather than an individually authored synthesis, took shape in my mind over the course of several years. I had worked since about 1984 on the indigenous currencies of Southern Cameroon and been inspired by an acquaintanceship with Marion Johnson. During the 1980s, when anthropology became definitively historical in approach, whatever I worked on seemed to pose with urgency and insistence the problem of "value," as created and recreated over time. Whether with respect to food prices in urban provisioning, taxes and public finance in the state sphere, intrahousehold income-management within production and consumption units, or the marriage payments within kinship and community groups (which I address in my own contribution), the volatility of the currency in relation to the creation of long-term value was strikingly evident. My first attempt at a general approach to money and value was a paper entitled, "'The Impact of Money' in Village Communities: Thoughts on Colonial Currencies and the Transformation of Values," written in 1987 for a conference on "New Perspectives on Colonial Africa," held at the University of Illinois at Urbana. The same paper was presented at a seminar at the Department of Anthropology, Cambridge University in 1988. There were many responses to this paper: positive, negative, and puzzled. And I was never satisfied with it. Suggestive though the directions of thinking might have been, the treatment was full of substantive gaps and conceptual weaknesses.

My experience of working with the twin difficulties of limited secondary sources and a very challenging conceptual problem that bridges the anthropology of value and the economic history of imperial capitalism persuaded me that a collection of papers by scholars who had access to primary sources in different places for different periods of history, and who had addressed the issues from different disciplinary standpoints and different national traditions of scholarship, would constitute a much richer contribution than possibly could be compiled at this stage by a single author. In particular, African colleagues clearly had a much more intimate sense of the idiosyncrasies of modern monetary history in local communities—having lived it—than all but the most focused of outside scholars. Their insights and descriptions add new information, a sense of life-challenge, and local idioms for everything from practical storage to poetic meaning, which are missing from accounts focused solely on economic analysis. Then as the late 1980s unfolded, currency instability in the wider world took on new prominence. Scholars who had already worked on currency issues found instability an increasingly plausible theme and those for whom the topic had been tangential found new inspiration to search their notes and field projects for relevant material. In general then, once some of the issues were posed, the potential contributors whom I contacted rose to—and far beyond—the initial agenda that I set from the vantage point of my own concerns.

Common themes have emerged from ongoing discussion, while at the same time the present volume preserves some of the variety of approach that I was hoping to garner. The contributors are Nigerian, Ghanaian, French, British, and American. By discipline, they are mainly anthropologists and historians, primarily although not exclusively with an emphasis on economic life. Manuh is a lawyer and social scientist; Mabogunje—a geographer by training—participates by virtue of his current chairmanship of the Nigerian National Board for Community Banks; Barber is a scholar of literature and performance.

The introduction and most of the papers in this collection were presented at a conference entitled "Instability and Values in West Africa: Currencies and Social Payments in Long Term Perspective," held at the Institute of African Studies, the University of Ghana, Legon, June 16–18, 1992. We all owe a debt to Professor Kwame Arhin, without whose enthusiasm for the project we would probably never have managed a meeting at all. He invited us to Legon, supported the proposal, organized the local arrangements and participated insightfully in all the sessions. Takyiwaa Manuh was the first colleague to suggest that we hold a meeting, and she generously helped to organize and host it, as well as make her own intellectual contribution. Felix Iroko enlivened our discussions in Legon but was unable to contribute to the book.

The workshop and some of the publication costs have been financed by the Wenner-Gren Foundation for Anthropological Research in New York. The attendance of Felicia Ekejiuba and Felix Iroko was generously supported by the Council for the Development of Social and Economic Research in Africa (CODESRIA) in Dakar. The manuscript was commented on in generous detail by Jan Hogendorn and Barbara Cooper. Marc Sommers helped with initial editorial work, and the final manuscript was expertly edited by Julie Croston.

The completion of this project owes everything to the commitment of these people, these organizations, and above all the contributors. Several participants have had pressing political and professional obligations in Africa over the two years of the project. Everyone has had many other concerns and deadlines. It is the critical nature of the currency issues that has kept us all engaged. As the final manuscript goes off to the press, the instability of currencies and the necessary inventiveness of their users have intensified, not only in Africa but elsewhere in the world. My colleague Sutti Ortiz has shown me a note printed and distributed independently by the government of the Argentinian province of Tucuman last year when the central currency allocations proved inadequate for regional transactions. The value of the *zaire* quoted in my introduction as 5 million to the dollar suddenly plummeted between October and December 1993 from 8 million to 110 million. Undeterred, money traders still gather in the narrow alley known as "Wall Street" across from the U.S. Embassy to speculate on the exchange rate.[1] Other cases keep emerging, from Serbia to Iran.

And the troubadours of popular culture keep up the tradition of commentary analyzed by Karin Barber for the Yoruba. When we gathered in Legon in 1992, one of Ghana's favorite songs was entitled "*Sika Asem.*" *Sika* is the Twi word for gold, which became the generic term for money in the twentieth century. *Asem*, roughly translated, means "matters." Because of the historical resonance of the Twi word, and because the sentiments of the song excerpted below capture the contemporary phase of the long history of money in communities that we broach in the collection, we used it as the inspiration for the title.

"It is a matter of money. It is a matter of money.
It is money which makes the elder become a child . . .
It is because of money that I am always travelling . . .
Because of money all my bright ideas are left unrealized . . .
It is a matter of money."[2]

Notes

1. Kenneth B. Noble, "Zaire Is In Turmoil After the Currency Collapses." *New York Times International,* December 12, 1993.
2. Lumba Brothers, "Sika Asem," 1990. Excerpts from lyrics translated by Takyiwaa Manuh.

Introduction: The Currency Interface and Its Dynamics

JANE I. GUYER

Over thirty years ago, Paul Bohannan proposed that the "impact of money" in Africa—that is, colonial currency—had been to dissolve old systems of currency use. "[I]n an African economy which had known only local trade and had used only special purpose money" that was designated by a moral code of acceptable equivalences for only certain kinds of exchange, general purpose money would come as "one of the shatteringly simplifying ideas of all time ... [which] creates it own revolution" (1959:492, 503). Historians took up and developed the concept of a "currency revolution" (Hopkins 1966; Ofonagoro 1979b). It is this terrain that our collection reexplores. The introduction takes a more distant vantage point, setting a historical and analytical context for compiling papers by scholars from different disciplines, covering a hundred years or more of historical change, for the circumscribed region of West and Equatorial Africa. The chapters focus closely on social, economic and cultural dynamics within particular local communities, over one phase or another, of the broad scope covered by the collection as a whole.

The concept of a currency revolution was profoundly provocative in the context of either the traditionalist theoretical focus of anthropology or the gradualist thinking of modernization theory. And certainly there have been critical moments in West African currency history. The further the colonial era recedes into the past, however, and the more closely one looks at communities rather than states, the less adequate seems the concept of "revolution," with its implications of two different states of being, one of which totally supplants the other. Advances in knowledge about African pre-colonial currency systems suggest that they had *more* modern "purposes" and characteristics than was thought in the past, and that twentieth century monies clearly have *fewer*. Bohannan himself noted that the metal rods that "hold a pivotal position" in Tiv exchange were "[o]riginally imported from Europe" (1959:498). Dorward (1975:438) points out that the Tiv-made cloth that circulated within the same indigenously defined "sphere of exchange" as the metal rods, was being exported for use as currency throughout Northern Nigeria, a region that had one of the most active commercial economies of the time, linked by long-distance trade to the entire Western Sudan and across the desert to North Africa (Dorward 1976). Pre-colonial currencies in Africa were often regional rather than local, and they were rapidly changing and developing throughout the era of the slave trade, potentially or actually permeating new "purposes" beyond those that can be satisfactorily contained within the designation of "special."

Colonial currencies, by comparison, were indeed "modern" in that they were issued and controlled by government and used for a wider variety of "purposes," notably including tax payment. But they were not *as* "all purpose" as twentieth-century European currencies, mainly—as I will explore in more detail later—in that the relationship between deposits of wealth and the creation of money through negotiable debt instruments was kept much less sophisticated for colonial currency than in the highly troubled but highly experimental metropolitan financial systems. In the immediate pre- and post-colonial period new financial institutions and new currencies were created, provoking both turbulent and cautious experimentation. For most of this period, however, money stayed within bounds set by relations to the former imperial power. Innovations were just picking up when the stability of the Bretton Woods era began to disintegrate and the currencies of the world became market goods. Suddenly the new post-colonial currencies of anglophone Africa became "soft," and thereby even more divergent from the current European hard currencies in the purposes that they fulfill and the capacities that they confer. A Swiss bank employee gave the extreme example: in the early 1990s, the currency of Zaire became unacceptable because in the era of electronic transfers in the vast money market of the world, when banks are staffed by highly paid experts, it would be prohibitively expensive simply to count the bills.

With this broader knowledge over the greater time depth now afforded us, it is no longer plausible to frame our thinking about African currency history in terms of the revolutionary replacement of an absolute difference between "primitive" and "modern" monies by a total victory of "modern" money. And not because, empirically, people may still use cowries—or iron anvils, or lengths of cloth, or enamel bowls—for certain transactions, but because, theoretically, the "modern" must be seen as intrinsically dynamic, continually creating new kinds of *relative* "primitiveness." Modern monies and the financial instruments that generate them continue to change, their capacities elaborated far beyond the simplicity of the classic "functions of money" defined by Aristotle and still repeated in texts: a store of wealth, a means of payment, a unit of account, and a medium of exchange (see, for example, Neale 1976). Even though the modern money systems of the 1950s—when Bohannan wrote his seminal article—fulfilled all these purposes, they are themselves primitive by comparison with the same currency systems in the 1990s. Africa's monies have developed, from almost as far back as can be traced, in a continuous though shifting relationship to these changing monies of Europe. While they have *never* been "primitive" in the absolute sense, they have *always* been—by various dynamics—"primitive" or "special purpose" relative to the capacities of their contemporary European counterparts.

African communities, therefore, have not so much braced or given in before an "impact." Rather, they have lived continuously, for several centuries, at an interface of econo-logical zones. As in the case of ecological borderlands, the compositions on each side and even the locations of the meeting zone have shifted, while the fact of a "divide" has been constant. Every few years throughout their entire history, Africans have incorporated currency change of varying provenance: radical shifts in the prices of goods, the range of goods to which money could be applied, the capacities of that money as a financial resource, the financial institutions to which they had access, and the physical nature of the acceptable currency. Zaire's recent experience with a forced return to something other than bank money has its own particularities, but it can serve as an extreme example:

> Zaire's banking association says the central African country's 12 commercial banks will close indefinitely on Monday because of cash shortage. The association said on Friday that it needed 10 trillion zaires a month for its clients, but only gets 480 billion monthly from the central bank. The zaire currency has become nearly worthless—the largest denomination bill, 100,000 zaire is worth less than $1. (*New York Times*, April 19, 1992.)

Less than a year later a 5-million zaire banknote was worth about $2, and was printed at an expense in Germany that must begin to creep up towards the face value of the bills. Merchants' reluctance to accept the new issue provoked violent confrontations in Kinshasa in which about 300 people are said to have died, the parliament buildings were taken over and "several hundred" members were held hostage (*New York Times*, February 26, 1993).

There have been other more local dramas, such as the recent large counterfeit issue of new Nigerian bills noted by Ekejiuba (see Ch. 6), probably printed in much lower quality and at much lower cost outside Europe. "Money Magicians" appear, promising extraordinary interest rates (*African Concord* 1992, 7:26). Most African countries outside the franc-zone have witnessed an abundance of smaller volatilities: bills issued with new faces on them (giving rise to a whole vernacular of monetary terms in Nigeria), new official names, new denominations, new colors, and new materials. Falling values require new means of bulking; one now works in uncounted and unpacked "briques" of notes in Zaire, and shops for anything substantial with a plastic bag of money in Ghana. The very state that was intended, with a certain heroic fervor, to reduce all the perceived uncertainties of pre-colonial currencies then seen as "riddled with imperfections" (McPhee 1926:234), now generates unpredictabilities by failing to pay altogether for the goods delivered by its own people. Witness the recent report from Northern Ghana that 30,000 farmers have not been paid for the cotton that they delivered to the Ghana Cotton Co. (a parastatal) due to the inability of textile companies to market their cloth (*West Africa*, January 11–17, 1993, page 25).

The longer historical record suggests that the present relatively chaotic situation can be seen—possibly analytically but certainly experientially— as a new phase in an old tale. Currency has been needed in large quantities to make relatively small payments before (see Law, Ch. 2); it has also been in short supply (see Arhin, Ch. 4), over-perishable, under-usable and straight counterfeit (see G. Dupré, Ch. 3). During moments when the supply "expanded spectacularly," people have worried about "boundless, baseless fortunes" and prayed for money to come in "little by little" (Barber 1982:431, 448, 450). For these reasons—changeability as an attribute and recurrent challenge as an experience —we orient this present collection to exploring the single most important aspect of the currency interface over the *longue durée,* namely its instability.

West and Equatorial Africa have a certain historical unity in this respect. Despite an internal diversity in currency history so vast as to have defied any integrated summary,[1] the entire area has been linked into European and transatlantic trade over very long periods in a way that the other economies of Africa have not. For the twentieth century also, the economic expansion is more similar within West and Equatorial Africa than it is across regional boundaries into East and Southern Africa. Colonial policies were regional: the West African Currency Board, founded in 1912, issued colonial currency for all of British West Africa (Hopkins 1970), and the franc of the Communauté Financière Africaine (CFA) was created for French West and Equatorial Africa in 1939, after interdictions had been placed on international trade and financial transactions between France and the "exterior" (Bourdin 1980; Vallée 1989). Although national monetary policies have diverged since Independence, a commonality of conditions continues to unite these countries: the importance of particular agricultural products and minerals to earn foreign exchange, links to the economies of the old colonial powers, substantial internal migration within the region from one country to another, highly permeable borders that have remained open to many old and new trade networks, and regional formal organizations such as ECOWAS and UDEAC.[2] Local communities across the region are linked into these networks in one way or another and find themselves deeply affected by shifts in the international exchange rates: pools of migrant farm labor are created or dry up overnight according to the exchange rate of the franc CFA against the anglophone-country currencies; the cattle trade across the Nigeria/Niger border orients itself north or south, and the rice trade across the Nigeria/Cameroon border orients itself east or west, in accordance with exchange rates; the Lobi—astride the Ghana/Burkina Faso border—store away or bring out their cowries, the Sierra Leone diamond trade surges or recedes, and the money changers in Maiduguri market or Ibadan's Sabon Gari adjust their rates. In spite of formal inconvertibility, and perhaps in some senses because of it, the networks of international linkage within West and Equatorial Africa are dense and their activities are lively (MacGaffey 1991). Again, there is a certain unity to regional history, and this justifies the geographical limits of our contributions.

The themes of the collection are oriented in one way or another around three main concepts, with greatest emphasis on the last: *the persistent interface* that has framed the relative "primitiveness" or "special purpose" character of African currencies, *the concomitant instability* of monetary conditions within Africa, and the resulting *ways in which money matters* within African communities. Because currency has not generally been described within this long-term framework, one of our main aims is empirical documentation. The contributors take social historical, cultural and policy approaches to the local communities in which anthropologists and social historians have generally worked—the contexts in which most people live most of their lives— rather than the macro-political and economic contexts in which some of the parameters of valuation are set. We address the linkage to the macro-arenas from the local vantage point. Our collective aim is to infer and to understand the principles by which changes and instabilities have been assimilated or embraced within communities.

Cumulatively, the chapters illustrate recurrent themes. Clearly the changes that we describe have not fulfilled—at least not yet and not in a dramatic cataclysm— Keynes' dictum that "There is no subtler, surer means of overturning the existing basis of society than to debauch the currency" (quoted in Ofonagoro 1979a:277).

Indeed, Africa exemplifies the possibility of a different condition of monetary existence that falls somewhere between florescence and collapse. But it is a much more subtle and difficult question whether or not chronic instability has been of a kind or a level to result—as Adam Smith said of the chronic uncertainties with which peasants lived under the French *Ancien Régime*—in a "fear of the arbitrary [that] did even more harm that its vexations" (quoted in Ardant 1965:204). Thinkers of Smith's era were acutely conscious of the dangers of unpredictability, in their own case largely associated with taxation. Von Thünen, for example, stated unequivocally "that taxes that are unequal are a far smaller evil than those that change frequently" ([1826]1966:210).

Does chronic instability stemming from the currency interface in the nineteenth and twentieth centuries in Africa have similar effects as the uncertainty stemming from capricious taxation in the eighteenth century in Europe? Some scholars imply, somewhat to the contrary, that Africans' long and complex experience with currency change has actually honed their skills at rapid adjustment to maintain the crucial equivalences of social life. If money has never been stable, possibly valuation is highly responsive, as Fernandez implies for Fang bridewealth: "Despite very great fluctuations in colonial currency, the real value of the woman had remained the same over the years . . . There were thus more enduring motifs and thematic values behind the busy buying and selling which took place" (1982:148). Georges Dupré also documents extraordinary persistence in the value of social payments (1982:336). If people have never lived under conditions in which money was really controled by a central power, possibly their imaginations are less bankrupt than their purses in the face of the Zaire kind of situation. Possibly, then, it is not the arbitrariness of instability but its seeming inescapability ("fear" as Adam Smith puts it) that produced the sullen atomism of peasant life noted by so many theorists of Europe. From simple experience, it would be hard to argue that West Africans have been utterly discouraged and defeated by instability. In fact, there has been a long slow process of growth in financial institutions predicated on inter-temporal transactions, some of them carefully planned and advocated in the political arena (see Mabogunje, Ch. 12). Hope seems to spring eternal in ways that need analysis.

On this major interpretive issue, we cannot summarize a single inference from our several contributions; the participants are probably of different minds and each chapter adds its own slant. But in struggling with the cultural meaning and systemic implications of currency instability, we do attempt to add to the analytical vocabulary and, most fundamentally, to open up questions that have remained secondary so far. Money may be *merely* the means by which characteristic surplus extraction takes place, as in the Marxist formulation, or *merely* an indicator of capacity and confidence in the neoclassical formulation (see Berry, Ch. 13). Money *can* be treated in this way, as an indicator rather than as a fundamental phenomenon in itself; and it can be treated much more literally, as an object invested by its users with a whole penumbra of meanings (Simmel [1900]1990; Crump 1981; Parry and Bloch 1989). But two facts encourage us to bring money forward again into a more political economic as well as cultural inquiry, and to try to marry the two. The first is its variety in the present world: a variety produced by state and supra-state institutions (Hart 1986), which gives rise to the interfaces on which most of the world lives. The second is that money is probably the single most important "thing/good" in ordinary people's ordinary lives. Thinking about it, planning, consulting about and paying bills, not to mention worrying (that is, producing a folk theory), takes more time and imagination than much else. And professional thinking about money is probably among the most obsessively concentrated activities that the human mind has every invented; a currency trader writes "there are weeks when I trade nearly around the clock . . . I'm hooked" (Krieger 1992:8). Inventions around money management have grown in startling surges: the Florentine banking system of the thirteenth century (Veseth 1990), the British financial revolution of the late seventeenth century (Dickson 1967), the liberal revolution in the nineteenth (Reddy 1987), the construction in the past twenty years of the biggest market in the world, the international currency market (Sampson 1990). Money is not *merely* anything. It is a vastly important reality to vast numbers of people, all but an infinitesimal number of whom have absolutely no idea of the official doctrines under which it "makes sense," but whose own constructions—the bases of "confidence"—are a necessary component of that "sense" as it works out in practice. In the metropolitan centers, ordinary people struggle to make their own sense of money in a world in which a given quantity "means utterly different things to different people" (Reddy 1987:32). Even intellectuals' commentaries are poised in "uneasy balance" between "[t]hese two ideas—of the fairness of money and of the inherent superiority of the wealthy" (Reddy 1987:32). For those living on currency interfaces, the imagination has to be yet more nimble.

We are not attempting, here, to grapple directly with the official doctrines, with what Crump refers to as "the esoteric tradition," in the theory of money (1981:29). But neither can the context in which money has been created over the past centuries be completely held in abeyance, as it seems to be in culturalist work (Appadurai 1986; Parry and Bloch 1989). Rather, we extend Hart's approach (1986) to the money of the state and the money of the market to include the money of people's experience, and use the latter to read into the other two, to reconfigure them from the concerns of anthropology and history. The remainder of this introduction explores in general terms (a) the permanent currency interface that sets the context for West African monetary studies, (b) the sources and kinds of instability that West Africa has seen, and finally (c) some of the empirical foci and analytical concepts relevant to the chapters.

The Permanent Currency Interface: A Brief Macro-History

To take instability as an empirical theme with respect to money is to work across the grain of the stated rationale for money to exist, namely that it is a medium for intertemporal transactions. Keynes cut to the core when he suggested that "money is a link between the present and the future" (Jevons 1875:31 quoted in Einzig 1949:368). In all functional analyses of monetary systems, the theoretical elaborations rest on the related premises that money is stable and thereby acceptable for deferred payments, and that it circulates in a closed system. Niehans' textbook summary can stand as an example: it is based on "a general equilibrium framework" and "analysis . . . confined to a closed economy in which all money is noncommodity or token currency supplied by the government" (1978:1, 200). The centrality of the idea of stability is very old, associated for centuries in Eurasian thought with gold. Marx begins his discussion of money: "Throughout this work, I assume for the sake of simplicity, gold as the money commodity" (Marx [1954] 1977:25). Einzig quotes Jevons on the attributes of money: utility and value, portability, indestructibility, homogeneity, divisibility, *stability of value* and cognizability (1949:330; my emphasis). Galbraith quotes Ricardo: "a currency, to be perfect, should be absolutely invariable in value" (Ricardo 1951:58, quoted in Galbraith 1975:37). Indeed, Melitz takes stability as the critical difference between primitive and modern monies.[3] Primitive commodity currencies can be over-produced at home or under-controled in their import from outside, and they may deteriorate rapidly in use. Melitz claims that "the advance of currency among primitives in the last hundred years is partly a reflection of the *relatively* greater stability of the value of modern currency than the major primitive monies over *most* of this period" (1974:125; emphasis in the original). Extraordinary ingenuity has gone into the attempt to make it so, following the demise of the gold standard: the Bretton Woods agreement reached towards the end of World War II (see Schweitzer 1972), superceded by a vast currency market in which changes in the second or third decimal point in a currency's value bring about a flood of transactions (Krieger 1992) and which is heavily critiqued by advocates of "alternative monetary regimes" (Campbell and Dougan 1986), who are deeply concerned about potential market instability. Stability is an absolutely vital component of modern economies that are predicated on negotiable debt instruments: not necessarily that money must always *be* stable, but that people *believe* stability to be its nature and wide fluctuation to be a treatable pathology. All evidence on the soft currencies to the contrary, economic development approaches have rested on a profound commitment to the notion that prices can be relatively stable, both over time, and to some degree and for important commodities, relative to each other. This is reflected in the concept of "rightness" in the 1980s aim of "getting the prices right."

If we start however, as anthropologists and historians, from people's experience, we can experiment with a different standpoint, from a different set of premises. West Africa's pre-colonial currency systems as we know them are not *ab initio,* or *sui generis* developments within closed systems, but rather configurations largely developed in the context of the Atlantic trade. Tokens used in various types of exchange do predate the trade: iron and then gold in Ghana (Arhin, Ch. 4), copper croisettes in the Southern Congo region (de Maret 1981), *nzimbu* shells in Kongo (Hilton 1985). But the historical record has illuminated such a vast currency import and currency production within Africa in subsequent centuries as to justify taking the interface as the condition of African monetary development for at least the past three centuries. Curtin suggests that West African gold was important in North Africa from at least the end of the first millenium (1983:241). For more recent centuries, as Hopkins writes tersely: "Traditionally, money required in West Africa for commercial purposes was supplied by the merchants who traded there. They ordered, shipped, and issued the various transitional currencies produced in Europe . . ." (1970:107). Sources for Equatorial Africa note the import of *mitakos* and neptunes, and the creation of tokens and company scrip (Vansina 1990; Coquery-Vidrovitch 1972; Samarin 1989; Antoine 1986; Eggert 1980; G. Dupré, Ch. 3). Hogendorn and Johnson give the figure of almost 36,000 tons of cowries (14 billion shells) shipped into Africa by five German and French companies between 1851 and 1869 alone (1986:75-6).

On the local production side, Herbert suggests as a "very conservative calculation" that the amounts of copper in use and circulation by the end of the nineteenth century, a substantial proportion of which was Africa-made, at 50,000 tons and possibly double that figure (1984:181). Warnier and Fowler (1979) were so impressed by the slag heaps from iron production in the Ndop Plains in Cameroon, some of whose product went into currency circuits, that they depicted it as a "Ruhr," after the center of German heavy industry. The currency collection from Equatorial Africa alone that is housed in the Belgian Royal Museum of Central Africa contains at least 120 different shapes and sizes of metallic currencies (Guyer 1993). The amounts of *nzimbu* shells and cloth currencies in use are simply incalculable. The two processes fed into one another: currency import, and local currency development through both domestication and production.

Given the interpenetrating synergies of these processes, conceptualizing them in a manner applicable to the whole moving configuration is a challenge. Rather than develop new words, I use here some familiar terms placed in a changed relationship to each other. The basic assumption is that of the "interface": a point of meeting where difference was maintained, albeit on changing bases and with changing terms. For currency constructions that were clearly formulated, or borrowed and successfully institutionalized, within African communities I use the term "original." For currency constructions in Africa that are clearly based on a contrast created by Europeans for use at the interface, I have been tempted to use the term "primitive," because their "limited or special purposes" were clearly envisaged and intended, relative to the contemporary European monies. While Europeans did use them, they were not convertible, could not be banked, and were not applicable to the acquisition of European assets. But given the meanings already attributed to "primitive money" and "special purpose monies," it is probably wise to avoid these terms, even though they quite precisely capture the nature of the currencies imported by Europeans for sole use within Africa. They are perhaps best referred to as "interface currencies": that is, currencies largely created from the outside, and whose capacities to permeate economic relationships across the borderland were kept limited.

If we focus on the interface, the major questions become: how have African currencies become interface currencies? How have they developed and retained their features in a changing monetary world? And what relationship have they had to the originalities of African currency constitution? One underlying hypothesis is that the interface currencies have induced instabilities, while the original qualities of indigenous currency culture may have—under some circumstances—the capacity to mitigate them. But this is only a hunch, only a working suggestion, a lens through which to see the world in a different way. The door is held open for a variety of other possible dynamics, and final conclusions are left open for debate.

On what changing qualities, then, has the special purpose nature of Africa's interface currencies rested? Braudel writes of the early modern period in Europe, "Like ocean navigation or printing, money and credit are techniques, which can be reproduced and perpetuated.... Money rushed to the service of monetary techniques" (1981:477). The metropolitan history of money and monetary management suggests the centrality of the ramifying techniques for creating and managing new relationships between, to use Keynes' definition, the present and the future: concretely, the institutional frameworks for debt. As Galbraith writes, the Bank of England "is to money as St. Peter's is to the Faith" (1975:30). According to a prominent banker (John Reed of Citicorp), three hundred years after the foundation of the Old Lady of Threadneedle Street, of the five billion people in the world, "probably 4.2 billion are living within societies that in some very fundamental way are not bankable" and "The new economic atlas left out large areas and populations from its money maps . . . it omitted almost the whole of one continent: Africa" (Sampson 1990:209, 217). In brief, African interface currencies have rarely played a full role in the credit and debt systems that underlie capitalism and are mediated by the banks.

Analytically this means that we need to go beyond listing the "functions of money" in an additive manner that is intellectually indebted to evolutionary frames of thought: the more advanced the money, the more functions are added. We need instead to ask about the changing relation amongst the functions. For interface currencies, some functions were always more important than others. Money earned for tax payment alone, for example, not only "had" only two functions—as a means of payment (of taxes) and a medium of exchange (for the produce bought)—but those two functions formed a short, closed, mutually reinforcing loop without passing through investment in assets and the generation of credit, or even in some cases, purchases for consumption. Neither was the money earned in amounts beyond what was needed for the function of "payment" amenable to all the purposes the holders of comparable metropolitan currencies would have had available.

The most critical relationship in capitalist systems is between money as a medium of exchange and stores of wealth. In the developed systems, there has been vast inventiveness in designating and institutionalizing those stores of wealth that can back the issue of money, and in which money can be invested in the endless cycle of debt creation and payment: stocks; bonds; house mortgages; insurance policies; pension payments; and a whole range of other assets, including educational investment, estimated earning power, and past history of bill payment (credit rating). At the fringe, there are antiques, art, baseball cards, and so on. In situations in which those institutions are *not* embedded in the banking system, the public debt and the law, the entire cycle between stores of wealth and media of exchange is radically contained in its potential, and open to a highly varied range of locally specific struggles and resolutions. The macro-picture of the history of the relationship between assets and money in West Africa lies outside our frame of reference, but the phases of its local and regional history form the essential context for our chapters about local struggles and resolutions, so they are outlined briefly below.

The basic reality of West African pre-colonial currencies is that, even though many were "issued" from European sources, they were not convertible and therefore could not be used to acquire European assets. Billions of cowries were used by European traders to purchase goods from Africans, but were unacceptable to purchase goods from Europeans or to invest in bank deposits (Hogendorn and Johnson 1986). For a very long period, Hogendorn and Johnson argue, the lack of evidence for inflation suggests that these uncontrollable waves of cowry imports were absorbed within African societies: in their own opinion, through expanded market exchange and, in Webb's (1982) formulation, possibly to vastly expanded hoarding by political leaders. Iroko (1987) describes such storage houses, a hundred meters long. In only one case, do the stores seem to have been transformed into loan sources: at very high rates of interest, and always subject to default, appropriation as forced tribute, and simple physical destruction. Eventually, however, inflation set in *pari passu* with the expansion of legitimate trade in export crops. Chapter 2 addresses some of the implications of nonconvertibility and value instability for Dahomey, where the state clearly pursued a currency policy and pooled money wealth. The case that Law describes had certain features that applied more generally: that the cowries, hoe blanks, copper mitakos and so on never entitled the holder to free purchase of either goods or assets at the interface with Europe, and they therefore surged through African channels of distribution with no escape.

By the time that Africa became part of the colonial world, the financial infrastructures of the colonial powers included: the Public Debt, central banks, and the joint stock company (developed in the late seventeenth century, see Dickson 1967), state-issued paper money (the assignats of the French revolutionary period), checks as credit instruments (early nineteenth century, see Bloch 1954), the promotion of municipal incorporation facilitating bond issue (nineteenth century, see Thane 1990) and state monopoly of currency issue (the early twentieth century, see Born 1984). Countries borrowed and adapted each other's financial instruments: England in the eighteenth century forged ahead with the Dutch system of a land registry to provide collateral and stimulate banking (Dickson 1967:5-7); Germany mobilized the Dutch-English system of long-term government bonds in the nineteenth century (Homer and Sylla 1991:502). Debt was built upon debt, backed ultimately by economic and political stability, the efficiency of state fiscal systems, the political ability to promote and protect trade, the value placed on land and access to international sources of capital. The proliferation of asset creation and credit instruments continued: insurance gradually developed over several centuries, mortgages and building societies for the expansion of owner-occupier housing in the early twentieth century (Daunton 1990), and eventually pension plans. At any one time, the financial system was therefore a highly dynamic configuration of instruments rather than a single coherent system of functions.

Policy was experimental, especially in the colonial world. Writing about the combinations of financial policies during a period often looked back to as a golden age of simplicity, the period of the international gold standard from 1870 to 1914 , de Cecco suggests that far from being logical and internally coherent, "international economic events followed a pattern which could not possibly be called automatic . . . [U]ncertain and even downright contradictory economic policies were adopted" (1984:61). In matters of finance, fine print could change the course of history, for small communities as well as great nations. As Hopkins (1973) points out, it was a part of the complex of fine print—the limited liability company, bankruptcy provisions and various institutional supports such as currency arrangements with the Mint— that gave the large European companies such a major advantage over African and other small business in the late pre-colonial and early colonial periods.

The imposition of colonial currencies entailed the abrogation of the pre-existing interface currencies, including the Asante gold system that actually already embodied some of the qualities of modern money; it was, by definition, on the gold standard, and it was controlled by the Asante state (see Arhin, Ch. 4). The heyday of colonial rule is marked by devastating currency dilemmas in Europe. By integrating the colonial economies directly into the circuit of metropolitan currency Europe opened itself not only to the repatriation of profits but also the dangers of losses and transported crises at a time when it was itself very vulnerable. If money circulating in the colonies was either hoarded or suddenly released, the shock waves would be felt in the domestic economy. Under these conditions, the metropolitan powers exercised extremely conservative policies with respect to their colonies' finances. At the time that it was introduced, the colonial cash that replaced the "indigenous" currencies was experimental, both in Africa and in the financial centers. Coins of various denominations and paper money were tried out for their convenience in market exchange and suitability for official payments, and their dynamics against the still-circulating older media were noted (McPhee 1926). More seriously for long term policy, the Treasury and Colonial Office in Britain and their counterparts in France were deeply concerned about over-issue of a currency in West Africa, which, in principle, could flood back into the mother country because of convertibility. To prevent instabilities in West Africa from causing instabilities at home, the currency supply to the colonies was strictly limited, and kept backed by the sterling reserves earned through trade (Hopkins 1970). This policy persisted more or less throughout the colonial period in British Africa, severely restricting the possibilities for the colonies to use their own assets in sterling to create credit.

It is worth pausing over these conditions because they do not figure very strongly in the social history of colonial Africa. If regulations had partially released colonial currency institutions from 100 percent liquidity in sterling, more lucrative and productive investments could have been made with the capital. The stock of francs CFA in circulation, still convertible with the French franc to the present, was and still (as of 1993) is pegged to the level of exports. Both policies have kept money supply low and credit institutions weak, not only because of any putative weakness of African economies but because of the possible repercussions of any rapid fluctuations in colonial money use, given convertibility, for the metropolitan money supply. Drawing attention to metropolitan banking history, a critic wrote "No banker finds it necessary to have his deposit liabilities covered by 100 percent liquid reserves. If this were so banking would never have started" (Analyst 1954:107). The strongest critiques came from the West Indies (see Analyst 1954; Hazelwood 1954; Earle 1954), but not until the 1950s, well after the major powers had set about, and substantially succeeded in, completely recreating the German and Japanese currencies and financial institutions after World War II. The capacities were clearly there to create assets, but only given conditions judged to justify long-term credit-worthiness.

Certain portions of the Empires—including Africa—were tied more tightly to reserves than others. Britain's currency relationship with India was very different from her relationship with West Africa and the West Indies; it was such a huge market, with a high demand for sterling coin, that it could perform the obverse functions of taking the pressure off over-issue of coinage in Britain (Hopkins 1970) and "keep-[ing] London the centre of the international monetary system" (de Cecco 1984:62). Kay makes a similar argument for private investment in Ghana, that the interests of particular London investors clearly affected the entire financial policy of the colonial government, promoting railway development at the expense of roads, building up seasonal pressures on the transport system, ultimately fierce competition and a decline in road haulage costs, and eventual political confrontations (1972:20–25,30). More broadly, it appears from the 1950s debates that during the Depression in West Africa, the amount of currency remaining in circulation was only about one fourth of the peak amount for the interwar years, a decline that was intensified by the requirement of 100 percent sterling backing which "amplified internal effects of swings in the balance of payments" (Hazelwood 1954:307). In brief, the currency situation in the colonial world was managed to meet the changing needs of the metropolis. Under conditions of convertibility, for Africa this meant severe restriction on money creation through credit.

Money wealth that was accumulated in Africa through new economic possibilities could hardly be stored, used, and leveraged for formal sector credit or future advantage. It was general practice by the foreign commercial banks throughout the colonial period to limit the access of African businessmen to credit. In Ghana, the Company Act of 1906 prevented the establishment of any local company to carry out any form of banking; the Act was only abrogated in the 1950s (Onoh 1982:95). Falola's chapter points out the strict limitations placed on money lending in Nigeria in the 1930s, so that banking functions could not be taken over from the established institutions. A Cameroonian businessman who founded his career during the colonial period pointed out to me that he was not allowed, on pain of administrative punishment under the *indigénat*, to carry more than a small amount of cash on his person (personal communication, Simon Bikie Noah, Yaoundé, 1984). In Nigeria in the 1950s, new pools of potential investment funds—such as regional government revenue funds and parastatal stabilization funds—were beginning to be controlled by Nigerians, fueled by nationalist discontent with the credit and banking situation and promoting the mushrooming growth in indigenous banks, many of which ultimately failed.[4] The Newlyn and Rowan Report of 1954 concluded that banks had little contact with Africans, a situation that had only shifted in fairly limited ways ten years later due to low confidence in the new indigenous banks and the decline of Post Office Savings (Brown 1964:183). As Mabogunje points out, Post Office Savings might have been a focus of financial asset creation for ordinary Africans, but the capital was entirely invested elsewhere instead of being used as a loan fund for the members. By design or default, and for a variety of reasons that included the retention of collective landholding and the assessment of African borrowers as high risk, formal sector credit was kept very limited. Even now in most cities of most African countries it is impossible to buy a house through a mortgage. The synergy of growth in production and growth in formal sector credit institutions that characterized, for example, British rural development in the eighteenth and nineteenth centuries (Pressnell 1956) has a very fitful and checkered history in Africa. For the colonial period, Africa had convertibility but not financial instruments at the interface. As Falola (Ch. 7) shows, people created their own modes of converting wealth into credit, within their own institutional frameworks.

This paucity of credit instruments applies in the long run to collectivities as well as to private persons. Formal sector collective funds were promoted in some places in Africa under colonial rule, but their history remains to be written. In Europe and America, the taxable capacity of municipal and local governments provided the "asset" against which bonds could be floated for capital projects (see, for example, McDonald and Ward 1984; Thane 1990). In Africa, it remains unclear how the Native Treasuries of the Lugard philosophy really functioned as financial institutions. African archives contain bookshelves full of vast ledgers of accounts: court fees, tax collections, fines, licenses, chiefs' salaries and allowances, all diligently recorded in copper-plate handwriting. But the treasuries seem to have been mechanisms strictly for the control of flows of funds on current account. Only illegally could they be used as sources of investment funds—by both Europeans and Africans alike, as graphically portrayed by Joyce Cary in *Mister Johnson* (1939). In francophone Africa, by contrast, the Provident Societies collected dues and loaned investment capital in the rural areas, achieving some major innovations, albeit largely through the direction of French administrators rather than local people. In Cameroun, the activities of the Provident Societies varied very widely by *département*, but as examples one can cite the large-scale rice milling enterprise in Nanga Eboko which actively promoted small-scale rice cultivation, dairying in Meiganga, and the creation of larger-scale plantations by Cameroonians in Nkongsamba (Guyer 1980). Most of these enterprises collapsed when the backing that had been constituted by the Common Fund was discontinued following Independence in the early 1960s.

Local government funds and parastatals instituted in the 1950s clearly created investment capital. Again, their financial histories remain to be written. Certainly state governments in Nigeria have become partners in many businesses, such as breweries, and in a few cases much larger multinational concerns.[5] But how the management of these funds relates to the financial opportunities or plans of communities remains to be explored. According to one authoritative summary, "In most countries in Africa, political independence saw the loss of juridical integrity of most urban centers" (Mabogunje 1990:159), which then implies loss of corporate capacity with respect to revenue generation and thereby to debt. Were these parastatals used as assets for credit generation, and if so, for what kinds of collective projects?

The creation of new currencies at the time of Independence gave governments and banks substantially increased control of credit formation, but the problem of convertibility set in almost immediately, greatly exacerbated by the profoundly competitive international money markets of the post-Bretton Woods era. For totally exogenous reasons to do with oil-money accumulation and banks' needs to lend, African "assets" were precipitously created in the mid-1970s in order to make governments credit worthy in international lending. The traditional, basic western assets such as land, corporate tax capacity and so on, were much too cumbersome and politically controversial to create quickly, so actual and potential trade revenues were used instead. When rapid declines in trade conditions set in, due to convertibility problems and unforeseen lurches in international prices, the debts incurred at the interface during that brief moment now seem largely unresolvable. The creation of domestic assets such as stocks, bonds, and land ownership still struggles with, amongst other things, a continuing lack of fiscal conditions and legal frameworks. Local communities have no way to invest in their own future earning power, except through their own original means (see Guyer 1992; and see also Mabogunje, Ch. 12).

The franc CFA differs in that it still reflects conditions of the colonial era. Its stability in international exchange with the hard currencies is linked to French policy, which restricts currency issue. But like the colonial era, the present conditions in francophone Africa profoundly discourage the development of domestic assets and local credit. The result of total convertibility is capital and consumer-spending flight to Europe on a scale said to be greater than also considerable private disinvestment in anglophone Africa. Vallée, citing an article published in *West Africa*, calls it: living in the "Fantasy Zone" (1989:73). With greater analytical rigor and much greater bitterness Tchundjang points out the continuing impoverishment of the financial infrastructure, where financing the campaign (for export crop purchase) is "the alpha and omega of banking" (1980:158). In fact, he argues that the CFA is still a "colonial money" and that the problems with nonconvertible currencies earns them the designation of "satellite monies" (1980:156). The fact that African currencies are still, at the end of the twentieth century, so largely made up of circulating media of exchange in the form of recognizable cash rather than credit instruments is clear evidence of their nature as "primitive" or "special purpose" interface currencies.

As indicated earlier, it is not the detailed dynamics of this macro-history that ultimately concern us here. My purpose is rather to set the frame of the ingeniously and flexibly constructed "special purposes" of persistent interface currencies around our descriptions of local originality. The logic of my own interpretation here is that the special purpose nature of interface currencies in Africa, and in particular the highly managed and deeply limited linkage between money as a means of payment/medium of exchange and asset creation/credit, has produced two major categories of effect: the instability in value that forms our central concern, and the persistent, radical challenge within Africa of how to link stores of value, constrained as these were by the limits on formal-sector asset creation, to the nominally "modern" media of exchange.

Currency Instability Within African Communities: A Brief Micro-History

A "people's view" of monetary history would include a long and heterogeneous list of situations and events, each leaving its own driftwood in the shape of membership cards in now defunct local savings institutions such as Post Office Savings Banks and Provident Societies,[6] receipts for failed deposits in fly-by-night banks, and a proliferation of terminologies for types of currency or crisis or illegal scheme. The tolafen ("threepenny" piece) and silfen ("sixpenny" piece) of the Cameroonian colonial period, is joined by the Muri (bill with Muritala Muhammed's likeness) of the Nigerian 1980s, the "affette" (goods "affected" by the economic crisis) of Ghana in the 1990s and the Nigerian "419" con-artists of the latest news (*African Concord*, February 24 1992; Ekejiuba, Ch. 6). A research report from Ghana in the 1930s (Field 1960) and newspaper coverage from Nigeria in the present, alike evoke the occult: "Watching Money Work Magic" (*Newswatch*, April 2, 1990). Informants in Cameroon remember throwing away now useless indigenous currency pieces, and in Nigerian communities they still use the terminology of the pound sterling and the counting system for cowries to refer to the ever-changing naira.

Ekejiuba (Ch. 6) offers a fine list of "instabilities" as seen from one local perspective. It outlines the major watersheds: the development of manilla and cowry multiple-currency systems in the early colonial period, forced demonetization in 1948, the issuance of Biafran currency during the Nigerian Civil War 1967–70, and the devaluation of the 1980s. But it also includes episodes of no theoretical monetary significance: high "allotment" payments in sterling made to World War II veterans, and the replacement of the entire paper currency stock in 1984 to flush out large-scale corruption and currency hoarding. People's memories may be hazy about the price fluctuations and exchange rates that would make up a standard economic history, but much less so about the personal dramas of trying to make a marriage or take a title under conditions of suddenly greater currency circulation, or of standing in endless lines at the bank, under strict deadlines, to face the inevitable unofficially demanded discount on the exchange of one's hard-earned savings into banknotes of a new design. And yet more localized or little publicized instabilities are extremely common. The blocking of all withdrawals for three months from a commercial bank in one area of rural Nigeria in 1991, the massive gambling scam in Kinshasa in 1991: all these happen now and have counterparts at earlier moments of history. Surely, over the late nineteenth and twentieth centuries, local philosophies of money and techniques of financial management have grown up, instigated and framed—but not entirely determined—by the formal sector's policies and implementation measures.

Recurrent currency change may also have been more characteristic of African pre-colonial systems than the stable spheres of exchange for special purpose monies that Bohannan posited. De Maret's (1981) work on a series of copper croisettes from the seventh to the eighteenth centuries—before the pervasive effects of the Atlantic trade—show dramatic changes in size. Arhin's contribution to this volume (Ch. 4) suggests that the famous Asante gold currency was a relatively late development, replacing an iron currency. During the period of the trade, the sheer quantities and varieties of currency goods introduced into Africa, taken together with the varied ethnographic hints about local practices, suggest that change was endemic.[7] Great surges of currency materials produced in Europe flowed into the Congo River exchange networks as European traders tried to penetrate deeper and deeper into the hinterland (Harms 1981). Neptunes, manillas, *mitakos,* and different types of cloth were all manufactured for export to Africa. Out-of-date rifles found a market there. Cowries by the billions were brought in from the Maldives and the East Africa Coast. All imported items circulated against indigenously produced currencies, and in fact often mimicked them in shape or material. Interface currencies and original currencies interpenetrated (M.-C. Dupré, Ch. 1; G. Dupré, Ch. 3).

For several years at the beginning of colonial rule, some of the components of this "bewildering jungle of currencies" (Quiggin 1949:92) were still accepted for tax payment, but by the end of World War I all tax responsibilities had to be met in cash. Some indigenous currencies were declared convertible up to a certain date only, and then only at disadvantageous rates for Africans (Lovejoy 1974). Beyond that, they circulated under conditions outside of government and official market control. The fate of stores of wealth held in iron, gold, cowries, copper, and cloth when they ceased to be usable in market or fiscal transactions remains one of the vast mysteries of modern African history, partly for empirical reasons, but partly because the *subtraction* of "functions" assimilates poorly to the dominant evolutionary, *additional* model of "special-to-general" purpose schema. Herbert (1984) wonders what happened to all the copper in the Equatorial region. In Southern Cameroon, people said that they gradually threw the iron currency away (Guyer 1986). McCaskie (1986) describes in some detail the dissipation of the gold dust and regalia in the Asante "Great Chest of the Treasury." Cowries given for taxes were physically destroyed by the French, especially in Borgu, and both personal fortunes and collective banking institutions were lost (Iroko 1987:606, 639, 642). The Igbo manillas were purchased at a low price and resold as scrap iron (Ofonagoro 1979b). Tio copper currency was deliberately ruined by the massive introduction of copper bars (M.-C. Dupré 1981–2). Physical remains of old currencies turn up from time to time. One hears that people are still accidentally discovering old cowry caches, buried long ago against the insecurities of war, theft, or confiscation. But the implications are still to be explored. Lovejoy summarizes the situation:

> many questions relating to economic change during the colonial period will
> need re-examination . . . the dissolution of the cowry system . . . [c]hanges in

the tax structure . . . [O]nly when the detailed research has been done will it be possible to evaluate the full significance . . . " (1974:583).

The full significance of this rupture of the connection between currencies and stores of wealth within African societies has hardly been fully elaborated conceptually and theoretically (see, however, Iroko 1987). To develop any generalizations depends on developing a *general* theory of the link between currencies as media of exchange and as constituting—or giving access to—stores of wealth (assets) on the other. There are bound to be variations. I have argued (Guyer 1993) that in Equatorial Africa, currency valuation in exchange created the singularity of *persons* rather than pools of money or material wealth that conferred or represented power in themselves. Surely the demise of a particular currency token and its replacement by another has less powerful reverberations in the former kind of case than in societies like the Asante where the material form of the Great Chest of gold dust was both symbol and means of national wealth and market trade (see Arhin, Ch. 4; Manuh, Ch. 8), or Dahomey, where cowry storehouses were at the center of the fiscal system (see Law, Ch. 2).[8] As long as we have no theory that links the "functions" of money to one another in the *various*—and not necessarily cumulative—combinations and permutations suggested by the comparative historical record, comprising both linkages and ruptures, then we cannot infer what the loss of a particular function has meant. The loss of asset formation, at a time when Western economic culture and practice were vigorously creating assets to underpin a ramifying system of credit, seems to me potentially devastating.

The development of strategies must follow. With a view to financing commerce, housebuilding or ceremonial, people probably have always kept, and still keep, quite large amounts of cash in personal coffers, as Cohen (1969) noted for the large-scale traders of the Ibadan cattle and kola markets, and as Shipton (Ch. 11) documents here. Certainly apocryphal stories attribute huge sums kept in mattresses, pillows and so on by the Nigerian wealthy caught out by the crack-down on cash in 1984. The demands of growth and the sources to finance it were in profound tension, which I would argue—following Falọla (Ch. 7)—put enormous pressure on the few possible assets that people could create in the formal sector, namely education, employment and status appointments such as chieftaincy titles (see also Arhin, Ch. 4), as a focus of investment and a source of collateral/surety in the credit market.

Some of the new functional linkages introduced by colonial cash were certainly intended, and others were probably foreseen. But by no means all the implications of monetary change were intended or even envisaged by those who instituted it. They resulted, rather, from experimental and clumsy groping at the interface between the changing originalities of African and European constructions, generously referred to as "working misunderstandings" (Dorward 1974) and, in Barber's marvelous phrase, as "ignorant but authoritarian" (1991:223). This must be more true of the diffuse processes of adjusting to instability than the higher-profile organizational processes of trying to shape asset creation. Predicting the operation of Gresham's Law, whereby bad money always drives out good,[9] was a matter of trial and error in situations where no one knew exactly what might be considered "bad" or "good." According to McPhee, with the first issue of banknotes in West Africa in 1916, all silver coins put in circulation disappeared into hoards, while bills were heavily discounted and ended up in equally unpopular bank accounts as the only thing one could do with them

(1926:240–6). Ekejiuba (Ch. 6) notes a similar and very familiar situation in present day Nigeria: that old naira bills are barely acceptable, despite government advertising campaigns to persuade people to the contrary.[10] Although the early advocates, such as McPhee, waxed enthusiastic about colonial currency and in contrast to indigenous ones, in the actual playing out of economic processes, the monies issued were themselves highly "imperfect" by local standards and to meet local agendas.

People's experience of currency instability must surely also be affected by price fluctuation: the rapid shift in the monetary value of one commodity versus another in people's portfolios of income and expenditure. It seems unlikely, for people whose experience with colonial currency was fairly short and their involvement in long-term money investments fairly limited, that they could tell the difference between price changes and changes in the value of the currency. In fact, the two were related in Eastern Nigeria, where a single commodity—palm oil—dominated the economy and the supply of the local currency—manillas—was strictly fixed (Naanen ms.). The present Nigerian inflation in response to the sudden decline in the exchange value of the naira in early March 1992, is just one phase in a long history in which prices and money are shifting at the same time. Clearly, the prices of imported items, or items integrated into international circuits will rise, unless controlled by government (like petrol). But the rates of change in the price of the different commodities reported in the press seem quite unpredictable: detergent up 20 percent, toothpaste up 25 percent, powdered milk up 50 percent, some automobile spare parts up 100 percent and so on (*African Concord*, March 30, 1992, pages 27–28).

While the full complexity of financial measures, unintended consequences and price fluctuations is often difficult to trace and integrate into a social or anthropological analysis, one cannot be naive about their direct relevance to local phenomena. Kwame Arhin (1976–7), for example, has traced out the implications of chronic cash shortage in Asante society in the colonial period, a shortage that was caused by a convergence of limited money supply, timid taxation policies for funding local government (Arhin 1974) and the growing needs of village populations and colonial chiefs to fulfil both old and new agendas. The massive growth in non-bank loans and debts in Asante seems quite different from dynamics during the same period elsewhere,[11] and cannot be understood comparatively without a full description of the financial context as well as the socio-cultural context. Quite largely starved of credit funds, having very limited assets and possibly also mistrusting all these formal institutions, African populations turned to money-lenders and exploitation of the few qualities that could function as assets (see Chapter 7). Indigenously controled "informal sector" institutions, such as rotating credit associations, began to grow in the vacuum (Nwabughuogu 1984). Capital mobilization in local communities has been very inventive in some places; Guyer (Ch. 5) suggests how marriage payments have shifted from a patronage-based system for mobilizing funds to an income/savings-based system, and Mabogunje (Ch. 12) describes a new attempt in Nigeria to bridge the formal/informal sector gap in savings and investment institutions through the adaptation of the Western "community bank."

With all these changes, it seems hardly possible that African populations have seen colonial and post-colonial cash as any more dependable than the currencies of an earlier period. But have these monies, then, in some senses been assimilated to familiar constructions and elaborated on original bases? The centuries-long policies of Europe have set certain parameters on African monetary history, but they have not entirely determined it. Changing monetary conditions have also been the product of local dynamics, and indeed the initiation and assimilation of change has been a marked quality in African society and history in general.[12]

Questions abound from thinking through the policy changes, the money/price fluctuations and the unintended-consequence scenario. How have sudden jolts been assimilated in African societies: culturally, politically, and simply in the organization of community life? Does the ordinary market-seller in francophone Africa have a concept of the meaning of the *mercuriale*, or more broadly, are there indigenous concepts of "the just price?" What does "worth" mean to people in relation to money valuation? Have the experiences of price fluctuation built up a series of resources and measures that now form part of the cultural and social repertoire, for both rich and poor, and do these differ from one society to another? How do people in different milieux relate the medium of exchange to the store of wealth? What counts as an asset—the qualities and things that can leverage further resources—is partly a creation of the collective reworkings of politics and culture, anywhere in the world.[13] The contributions of Barber (Ch. 9), Shipton (Ch. 11), and Mabogunje (Ch. 12) examine the meaning of wealth and the implications of the uses to which pools of wealth are put. For more modest levels of assets, all the chapters on the colonial and postcolonial situations contain relevant material, even where the author may not take the interpretation in that direction.

Cultural and social resources for each of these processes have been present in West African repertoires for centuries, albeit with very different components from the metropolitan repertoire, and from the "policies at the interface" that have been reviewed in previous sections. People have continued, but in new ways, to devote some funds to the social payments that probably developed and elaborated alongside the growth in pre-colonial currency systems: bridewealth (see Guyer, Ch. 5; Manuh, Ch. 8), varied labor arrangements within and across family lines (Berry, Ch. 13; Mikell, Ch. 10), and chieftaincy (Arhin, Ch. 4). Shipton (Ch. 11) reviews the entire inventory of Gambian modes of saving. And the whole configuration is evaluated continually in moral and descriptive terms (see Barber, Ch. 9; Barber, 1982). Can one see such processes developing and transforming over time, underlying and helping to explain current monetary practice? What intellectual resources exist for tracing out an answer to this question?

Conceptual and Interpretive Issues in the Study of African Currency Use

The subject of money keeps returning us to the basic problem of inter-temporality: money as a link between present and future, and the implications of that link being— for whatever reason—a fragile one. Standard economic theory suggests that the greater the fragility, the quicker the turnover, the weaker the rationale to use money at all, and the greater the incentive to develop stores of wealth in a form that has greater stability (Melitz 1974:35). This kind of argument is based on rational choice theory. Humphrey (1985, 1991; Humphrey and Hugh-Jones 1992), for example, argues convincingly that the possibility of barter is a constant element in economic and cultural repertoires, applicable to situations where the temporal frames for monetary transactions have been cut down. People exchange the goods alone in a dyadic and momentary transaction that has no necessary links to wider circuits nor to longer series of ramifying exchange. Purchase with cash, then, is a type of transaction characteristic of conditions where some degree of social breadth and temporal reach can be predictably envisaged.

Rather than defining *types* of transaction (purchase, barter, investment, and so on) Simmel offers a general framework for thinking of the differing temporalities of exchange as a *continuum*. Money, he argues, "tends to prolong the teleological series for what is close to us"; it also and at the same time tends to "shorten the series for what is remote" ([1900] 1990:208). Consumption becomes more indirect at the same time as valuation of timeless assets is brought into a calculable temporal zone. Money transactions therefore cover a particular range of the exchange continuum whose reach may change over time. The rational model would suggest that the greater the *instability* of money, the more likely that some transactions—for "what is close"—would be shortened to self-provisioning and barter, and that others—for goods that are "remote"—would be extracted from the money nexus at the other end of the continuum and consigned to the category of priceless (that is, timeless) valuables. This model is clearly a dynamic version, phrased in terms of rational theory, of the moral-cultural model of spheres of exchange. The greater the stability of currency, the wider its range of application is liable to become and the more prices and values will appear to be like a continuum; conversely, the greater its instability, the narrower the applicability of currency to the range of transactions and the more the system will look like discrete spheres of exchange, with valuables at the top and self-provisioning and barter at the bottom.

It is very helpful to use such logical models as a reminder of how sharp cultural distinctions may represent only a moment in a history. But there is a complementary descriptive and analytical task here because neither rational theory nor spheres of exchange theory explains which goods fall where on the temporal/cultural scale. While the segregation of certain items on Simmel's continuum *can* be thought of for theoretical purposes as outside of history and culture—food and basic needs at the "close" end and sacred items at the "remote" inaccessible end—in fact, they and the entire continuum of valued goods are culturally constituted and constantly renewed, and for reasons other than relative security. Before the Reformation, God's pardon for some sins (but not others) was indeed "remote" in that people did not need it three times a day, but it was not so unique a lifetime need that it was unattainable by the occasional dispensing of money. It was an intermittent need, valued in cash. Protestantism returned it to the category of timeless valuable, to be attained exclusively outside the cash nexus. No economic theory can explain why pardons—or sex or votes or bridewealth goods—fall where they do, or move around as they do over time, on the value continuum of particular peoples.

Again we are returned to the question of assets, of the nature of values that are projected by people themselves over the longest term that they envisage, and of the relationship of assets to cash purchase and exchange. This topic has fallen between the cracks in anthropology. For non-Western economies, the "spheres of exchange" model has encouraged more attention to the cultural categories and their boundaries than to the historical processes whereby the categories are filled with goods. And for capitalist economies, anthropological writing has concentrated on production and exchange: on the commodity form (e.g., Appadurai 1986) and the moral frameworks in circuits of exchange (Parry and Bloch 1989). That is, we have focused on the *short* temporal cycles and circuits when we write about capitalism, leaving out analysis of the composition of the very long cycles that coexist with them, and indeed—through the capital/credit nexus—make them possible. And those very long cycles of relatively timeless value do exist in capitalism, as they do in other types of economy, and even more critically because the entire edifice of credit depends on them. Capitalism is about capital, not only about commodities and labor. The households and local populations that we study in anthropology are only a part of differentiated systems that also include corporations and government. Classically, it is government that frames, controls, and guarantees the capitalist assets that are on the longest temporal frames: assets kept "as safe as the Bank of England" (and other central banks), the royal wealth, governmental tax capacity, long-term bonds issued against government at all levels, and national treasures of art and architecture.

Ordinary populations, with limited access to assets in this category of goods but with certain aspects of their collective life guaranteed by them, are necessarily involved in purchase and creation of different, smaller assets of their own, on shorter temporal schedules. Even though they may hardly understand how the larger system works, the investments under their own control are only ever a small part of what shapes their cultural and social life, and above all, their security. Their situations are also framed by the existence and nature of the stable "treasures" in the background. Does the stationmaster or porter employed by British Railways know that a famous piece of Fang statuary was owned by their pension fund and used as an investment to earn the returns that would underwrite their own capacity to live adequately in old age? And if they did, would they have any idea at all how or why it was worth over half a million dollars when it was sold at Christie's in New York in 1992, or how the statue's value on the auction block affected their personal life-long security?[14] Ordinary people in the capitalist orders have to worry only about the time frames of their own assets and their own consumption decisions, and are rarely concerned about the collective assets of state and society as a whole. Indeed, the great collective assets are taken care of by processes that seem so self-evident that we can speak of them in naturalistic terms: taxes, inevitable like death; corporate community structures, achieved according to political ideology by the rational will of free social contractors; a people's birthright in the products of its own communities' geniuses. In fact, of course, collective and private capital is byzantine in its complexity and highly inventive and dynamic, far beyond the possibility of summarizing in rational-choice terms, and does not have to be understood by ordinary populations to be critically important to their lives.

In societies or under conditions in which formal sector state and social assets of the very long term barely exist at all, or cannot be accessed by ordinary people even as indirectly as through the holdings of their pension funds, we need to understand whether and how people envisage long-term assets. In these cases, and at times when the currency is also at the same time unstable, Simmel's ([1900] 1990) "generic" processes through which money creates a play on economic temporalities may be driven to great intensity by two contradictory logics: first, the predictable need to shorten the time frame of transactions to minimize losses (see also Melitz 1974), but secondly, the simultaneous and urgent need to create and protect very long-term personal and collective assets. It is a rather functionalist assumption that individuals and communities do search to create long-term assets, to place a lien on the longer term future, but it is a provocative one. Sharp and irregular pulsations must create great uncertainties about what may or may not have long-term value, about who will decide that and how the rest will link their own economic and social processes to it. Community gatekeepers may seek to neutralize income surges by turning disproportionate amounts into immobile assets (see Guyer 1993), allowing them to keep political control on distribution networks while at the same time moderating the flow. It is surely sociologically different for a given wealth to come in, or be otherwise generated, slowly and regularly so that collective processes of valuation and legitimation have time to consolidate.

When instability is a regionally specific phenomenon and money can be transferred to the outside, one method of internal immobilization of wealth is external transfer: the removal of long-term wealth out of their own unstable system to put it elsewhere. The need to lengthen temporalities then results in asset transfer, as is obviously happening in the case of capital flight in present-day Africa. But is there another process, for those people whose options are contained *within* local economies, whereby the means of long-term stabilization of some assets develops alongside rapid transactional turnover? This is an almost completely unexplored problem: the ways in which *collective* assets of the long term are built up under conditions of long-term instability and the levels of collectivity at which this investment takes place in situations where the state-level corporate institutions do not or cannot fulfil this function.[15]

Berry (1989) has suggested that we think of investment in social relations in this kind of framework; she expands the argument in Chapter 13 in this volume. Shipton (Ch. 11) examines the forms of savings in the Gambia. Mabogunje (Ch. 12) outlines a new formal sector innovation for community asset creation in Nigeria. Suffice it here to suggest that all logic points to a profound dilemma in African local economies. It may be couched in terms of their own original idioms of conversion, spheres of exchange, social payments, and indigenous financial organization, but it must also be understood as framed by the special purpose currencies at the interface, and monetary instability as a continuing condition. The following are some of the processes that may be relevant.

Multiple Currencies, Spheres of Exchange and Convertibility

The convertibility of national currencies is just one of a class of phenomena, the general principle of which has clearly been familiar in African economies for a long time. Paul Bohannan put the phrase "spheres of exchange" into the anthropological repertoire in 1955, to indicate that in the Tiv economy exchangeable goods were classified into discrete categories, which were ranked in a moral hierarchy. Goods and currency in one sphere could be "conveyed" against one another, but with difficulty and a certain moral opprobrium "converted" into items in other spheres. The term has been found applicable by others in a host of different situations, with or without "general purpose" currencies, where there are discernible subsectors. The subsectors are often marked by different technologies of some sort: different legal instruments with attendant constraints and entailments; different explicitly theorized moral underpinnings; different objects as media of exchange; and different origins, pathways, and destinations. There is a similarity between Bohannan's spheres and, for example: the medieval Mediterranean system, whereby some transactions were in precious metal coins, others in base metals and others in kind (Cipolla [1956] 1967),

Walzer's (1983) social philosophical discussion of moral spheres in the uses of money in capitalist economies, Shipton's (1989) discussion of "bitter money" among the present-day Luo, and even descriptions of Gresham's law where the "driving out" of good money by bad actually amounts to their increasingly differential uses, the "good" for transactions in low-velocity/high-security circuits (and their logical end point in stores of wealth) and the other for high-velocity/low-security circuits.[16] If this kind of economy is understood broadly, as comprising multiple and contingent circuits, rather than understood narrowly as comprised of morally bounded spheres of exchange, then the multiple currencies of many pre-colonial African economies become perhaps the most strikingly representative case of a general class.

I cannot rehearse and critique here the entire long and tangled history that explores the factual and interpretive literature on the multiple and changing currencies of West and Equatorial Africa, assortment bargaining, and the constant assimilation of new "commodities" into intricate frameworks of equivalence. One conclusion, however, is that the maintenance of a single type of currency for a breadth of transactions seems to have been achieved in pre-colonial Africa only under very limited conditions, one of which was political centralization.[17] Given the apparent profound propensity for currencies to proliferate,[18] colonial currency must have presented a difficult logistical challenge to populations not accustomed to monopoly. The resistance of the highly commercial Igbo populations to a drastically reduced latitude in currency use may reflect a somewhat more general process (Ofonagoro 1979a, 1979b) of keeping colonial money in its place and retaining other circuits of exchange. Because the multiple-currency systems are no longer functioning, the sources are not detailed enough for us to reconstruct exactly how they worked. One gets fleeting glimpses of the circuits for the pre-colonial period, but rarely an entire chain of transactions.

Neither are we sure how price responsiveness along one currency vector interacted with multiplicity along several vectors.[19] Even for the well described multiple-currency systems[20] and for spheres of exchange, the actual nodes of control for the circulating commodities and currencies are not fully illuminated. It seems from the studies of early colonial Eastern Nigeria that the Arochukwu traders were instrumental in keeping colonial currencies out of the hinterland. Particularly shrewd merchants made handsome profits on money exchange as well as trade (Ekejiuba 1967). In the 1930s, the organizers of regionally based rotating credit associations made similar profits from accepting contributions, making payments, and generally mediating people's complex monetary needs in more than one currency (Nwabuguoghu 1984). There is obviously a sociology that corresponds to multiple currencies, but the question of how these systems worked over time is unclear. Even though most indigenous currencies no longer circulate widely, the philosophy and sociology of multiple circuits is probably still very lively, as are people's expectations that there are potential gains to be made in conversion.

There is one further possible rationale to the preservation of indigenous currencies, besides the advantages of multiplicity, and that is protection from counterfeiting. All sources point out that the cowry's greatest asset as a currency was the impossibility of copying it successfully. We know, also, that there was great expertise within African societies about the authenticity of metals and other commodities. For populations with such expertise the importance of "commodity currencies" may not only have been that objects had alternative "use values"—as clothes, drink, tools, or weaponry—but that counterfeit was so easy to detect. Those circuits in which the currency unit potentially passed through a utilitarian function allowed for continuous verification of authenticity. Although no one (as far as I know) has written a history of counterfeiting of colonial currencies, the possibilities were surely too tempting, and have been seized too often elsewhere in the world, to have been bypassed altogether in West Africa. "Fake Currency Notes Flood Benin City" warns a recent newspaper headline (*Sunday Concord,* May 5, 1991, page 2).

It seems, then, a useful working assumption to make, especially when exploring strategies for containment of the damage of currency instability as well as exploitation of its potentials, that West and Equatorial African populations already had institutions such as multiple circuits in their repertoires that had potential buffering, rationing, blocking effects on a simple price logic and that provided for the accumulation of pools of wealth. The concept of "spheres of exchange" places nonrational metaphors of qualitative distinction at "breakpoints" along Simmel's temporal continuum. Do the continuing strategies of monetary circuitry that are manifestly influenced by a more self-conscious strategizing in the context of instability draw on similar logics and similar metaphors, and do they work in similar ways? And if so, how are they constructed experientially and how can they be understood analytically? In various ways, all the contributors explore the changing nature and meaning of conversions. And the contribution by Law on cowries (Ch. 2) and Arhin on the transition from gold (Ch. 4), examine currency change in two of the more powerful pre-colonial states, in which multiple currencies were not present and not countenanced. Their chapters address the particular challenges posed by currency change in the more unusual monopolized systems.

Wealth and the Creation of Assets

As noted above, one of the commonly cited functions of money is as a store of wealth. Although many authoritative interpretations of pre-colonial Africa suggest that the ultimate purpose of material wealth was to transform it into personal allegiances,[21] there are still many indications that material wealth was also stored, guarded, and sometimes displayed. Vansina hinges parts of his interpretation of the long-term development of Equatorial kinship and political systems on "the inheritance of the treasury" (1990:152). Igbo compounds had entire storerooms for manillas and cowries (Ofonagoro 1979b). One of the central symbols of the Asante state and a means of economic control was the treasure chest (Garrard 1980:188–192).

Iroko (1987) reviews the whole range of storage methods for cowries: the 70-meter-long storehouse at Abomey "the walls . . . completely decorated in the precious shells" (quoted from Laffitte, in Iroko 1987:465), buried jars, and the secured deposit banks of the very wealthy of the Slave Coast. Alone amongst the stores of material wealth of pre-colonial Africa, this institution seems to have served the interests of merchants rather than political leaders, and to have allowed the use of accumulated currency as financial—as distinct from political—assets. A special architecture to the storehouse protected the cowries from damage; accounts were kept; interest rates were set by the year (a part of the year assimilating to the year); and the rates were extremely high (200–250 percent) to cover the great risks of loss and the problems of liquidity (Iroko 1987:394–439). Not the least danger to these enterprises, like comparable stores of independent wealth the world-over, were the demands of impecunious authoritarian rulers who imposed (or otherwise extracted) loans and subventions without interest or engagement to repay. The *radio-trottoir* in Africa has carried modern-day versions of this old story, where leaders "shake-down" the wealthy in times of liquidity crisis. In fact, historical studies stress that the institutionalization of banking in Europe depended on a strong concept or practice of republicanism (Dickson 1967; Veseth 1990). Personal rule accommodates independent financial power with difficulty, elsewhere as well as in Africa. Doubtless part of the history and sociology of stores of independent wealth, as distinct from political wealth which may be displayed, is an intricate web of secrecy about where they are and how much is there.

The wisdom on what happened to stores of wealth during the currency revolution and colonial conquest is that they were completely dissipated, either by theft or demonetization. But some new wealth was accumulated. For certain leaders, the amounts are vast and some of the uses clearly theatrical. Because this wealth is in cash, study of its storage and use tends so far to have drawn on an implicit "money economy" frame of interpretation, using terms such as accumulation, investment, and corruption. Rather few are the studies that have tried to understand great wealth ethnographically, that is as intricate technologies of acquisition, storage, access, and deployment along lines comparable to those followed by Iroko for cowry wealth.[22] Michelle Gilbert's "Sudden Death of a Millionaire" (1988), Belasco's book on Yoruba entrepreneurs (1980) and Forrest's work on Nigerian businessmen (1993) begin to add analytical work to the journalistic near monopoly on this critically important topic.[23]

For the storage and deployment of smaller-scale wealth by ordinary people there are more sources and more potential topics: bridewealth payments, the finance of funerals, the raising of funds for court costs, mobilization of funds for title-taking, and so on. Reputation is everywhere an asset that leverages credit. The question is, what kind of reputation, what kind of asset, and what kind credit work together under the originalities of particular African systems. Because many of our chapters deal with these topics, suffice it here to add one comment and one question. First, there are enough data to show that however poor African populations are, however apposite seems to be the concept of "coping" in understanding their finances, it is still impossible to be a social adult in most places without the capacity to mobilize sums of money that are quite substantial relative to people's incomes. Under unstable and, in recent years, declining circumstances how are the acceptable levels, compositions, priorities, and frequencies of these social payments reworked? With what implications? And how do people build up assets against which claims can be made in case of substantial need? The social relations of communities are not a natural resource, a simple direct outcome of birth and contiguity as naturalistic "subsistence" assumptions about "communities" tend to imply. They constitute an achievement of Byzantine complexity, built up from myriads of attentive acts, imaginative rethinkings, interventions by the powerful, and selective avoidances by the powerless (see Mikell, Ch. 10; Berry, Ch. 13). What then have been the patterns and possibilities produced by the conjuncture of currency stabilities and instabilities with the uses to which large and small wealth has been put?

Cultural Constructions and Social Organizations for Money Management

Differentiated circuits rest on a conceptual theory of differentiation and combination. The concepts through which prices operated in West Africa seem to have the remarkable qualities of, on the one hand, fine discrimination and price sensitivity by type of object, and on the other, conceptual stability in collections and combinations. The prices of particular goods rose and fell, but the collective concepts and equivalences remained relatively steady. Careful analysis has shown that the conceptual stability veiled price changes.[24] But over the long term, the sheer staying power of conceptual stability demands its own attention. In Western Nigerian markets in the present day, an enamel bowl of cassava flour hardly changes in price over the seasons, but its volumetric content changes; an acre of land costs a certain fixed amount to plow, but the area may change; the collective term "bag" that comes out of the cowry lexicon has been applied first to pounds sterling and then to naira; an interest rate can be a fixed ratio between interest and principal, regardless of the time frame of the loan (see Chapter 7), in exactly the same way as Shipton (1990) describes for the Gambia. In Cameroun, a small bundle of metal rod currency pieces was named after the raffia binding; as the currency inflated, bundles became bigger and individual pieces smaller, until the term for a bundle became the present numerical concept for "a hundred" (Guyer 1986). Through linguistic terminologies and bargaining practices, fluctuations and mutations are assimilated to stable categories.

This much is well known; but what does it mean? Is the practice of conceptual stabilization actually pervasive in particular economies, or does it only apply to certain items or certain circuits? Where it does apply, does it stabilize anything at all, and if so what?—given that transactions are only concluded through ardent bargaining. And are the items to which it applies in any way special? In short, there is an entire cultural underpinning to monetary circuits: classification of goods and transactions, numerical systems, and connotations of the active verbs through which money and commodities circulate. There are few studies that have tried to trace out the cognitive categories that organize economic life in Africa in the present: Chilver and Kaberry (1960) show how the Nso ruler chose between two plausible indigenous terms to designate colonial taxation; the Asante literature follows through the history of the term for a man wealth (*asikafo*) and achievement (*obirempon*), over a 200-year period (Arhin 1983; McCaskie 1986). But we have little to go on with respect to the derivations and connotations of concepts of current monies themselves, their denominations, and appropriate verbs (*save, earn, spend, sell, profit,* and so on).

Anthropological work has been stronger on the moral criteria underlying knowledge about money (see Parry and Bloch 1989) than on the classificatory or cognitive criteria. Much of this work focuses on the moral ambiguity, if not downright evil, of the promiscuous transformations that money makes possible. Exemplary of this line of analysis is Shipton's (1989) monograph on Luo "bitter money," that is, the money that is earned through selling morally questionable goods (such as tobacco or cannabis) or selling things that should not be sold (such as land). Behind such judgments lies a system of classification. Barber's contribution here, however, suggests a completely different construction among the Yoruba.

There is one further topic in the analysis of cultural categories that is critical to the study of change, namely the ways in which new elements have been assimilated into the culture of money. Commoditization could not advance without cultural improvization with the words that apply to transactions and the categories that classify saleable items. The force of the state alone could not insert taxation and court fines into the routine of life without people applying themselves to cultural invention and moral commentary. People themselves could not allow money valuation to penetrate new relationships without rethinking them, probably contentiously (see

Mikell, Ch. 10; Berry, Ch. 13). Cultural repertoires must have receptor concepts for assimilating and domesticating "outside knowledge" (Barnes 1990), or the outsiders have to provide the mental categories and persuade people of their power. The state and the church/mosque surely have commented at length on the meaning and morality of money in the present day; financial obligations to community and congregation, the just deserts of life, and the meaning of wealth. How skillfully they use, or create afresh, receptor concepts in local cultures must be a critical aspect of the drama of market penetration, both before and after colonization.

One context in which Simmel's ([1900] 1990) cultural constructions can be combined with calculating models is in the relationship between money and time in credit institutions (see Berry, Ch. 13, in particular; but see also Barber, Ch. 9; Falola, Ch. 7; and Shipton, Ch. 11). Should one save first and then spend, as the Victorian wage-earner was encouraged to do, or borrow first and pay back, as the Victorian manufacturer, the twentieth century home-owner, and the Yoruba debt-pawn have been encouraged to do? Does the passage of time weaken or strengthen obligation, and why? How are financial obligations inherited, in the case that human frailty or death cancels out the possibility of the use of savings or the repayment of debt by the original party? Are savings and debts inherited differently? What constitutes default and what are its repercussions? All these questions revert ultimately to classic issues in the anthropology of exchange, namely how personhood and its inevitable growth and decay over time are conceptualized (see Appadurai 1986; Strathern 1988; Weiner 1992) in relation to the timeless value of assets and the conceptual stabilization in African modes of exchange.

Final Comment

Not all of these questions about African money can be answered, but they do need to be asked. Money is mundane, but it is a mundane mystery to most who use it: a small miracle that grows people and creates relationships (Barber, Ch. 9), contributes to the destruction of state leaders (Law, Ch. 2) and demands intricate systems of dykes and channels to prevent the forces of destruction from eroding growth. African economies are at present in what is probably their most serious state of crisis in this century. The commitment we have made in the chapters of this book is to describe money management over that century, and to lay out some of its originalities in their larger context. The "impact of money" has resulted in neither a successful revolution nor the kind of gradual directional change implied by terms such as commercialization or the penetration of market relations. But it has traced out a history whose form underlies the sequence of the chapters.

Notes

1. Although several important summary works have been devoted to Nigeria: Jones 1964, Johansson 1967, Kirk-Greene 1960, and Eyo 1979. Nothing published in English compares in comprehensive coverage to the work of Rivallain (1987).
2. Economic Community of West African States; Union Douanière et Economique de L'Afrique Centrale.
3. In fact, there is some confusion and shading of referent in the literature on "primitive"

monies. Although Melitz gives an analytical definition of money in terms of the underlying rationality for its use—"to economize on transaction costs" (1974:77)—he also suggests that "[b]y primitive money, we shall mean, quite simply, the moneys of primitive societies" (1974: 85). The slippage from analytical discriminations based entirely on the attributes of the currency in question to intuitive discriminations based on supposed attributes of the people who use it is not unusual in this literature.

4. For a fascinating case study, see Brown 1964.

5. A list of industries published by the Manufacturers Assocation of Nigeria includes, for example, a Daimler/Benz factory partially owned by the federal government and three state governments, an asbestos factory partially owned by a German company and one state government, and a cement company partly owned by BCI, the federal government and three state governments (Manufacturers Association of Nigeria 1984).

6. Post Office Savings has not been as important in West Africa as in Southern Africa, where it was developed for facilitation of the remittances of migrant workers to mines and plantations. It seems an understudied topic. One brief reference is to the Federation of Rhodesia and Nyasaland where the Post Office has been an important African institution "with its large branch coverage and its willingness to accept deposits of small sums of money" (Sowelem 1967:187), albeit at the very low interest rates and sterling investment that Tchundjang argues makes African savings a losing proposition all around: to the saver, because interest does not keep up with inflation, and the prospective borrower/investor because s/he has no access (1980: 81). For a summary of the short meteoric history of the Provident Societies in Cameroun, see Guyer 1980.

7. The sources are voluminous here: Hogendorn and Johnson 1986 and Iroko 1987 on cowries; Polanyi 1964 and Johnson 1966 assortment bargaining and the ounce trade; Garrard 1980 on gold; Herbert 1984 on copper; Goucher 1981, Warnier and Fowler 1979 and Guyer 1986 on iron; and regional summaries by Mahieu 1923, Quiggin 1949, Jones 1964 , Kirk-Greene 1960, Lovejoy 1974, and Curtin 1983.

8. Other implications of colonization for value and asset formation may be equally destructive, however, in systems in which people represented value. Whereas the demonetization of physic al objects used as currencies may not entail much loss, demographic collapse may undermine entire structures of long-term valuation and exchange.

9. For an explanation, anthropological/historical critique, and application to the Caribbean, see Mintz 1964.

10. There is a whole topic here. In my own experience, the naive foreigner is seen as a potential recipient of otherwise unacceptable bills, preferably hidden in the middle of a stack. A torn bill may not even be acceptable in official contexts—such as, in my case, a one-naira admission to the National Museum in Lagos.

11. Unless, of course, our documentation for other places is so limited as to be inadequate for making comparisons.

12. Kopytoff (1987) argues that the constant change has been essentially conservative, whereas Vansina (1990) is inclined to stress growth—but the pervasiveness of indigenously inspired change is no longer a controversial point.

13. I am sceptical about the utility of both the Marxist labor theory of value and accumulation processes, and the neo-classical theory of the market, when it comes to understanding asset creation. In the first case, stores of money accumulated through the capitalist labor process are not the only form that assets have taken in capitalist history: personal reputation, the fiscal power of the state, and land value have all been used to generate credit. And in the second case, it does not seem historically accurate that land operated as an asset relative primarily to its market value, but rather to the value given to la nd in the feudal definition of its tax-bearing capacity. Loaning against land developed in England *before* there was an active land market to price its value in strictly supply and demand terms (see Dickson 1967).

14. I am indebted to Christraud Geary of the National Museum of African Art, The Smithsonian Institution, Washington, D.C., for these details. The sale is recorded in Christie's catalog entitled "Important Tribal Art and Antiquities from the Collection of William McCarty-Cooper," May 19th, 1992, and refers to item #134, page 70-1.

15. Note that demographers have seen that the nature of social institutions that provide a real or felt sense of security (explicitly including financial institutions) may be critically important in determining fertility. Bearing more children, and seeing them as assets-of-the-long-term is one plausible response on the part of very small collectivities such as families to the absence of other long-term assets (Smith 1986). Investment in ethnicity and religious congregations may be another response, for larger groups.

16. See Mintz 1964 for a fascinating discussion of slaves' money and other monies in the Caribbean in the eighteenth century.

17. For the gold dust of the Asante see Wilks (1975), Arhin (1967), and Garrard (1980); and for the cowries of Hausa, Yoruba and Dahomey, see Iroko (1987).

18. By using the active voice, I don't mean to imply that there was some intrinsic process. By logical inference from what we know already about the monetary ingenuity of the Western merchants and the detailed discriminations of Africans, there must have developed a familiarity and facility from continually dealing with multiplicity and novelty.

19. The reading of the sources on this is very difficult, especially when—as will be discussed below—concepts were more stable than content. See Law (1991); and Law (1992).

20. The Igbo literature is the best: Jones (1964), Ekejiuba (1967), Henderson (1972), Northrup (1978).

21. Miller writes of Equatorial Africa: "A wealthy man increased productivity by organizing and controlling people ... [by] aggregating human dependents" (1988:43, 47). Vansina confirms this view: "After centuries of trading, goods still retained their value as items for use rather than for exchange. Whenever possible, wealth in goods was still converted into followers" (1990:251).

22. One example is Gilbert's (1988) paper on the death of a Ghanaian millionaire; another is Karin Barber's (1982) discussion of popular representations of the morality of the petro-naira.

23. The Nigerian press is full of stories of individual wealth and its uses, complete with naira amounts, sources, costs of items, contributions to causes, and so on. In fact, money seems to be to the Nigerian popular press what personal scandal is to the American.

24. For a detailed argument against the assumption that Dahomean administered prices and stable exchange concepts such as the galina corresponded to prices in actual transactions, see Law 1992. In the context of entire sets of prices, those remaining stabilities—such as wages in this case—can no longer be interpreted as due to "the operation of traditional notions of a reasonable rate of remuneration, but a cheapening of the cost of labour to the benefit of European and African employers."

Sources

Analyst [pseud.]. 1954. "Rejoinder to Mr. Earle." *Social and Economic Studies*, 3:105–108.

Antoine, Régis. 1986. *L'Histoire Curieuse des Monnaies Coloniales*. Paris: Editions A CL.

Appadurai, Arjun. 1986. "Introduction: Commodities and the Politics of Value." In *The Social Life of Things: Commodities in Cultural Perspective*, ed. Arjun Appaduri, 3–63. New York and Cambridge: Cambridge University Press.

Ardant, Gabriel. 1965 *Théorie Sociologique de l'Impôt*. Paris: S.E.V.P.E.N.

Arhin, Kwame.1967. "The Financing of the Ashanti Expansion (1700–1820)." *Africa* 27:283–90.

———. 1974. "Some Asante Views of Colonial Rule: As Seen in the Controversy Relating to Death Duties." *Transactions of the Historical Society of Ghana* 15:63–84.

————. 1976-77. "The Pressure of Cash and its Political Consequences in the Colonial Period." *Journal of African Studies*, 3:453-68.

————. 1983. "Rank and Class among the Asante and Fante in the Nineteenth Century." *Africa* 56:2-22.

Barber, Karin. 1982. "Popular Reactions to the Petro-Naira." *The Journal of Modern African Studies* 20:431-450.

————. 1991. *I Could Speak Until Tomorrow: Oriki, Women, and the Past in a Yoruba Town.* Washington, D.C.: Smithsonian Institution Press.

Barnes, Sandra T. 1990. "Ritual. Power, and Outside Knowledge." *Journal of Religion in Africa*, 20:248-268.

Belasco, Bernard. 1980. *The Entrepreneur as Culture Hero: Preadaptations in Nigerian Economic Development.* New York: Praeger.

Berry, Sara S. 1989. " Social Institutions and Access to Resources." *Africa* 59:41-55.

Bloch, Marc. 1954. *Esquisse d'une Histoire Monétaire de l'Europe.* Paris: Armand Colin.

————. 1966. "Natural Economy or Money Economy: A Pseudo Dilemma." In *Land and Work in Medieval Europe*, ed . M. Bloch, 230-43. Berkeley, CA: University of California Press.

Bohannan, Paul. 1955. "Some Principles of Exchange and Investment among the Tiv." *American Anthropologist* 57,1:60-70.

————. 1959. "The Impact of Money on an African Subsistence Economy." *The Journal of Economic History* 19:491-503.

Born, Karl Erich. 1984. *International Banking in the 19th and 20th Centuries.* New York: St. Martin's Press.

Bourdin, Joel. 1980. *Monnaie et politique monétaire dans les pays africains de la zone franc.* Dakar: Nouvelles E ditions Africaines.

Braudel, Fernand. 1981. *The Structures of Everyday Life: The Limits of the Possible.* Vol. 1 of *Civilization and Capitalism 15th-18th Century.* New York: Harper and Row.

Brown Charles V. 1964. *Government and Banking in Western Nigeria: A Case Study in Economic Policy.* Ibadan: Oxford University Press for NISER.

Campbell, Colin D. and William R. Dougan. 1986. *Alternative Monetary Regimes.* Baltimore,MD: Johns Hopkins University Press.

Cary, Joyce. [1939]1962. *Mister Johnson.* New York: Time Inc. Reprint.

Chilver, Elizabeth. and P. M. Kaberry. 1960. "From Tribute to Tax in a Tikar Chiefdom." *Africa*, 30:1-19.

Cipolla, Carlo M. [1956] 1967. *Money, Prices and Civilization in the Mediterranean World: Fifth to Seventeenth Century.* New York: Gordian Press.

Cohen, Abner. 1969. *Custom and Politics in Urban Africa: Hausa Migrants in Yoruba Towns.* Berkeley, CA: University of California Press.

Coquery-Vidrovitch, Catherine. 1972. *Le Congo au Temps des Grandes Compagnies Concessionaires 1893-1930.* Paris: Mouton.

Crump, Thomas. 1981. *The Phenomenon of Money.* London: Routledge and Kegan Paul.

Curtin, Philip D. 1983. Africa and the Wider Monetary World, 1250-1850. In *Silver and Gold Flows In the Medieval and Early Modern Worlds*, ed. John F. Richards, 231-68. Chapel Hill, NC: University of North Carolina Press.

Daunton, M. J. 1990. "Housing." In *The Cambridge Social History of Britain, 1750-1950*, Vol. 2, ed. F.M.I. Thompson, 195-250. New York and Cambridge: Cambridge University Press.

de Cecco, Marcello. 1984. *The International Gold Standard: Money and Empire.* New York: St. Martin's Press.

de Maret, Pierre. 1981. "L'évolution Monétaire du Shaba Central Entre le 7e et le 18e Siecle." *African Economic History*, 10:117-49.

Dickson P. G. M. 1967. *The Finan·ial Revolution in England: A Study in the Development of Public Credit 1688-1756.* New York: St. Martin's Press.

Dorward, D. C. 1974. "Ethnography and Administration: A Study on Anglo-Tiv 'Working Mis-understanding'." *Journal of African History*, 15:457–77.

———. "An Unknown Nigerian Export: Tiv Benniseed Production, 1900–1960." *Journal of African History*, 16:431–59.

———. 1976. "Precolonial Tiv Trade and Cloth Currency." *International Journal of African Historical Studies* 9:576–91.

Dupré, Georges. 1982. *Un Ordre et sa Destruction*. Paris: ORSTOM.

Dupré, Marie-Claude. 1981–2. "Pour Une Histoire des Productions: La Métallurgie du Fer chez les Teke." Cahiers de l'ORSTOM serie def Sciences Humaines 18:195–223.

Earle, A. F. 1954. Colonial Monetary Theory. *Social and Economic Studies*, 3:96–105.

Eggert, R. K. 1980. "Zur Rolle des Wertmessers (mitako) am Oberen Zaire, 1877–1908." *Annales Aequatoria*, 1:263–324.

Einzig, Paul. 1949. *Primitive Money in Its Ethnological, Historical and Economic Aspects*. London: Eyre and Spottiswood.

Ekejiuba, Felicia. 1967. "Omu Okwei, the Merchant Queen of Ossomari: A Biographical Sketch." *Journal of the Historical Society of Nigeria*, 3:633–46.

Eyo, Ekpo. 1979. *Nigeria and the Evolution of Money*. London: Ethnographica.

Fernandez, James. 1982. *Bwiti: An Ethnography of the Religious Imagination in Africa*. Princeton, NJ: Princton University Press.

Field, Margaret J. 1960. *Search for Security: An Ethno-psychiatric Study of Rural Ghana*. Evanston IL: Northwestern University Press.

Forrest, Tom. 1993. *Politics and Economic Development in Nigeria*. Boulder, Colorado: Westview.

Galbraith, J. K. 1975 *Money, Whence It Came, Where It Went*. Boston, MA: Houghton Mifflin.

Garrard, Timothy F. 1980. *Akan Weights and the Gold Trade*. London: Longman.

Gilbert, Michelle. 1988. "The Sudden Death of a Millionaire: Conversion and Consensus in a Ghanaian Kingdom." *Africa*, 58:291–313.

Goucher, Candace. 1981. "Iron is Iron 'Til It is Rust: Trade and Ecology in the Decline of West African Iron Smelting." *Journal of African History*, 22:179–89.

Guyer, Jane I. 1980. *The Provident Societies in the Rural Economy of Yaoundé: 1945–60*. Boston, MA: Boston University African Studies Center, Working Paper No. 48.

———. 1986. "Indigenous Currencies and the History of Marriage Payments: A Case Study from Cameroon." *Cahiers d'Etudes Africaines*, 104:577–610.

———. 1987. "'The Impact of Money' in Village Communities: Thoughts on Colonial Currencies and the Transformation of Values." Paper presented to the conference, "New Perspectives on Colonial Africa." Urbana, Illinois.

———. 1992. "Representation without Taxation: An Essay on Democracy in Rural Nigeria 1952–1990." *African Studies Review*, 35:41–79.

———. 19 93. "Wealth in People and Self-Realization in Equatorial Africa." *Man* (n.s.) 28:243–65.

Harms, Robert. 1981. *River of Wealth, River of Sorrow: The Central Zaire Basin in the Era of the Slave Trade, 1500–1891*. New Haven, CT: Yale University Press.

Hart, Keith. 1986. "Heads or Tails? Two Sides of the Coin." *Man* (n.s.) 21:637–58.

Hazelwood, Arthur. 1954. "The Economics of Colonial Monetary Arrangements." *Social and Economic Studies*, 3:291–315.

Henderson, Richard N. 1972. *The King in Every Man: Evolutionary Trends in Onitsha Ibo Society and Culture*. New Haven, CT: Yale University Press.

Herbert, E. W. 1984 *Red Gold of Africa. Copper in Precolonial History and Culture*. Madison, WI: University of Wisconsin Press.

Hilton, A. 1985. *The Kingdom of Kongo*. Oxford: The Clarendon Press.

Hogendorn, Jan and Marion Johnson. 1986. *The Shell Money of the Slave Trade*. New York and Cambridge: Cambridge University Press.

Homer, Sidney and Richard Sylla. 1991. *A History of Interest Rates*. New Brunswick, CT: Rutgers University Press.

Hopkins, A. G. 1966. "The Currency Revolution in South-West Nigeria in the Late Nineteenth Century." *Journal of the Historical Society of Nigeria*, 3:471–83.

————. 1970. "The Creation of a Colonial Monetary System: The Origins of the West African Currency Board." *International Journal of African Historical Studies*, 3:101–32.

————. 1973. *An Economic History of West Africa*. New York: Columbia University Press.

Humphrey, Caroline. 1985. "Barter and Economic Disintegration." *Man* (n.s.) 20:48–72.

————. 1991 "'Icebergs,' Barter, and the Mafia in Provincial Russia." *Anthropology Today* 7:8–13.

Humphrey, Caroline and Stephen Hugh-Jones, eds. 1992. *Barter, Exchange and Value: An Anthropological Approach*. New York and Cambridge: Cambridge University Press.

Iroko, A. Felix. 1987. "Les Cauris en Afrique Occidentale, du Xe au XXe siècle." Thèse Sorbonne, Paris.

Jevons, W. Stanley. 1875. *Money and the Mechanism of Exchange*. London, England: Kegan Paul, Trench, Trubner and Co.

Johansson, Sven-Olof. 1967. *Nigerian Currencies: Manillas, Cowries and Others*. n.p., Sweden: Alfe-Tryk.

Johnson, Marion. 1966. "The Ounce in Eighteenth-Century West African Trade." *Journal of African History* 7:197–214.

Jones. G. I. 1964. "Native and Trade Currencies in Southern Nigeria during the Eighteenth and Nineteenth Centuries." *Africa*, 28:43–54.

Kay, G. B. 1972. *The Political Economy of Colonialism in Ghana: A Collection of Documents and Statistics*. New York and Cambridge: Cambridge University Press.

Kirk-Greene, A. H. M. 1960. "The Major Currencies in Nigerian History." *Journal of the Historical Society of Nigeria*, 2:132–50.

Kopytoff, Igor. 1987. *The African Frontier: The Reproduction of Traditional African Societies*. Bloomington, IN: Indiana University Press.

Krieger, Andrew J. 1992. *The Money Bazaar: Inside the Trillion-Dollar World of Currency Trading*. New York: Times Books.

Laburthe-Tolra, Philippe. 1981 *Les Seigneurs de la Forêt*. Paris: Sorbonne.

Law, Robin. 1992. "Posthumous Questions for Karl Polanyi: Price Inflation in Precolonial Dahomey." *Journal of African History*, 33:387–420.

————. 1991. "Computing Domestic Prices in Precolonial West Africa: A Methodological Exercise from the Slave Coast." *History in Africa*, 18:239–57.

Lovejoy, Paul E. 1974. "Interregional Monetary Flows in the Precolonial Trade of Nigeria." *Journal of African History*, 15:563–85.

MacGaffey, Janet. 1991. *The Real Economy of Zaire: The Contribution of Smuggling and Other Unofficial Activities to National Wealth*. Philadelphia, PA: University of Pennsylvania Press.

McCaskie, T. C. 1986. "Accumulation: Wealth and Belief in Asante History, 2. The Twentieth Century." *Africa*, 56:3–23.

McDonald, Terrence J. and Sally K. Ward. 1984 *The Politics of Urban Fiscal Policy*. Beverley Hills, CA: Sage.

McPhee, Allan. 1926. *The Economic Revolution in British West Africa*. New York: Negro Universities Press.

Mabogunje, Akin. 1990. "Urban Planning and the Post-Colonial State in Africa: A Research Overview." *African Studies Review*, 33:121–203.

Mahieu, A. 1923. "Numismatique au Congo." *Congo*, 1:1900–9.

Manufacturers Association of Nigeria. 1984. *Who Makes What in Nigeria*. Lagos: Academy Press.

Marx, Karl. [1977] 1954. *Capital*, Vol I. Moscow: Progress Publishers.

Melitz, Jacques. 1974. *Primitive and Modern Money: An Interdisciplinary Approach*. Reading, MA: Addison-Wesley.

Miller, Joseph. 1988. *Way of Death: Merchant Capitalism and the Angolan Slave Trade, 1730-1830*. Madison, WI: University of Wisconsin Press.

Mintz, Sidney. 1964. "Currency Problems in Eighteenth Century Jamaica and Gresham's Law." In *Process and Patterns in Culture*, ed. Robert A. Manners, 248-265. Chicago: Aldine Press.

Naanen, Ben. "Economy Within An Economy: Manilla Currency, Exchange Rate Instability and Social Conditions in Southeastern Nigeria, 1900-1948." (Unpublished ms.)

Neale, Walter C. 1976. *Monies in Societies*. San Francisco, CA: Chandler and Sharp.

Niehans, Jurg. 1978. *The Theory of Money*. Baltimore, MD: The Johns Hopkins University Press.

Northrup, David. 1978. *Trade without Rulers: Precolonial economic development on Southeastern Nigeria*. Oxford: Clarendon Press.

Nwabuguoghu, A.I. 1984. "The Isusu: An Institution for Capital Formation and the Ngwa Igbo: Its Origin and Development to 1951." *Africa*,54:46-58.

Ofonagoro, Walter Ibekwe. 1979a. *Trade and Imperialism in Southern Nigeria, 1881-1929*. New York: Nok.

———. 1979b. "From Traditional to British Currency in Southern Nigeria: Analysis of a Currency Revolution 1880-1948." *Journal of Economic History*, 39:623-54.

Onoh, J. K. 1982. *Money and Banking in Africa*. London: Longman.

Parry, J. and M. Bloch. 1989. *Money and the Morality of Exchange*. New York and Cambridge: Cambridge University Press.

Polanyi, Karl. 1964. "'Sortings' and 'Ounce Trade' in the West African Slave Trade." *Journal of African History*, 5:154-69.

Pressnell, L. S. 1956. *Country Banking in the Industrial Revolution*. Oxford: The Clarendon Press.

Quiggin, A. H. 1949. *A Survey of Primitive Money: The Beginnings of Currency*. London: Methuen.

Reddy, William M. 1987. *Money and Liberty in Modern Europe: A Critique of Historical Understanding*. New York and Cambridge: Cambridge University Press.

Ricardo, David. 1951. *Pamphlets: 1815-1823*. Vol. 4 of *The Works and Correspondence of David Ricardo*, ed. Piero Sraffa. New York and Cambridge: Cambridge University Press.

Rivallain, Josette. 1987. "Etude Comparée des Phénomenes Prémonétaires en Protohistoire Européenne et en Ethnoarchéologie Africaine" Thèse d'Etat. Sorbonne, Paris.

Samarin, W.J. 1989. *The Black Man's Burden: African Colonial Labor on the Congo and Ubangi Rivers, 1890-1900*. Boulder, CO: Westview Press.

Sampson, Anthony. 1990. *The Midas Touch: Understanding the Dynamic New Money Around Us*. New York: Dutton.

Schweitzer, Pierre-Paul. 1972 . "A Report on the Fund." In *Bretton Woods Revisited*, eds. A. L. K. Acheson, J. F. Chant, and M. F. J. Prachowny, 121-128. Toronto: University of Toronto Press.

Shipton, Parker. 1989. *Bitter Money: Cultural Economy and Some African Meanings of Forbidden Commodities*. American Ethnological Society Monograph Series no. 1. Washington, D.C.: American Ethnological Society.

———. 1990. "Borrowing and Lending in The Gambia. Local Perspectives on Formal and Informal Finance in Agrarian West Africa." Unpublished manuscript.

Simmel, Georg. [1900] 1990. *The Philosophy of Money*. New York: Routledge.

Smith, R. M. 1986. "Transfer Incomes, Risk and Security: The Roles of the Family and the Collectivity in Recent Theories of Fertility Change." In *The State of Population Theory: Forward from Malthus*, eds. D. Coleman and R. Schofield, 188-211. Oxford: Basil Blackwell.

Sowelem, R. A. 1967. *Towards Financial Independence in a Developing Economy. An Analysis of the Monetary Experience of the Federation of Rhodesia and Nyasaland 1952-63*. London: George Allen and Unwin.

Strathern, Marilyn. 1988. *The Gender of the Gift: Problems with Women and Problems with Society in Melanesia*. Berkeley, CA: University of California Press.

Tchundjang Pouemi, Joseph. 1980. *Monnaie, Servitude et Liberté: La répression monétaire de l'Afrique*. Paris: Editions j.a.

Thane, Pat. 1990. "Government and Society in England and Wales, 1750-1914." In *The Cambridge Social History of Britain, 1750-1950*, Vol. 3, ed. F. M. L. Thompson, 1-61. New York and Cambridge: Cambridge University Press.

Vallée, Olivier. 1989. *Le prix de l'argent CFA: heurs et malheurs de la zone franc.* Paris: Karthala.

Vansina, Jan. 1990. *Paths in the Rainforests: Toward a History of Political Tradition in Equatorial Africa.* Madison, WI: University of Wisconsin Press.

Veseth, Michael. 1990. *Mountains of Debt: Crisis and Change in Renaissance Florence, Victorian Britain, and Postwar America.* London: Oxford University Press.

Von Thünen, Johann Heinrich. [1826-63] 1966. *Von Thünen's Isolated State.* Oxford: Pergamon Press.

Walzer, Michael. 1983. *Spheres of Justice: A Defense of Pluralism and Equality* New York: Basic Books.

Warnier, Jean-Pierre and Ian Fowler. 1979. "A Nineteenth Century Ruhr in Central Africa." *Africa*, 49:329-51.

Webb, James L. A. 1982. "Toward the Comparative Study of Money: A Reconsideration of West African Currencies and Neoclassical Economic Concepts." *International Journal of African Historial Studies*, 15:455-66.

Weiner, Annette. 1992. *Inalienable Possessions: The Paradox of Keeping-While-Giving.* Berkeley, CA: University of California Press.

Wilks, Ivor. 1975. *Asante in the Nineteenth Century.* New York and Cambridge: Cambridge University Press.

PART I

PRE-COLONIAL CURRENCY DYNAMICS

No aspect of African political culture and economic valuation could have been more inventive during the eighteenth and nineteenth centuries than monetization. Hogendorn and Johnson's figures suggest cowry imports in the eighteenth century of just under 13,000 tonnes, or about 12 billion (thousand million) *moneta* shells (1986:62). The figures for the nineteenth century are very much higher, diversified into *annulus* as well as *moneta* and reaching a "frenzied climax" (1986:78) around 1880. It was in the eighteenth century that the Ashanti state suppressed the use of iron rods and imposed a gold-dust currency (Arhin, Ch. 4). And in Equatorial Africa these centuries saw the continuing growth and change of the variously shaped metallic currencies: copper croisettes, iron rods, spear-heads and aggressively imported wires and plates. These circulated in some places alongside the raphia-cloths, whose origins as currency may never be amenable to exact dating. Far from their practices representing "tradition" in its conventional sense, West and Equatorial peoples of the immediate pre-colonial centuries were probably—in many cases self-consciously—engaged in massive experimentation.

The papers in this section focus on the multiple tensions and innovations in two different areas, one in West Africa and the other in the Equatorial region. In both areas, there was a previous history of multiple and changing currencies well before the eighteenth century, but the authors point out how scanty the sources are for reconstructing a plausible account of how they worked. Law (Ch. 2), for example, reports how the famous ounce trade in assorted goods may well be seen not as a concession to already established "African traditions of fixed prices," but as a specific response to currency instabilities in the mid-eighteenth century, instituted by both European and African traders in their own interests. M.-C. Dupré (Ch. 1) is inclined to eschew any attempt to summarize the total complexity of the currency dynamic among the Teke because of the limited direct sources about a regional system that included, at the very least, various iron objects, salt, copper, and multiple kinds of raphia-cloth. She proceeds instead by focusing on the way in which the circulation of

various types of one key currency, namely raphia-cloth, reflected a persistent political tension along whose fault-line Teke history itself was reproduced.

These authors' caution about assuming a fixed "tradition" must inform all of the
other contributions. We are clearly all dealing with phases and eras in the shaping of
monetary experience and institutions, and not with an episodic history for which
one episode can be confidently designated—beyond a few simple points—as the status quo ante. Law suggests that Western conceptions of an African diffidence about
market sales that were much debated as a cultural characteristic in the mid-twentieth
century may well stem from the era of the Great Cowry Inflation after 1880, when
people withdrew into barter and subsistence, and credit became much more risky.
On the eve of colonial rule, the cowry zones of Africa were suddenly less commercial
than they had been for the previous two centuries. In Equatorial Africa, the late nineteenth century also saw a flood of currency imports, but in addition to external influences M.-C. Dupré (Ch. 1) sees pressures and "shocking innovations" from within:
the creation of new categories of raphia-cloth that—by virtue of difference—were
able to escape the intricate circulatory flows that kept imported and home-woven
cloths in separate and noncompeting channels. Certainly, the cultural sources discussed by Barber (Ch. 9) suggest that a fundamentally positive Yoruba notion of
money as a means of "self-realization" had gone through mutations that were
already elaborated well before the imposition of colonial rule.

By concentrating on changing tensions, both papers suggest a theme that recurs
in several others: the social and political challenges of running an open economy. In
a vast continent with a mobile population and constant engagement with the exigen-
cies of external trade, currency change was at the cutting edge of social change. Political leadership struggled to control the flow of goods and their valuation with a multiplicity of weapons, but many of them were ultimately impossible to sustain. By
mandating cowry exchange, the Dahomey state could control taxes and the stores of
private wealth, but only as long as cowries retained their value. By mandating types
of raphia-cloth, and the conditions of their production and use, the Teke leadership
could sustain the structural tensions of a system at once autonomous and deeply
integrated into regional trade, but only as long as new cloth types did not proliferate.
Both sudden lurches and otherwise mysterious quietude in the levels of social payments seem to result from these struggles. In Dahomey, bridewealth apparently
withstood the cowry inflation, possibly because—as Ekejiuba (Ch. 6), Manuh (Ch. 8)
and Guyer (Ch. 5) point out in their contributions—the multiple sources and destinations of marriage payments are linked to the creation of long-term relationships,
making other more dependable media perhaps more sought after by an ordinary
agricultural population, interested in solid alliances and secure resource access. Here
home-produced cloth holds its own as a component of payments. On the other
hand, the political nature of bridewealth control among the Teke meant that relax-
ation of controls left a space for sudden and intense competitive innovation in the
early twentieth century.

Conditions of convertibility, whether between local groups as in the Equatorial
case, or between Europeans and Africans in the Dahomey case, were politically mediated but also controllable only ephemerally. The interface had a changing ecology,
due as much to the backward linkages into such conditions as metal production and
use, and financial policy in Europe, as it did to the negotiations of actors on the scene.

Sources dried up; goods became available; different nationalities of Europeans had different and changing possibilities for substituting commodities for precious metals in the African trade.

With these papers, then, the authors leave behind a model of a morally framed system of exchange spheres in pre-colonial West and Equatorial Africa in favor of a historical view of highly dynamic, constantly challenging, tenuously controllable innovations. It was less the culturally defined nature of the goods than the shifting vectors of power that differentiated currency flows (see also Arhin, Ch. 4). In light of this work on the pre-colonial period, the vast currency interventions of the twentieth century that are addressed in subsequent sections must be seen as new eruptions in a long series of shifts, each of which caught particular communities at a different juncture of their own social and cultural history. The "beginnings" of these, as of most of the other papers, therefore reflect the sense of a story picked up in the middle of its course.

1

Raphia Monies Among the Teke: Their Origin and Control

MARIE-CLAUDE DUPRE

Introduction

Among the Teke, raphia coexisted with other monies of shell, copper, and iron, but these have disappeared before anthropologists could observe them. In the zone between the Ogooué and the Zaire Rivers, the diversity of objects used as money marks the identity of groups and peoples who define themselves as different one from the other. In order to preserve for money the definition that applies in western societies—as a neutral and universal means of exchange—anthropologists have spoken of closed or quasiclosed spheres, of restricted exchange, of social transactions, of subsistence economies, of reduced convertibility, and of variable equivalences. What I have been able to learn of the history of raphia shows, above all, the Teke strategies for preserving control over their means of exchange. Could we not revise our view of the data on these bases?

Raphia in the Monies of Lower Zaire

Raphia cloth circulated in all the Teke groups. In the kingdom of Kongo, it existed side by side with shells collected on the Island of Luanda. It could also be found in the kingdom of Loango, and, despite the paucity of the historical sources both written and oral, amongst the peoples of the Niari basin. And everywhere between the Ogooué and the Zaire, it coexisted with other objects of exchange. The Teke also had a currency made of copper from the Mindouli mines; the Kukua had shells coming from the northwest and small, iron arm-rings. The metal-working peoples of the Chaillu Mountains used salt that came from the coast, as well as their iron objects, anvils and adzes. Small iron bars circulated in Lower Zaire at the beginning of the twentieth century, as described by K. Laman (1953) and, judging from the study undertaken among the Beembé, gunpowder, salt, palm wine, and groundnuts were periodically the object of controlled equivalences in the numerous markets of the

39

country (G. Dupré 1985:112). At the end of the nineteenth century, among the Teke of Pumbu, there were alongside one another cotton and raphia cloth, brass bars, beads, shells, dishes, fire-arms and salt (Vansina 1973:268).

The history of West Central Africa, from the Ogooué to Luanda, since the fifteenth century is marked by the introduction of false money oriented towards guaranteeing the maximum profit for the European merchants. First of all, there were shells from the Brazilian coast—similar to the *nzimbu* from the Isle of Luanda—that were introduced by the Portuguese. Then raphia cloth passed back and forth between the coast of Loango and the Kingdom of Kongo. After the French arrived in Pumbu in 1882, the copper *ngiele* were replaced within a few years by brass rods called *mitakos*.[1] In 1905, finally, the evaporation of salt was prohibited along the whole Atlantic Coast, and it was salt imported (from where, one is not sure) by the concessionary companies that was used to buy the rubber from the peoples in Chaillu Mountains. Each time, foreigners tried to appropriate the origin of the currency for themselves. And this same process continues today, under the advice of the International Monetary Fund (IMF).

Places and Periods

The groups with various names that today claim Teke identity inhabit a continuous area in the savannas that stretches from the Zaire to the Alima in Congo, and crosses over into Zaire in the south and Gabon in the north (see Figure 1.1). Brazzaville and Kinshasa were built in Teke territory and Franceville is very close to the limits of the Teke region in Gabon. Several centuries ago, some Teke groups settled in the forests of the Chaillu Mountains. At the beginning of the twentieth century, even though they had become mixed with Sundi groups, the Teke were still masters of the zone that stretched from the right bank of the Zaire, between Mindouli and its copper mines and Kingoue; nowadays the territorial advance of the Lari is taking place well to the north of Brazzaville. At least ten different groups (among which are some, identified by linguists, which now are represented by only a few speakers) have been studied by observers of diverse origins: linguists, geographers, anthropologists, archeologists, historians, art historians, and musicologists. This list is offered to illustrate how diverse is the Teke subject matter and how varied are the available sources in both quantity and kind.

The reality of a Teke culture, whose linguistic links have been partially explored by the CRLS[2] at Lyons, is affirmed by members of diverse groups now divided amongst the three countries. I suggest, after confronting a series of anthropological studies, that all Teke groups possess a single political structure characterized by restricted territories, within which two ideals interface, represented by two political chiefs: the master of the land and the master of the people.

This Teke political structure and its concrete manifestations vary a little from one group to another, but all are generally characterized by strong bipolar political power. This particular political mode is based on a bicephalous chieftaincy, exercized internally within small territories, regrouping a few hundred or a thousand people. At any moment of their history, the inhabitants of each "territory" find themselves confronted by alternatives defined by the powers held by each chief, called *nga*, "owner of." The master of the land, *nga nstie*, offers an ideal of economic and political development which could—and did—go as far as a hierarchical type of kingdom. He

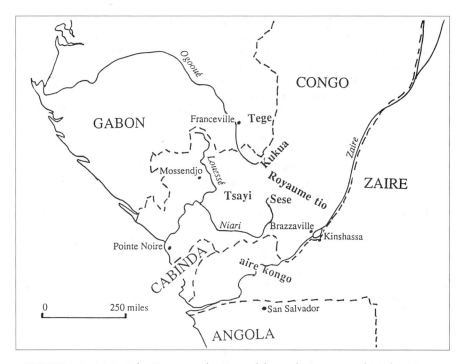

FIGURE 1-1 Main Teke Groups at the Turn of the 20th Century and Modern States (Broken Lines).

"possesses" the products of the land, and by extension the products of agriculture, craftwork, and commerce. He alone is authorized to accumulate material goods, which are mostly destroyed at his death. The masters of people, *nga bate*, (or *nga nzo*, masters of the "house," lineage segment, maternal uncle [*ngu balaga*] or "male mother") possess the people of their lineage and have power over their health and fertility. They offer an ideal of human health and prosperity based on frugality, obedience, and social peace. The dynamic of Teke history is, at one and the same time, the permanent tension that exists internally between the two chiefs (defined as homologous *and* opposed) and the different pressures exerted externally by the surrounding peoples. According to historical period, the Teke country may be exporter of goods, in transition, or autarchical. Teke political theory puts only one, extreme, limit on the rivalry between the two masters: anyone who managed to destroy the ideal of his rival would destroy the fundamental principle of Teke society.

In spite of the widespread existence of "masters of the land" in all of sub-Saharan Africa, a relationship of this bipolar type has never been described. It is possible that it only exists in a visible fashion—and theorized—amongst the Teke, and in the Teke area of influence such as the Tsayi. The latter migrated "recently" into the Chaillu Mountains and the past several centuries have not left time for new practices to sediment as much as in related groups. The dialogue between the two *nga* was therefore more clearly observable in the places in which I did fieldwork. In all areas, the transformations of Teke contradictory structure—the successive developments of the *nga ntsie* pole—leave at each juncture the *nga bate* pole to try to reconstitute the bipolarity facing a new political chief. The Tsayi and the other Teke, held within this constraining bipolar structure, have created their history in grand oscillations, with periods of expansion followed by periods of greater austerity when the masters of people regained their supremacy (M.-C. Dupré 1987, 1992). Among the Tege in Gabon, rooted on the plateau for many centuries and maybe at the origin of Teke society, it would be the *kumu* that replaced the *nkani*, having himself partially supplanted the *nga ntchie*. Nowadays, among the Kukua, the lord of the sky—two centuries after his "creation"—seems to have almost the same powers as the lords of the land. The lords and squires of the Tio Kingdom, *mubial* and *nga ntsie* among the Tsayi have managed to rebuild the structural antagonism. The opposition between the two ways of controling people is affirmed right from the foundational period amongst the Tsayi. It is infused with a concept of dynamic contradiction whereby the welfare of people is put in danger by the accumulation of "riches."

These peoples are known for their raphia weaving, which they have taught to all their neighbors, even the Kongo-Sundi of the present-day Congo. The groups included here are the Tsayi of the forest of Chaillu, studied by myself, their neighbors, the Lali, and the Tege of Gabon visited by Löffler (1975), the Tio kingdom made so well known by Vansina (1973) and the Kukua mainly described by P. Bonnafé (1978, 1987, 1988).

For What Period of History?

Archeologists have inventoried and dated the iron-work sites in the Teke savannas of Congo, tracing back the ancient origins of metallurgy to the beginning of the Christian era (Pinçon 1991), and linguists have started to examine the linguistic affinities in order to date the appearance and patterns of dialect variations. But other observers have been much more limited. The beginning of the eighteenth century seems to form an impassable barrier, as much for the anthropologists as for the historians, even if the dynamic particular to the Teke—formed by repetitions and alternations—allows us to outline the movements of earlier centuries.[3] The period principally addressed here, then, bears on the past 150 years.

What Sort of Cloth?

The variety of cloth was, in theory, immense. From the basis of lengths of cloth woven one by one, cloths of three, six, nine, and twelve pieces, then multiples of four, and cloths of six or more pieces could be made by sewing them together. In addition, each piece differed according to the fineness and the length of the threads cut from the raphia foliole, and according to the stylistic working of the fringes. Color also contributed—natural, black and different nuances of yellow, red, and brown—as did the different possible checkerworks. Finally, from at least the eighteenth century, the Kukua wove for their "lords of the sky" velours formed of two wefts superimposed, for which the variety of motifs was even greater.[4] Each Teke group had its own classifications and names. And local histories have contributed, as we shall see, to augment the variety yet further.

For What Uses?

This question cross-cuts the previous one, while at the same time including another element, namely the weaver, his identity, and status. And it leads back into the basic sociology of Teke groups.

These four questions lead us finally into the question at the heart of the subject: in a variable situation, created by regional diversity, stirred up by the parallel histories of related groups, how is it possible to infer the characteristic of "money" from a raphia cloth production as abundant as it was varied, even when the topic is narrowed down to one and a half centuries and focused on specific groups? Or, to formulate the question in another way, how were exchanges internal to a regional ensemble considered? And how were acceptable regional currencies developed, based on reciprocally fruitful relations? The answers emerge from information collected by anthropologists, that is, through maximum recourse to testimonies given by the various Teke groups.

Raphia Cloth: From Nature to Culture

Balandier wrote of a "raphia civilization," in relation to the Kingdom of Kongo in the fifteenth and sixteenth centuries ([1965] 1992:77). But since his study, archeologists have found traces of palmnut shells from well before 2500 BP in sites in Cameron, and abundant remains in neolithic sites in Gabon, Congo, and Zaire, between 2500 and 2000 BP (Lanfranchi and Clist 1991:182). The Teke, for their part, give great emphasis to the importance of the palm trees that they tend, using methods sometimes very close to proto-agriculture, for the fruits, sap, leaves, and woody parts. They have used many subspecies of palm for weaving. Certain groups prefer the trees that grow in the marshes, others those that grow in dry sand, while the Teke who have migrated into the forest cut out the small trees in the surrounding vegetation to give the palms more light. Yet other Tsayi went to the Tege area to find a type of palm most valued because of the length of the folioles, a quality that was appreciated enough to override their lesser resistance to ecological conditions. Furthermore, all the villages were planted with palms. These trees formed the heart of the copse that, many years later, would mark the trace of a human habitation long forgotten[5] and handed over to the invisible powers.

The geographical specificities and the cycle of the seasons had their role to play. The young leaves were picked at a certain stage of their development. For the palms growing in the marshes to the north of the Kukua plateau, the folioles cut from the central spine were scraped, after having been retted. The leaves were dried, on the roof according to the Kukua, next to the fire during the rainy season according to the Tsayi. The foliole, of variable dimensions according to the source tree, was divided into blades of variable width. This operation was carried out by hand when the fiber was destined for a coarse weave, or with a special tool when the thread was meant to be very fine. The creation of the warp was a delicate operation: for each piece of cloth to be produced (a rectangle of about 50 x 70 cm), the loom had to be mounted vertically with a row of warp-threads; only the end-beams were fixed. The weaver spent more time setting up the frame than weaving.

Another bottleneck was imposed by the number of days on which a person could work. The Teke lived according to a four-day week with one entire day, *mpika*, dedicated to ceremonies and political meetings, during which it was forbidden to work, hunt, or cultivate. The Tsayi recognized a second day when work was restricted. The Tege of Gabon, by contrast, followed a six-day week and have a reputation for being prolific producers.

The Tsayi trace the invention of weaving back to a time that preceded their creation as a society. When Mukaga nga Kabela crossed the Upper Ogooué and divided the land among his children, weaving was already known. Arrival in the forest provoked an addition to the technical chain: Mukiki the Pygmy taught them how to dry the fibres close to the fire so that they could weave in all seasons (M.-C. Dupré 1984). Among the Kukua, the technique of weaving goes back to the creation. In spite of the existence all over present-day Zaire of peoples whose raphia-cloth production is greater today than that of the Teke (Loir 1935; Meurant 1987), the Kukua claim that the diffusion and the perfection of palm varieties and weaving techniques originates within the Teke sphere. Only for the velours is their origin unknown.

All the men wove, affirm the Teke unanimously. Research modifies this proposition, even for pre-colonial times. Apprenticeship was general, occurring between the ages of seven and ten years, but it is possible that certain marginal people were excluded. And even if all male children actually learned how to weave, only certain adults devoted themselves to weaving. During the 1960s, each Tsayi village still harbored an old weaver. Possibly this is the simple reason why a young anthropologist notes that few Kukua weavers remain vigorous and that the artisan is often too tired by evening to fulfill his conjugal duties (Ngoulou 1985). Among the Lali, people said bluntly that young adults could not touch the weaver's shuttle without becoming sterile. This opposition between artisanal production and the production of children may explain why the technique was practiced in the later years of life. But then, how were the periods of high production noted by historians managed, when the exchange of cloth between Teke groups and beyond was so important?

Today, and for several decades, the weaver works alone in his house. But people remember times when the fixed part of the looms, the upper and lower beams, were on the roof ledges of houses placed at the center of the village. Tsayi, Lali, and Kukua wove in public, and it was an occasion for visits, observations, commentaries, and diffusion of techniques for perfection of the craft. Information on the number of pieces made and the identity of the artisans was constantly watched over by the elders, because, as Bonnafé has emphasized, the artisan never wove for himself but always for his seniors.

A Constraining Political Organization

We have not yet addressed the question of currency. But already, in the conditions of production of a single piece of raphia cloth, one can judge the influence of social hierarchies, religious conceptions, political structure, historical memory, and myth at all stages of weaving. The importance of the controls placed on this object of human fabrication made of it, as the Teke always point out, the emblem of an identity that nevertheless required continual affirmation and preservation. This identity was manipulated by the elders, because up to an advanced age and well past the age of marriage and paternity, the young men were entirely submitted to the authority of those senior to them. The power of the uncle, or *nga bate*, was the most impressive; it was often relieved by the more cordial authority of the father, with whom a son lived.[6] All products of a house, whether from the hunt, gathering, agriculture, or craftwork belonged entirely to the elders. Other leaders, masters of the earth and—among the Kukua—the lords of the sky, who were installed in the eighteenth century, appropriated an important part of the raphia-cloth production in the form of fines that they inflicted on those declared guilty of delicts.

With respect to raphia cloths or other nonperishable goods defined as riches, it was unthinkable that a young man should keep the smallest part. In return, the elders, uncles, fathers, masters of the earth, and lords of the sky who owned all of material production were obliged to redistribute it. About the end of the nineteenth century, during a period of flourishing production and exchange, Bonnafé (1987:78–80) noted an increase in the variety and quantity of food imported to the Kukua plateau, in particular animal protein. Apart from this kind of material redistribution that was largely regulated by the local markets,[7] the elders directly regulated the health and fertility of their own people. Every accident of health, every delay in the spacing between births (about 53 months for the Kukua, according to Guillot 1973) was attributed to their displeasure, and people searched for those who might be responsible for such disharmony. The guilty party was the one who had not offered the totality of his gains, or who—more seriously—had tried to exercise some kind of social responsibility without having been authorized to do so. These two accusations were often formulated in terms of sorcery; the guilty party had abrogated the obligations of his subordinate status and, in so doing, entered the extra-natural order manipulated by his elders, those who very literally "possessed" him (Bonnafé 1978, 1988; M.-C. Dupré 1984, 1987).

Varieties of Raphia Cloth and Control of
the Means of Exchange

Cloth as a Representation of the Person

In the abundant cloth production of the different Teke groups, those pieces that served as reference points in exchange and social transactions were, amongst the Tsayi, the crude length off the loom and the non-dyed cloth made up of twelve pieces. The first served as an introductory gift to other transactions, the payment for a musician or a dancer during their performance, and small purchases in the market. The second was put into circulation for matrimonial compensations, fines, and blood payments. In both cases, the cloth was new; it was presented carefully folded in accordion style or rolled into a bale, sometimes sewn. In everyday life, one piece served as headcovering or a ceremonial cloth for ordinary people, and was then no longer exchangeable.

Among the Tsayi, like the Kukua, it was the largest cloth that served for the acquisition of slaves: *kevota* (up to 48 pieces) for the former, *nzuona* for the latter.

Internally, the cloths were intensely representative of human equivalence (marriage, adultery, and murder), a recognition of political order (fines for transgressions), an opening gift for the negotiation of social relations, in a fashion that is still a given of social life today. Even in the case of a 5F coin, the smallest modern unit of account, one must rub it on the arm of the patient before bringing it to the healer to solicit his services. What matters is the quantity of information it carries, not its "objective" value.

It was in the context of contact with neighboring groups, and then with peoples of different origins, that cloths were used for exchanges in their strict sense. They then left the internal sphere. Bonnafé (1987) dates to the eighteenth and nineteenth centuries the growing gap between the needs of houses and the circuits of "produce values" that developed when the reservoir of nonmatrimonial exchanges broadened for the last time in Kukua history.

The Cloth as an Extension of the Person

One cloth that had considerable importance in the nineteenth century was the particular type that served as a shroud. The Teke custom is well known, being shown in old photographs, whereby important men were buried after being wrapped in multiple layers of cloth, to the point where the entire bale attained a diameter of two meters or more. Very early, at least before the 18th century, among the Kukua as among the Tsayi, shrouds were imported from the Tege. The *muta* were much larger; they were also much more crude, loosely woven with broad threads and not tightly woven. These cloths, coming from another Teke group, were not used for bridewealth, so that the internal circulation of wives was kept separate from the accumulation of goods through exchange. Among the Tsayi, at the dawn of the twentieth century, the size of the funeral bale had come to depend on the number of "commercial partners" of the deceased, who arrived over a period of months to recognize the heir and make clear their intention of maintaining the chain of exchanges. Even for this material form of riches, accumulation ought not to excede the space of a single life. The destruction of *muta* manifests the priority given to the person against the acquisition of things.

Cloth as a Manifestation of Teke Identity

The Teke habitat coincides in large part with the sandy plateaus that form a large island in the middle of the equatorial forest, and their language is—as far as linguists know—very close to proto-Bantu. What we know about the migrations of various forest peoples over the past centuries suggests that they did not cross into the Teke sands. This boundedness did not prevent constant movement and quasi-individual migrations within the Teke area. Soret (1973:203-5) has been the only scholar to remark on this strange drift across the Congo Plateau from northwest to southeast, which he interprets as a migration by stages towards Brazzaville. But in the eighteenth century or earlier, the diffusion of the *nkobi* charm that legitimized the existence of new leaders in the Tio kingdom, followed the same broad path. People told me that nuclear families or individual men, coming from the savanna to settle in Tsayi country, defined themselves as Teke, and of course adopted the local rules. This constant mobility was reminder of the importance, for each man, of all four lineages from which he descended; in this way he was assured of finding along the way at least one lineage to whom he could offer obedience, because it was the elder who protected against the invisible powers.[8] When the new settler could not find a lineage to accept him, he turned to the master of the land. The masters of people only "possessed" those of their own lineages and could not control all the newcomers. Masters of the land thus had an opportunity to augment the number of their followers.

Vansina (1973) notes for the Tio kingdom that the low population density encouraged individual men to move, and that the masters of the land competed amongst each other to offer the inhabitants the best conditions of life in order to keep them in place. In particular, they made every effort to prevent manifestations of sorcery. His description of the "little society" evokes, for me, one of the states of the bipolar system, where the welfare extolled by the master of people was reinforced by the master of the land. Even if the spirit of competition and the desire for acquisition existed, the system would connect with difficulty to economic demands dominated by trade and the accumulation of wealth, because such a connection entails an inversion of values or their disjuncture.

The Tio kingdom has never been truly centralized; the economic development of the seventeenth century encouraged the creation of quasi-independent lords[9] who united several territorial units. The bipolar structure that I have built up from observations among the Tsayi presupposes a certain territorial autonomy to maintain it. As a result, the Teke area as a whole appears submitted to contradictory pressures: the autonomy of territories necessary for the authority of the master of people was just as important as the external relations encouraged by the master of the land. The diversity of raphia cloth came, as if naturally, to distinguish between neighboring Teke groups, while at the same time offering a recognized common basis, usable for exchanges amongst them. Outside the limits of the Teke area, the cloths became export items. The convertability sketched in at the end of the nineteenth century in the Chaillu mountains between "monies" of raphia cloth, iron, and salt was accompanied by an effort to produce a certain cultural cohesion. Different peoples invoked a common female ancestor, Ngunu, and clans with diverse names declared themselves related. To come back to the Teke, this diversity internal to their culture area can be used *a posteriori* by the historian. The Tege became those to whom neighboring groups went to buy *muta*; the Kukua were at the origin of velour cloth; the Sese of the Upper Niari actively participated in the regional exchanges stimulated by trade by exporting a great amount of raphia. Weaving was not only the distinguishing emblem of the Teke; it was also the trademark of a regional commerce controled by local groups, which was developing both along the lines of the slave trade and in opposition to it. Rubber, ivory and humans were the products that these societies could give up without diminishing themselves. Recall that the export of slaves to the New World was tied to an ancient usage of banishing far away the fomenters of trouble, who negated the ideal of harmony proper to the masters of people.

During the period considered here, the nature of these negative or superfluous goods traded out reflected the economic regulations and ethics of the bipolar Teke system. The simultaneous development of local exchange, where raphia cloth retained its original function, contributed to the contradictory development of a structure that was itself contradictory. The welfare of people grew through a multiplication of goods, most of which were for consumption; the political systems grew in complexity and in capacity for intervention; the Tio lords, the Kukua masters of the sky, the Tege *kumu* (Löffler 1975), and the Tsayi *mubial* controled vaster areas, had their judicial powers extended, and disposed of new means of coercion. At the same time, and inversely, according to the logic of the bipolar structure, the masters of people— placed at the interface between the individual and the system—were vigilant to maintain their control over local production, notably through strict obedience on the part of producers and through destruction of material goods at funerals. The diversity of sources for raphia cloth—these "product-values" as Bonnafé (1987) so well named them—accompanied by knowledge of their origin, contributed to maintaining pride in being Teke, engendering consciousness of belonging to an entity both vast and specific. My first information gathered among the Tsayi consisted of lists of names, the diverse known Teke groups, followed by precise localizations.

Under these conditions, the diverse "monies" of raphia, while playing fully their role as identity markers, contributed to strengthening those regional exchanges that were opposed to the devastating effects of trade as it became at the turn of the twentieth century: a time when the trading peoples lost control over the origin of the means of exchange that then became simply monies: manipulated, counterfeited, and degraded by the pre-colonial powers.

Cloth as a Control on Exchange

The last two thirds of the nineteenth century were marked amongst all the Teke groups by a strong development of commercial relations. Beside the slave trade, which continued legally to the south of the equator, migratory peoples settled on the borders of the Teke bloc, close to the Tsayi, and formed chains of exchange converging on the Atlantic for trading ivory, gum, dyes, and then rubber. An entire region developed, with its own specificities, and local monies now became convertible (G. Dupré 1972).

For a long time, long-distance trade remained embedded in a very active regional exchange. The pre-existing prosperity had depended on control over the origins of money by the peoples who were the traders. The Tsayi used to export to the Niari valley, besides the ivory and rubber that they obtained from neighboring peoples who had infiltrated into their territory, raphia cloth, bushmeat hunted by the pygmies, poultry, groundnuts, and iron produced in their mines. Equivalences were established between salt, raphia, and iron that were quite stable in the entire commercial area between the Tsayi and the coast. In the Tsayi area, where the only person allowed to become rich was the master of the land, the increase in traders had a direct effect on the production of cloth. The cloths were made bigger and more colorful; the prices rose, and the leaders made an effort to maintain use of the most beautiful cloths within a restricted circle. Only the richest individuals had the right to add them to bridewealth and, in order to be dressed in fine cloths on ceremonial days, they had to request permission from the master of the land. When the velours spread throughout the forest, they were woven in secret, out of sight, by a young kinsman of the master of the land.

This was a shocking innovation, running against previous weaving practices. It marks in fact a rupture in the political legitimacy that until then and with a certain dose of hypocrisy, presented the chief as "first among equals," to use an expression employed by the earliest anthropologists. Hereafter, the leader aspired to distinguish himself from the other leaders. Yet, this escape of political creativity from the contradictory structure coexists with the need to control an emblematic product by withdrawing it from exchange. The Teke cloths were caught up in a permanent dilemma: to materialize an identity and to stake out the life of people or to serve as money equivalent, neutral and depersonalized.

The Birth and Control of Bridewealth Inflation

Politically, the Tsayi country remained divided into small territories in which two distinct types of chiefs tried to impose two antagonistic ideals. The master of the land, who encouraged the development of exchange and production, was buried with his riches, in the hope—vain in periods of prosperity—of re-establishing the *status quo ante* more in harmony with the needs of health and fertility.

For the historian, the size of the reference type of cloth is witness to preceding states of prosperity. In the west of the Tsayi country, at the end of the nineteenth century, bridewealth cloths had only 9 pieces; in the east, already affected during the eighteenth century by a commercial thrust due to export of iron, they consisted of 12 pieces. And in the latter zone, at the end of the nineteenth century, fathers and uncles demanding for bridewealth cloths of 16, 18, or even 24 and 36 pieces. The riches of commerce gained on the sphere of social transactions and instigated bridewealth inflation.[10] From the 1920s, Tsayi country fell again into stagnation. The tax war of 1913-19, which almost annihilated the Tsayi, was caused by a revolt against "fine" that had to be paid every year out of the money obtained from rubber, even if one had worked well (M.-C. Dupré 1993). Bridewealth in 1960 stayed at a low level, about one tenth the level among the Kukua who had become prosperous cultivators of tobacco. Rolls of cloth (fixed at 12 pieces) still figured compulsorily in Tsayi payments, representing about half of the total amount offered.

In the Tio kingdom, the obligatory stop along all the exchange routes from Upper Zaire to the coast, Vansina notes the persistence of raphia cloth for social transactions between 1880 and 1892, as if the variety of monies was used there to preserve the original specificity of raphia, protected from commercial trade. By taking raphia and *ngiele* out of the sphere of exchange, the Tio accentuated the gap between the opposed social conceptions of the master of the land and the master of people. The *mitakos*, of foreign origin and denuded of intrinsic value, lent themselves perfectly to this division; they were excluded from social transactions. Vansina notes that the ideal of frugality and social harmony was in some ways preserved in the villages of the savanna, where people maintained the ideals of the small society, while the exercise of trade was confided in certain dignitaries installed on the banks of the Malebo, who were surrounded by slaves and nonkinsmen. The resistance to trade, following along the lines of the logic of the bipolar dynamic, kept familial relations in a category apart.[11]

Conclusion

The monetary uses of raphia seem to arise out of the confrontation between diverse groups. Internally to each Teke group, the oppositional structure that governs social life contains this emblematic product within its function of marking identity: the raphia cloths mark, first of all, the existence and rhythm of social transactions, welcome as alliances or disturbing, but inevitable as quarrels and transgressions. Recourse to the production of neighboring groups marks, from the beginning, the efforts of the leadership to maintain on their own territory the link between cloth and the Teke person that they "possessed." For accumulated surpluses there existed regulation through funerary destruction. Dissociation between raphia and other means of exchange appears to be the last recourse of the merchants of the Tio kingdom, to maintain the ancient practices in which raphia accumulated diverse, but not yet contradictory, roles.

It is difficult to evaluate the importance of monies that have disappeared—shells, copper, and iron bars—and impossible to reconstitute their coexistence with raphia. But one can imagine that the monetary uses of raphia, even if contemporary with the first piece ever woven, long ago have been considered secondary, even unthinkable, in the political life of Teke groups. For the leadership, the cloths received on the occasion of matrilineal alliances or payment of fines were testimonies of their authority; they were, as numerous anthropologists have pointed out, "frozen." As relations became increasingly dense within the Teke area, the first cloths that circulate are Teke shrouds, destined for destruction. The velours that appear later are strictly reserved for the *mubial* and other, most entrepreneurial, masters of the land.

Contrary to the liberal theories of western economy that promote the use of a money devoid of intrinsic value, [12] the Teke theory superimposed both of the recognized and antagonistic needs simultaneously: the two means of origin, exchange and use. For them, the source of what we consider to be "pure" money, the basis of its value that served at the same time to guarantee the efficacy of its use, was the human being, the only fundamental wealth. And by means of their antagonistic political structure, they controled both the human being and the emblematic product.

Notes

1. To the point of accomplishing the complete disappearance of the *ngiele*. A large sculpture was dedicated to it in Brazzaville in 1988, inspired by two pieces deposited in the Musée de l'Homme.
2. Centre de Recherches Linguistiques et Sémiologiques, University of Lyons II. Since 1984 one volume of "Pholia" per year has been published by the Centre.
3. I am using bipolar dynamics to explore in a "retro-prospective way" Tio political movements for the past millenium, leaning on archeological findings. See Dupré and Pinçon, (in press).
4. These velvets are also referred to as cut-pile cloth, and *Raffiaplüsche* in German.
5. No written source consulted names the palms clearly. Infragenetic multiplicity still has to be reduced to botanical order. One should note for the moment that the raphia *Hookeri* has its variants *angolensis, gigantea,* and *maxima,* the last identified in Loango in 1876, and no longer recognized. *Hookeri* prefers inundated land, produces a lot of sap and fibres for weaving, but the author omits to report the length of the folioles. *Raphia vinifera* , with its variants, *gracilis africana* and *Laurentii,* also gives fruits rich in oil, and its folioles are long, from 1750 to 1850 mm, and 50 to 55 mm wide (Otedoh 1982). The raphia *textilis,* identified in Gabon in 1864, has disapeared from botanical lists, replaced by *Hookeri.* The *textilis* folioles were 950 mm long and 50 mm wide. As for *elaeis Guineensis,* it has short folioles, from 300 to 450 mm, which should not endear it to weavers. According to Francois Sita, of ORSTOM in Brazzaville, *Hookeri* should correspond to the Tsayi *piki* and the Tsogho (Gabon) *epoko,* while *vinifera* should be the Tsayi *tuomi,* a wild plant, and the *babi* of the Tege.
6. The Teke are matrilineal. Those of the Congo plateaus that were interviewed by Vansina and Bonnafé emphasize the importance of the paternal line. Moreover, they use the resources offered by the lineages of both their paternal and maternal grandfathers. Any study of kinship or alliance that does not take into account the paternal lineage or the existence of preferential marriage, ends up contradicting its own claims.
7. Markets did not exist in all Teke groups. It seems that this institution is of Congo origin.

8. A similar importance of all four lineages appears among the Nzabi, supported by the four names given to newborns. The young adult could thereby change identity to facilitate a change of residence (G. Dupré 1982:164–5).
9. Vansina (1973) calls the new chiefs "lords," by contrast with the already existing "squires," masters of the land. The same economic evolution, at the same period, fostered the creation of lords of the sky among the Kukua and, in the eastern part of Tsayi country, the *mubial*, who have affinity to the lords of the sky. These new leaders attempted to bring together the powers of the masters of the people and those of the masters of the land, and unified several territories under one system of control. In other words, as soon as Teke history opens up to long-distance relationships, the bipolar structure tends to break up. It has, however, been maintained right up to the present.
10. It was the same among the Kukua where, parallel to the increase in bridewealth, Bonnafé (1987: 80) notes the mastery of a very ancient, previous, inflation through the variability of cloths that become larger a nd larger and more and more ornate. Bridewealth cloths had 16 pieces in 1965.
11. One finds a similar division in our own case, as soon as one needs to calculate the monetary value of familial production. It seems unthinkable that a mother should make her baby pay for her milk. Meanwhile the development of certain enterprises rests on such a monetization, not without risk for the nursing baby.
12. The gold standard has been abandoned only two decades ago. Our advertisements continue to represent gold jewelry as proof of affection.

Sources

Balandier, G. [1965] 1992. *La vie quotidienne au royaume de Kongo du XVI au XVIII Siècle*. Paris: Hachette.

Bonnafé, P. 1978. *Nzo Lipfu, le lignage de la mort. La sorcellerie, idéologie de la lutte sociale sur le Plateau Kukuya*. Nanterre: Service de publication, Laboratoire d'ethnologie et de sociologie comparative, Université de Paris X.

———. 1987. *La Terre et le Ciel*. Vol. 1 of *Histoire sociale d'un peuple congolais*. Paris: ORSTOM.

———. 1988. *Posseder et Gouverner*. Vol. 2 of *Histoire Sociale d'un Peuple Congolais*. Paris: ORSTOM.

Dupré, G. 1972. "Les échanges entre sociétés segmentaires." *Cahiers d'études africaines*, 12:616–658.

1982. *Un ordre et sa destruction: économie et politique chez les Nabzi du Congo*. Paris: ORSTOM.

———. 1985. *Les naissances d'une société: espace et historicité chez les Beembé du Congo*. Paris: ORSTOM.

Dupré, M.-C. 1984. "Naissances et renaissances du masque Kidumu: art, politique et histoire." Paris: Thèse D'État. Université de Paris V.

———. 1987. "Place du serment dans une structure politique duale: Le cas des Teke Tsayi de la république populaire du Congo." *Droit et Cultures*, 14:17–28.

———. 1992. "Efficacité et permanence de la tradition orale: Teke-Tsayi du Congo." In *Lire le Droit: Langue, Texte, Cognition*, ed. D. Bourcier and P. Mackay, 409–422. Librarie Generale de Droit et de Jurisprudence.

———. 1993. "La Guerre de l'impôt dans les monts du Chaillu, Gabon, Moyen Congo, 1909–1920." *Revue Francaise D'Histoire D'Outre Mer*, 80:409–23.

Guillot, B. 1973. *La Terre Enkou (Congo): Atlas des structures agraires au sud du Sahara*. Paris: Ecole Pratique des Hautes Etudes.

Hogendorn, Jan and Marion Johnson. 1986. *The Shell Money of the Slave Trade*. New York and Cambridge: Cambridge University Press.

Laman, K. E. 1953, 1968. *The K ongo*. 4 Vols. Uppsala: Studia Ethnographica Uppsalienia.

Lanfranchi, R., and B. Clist. 1991. *Aux origines de l'Afrique centrale*. Libreville: Centres Culturels d'Afrique Centrale et Centre International des Civilisations Bantu.

Löffler, I. 1975. *Beiträge zur Ethnologie der Tege*. Mainz: J. Gutenberg Universität.

Loir, H. 1935. "Le Tissage du raphia au Congo belge." *Annales du Musée du Congo Belge*, Tervuren, serie 3, T3, 1–68.

Martin, Phyllis M. 1987. "Power, Cloth and Currency on the Loango Coast." *Muntu* 7:13 5–48.

Meurant, G. 1987. *Abstractions aux Royaumes des Kuba*. Paris: Fondation Dapper.

Ngoulou, S. 1985. *L'artisanat textile kukua: tradition et évolution contemporaine*. Brazzaville: Memoire DES, Faculté des Lettres et Sciences Humaines.

Otedoh, M. O. 1982. "A Revision of the Genus Raphia Beauv (Palmae)." *Journal of the Nigerian Institute for Oil Palm Research*, 6:145–89.

Pinçon, B. 1991. "Archéologie des plateaux et collines teke (Republique Populaire du Congo): De Nouvelles Données." *Nsi-c iciba*, 8/9:24–32.

Soret, M. 1973. "Les Teke de l'est: essai sur l'adaptation d'une population à son milieu." Lille: Service de réproduction des Thèses.

Vansina, J. 1973. *The Tio Kingdom of the Middle Congo, 1880–1892*. London: Oxford University Press.

2

Cowries, Gold, and Dollars: Exchange Rate Instability and Domestic Price Inflation in Dahomey in the Eighteenth and Nineteenth Centuries

Robin Law

This chapter considers the question of the instability of currency values in a precolonial context, with reference principally to the kingdom of Dahomey, in the modern Republic of Bénin (but also, to some extent, to neighboring areas), during the eighteenth and nineteenth centuries. Dahomey was probably founded in the early seventeenth century, but emerged as a major power only in the 1720s, when it conquered the kingdoms of Allada and Whydah to the south, and thus established direct contact with the European traders at the coast. Thereafter, Dahomey was a major supplier of slaves for the Atlantic trade and, after the mid-nineteenth century, of palm oil for European industrial markets.

The currency of Dahomey, as of Allada and Whydah earlier, consisted of cowry shells, imported ultimately from the Indian Ocean, and brought to West Africa immediately from Europe.[1] The operation of the cowry currency, in a general West African context, has been the subject of considerable detailed study, especially by Jan Hogendorn and Marion Johnson (1986) and by Félix Iroko (1987); some aspects of its operation in the specific case of Dahomey, including especially its exchange rate against gold and the inflation of domestic prices, have been treated in recent publications of the present author (Law 1990a, 1991a, 1992). For the purposes of this chapter, it should be noted that cowries in Dahomey were counted in units of 40 (called a "string") and 200 (a "galina"); in the eighteenth century, there was also a higher unit of 4,000, called a "grand cabess," but in the nineteenth century this was superseded by a "head" of 2,000.

Already in the seventeenth century, exchange in local markets in this region was fully monetized. The English trader Thomas Phillips, at Whydah in 1694, thus noted that "when they go to market to buy anything they bargain for so many cowries. . . and without these shells they can purchase nothing" (1732:228). Likewise in the mid-nineteenth century at Badagri, further east along the coast (and beyond Dahomian political jurisdiction, although part of the same cultural area), as the American missionary Thomas Bowen observed, "neither is it possible to pay for provisions and labour in any kind, barter being unknown, and cowries demanded for everything" ([1857] 1968:98). In addition to market transactions, a wide range of political and social payments were also made in cowries. In Dahomey, for example, the tolls levied on goods passing along the roads were paid in cowries[2]; and the principal form of direct taxation levied on "the black merchants, or trading men, and indeed every head of a family" consisted of "a quantity of cowries, proportionate to their circumstances," paid annually at the "Annual Customs," the principal public ceremony of the Dahomian monarchy.[3] Social payments such as bridewealth were likewise at least partially monetized. Recent ethnographic literature refers to two distinct forms of indigenous marriage that existed in Dahomey, one involving a gift of cloth to the bride's family (in which the wife was called *avonusi*, or "wife for cloth") and another involving the payment of cowries (where the wife was called *akuenusi*, "wife for money").[4] The inference that the monetized form of payment was more recent is supported by the fact that seventeenth-century accounts of marriage in Allada and Whydah refer only to gifts of cloth; but an account of Whydah in the early eighteenth century, shortly before its conquest by Dahomey, already notes the payment of "a certain quantity of cowries," as well as cloth (Dapper 1676:2nd pagination, 117; Phillips 1732:220; Relation n.d.:71).

As Hopkins has observed (with reference to the case of Lagos and Yorubaland in the nineteenth century), "the fundamental weakness of a monetary system dominated by the cowrie was the lack of control exercized over the supply and issue of currency . . . instability was virtually built into the monetary system" (1966:473). Although Karl Polanyi, in his classic study of the economic organization of Dahomey, claimed that the Dahomian state exercised control over the importation and issue of cowries (1966:189), this is not borne out by the detailed evidence. The only recorded instance of government intervention in the money supply in Dahomey, in fact, relates to a prohibition on *exports* (i.e., to other African countries) rather than imports, imposed when a blockade of Dahomey by the British navy in 1851-2 threatened supplies of cowries (Reid 1986:301). The quantity of money entering the local economy was determined by the value of exports (and by the proportion of their purchasing price paid in cowries), rather than regulated by the local authorities.

This lack of control over the money supply was compounded by the fact that cowries were effectively a nonconvertible currency; although European traders did occasionally sell goods (or even slaves) to Africans for cowries, which they required for meeting their local living expenses, they would not take them away with them, so that once imported, cowries remained within West Africa (Cf. Hogendorn and Johnson 1986:111). Imports were to some degree offset by the re-export of cowries in payment for imports from other areas of West Africa (Cf. Lovejoy 1974). But because there was no guarantee that re-exports would balance new imports of cowries, there was an inherent tendency towards oversupply of cowries, reflected in periodic depreciations in their value.

Assessing the stability or otherwise of the value of the cowry currency presents a number of difficult methodological problems (Law 1991a). Although many contemporary European accounts from the late seventeenth century onward give figures for the value of cowries in terms either of gold or of various European (or American) currencies, these are frequently difficult to interpret. Values in European currencies sometimes refer to the cost price of cowries in Europe (which of course itself varied) rather than to their exchange (or "trade") value on the West African coast; and "trade" values, although originally tied to the value of gold (reckoned at the normal U.K. rate of £4 sterling to an ounce; although the actual purchase price of gold, again, sometimes fluctuated), eventually became artificial units of account whose real value varied (and tended to decline). The "ounce trade" (ultimately fixed at four grand cabess, or 16,000 cowries) thus originally represented the purchase price of an ounce of gold, but fell in the later eighteenth century to only half the value of a gold ounce (see Johnson 1966). The grand cabess of 4,000 cowries likewise was valued at £1 "trade" because it would buy a quarter of an ounce of gold, but retained this nominal value long after it had ceased to do so. Likewise in the nineteenth century, when cowry values were normally given in terms of the silver dollar, they were originally exchanged at 2,000 to the dollar, and Dahomians continued to refer to a "dollar" of 2,000 cowries even after their exchange value against actual dollars had depreciated.

Although the value of cowries has usually been discussed in terms of their exchange value against gold (or, in the nineteenth century, the silver dollar), it is also possible to trace their changing value through analysis of reported prices of commodities in local markets. Because local prices also are often expressed in terms of European currencies rather than numbers of cowries, they present some of the same problems of interpretation as exchange rates. They are, however, more directly illuminating for evaluation of the impact of currency depreciation on the indigenous population. Although Polanyi (1966) posited that prices were not only set by the political authorities (which seems to have been in principle true), but also remained fixed at constant levels over long periods, the detailed evidence shows conclusively that prices were subject both to short-term fluctuations, reflecting variations in supply and demand, and to substantial long-term inflation (for a detailed analysis, see Law 1992).

Although there was almost certainly some depreciation of cowry values in the Dahomey area during the seventeenth century, the evidence for this is fragmentary and its consequences difficult to assess. More detailed information is available, however, for two later periods of instability, during the early and mid-eighteenth century (when cowries depreciated substantially against gold) and during the second half of the nineteenth century (when they fell even more drastically against the silver dollar). This chapter attempts to reconstruct the course and causes of these depreciations, and also (albeit necessarily more speculatively) to consider the problems that they posed for the African states and societies involved.

The Eighteenth Century: Cowries and Gold

The Dahomey area was not, of course, a producer or exporter of gold like the Gold Coast to the west. Gold (in the form of gold dust) was imported into Allada and Whydah, and later into Dahomey, mainly by European traders, initially from the

Gold Coast and from the 1700s, mainly from Brazil; although there was also some overland importation from the hinterland of the Gold Coast, conducted by African merchants (Law 1990a). In the late seventeenth century, gold was evidently imported only in small quantities, and did not function as a circulating currency. By the end of the century, indeed, imports of gold appear to have ceased altogether, the Dutch trader Bosman in c.1698 declaring that gold was altogether unknown at Whydah ([1705] 1967:350).

With the beginning of imports of Brazilian gold in the 1700s, gold evidently became much more common in Whydah, and was adopted as a monetary standard, operating alongside (and interchangeable into) cowries. In the early eighteenth century, gold in Whydah was normally valued at four galinas (800 cowries) to the acky (one sixteenth of an ounce; i.e., 12,800 to the ounce), or five ackies of gold to the grand cabess of 4,000 cowries; at the conventional rate of £4 sterling to the ounce of gold (or five shillings to the acky), this gave the grand cabess a "trade" value of £1 5s. (25 shillings).[5] This rate was, however, difficult to sustain in the face of fluctuations in the supply of cowries or of gold. James Houstoun, an employee of the English factory at Whydah, thus complained that the factory's governor, Ambrose Baldwin, in 1722 had sold so many cowries to Portuguese traders (in exchange for their gold) that he had "lowered the price of cowries," from the earlier rate of five ackies of gold for a grand cabess, to only three ackies (i.e., 21,333 cowries to the ounce of gold) (1725:32). After a period of instability, cowries settled during 1725 at five galinas (1,000 cowries) to the acky (16,000 to the ounce of gold), or four ackies of gold (£1 "trade") to the grand cabess of cowries, a depreciation of 25 percent from the earlier rate.

This fall in the value of cowries in 1722–5 was clearly the result of the oversupply of cowries; although Houstoun's account quoted above blames the particular transactions of Governor Baldwin, it reflected more generally the large scale of cowry imports, which reached unprecedented levels in the 1720s (with a peak in the specific year 1722) (Cf. Hogendorn and Johnson 1986:59). The new rate of 16,000 cowries to the ounce of gold applied, indeed, not only in Whydah, but also elsewhere on the coast, being attested likewise at Accra to the west (Hogendorn and Johnson 1986:134).

Information on prices in local markets indicates that the local purchasing power of cowries also fell, with palm oil in Whydah for example rising from 3,400 to 4,000 cowries per pot, an increase of 17.5 percent, roughly in line with the decline in the cowry/gold exchange rate (Law 1992:409–10). The social and political effects of this depreciation within Whydah are more difficult to grasp. It should be noted, however, that prices in the Whydah market were set, and varied from month to month, by action of a royal official.[6] It might be supposed, therefore, that royal administration rather than market forces took part of the popular blame for these price increases, which may therefore have played some role in the growth of political opposition to the King of Whydah in this period, which is known to have undermined the resistance of the kingdom to its conquest by Dahomey in 1727.

The reckoning of the grand cabess of 4,000 cowries at £1 "trade," established in 1725, was thereafter maintained throughout the eighteenth century; but it is clear that this became a purely nominal value, increasingly at variance with the real purchasing power of cowries relative to gold. In fact, a further period of instability in gold/cowry exchange rates followed the Dahomian conquest of Whydah in 1727. In 1728, French traders at Whydah were reported to be offering six grand cabess of cowries (i.e., 24,000) for an ounce of gold and were unable to obtain gold even at this inflated price.[7] By the beginning of 1733, the rate had fallen back to five grand cabess (20,000 cowries) to the ounce of gold but a French ship at Whydah later in that year had to increase its price for gold to seven grand cabess (28,000) to the ounce, and even so was unable to dispose of all its cowries.[8] Although the cowry price of gold did eventually stabilize, this was at a significantly higher price than before the Dahomian conquest. By 1746, the normal price of gold was again said to be five grand cabess, or 20,000 cowries, to the ounce, 25 percent above the rate of 1727.[9]

This rise in the price of gold was accompanied by a marked unwillingness on the part of Africans to sell any. The English factory at Whydah in late 1727 thus reported that "very little gold circulates . . . the natives not careing [sic] to lay it out any more than just for their bare subsistance"; and again in December, "as for gold there is none stirring." It was not that no gold was being imported: indeed, the English factory noted in February 1728 that "there is perhaps as much gold in Whydah Road now as there has been for these severall years past," but the Europeans could not buy any of it.[10] This unwillingness to sell gold may have been due in part to the disturbed conditions following the Dahomian conquest, because gold was more easily transported and concealed than an equivalent value of cowries. But it also seems likely that it reflects the depreciating value of cowries; rather than the increased demand for gold forcing up its price in cowries, it may be that the falling value of cowries caused the increased preference for gold. The disappearance of gold from the Whydah market might thus be an instance of Gresham's Law (according to which, bad money drives out good).

It may also be suggested that this decline of cowries relative to gold has some relevance to the origins of the Dahomian conquest of Whydah. Although the motives of King Agaja of Dahomey in attacking Whydah in 1727 are a matter of some historical controversy, the weight of the evidence suggests that he was interested in more direct and effective access to the trade with the Europeans, and some evidence indicates that he was interested more particularly in trading for gold (Henige and Johnson 1976). Certainly, several contemporary European observers remark that Agaja was especially eager to acquire gold. In 1727, for example, shortly after his conquest of Whydah, it was noted that Agaja preferred to sell his slaves to the Portuguese rather than the English, because he was "very desireous of the Portuguese gold"; and again later in the year that "the Dahomme King is very eager to acquire this metal."[11] Early in the following year, 1728, it was reported that King Agaja "engrosses all the gold in his own hands."[12] Legally, in fact, the gold trade at Whydah under Dahomian rule became a royal monopoly, private trading in gold becoming a capital offence (Law 1990a:110). It may therefore be that Agaja's conquest of Whydah was in some part a response to currency instability, an attempt to secure access to the harder currency of gold in the face of the depreciation of cowries.

The exchange value of cowries against gold was further disrupted by the effective cessation of imports of Brazilian gold after the mid-eighteenth century, which made it once more a rarity in the Dahomey area. At the same time, the price of gold was rising elsewhere in West Africa, including the Gold Coast to the west (Cf. Johnson 1966:202–4). In 1765, the English factory at Whydah recognized this appreciation of gold by raising its conventional valuation of it from £4 to £8 "trade" per ounce (Law 1990a:113; 1991b:244). Cowries, on the other hand, remained valued at £1 "trade" to the grand cabess, giving gold a price of eight grand cabess, or 32,000 cowries, to the ounce; the "ounce trade" continued to be reckoned at four grand cabess, or 16,000 cowries, but was now equivalent to only half an ounce of gold. This doubling of the price of gold is, however, obscured in many contemporary accounts, because most traders seem to have preferred to abandon the conventional "trade" valuations, and instead base their calculations on the U.K. price of gold, at £4 per ounce; on this basis, the grand cabess of cowries was now worth only ten shillings "gold price," and the "ounce trade" only £2. The impression is thus given that, rather than the price of gold being doubled, that of cowries had been halved. In fact, the apparent lowering of the value of the grand cabess from £1 to 10s. reflects merely a change in accounting conventions, from "trade" to "gold price," and the two are in fact equivalents. This valuation of cowries against gold, in turn, persisted into the first half of the nineteenth century, when, as will be seen below, the "head" of 2000 cowries (half the old grand cabess) was equated with the silver dollar, itself conventionally valued at five shillings.

This appreciation of gold against cowries after the 1720s (and the consequent distinction between "gold" and "trade" prices) was, again, not confined to Dahomey, but occurred also at Accra to the west, where cowries continued to be reckoned at 1000 for a rijksdaler (equivalent to 5s.), but by the 1780s, the rijksdaler "gold price" was equivalent to two "rijksdalers cowries," giving the ounce of gold (at £4) there also a value of 32,000 cowries (Isert 1992:85; cf. Nørregård 1966:161). Although this valuation was strictly an accounting convention, rather than the actual purchase price of gold (which European traders, in fact, no longer normally purchased locally), it was evidently more or less in line with the rate at which gold passed in local markets. The British official Joseph Dupuis, visiting Kumase, the capital of Asante, in 1820, was thus told by Muslim merchants there that gold was exchanged in Dahomey at one mithqal (equated with two thirteenths of an ounce) to 4,500 cowries, giving a rate of 29,250 to the ounce of gold ([1824] 1966:cxv); the slight discrepancy from the European rate may reflect the fact that cowries appreciated in value from the coast towards the interior.

With the increasing rarity of gold in Dahomey from the 1760s onwards, however, it effectively ceased to function as a circulating currency. Thus, the British trader John M'Leod, visiting Whydah in 1803, noted that, although it was used in the manufacture of ornaments, gold was "not used in the shape of money" ([1820] 1971:92). In the nineteenth century, gold seems to have been imported into Dahomey mainly in the form of coins, especially doubloons (Spanish double-crowns, worth $16). Such imports of gold remained a royal monopoly: the British Consul Richard Burton in 1864 reported that when doubloons were paid for slaves "the monarch monopolises all the gold" (1864, 1:178n) In this period, however, as will be seen below, gold was superseded in importance, both as an imported commodity and as a standard for valuing cowries, by imported coined silver, in the form of the Spanish dollar.

The appreciation of gold from 16,000 to 32,000 cowries per ounce between 1727 and 1765 clearly reflected principally to the rising value of gold in West Africa, the valuation of cowries in fact remaining constant (at £1 "trade" per grand cabess) throughout. It seems probable, however, that there was also some decline in the value of cowries, which is masked by the stability of their nominal "trade" value. It is noteworthy that, whereas down to the 1720s, European observers generally stressed the preference of Africans in Whydah for payment in cowries (e.g., Bosman [1705] 1967:364a), by 1750, cowries were said to be sometimes out of demand.[13] There is also some evidence for substantial increases in domestic prices in this period, with chickens in particular almost doubling in price from 160 cowries each in 1721 to around 300 by 1752.[14] Rising living costs may also be reflected in a strike of porters at Jakin, east of Whydah, in 1727 (shortly after the Dahomian conquest), demanding double the normal pay, though the Governor of Jakin intervened to induce them to accept the existing rate (Snelgrave [1734] 1971:83–5). In Whydah under Dahomian rule, however, porters' wages were maintained at 120 cowries per job, the same rate which they had obtained before 1727, throughout the eighteenth century, presumably representing a significant fall in real wages, and a cheapening of the cost of labor (Law 1992:416–7).

The instability of the cowry values between the 1720s and 1760s is probably also relevant to a change in the nature of the "ounce trade" in Dahomey, which has been noted in earlier analyses (Johnson 1966; Peukert 1978:108–9). In the first half of the eighteenth century, as has been seen, the "ounce trade" was merely the quantity of goods that could be exchanged in West Africa for an ounce of gold, which fluctuated with market conditions; but by the 1770s, the value of goods in "ounces" (and therefore also their values relative to each other) were fixed at, for example, 4 grand cabess of cowries (16,000 cowries), 4 iron bars, 1 roll of Brazilian tobacco, and 8 pieces of linen cloth to the ounce. Although Polanyi supposed that fixed ounce values represented a European concession to African traditions of fixed prices (1966:154–69), they were in fact clearly an innovation of the 1760s, and more probably a response to the instability of the price of gold in the preceding period, fixed ounce values serving the convenience of European as well as African traders.

The Nineteenth Century: Cowries and the Silver Dollar

As noted earlier, in the nineteenth century, cowry values were normally cited in terms of European (or American) silver coin, especially the Spanish or South American silver dollar (alternatively called the "piastre," "peso," or "piece of eight"—the last from its being equivalent to eight Spanish reales), rather than in gold.

Coined silver had, in fact, already been imported into the Dahomey area as early as the seventeenth century. The French merchant Delbée, visiting Allada in 1670, noted that silver as well as gold could be sold there, recommending in particular the importation of Dutch or English "crowns [écus]"; a slave of superior quality could be bought for ten Dutch "crowns [i.e., rijksdalers]" (£2 10s. sterling), which he regarded as "very advantageous" (1671:449). This importation of European silver coins was, however, apparently not sustained, at least in significant quantities. Although Bosman in the 1690s cited the prices of local commodities and taxes in Whydah in Dutch rijksdalers and stuivers ([1705] 1967:362, 389, 392), this apparently relates to money of account rather than actual coins, because he also noted explicitly that the Whydahs were unacquainted with silver, as well as with gold (ibid.:350). Likewise, the Englishman John Atkins, at Whydah in 1721–2, although giving prices in English money (in crowns, or five-shilling pieces, and pence), notes explicitly that purchases were actually made with cowries. Unlike Delbée earlier, Atkins regarded the importation of European coins as unprofitable: "coin is the dearest way of buying, at distance from Europe" ([1735] 1970:112). Although it remained conventional to value goods in sterling later in the eighteenth century, this clearly represented a money of account, related to gold (or from the 1760s, to the "ounce trade") rather than referring to transactions in actual English money.

The importation of silver coins in significant quantities appears to have begun only in the nineteenth century, and arose from the predominance in the slave trade (after its legal abolition by Britain and other European nations) of Brazilian and Cuban traders, who often brought coins (primarily silver dollars, but also—as noted above—gold doubloons) to pay for slaves (Cf. Newbury 1961:40; Manning 1982:47). The British trader Francis Swanzy thus told the 1842 Select Committee on the West Coast of Africa that during the past six or seven years, slave ships had adopted the practice of paying for their slaves with "dollars and doubloons" rather than goods.[15] The important role played by specie in the Dahomian slave trade at this time is also illustrated by the surviving correspondence of José Francisco dos Santos, a Brazilian trader settled at Whydah. In 1845, for example, when the selling price of Brazilian tobacco was low, dos Santos asked for a sum due to him from Brazil to be remitted in specie, "patacons [i.e., Brazilian silver coins], Mexican ounces [i.e., gold doubloons], or pesos [dollars], I don't care which." Later in the same year, he requested payment in "money of any sort except Spanish ounces"; and in 1847 in "silver pesos."[16]

This move towards payment in specie seems to have been due, in part, to the need to expedite business, in order to reduce the danger of detection by British anti-slaving naval patrols; but it also reflected the difficulty which slave-traders had in obtaining manufactured goods of European origin. The Scots explorer John Duncan, visiting Whydah in 1845, thus noted that the Spanish and Portuguese slave-traders at Whydah were obliged to pay for their slaves in cash, because they were unable to obtain manufactured goods as cheaply as the English and French merchants trading for palm oil ([1847] 1968, 1:138). Much of the imported specie was, in fact, promptly re-exported in exchange for goods. Other witnesses to the 1842 Select Committee reported supplying goods to Francisco Felix de Souza, the principal Brazilian trader established at Whydah, in exchange for "dollars and doubloons."[17] (Later in the 1840s, slave-dealers solved this problem by themselves supplying palm oil to European traders in exchange for goods, which they then used for the purchase of slaves.)

There was, however, also an indigenous demand for silver coin, some of which therefore stayed within the Dahomian domestic economy. For the most part, at least initially, this silver was used as bullion rather than as currency. Already in 1803, John M'Leod reported that both gold and silver, although not used as money, were "manufactured into ornaments" ([1820] 1971:92). The French officer Bouet, visiting Dahomey to negotiate a commercial agreement in 1851, observed that dollars and doubloons were melted down or worked by the royal smiths and jewellers (1852:62n). The British Consul Richard Burton in 1864 likewise noted armlets and cane-heads made from beaten dollars, and that the king's silversmiths made dollars into "chains, rings and crucifixes" (1864, 1:148n, 185; 2:34).

Eventually, silver dollars did become accepted as current money in Dahomey, but how early this occurred is unclear. One witness to the Select Committee of 1842 already claimed that "dollars are in circulation throughout the whole [West African] coast; as far as a metallic currency exists at all, it is principally in dollars."[18] John Duncan in 1845 likewise noted that both cowries and dollars were current at Accra, west of Dahomey ([1847] 1968, 1:85). But the situation further east along the coast is less clear. At Whydah in 1850, the British officer Frederick Forbes noted that although gold and silver (in the context, referring evidently to coins) were "current at valuation," they were "scarce" ([1851] 1966, 1:36). At Badagri, further east along the coast, around the same time, the American missionary Bowen reported that "silver and gold are not current here," as the [European?] merchants would only accept cowries or palm oil in exchange for goods ([1857] 1968:98). In the Yoruba interior, northeast of Badagri, silver dollars appear to have come into general use only during the 1850s: another American missionary, W. H. Clarke, who travelled there in 1854–8, noted that with the growth of trade "the disposition to use silver currency also increases"; whereas "four and five years ago [i.e., presumably, at his original arrival in 1854] it was with great difficulty that silver could be exchanged at anything like a fair value at Ijaye," "now" both there and at Abeokuta "silver . . . is in considerable demand" (1972:268).

The attractiveness of dollars as currency was partly that they would be readily received back in payment by European merchants and were thus not, like cowries, effectively inconvertible. In addition, they were more convenient than cowries in large-scale transactions, especially where large sums had to be physically transported. One of the great disadvantages of cowries for large-scale transactions was their sheer bulk, at a weight of 400 to the pound. As Bowen remarked, "the iron money of Lycurgus was not more cumbersome" ([1857] 1968:98). The standard load for a female carrier was ten heads (20,000), or 50 lb; at 2,000 cowries to the dollar, therefore, as Forbes noted in 1849, "to carry fifty dollars, we had to hire five women" ([1851] 1966, 1:51). By contrast, as explicitly noted by Clarke, one advantage of dollars was their relative "portability" (1972:268). Conversely, however, dollars (and imported coins more generally) were units of too high value to serve for small-scale exchange in local markets. As a witness to the Select Committee on the Western Coast of Africa in 1865 remarked, although the replacement of cowries by a metallic currency might be desirable, "we have not coins small enough."[19] (In British West Africa, this problem was not resolved until the introduction of coins with the low value of one tenth of a penny, in 1907.) The pattern that emerged, therefore, was for silver coin to be used in wholesale transactions, while cowries continued in use in local retail markets.[20]

Before considering the exchange value of cowries against the silver dollar during the nineteenth century, some preliminary remarks about the valuation of the latter need to be made. In principle, the dollar was an ounce of silver (as the doubloon was an ounce of gold), silver being valued conventionally at one sixteenth of the value of gold (and dollars being therefore reckoned at sixteen to the doubloon). In West Africa by the end of the seventeenth century, the silver dollar was being equated with the acky, or one sixteenth of an ounce of a gold, valued conventionally at 5s. sterling (and giving $4 to £1 sterling).[21] This, in fact, involved a slight overvaluation of the dollar, by comparison with European values, since the dollars (and doubloons) current in West Africa were on the standard of the Spanish ounce, which was slightly smaller (420 as against 480 grains, or seven eighths) than the Troy ounce in which gold was normally reckoned in West Africa (and valued at £4 sterling to the ounce). During the eighteenth century, in fact, the silver dollar was officially valued in British colonial possessions at only 4s. 6d. sterling (4 and one half shillings, or 54 rather than 60 pence) ([Pennington] [1848] 1967:25). This slight overvaluation of the dollar in West Africa probably reflects the higher value there, comparative to European prices, of silver against gold.

In the nineteenth century, the valuation of the dollar at five shillings continued to be employed, but this was now a conventional (or "currency") rate, which no longer corresponded with its exchange value against English money.[22] The official value of the dollar in Britain's West African colonies was, in fact, lowered further in this period, to 4s. 4d. (52 pence) in 1825 and to 4s. 2d. (50 pence), giving $4.80 to £1 sterling, in 1843 ([Pennington] [1848] 1967:39–40).In West Africa, however, silver continued to command a premium, and the actual exchange value of dollars against sterling was therefore somewhat higher than this, a rate of 4s. 6d. being cited as the "normal price," for example, in the 1860s.[23]

Interpretation of values for cowries given in nineteenth-century English sources is very much complicated by these variant values for the dollar. Forbes in 1850, for example, generally equated the Dahomian string of 40 cowries with the English penny, suggesting that he took the dollar (then equivalent to 2,000 cowries, or 50 strings) as worth 4s. 2d. (50 pence), which was the official rate ([1851] 1966, 1:110). Burton in 1864, however, writing when the dollar was worth 2 1/2 heads of cowries (5,000 cowries) in Dahomey, gave the value of the head as 1s. 9 1/2, following the market price of 4s. 6d. rather than the official rate of 4s. 2d. to the dollar ([1864], 1991 1:143n); but elsewhere in the same work, he equates the head with two shillings, according to the "currency" valuation of the dollar at 5s. (1864, 2:4n; 222–3).[24] Similar ambiguities apply to valuations of dollars in French currency. Strictly, the French franc at this period was worth about 9 1/2 English pence (1s. sterling = 1 fr. 25), and the five-franc piece about nine tenths of a dollar ($1 = 5 fr. 50). As a money of account in West African transactions, however, the franc seems often to have been equated with the English shilling, and five francs therefore with the dollar (e.g., Bouet 1952:42). At 2,000 cowries to the dollar, therefore, the franc was regularly equated with 400 cowries (Law 1991a:246).

The question of dollar values was further complicated by the substantial decline in the price of silver relative to gold in world markets that occurred from the 1870s onwards. The problems that this created led to the official demonetization of the dollar (and other non-British silver coins) in Lagos in 1880 (see Hopkins 1966). By the 1880s the dollar was being reckoned at Whydah at only four shillings ($5 to £1 sterling).[25]

In the nineteenth century, as noted earlier, cowries were initially valued against silver at 2,000 to the Spanish dollar. This rate is first attested by the British explorer Clapperton in 1825/6; although he cites it with reference to the Yoruba city of Oyo in the interior, it presumably reflects conventions at the coast (perhaps specifically at Badagri, where he had landed en route to Oyo) (1829:59). The same rate is given for the Dahomian port of Whydah by Duncan in 1845 ([1847] 1968, 1:254; 2:286); and by Archibald Ridgway in 1847 (1847:410n) and Forbes in 1849–50 ([1851] 1966, 1:36, 51, 122).[26] A rate of 2,000 cowries to the "piastre" or dollar at Whydah is also given by the French officers Bouet in 1851 (1852:39n), and Vallon in 1856–8 (1860–1, 1:334 n.1); and indeed the "piastre cauris" or "cowry dollar" was still cited as 2,000 cowries there in the 1880s (d'Albéca 1889:157; Chaudoin 1891:78). The same rate was also current in areas outside Dahomian jurisdiction in the mid-nineteenth century, such as Badagri and Lagos (Bowen [1857] 1968:98; Hutchinson [1858] 1970:77).

This apparent stability of the cowry/dollar exchange rate is, however, illusory, because other evidence shows that the value of cowries against the dollar, in Dahomey and elsewhere in West Africa, fell substantially during the second half of the nineteenth century. This phenomenon has been studied especially by Marion Johnson, who termed it the "Great Inflation" (Hogendorn and Johnson 1986:138–43). Even by the mid-nineteenth century, indeed, it is clear the rate of one dollar per head of cowries was already only a nominal value, and the discrepancy between it and the actual exchange value of cowries against dollars grew during the second half of the century. Forbes in 1850 distinguished explicitly between the "nominal" value of one head of cowries per dollar and the actual exchange value of the dollar, which was 2,400–2,600 cowries, or 20–30 percent above its nominal value ([1851] 1966, 1:36). In computing the king's expenditure at the Annual Customs, he accordingly deducted "one fourth the difference" to convert heads of cowries into dollars.[27] A similar depreciation occurred elsewhere in the cowry using area, outside Dahomian political jurisdiction. At Accra to the west, for example, the rate in the early 1850s was 2,400 cowries to the dollar; and at Badagri to the east in 1850 it was likewise noted that although it was "usual" to value cowries at 2,000 to the dollar, "of late they are cheaper on the coast" (Cruickshank [1853] 1966, 2:44; Bowen [1857] 1968:98).

During the 1850s, the value of cowries fell more precipitously. Vallon in 1856 noted that although cowries were current in Whydah at 2,000 for a "piastre" or dollar (equivalent to 5 francs), the French factory there would only accept them back at between 2 fr. 50 and 3 francs, suggesting that cowries had fallen to around half their nominal value (1860-1, 1:360). This parallels the decline recorded during the same period in Lagos and its Yoruba hinterland to the east, where cowries were reckoned at two heads (4,000) to the dollar by the late 1850s (Clarke 1972:268; Crowther and Taylor [1859] 1968:211; cf. also Hopkins 1966:476; Newbury 1961:59).The decline continued during the 1860s, 1870s, and 1880s. Burton in 1864, as has been seen, gave the rate in Dahomey as 2 1/2 heads (5,000 cowries) to the dollar, or two shillings to the head (1864, 1:143n.; 2:4n, 222–3). In the 1870s, 2,000 cowries were valued at 1 to 1.25 francs, here probably equivalent to one shilling "currency," and implying a rate of 10,000 cowries to the dollar.[28] By the 1880s, the silver dollar was equivalent in value to no less than ten "cowry dollars [piastres cauris]," or 20,000 cowries, making the head or nominal "dollar" of 2,000 cowries now worth only ten cents, six English pence (evidently at the nominal "currency" rate of 5s. to the dollar, rather than the actual sterling value of the dollar), or 0.63 French francs (d'Albéca 1889:57). At this rate, cowries were at only 10 percent of their pre-1850 value (and the cowry price of the dollar had risen by 900 percent); and given the fall in value of the dollar itself (noted above), the real decline was even greater.

There is no doubt that the principal reason for this catastrophic decline in the value of cowries was their oversupply through the European trade. Importations of cowries into West Africa, after collapsing in the early nineteenth century with the legal abolition of the slave trade, had recovered with the rise of the new trade in palm oil, and reached new record levels by the 1840s (Hogendorn and Johnson 1986:66–9). The demand for cowries was even greater in the oil trade than in the slave trade, apparently because much of the oil exported was supplied by small-scale producers and traders.[29] Cowries were more suitable than any other available currency for such small-scale trade, because they could be paid out in units of very small value. Several contemporary accounts of the palm oil trade in Dahomey observed that the counting out of cowries was a prominently visible feature of it: Ridgway in 1847, for example, recording the purchase of palm oil in the English factory at Whydah, saw "a number of women who were occupied in counting out a cask of cowries" (1847:196); Forbes in 1850, visiting the factory of the Brazilian José Francisco dos Santos, observed that "dozens of his own slaves were counting out cowries to pay for the produce" ([1851] 1966, 1:114); and the Frenchman Repin in 1856 reported that "the French factory keeps I don't know how many individuals employed in counting cowries" (1863:69). The counting (as opposed to weighing, as in the slave trade) of cowries in these trans- actions evidently implies that many of the payments made were small in scale. The connection between oil exports and cowry imports was, indeed, made more explic- itly by the British official Brodie Cruickshank, with reference to the take-off of the palm oil trade on the eastern Gold Coast in the 1830s: this had only been possible, he argued, because of the introduction there of the cowry currency, which was "capable of great sub-division" and therefore adapted for payment to small-scale producers ([1853] 1966, 2:43). At the same time, the fact that palm oil was produced exclusively near the coast rather than (like slaves) brought from the remoter interior, may have meant that a greater proportion of the cowries imported were retained in the coastal areas rather than re-exported, thereby undermining what had been the principal constraint on the growth of the money supply.

The oversupply of cowries for the palm oil trade was further exacerbated by the exploitation by European traders of cheaper supplies of cowries. Hitherto, the cow- ries sold in West Africa had come, virtually, entirely from the Maldive Islands, but now the main source shifted to the East African coast opposite Zanzibar, where they could be obtained much more cheaply (Cf. Hopkins 1966; Hogendorn and Johnson 1986:71–77). The first shipment of Zanzibar cowries to Whydah was made by a Ham- burg firm in 1845; its arrival is noted in the dos Santos correspondence.[30] The willing- ness of African traders in Whydah and elsewhere to accept Zanzibar cowries in pay- ment presents something of a puzzle, because they were of a different and larger species than the Maldive shells, and earlier cowries of large size had been considered unacceptable: the English factory at Whydah in 1684, for example, reported that "Great bouges [cowries] will not do there, small is most esteemed."[31] (Because cow- ries in the slave trade were generally paid out by weight or measure rather than by number, the inclusion of larger shells had the effect of reducing the local monetary value of the price received for a slave.)

There does, indeed, appear to have been some initial resistance to the Zanzibar cowries in Whydah. Dos Santos, soon after the Hamburg shipment of 1845, reported its deleterious impact on trade at Whydah, in 1846 blaming "these cursed cowries" for the poor condition of trade, and in 1847 reporting that "they are fed up with [cowries] here . . . the Blacks are reluctant to accept cowries and hardly make any effort to get them."[32] This might perhaps be taken to mean that the introduction of cowries in large numbers had lowered their local price, rather than that Africans were unwilling to accept the Zanzibar cowries as such; but some hostility to the Zan- zibar shells is also suggested by a clause in the commercial treaty between France and Dahomey in 1851, which stipulates that payments for permission to trade should be made in "white [i.e., Maldive] cowries."[33] In the long run, however, the critical point was that Zanzibar cowries were so cheap that European traders could afford to increase the quantities paid, by more than enough to compensate for their greater weight. The Zanzibar cowries were, indeed, soon reported to be having an inflation- ary impact on palm oil prices: Forbes in 1850 noted that the French traders at Why- dah were outbidding the English, driving up the price of palm oil from 5 to 7 dollars (referring presumably to "cowry dollars" or heads of cowries; i.e., from 10,000 to 14,000 cowries) per measure (18 gallons) in the space of 6 months, and explaining that they were able to do this because "their shells are of a cheap kind, and not actually cowries."[34]

In the end, the depreciation of the cowry currency was self-correcting, because by the 1880s the value of cowries in West Africa had fallen so low that importation even of the cheaper Zanzibar shells was no longer profitable. This effective cessation of European imports evidently led to a stabilization of the value of the currency, because in the early colonial period, cowries were valued at 4,000 for one French franc, only marginally below the rate recorded in the 1880s (or indeed, if the franc is taken as equivalent to one fifth of a dollar, identical with it) (Le Herissé 1911:84). By the 1930s, indeed, cowries were reportedly passing in Dahomey at only 1,000 to the franc, but this reflected a decline in the value of the franc (which fell to around 35 to the U.S.A. dollar at this period) rather than an appreciation of the real value of cowries (Quénum 1983:134).

The substitution of the heavier Zanzibar for Maldive cowries, of course, exacerbated the problem of their relative nonportability. Already by 1850, the weight of 10 dollars' worth of cowries (20,000) was being cited as 50 to 70 lb, rather than the 50 lb that had been standard for the Maldive cowries (Bowen [1857] 1968:98). The problem was further compounded by the subsequent depreciation of cowries, and doubtless helps to explain the tendency towards adoption as currency of the more portable silver dollars during the second half of the nineteenth century, which was noted earlier. The possibility of substituting a metallic currency for cowries altogether was, indeed, at least occasionally considered in Dahomey in this period. At the time of the British naval blockade of 1851–2, which threatened to cut off Dahomey's supply of cowries, King Gezo declared that Dahomey could make its own coins if necessary (Reid 1986:301). Later in the 1850s, however, when French officials visiting Dahomey asked Gezo why he did not adopt coins, he replied that cowries were preferable because, unlike coins, they could not be counterfeited, but also that the very bulk of cowries made it impossible to conceal accumulated wealth, and therefore to evade royal taxation on it (Vallon 1860–1, 1:343).

In addition to the considerations cited by Gezo on this occasion, it should be stressed that, while cowries had become increasingly inconvenient for large-scale (and long-distance) transactions, they never completely lost their utility as a currency for small-scale, local exchange. At the depreciated rate of the early colonial period, the lowest-denomination French coin (one centime) was equivalent in value to 40 cowries. In practice, moreover, there was a chronic shortage in Dahomey of the lower-denomination French coins (Cf. Manning 1982:160). Cowries therefore remained more convenient for many aspects of local trade. Although the French authorities officially demonetized cowries (in the sense of refusing to accept them in payment) in 1907, they continued in use in local markets for some time thereafter (Iroko 1987, 2:588). By the 1930s, however, although they were still sometimes accepted in payment by merchants in Dahomey, the demand for them was reportedly sustained only by their continued use in offerings to shrines (Quénum 1983:134).

This decline in the exchange value of cowries during the nineteenth century was clearly paralleled by an inflation of local prices, although the latter cannot be traced in equal detail. Hopkins, in his study of cowry depreciation in Lagos and Yorubaland, thought it "unlikely that there was widespread and extensive inflation" (1966:478), but the evidence from Dahomey suggests otherwise.[35] Most explicitly, Burton in 1864 noted that prices had doubled at Whydah during the last ten years, "and despite the complaints of commercial depression the value of coin still diminishes"; and he found provisions even dearer at Abomey, the Dahomian capital inland, where prices had quadrupled during the last six years (i.e., since the accession of the then-reigning king, Glele, in 1858) (1864, 1:66; 2:242). In addition to these general observations, Burton noted in particular that the price of a cankey (maize paste) ball had risen from 3 cowries under the previous king Gezo, to 12 by 1864 (1864, 2:244); and that the charge made by prostitutes had also risen fourfold, from 20 cowries to 2 strings, or 80 (1864, 2:221).

The rise of prices reported by Burton is corroborated by comparison of the prices that he gives for goods in the market at Abomey in 1864 (1864, 2:243) with those given by Forbes for 1850 ([1851] 1966, 1:110). These two lists of prices are not strictly comparable; while Forbes gives his prices in cowries, Burton gives his in currency (in dollars, or sterling). But the latter can be converted into cowries at the rate of 5,000 to the dollar (or 1,000 to the English shilling), which Burton himself gives elsewhere. Also, Forbes' prices relate to Whydah rather than Abomey, and Burton himself notes that prices in 1864 (and the preceding price rises) were higher at Abomey than at Whydah; the comparison will therefore overstate the rate of inflation at Whydah, while presumably understating that of Abomey. The comparison (Table 2-1) is nevertheless illuminating, and tends to confirm a price rise of around 100 percent (though the case of chickens, whose price rose over sevenfold, is aberrant):

TABLE 2-1   Prices of Goods in Dahomey

	Whydah, 1850	Abomey, 1864		
	Cowries	Dollars	Cowry Equivalent	Increase, 1850/1864
Bullock	25,000	$10–16	50,000–80,000	100–160%
Sheep	5,000	$2	10,000	100%
Turkey	4,000	$1.50	7,500	87.5%
Guinea fowl	1,000	2s. 6d.	2,500	150%
Chicken	280	2s.	2,000	614%
Egg	10	$0.75	33	233%

A comparison can also be made between rates of subsistence paid to workers at Whydah, as reported by Forbes and others in the mid-nineteenth century and by the French officer Chaudoin in the 1880s. Forbes in 1850 records the rate of subsistence paid to his hammock-bearers and porters (over and above their pay) as 3 strings or 120 cowries per day for men, and 2 strings/80 cowries for women ([1851] 1966, 2:81).[3] The French officer Bouet in 1851 also records that his porters and hammock-men (who were technically slaves of the French factory) at Whydah were paid subsistence at a rate of 6 galinas of cowries (i.e., 1,200) for 10 days, which is likewise 120 per day (1852:42). In the 1880s, however, Chaudoin gives the subsistence rate for French factory slaves as 2 "cowry dollars [piastres cauris]," that is, 4,000 cowries, per week, which gives a daily rate of around 570, 375 percent above the rate of 1851 (1891:78).

It is less clear whether social payments in Dahomey were subject to a comparable inflation. The only series of figures for such payments spanning the period of the "Great Inflation" that is available relates to bridewealth. The English trader Robert Norris in the 1770s reports that men who obtained wives as gifts from the King at the Annual Customs paid him 5 cabess, or 20,000 cowries, per wife ([1789] 1968:88); an account of the same practice in the 1850s, by the French officer Guillevin, however, gives a figure of 30,000 cowries, or 50 percent higher (1862:292). Burton in the 1860s, speaking of marriage more generally, cites the going rate for bridewealth as 10 to 40 heads, or between 20,000 and 80,000 cowries, which (assuming that payments to the King would be no less than to the generality of his subjects) might seem to suggest a significant degree of inflation (1864, 2:162). In the early colonial period, however, the rate is reported as 6 fr.50, which at 4,000 to the franc gives a figure of only 26,000 cowries (Le Herissé 1911:206). Despite the fragmentary character of this evidence, the inference that bridewealth had, at least, been significantly less subject than market prices to inflation seems permissible.

While it seems clear that the basic reason for these price increases, as for the decline in the exchange rate of cowries against the dollar, was the oversupply of cowries, exacerbated by the introduction of the cheaper Zanzibar cowries from the 1840s, it is less clear how far the Dahomians, or indeed the Europeans who dealt with them, understood the monetary causes of this inflation. Forbes in 1850, for example, thought that the premium on the dollar reflected "the scarcity of a metallic currency," rather than the oversupply of cowries ([1851] 1966:36). Interestingly, Forbes also reports a discussion among the king's advisers at the Annual Customs, relating to "the agricultural condition of the kingdom," in which one participant suggested that "the corn grounds were insufficient in extent to meet the demands," especially as war with Aja, to the west, had cut off supplies that had normally been brought from that market, and another asserted that "where goats were formerly plentiful in the market, they were now scarce, and that fowls and poultry were dear" ([1851] 1966, 2:102). This suggests that rising prices were already beginning to cause concern, but that the causes were seen as deriving from insufficiency of supply rather than monetary inflation.

A similar ambiguity appears in the account of Burton in 1864. At one point, he did note that cowries "are merchandize, and the price varies accordingly: at present they are abundant, and therefore cheap" (1864, 1:143n). He did not, however, explicitly connect the "abundance" and cheapness of cowries with the price rises that he also reported. Indeed, he attributed the latter rather to "the effects of an ultramilitary policy" (1864,2:242). This alludes to the claim that Glele, who had come to the Dahomian throne in 1858, had reasserted Dahomey's traditional militaristic policies, undermining agriculture through the diversion of labor from agricultural production. Here again, therefore, the problem was seen as insufficiency of supply.[37] It may well be, indeed, that such factors played some role in the price rises attested by Burton (perhaps explaining in particular why price rises were more severe in Abomey, where the mobilization of military forces would have had greatest impact, than in Whydah).

As regards the impact of these price rises on the domestic economy and society, the observation of Hopkins (relative to Lagos and Yorubaland) that "lack of detailed information at present encourages speculative rather than definitive comment" (1966:477), remains thus far applicable to the case of Dahomey. It may be speculated, first, that declining confidence in the currency tended to discourage people from offering goods for sale, thus undermining the market sector of the local economy. Burton in 1864 noted that "often, as in a famine, no inducement will make men part with their store"; and although Burton himself clearly thought that it was this unwillingness to sell that was forcing up prices, it may be that in fact the connection was reversed, the decline in the value of money driving sellers from the market (1864,

2:242). Certainly, the depreciation of cowries must have made people increasingly reluctant to accept them in payment. Traditions recorded by Iroko recall that cowries were sometimes refused in Whydah, while in the capital Abomey, it was made an offence, punishable by imprisonment, to refuse to accept cowries; and although this story is not explicitly connected with the inflation of the nineteenth century, it makes best sense in that context (1987, 1:453–4). The reluctance to accept cowries may also have affected social payments, such as bridewealth, as well as market transactions; it is at any rate suggestive that Burton in the 1860s, while recording bridewealth payments in heads of cowries, observes in passing that "dollars, however, are not refused" (1864, 2:162).

The depreciation of the currency must also be supposed, as Hopkins pointed out, to have injured those who held large stocks of cowries (whose real value now fell), and to have favored debtors over creditors (insofar as the value of debts was not adjusted upwards to take account of inflation) (1966:478). In the case of Dahomey, however, it is not clear how these tendencies would have affected the balance of wealth among different sections of the community. Although the monarchy had traditionally held large stores of cowries (for distribution at public ceremonies and defrayment of other expenses), this may no longer have been true in the second half of the nineteenth century, when the royal finances had been undermined by the ending of the Atlantic slave trade, and European observers regularly remarked upon the poverty of the Dahomian state (e.g., Serval 1878). On the other hand, although the king in this period was chronically in debt to traders at Whydah, he probably did not benefit from the devaluation of debts through inflation, as he would normally have settled his own debts in slaves or palm oil rather than cowries.

It seems likely, in fact, that the cowry inflation itself posed problems for the Dahomian state's revenues. Although the evidence is not entirely clear, it seems probable that taxes (whether on trade, wealth, or income) were levied at conventional set rates, rather than as a percentage of current market prices. Price inflation therefore undermined the real value of government revenues, and made necessary periodic upward revisions of the rates. It is noteworthy that complaints were recorded in the 1850s of increasing levels of taxation in Dahomey, especially upon the production and trading of palm oil.[38] Although this probably reflects in part an increase in taxation of the oil trade, to compensate for the loss of revenues from the decline of the slave trade, the racking up of taxes to keep pace with inflation may also have played a role.[39] Politically, however, it must have been difficult to increase tax rates sufficiently continuously to maintain their real value. Inflation also may therefore have contributed to the impoverishment of the Dahomian monarchy, which was reported in the later nineteenth century.

The most serious political problem posed by price inflation, however, was probably the fact that in Dahomey, as in Whydah earlier, prices were set by royal officials, albeit with regard to market conditions. Burton, for example, makes clear that the increase in prostitutes' charges from 20 to 80 cowries per session was authorized by the king "at the representation of the ministers" (1864, 2:221). The monarchy would thus have been seen, by those who did not fully understand the economics of the free market, as directly responsible for the price increases that were occurring. King Glele of Dahomey, in the 1860s, apparently responded not by denying his responsibility but, in the manner of governments in other countries and ages, by holding out the prospect of better times to come. At any rate, Burton in 1864 offers the intriguing comment that, "It is said that Gelele has resolved to grind the faces of his countrymen for ten years, of which six are now elapsed [i.e., since his accession in 1858]. After that time they will be applied to honest labour, and a man shall live on a cowrie a day, so cheap will provisions become" (1864, 2:85n). When this deflationary utopia failed to materialize, it must be supposed that disillusionment with the monarchy was heightened. It is difficult not to feel sympathy with Glele, who complained in a remarkably self-pitying public speech reported by the British explorer Skertchly in 1871, that "During the reign of Gezu [his predecessor, Gezo] everybody was happy, and there was plenty of trade, and everything prospered . . . Now, however, his people had become stiffnecked and perverse . . . If any person was desirous of becoming king, thinking that he would have nothing to do, let him come and try it, even for one moon. He would find that he would get no rest, night or day, but would be constantly receiving and sending messengers, and if he made any mistake great palavers would arise" (1874:379–80). Although Glele seems to have been thinking primarily of recent military failures, the problems of his economic administration cannot have helped his mood.

Notes

1. Although cowries had been imported into West Africa overland, across the Sahara, even before the beginning of European imports of cowries by sea in the sixteenth century, it is doubtful whether they reached the Dahomey area in any quantity prior to the opening of the European maritime trade.
2. For details of toll rates on various goods in the 1860s, see Burton ([1864] 1:43n).
3. Norris ([1789] 1968:87). A later account speaks not of a graduated tax, but of a poll tax levied at a fixed rate (4,000 cowries per head, in the late nineteenth century) on all adult males. (Le Herissé 1911:83–4).
4. In the former, children of the marriage belonged to the wife's family, whereas in the latter, they belonged to the husband (Le Herissé 1911:203–10).
5. For the exchange value of cowries in the 1720s, see Law (1990a:114; 1991a:244).
6. As was explicitly noted by a French visitor in 1704 (Doublet 1883:258).
7. Thomas Wilson, Whydah, 24 Feb. 1728 (in Law 1991b:no.15).
8. Archives Nationales, Paris (hereafter, AN) C.6/25, Levet, Whydah, 26 Aug. and 21 Nov. 1733.
9. AN C.6/25, Levet, Whydah, 1 Feb. 1746.
10. Abraham Duport, Whydah, 12 Nov. and 23 Dec. 1727; Thomas Wilson, Whydah, 24 Feb. 1728 (in Law 1991b:nos. 5, 11, 15).
11. Snelgrave [1734] 1971:89; Van Dantzig (1978:no.257 [Elmina Journal, 15 Dec. 1727]).
12. Thomas Wilson, Whydah, 24 Feb. 1728 (in Law 1991b:no.15).
13. AN C.6/25, Pruneau and Guestard, Whydah, 18 March 1750.
14. Atkins ([1735] 1970:112) (5 chickens for a crown, i.e., 5s., or 800 cowries); AN C.6/25, Conseil de Direction, Whydah, 18 Dec. 1752 (12–15 chickens for a grand cabess, or 4,000 cowries); Cf. also Law (1992), for other evidence of price rises.
15. Parliamentary Papers, London (hereafter PP): Report of the Select Committee on the West Coast of Africa (House of Commons, 1842): Minutes of Evidence, 735–46.
16. Dos Santos, Whydah, 25 May and 30 Dec. 1845; 16 Sept. 1847 (Verger 1952:nos 9, 25, 73).
17. PP: Report of the Select Committee on the West Coast of Africa, 1842, Minutes of Evidence, Captain Dring, 2200; cf. also J. A. Clegg, 1756; Capt J. Courland, 2375.
18. *Ibid.*: Minutes of Evidence, M. Forster, 10609.
19. PP: Report from the Select Committee on the Western Coast of Africa, 1865: Minutes of Evidence, W. McCoskry, 1875.

20. Cf. Staudinger (1990), 1:14 (referring to Lagos in the 1880s).

21. Cf., e.g., Phillips 1732:232; Barbot 1992, 2:737–8 (both referring to the Portuguese island of São Tomé (where silver dollars were current) in the 1690s.

22. Cf. Hogendorn and Johnson (1986, 137). Although gold continued to be reckoned in West Africa at £4 per ounce "currency," it was now valued against sterling at only £3 12s. (72 rather than 80 shillings); in consequence, English silver coins had a local or "currency" value of rather more than 10 percent above their face value.

23. Burton [1863], 2:234; Cf. Hogendorn and Johnson 1986:137. It should be noted that English silver coins were now (since 1816) token coins (i.e., containing less than their face value in silver); sterling coins, therefore, did not benefit from the West African premium on silver.

24. Burton [1863] further compounds the confusion by giving the value of the string of 40 cowries as 1 1/2, and that of a "cent" as 8 cowries; the former of these figures must be an error for halfpence, while the latter probably refers to the French centime.

25. d'Albéca (1889, 157).

26. The figure of $1 for 1,000 cowries given by Newbury (1961:40–1), based on dos Santos, Whydah, 20 Jan. 1847 (in Verger 1952:no. 49) is aberrant and clearly a misinterpretation.

27. PP: Papers Relative to the Reduction of Lagos, 1852, incl. 3 in no.13: Journal of Lieutenant Forbes, 2 July 1850 (giving 32,000 heads of cowries as equivalent to only $26,000).

28. Bouche (1877:164–5). Another source of this period gives 4 heads to the dollar, but also states that the size of the string had been increased from the earlier 40 cowries to 50, making the head (50 strings) therefore 2,500 rather than 2,000 cowries, and thus also a rate of 10,000 cowries to the dollar (Skertchly 1874:28).

29. As argued, most influentially, by Hopkins (1973).

30. Dos Santos, Whydah, 19 Dec. 1845 (in Verger 1952:no. 22).

31. John Carter, Whydah, 26 May 1684 (in Law 1990b:no. 16); cf. also Hogendorn and Johnson 1986:89.

32. Dos Santos, Whydah, 3 March 1846; 20 Jan. 1847 (in Verger 1952:nos. 29, 49).

33. Treaty of 1 July 1851, quoted in Cornevin 1962:279–81. Zanzibar cowries were known as "blues" (Cf. Burton 1864, 1:143n).

34. PP: Correspondence Relating to the Slave Trade, 1850–1, vol. 1, incl.3 in no.198: Lieutenant Forbes to Commodore Fanshawe, 6 April 1850.

35. For more complete documentation, see Law (1992). In fact, there was surely price inflation in Lagos also, where it was complained that between 1853 and 1857 laborers' wages had risen from 3 to 15 strings of cowries (i.e., 120 to 600 cowries) per day (Public Record Office, London, FO.84/1141: British and Foreign Anti-Slave Trade Conference, 15 June 1861: my thanks for this reference to Caroline Sorensen). Although this probably represented in part a rise in the real cost of labor (due to an expansion of demand for wage labor in the developing semi-colonial economy of Lagos), it probably also reflected in part a rise in the cost of living resulting from cowry depreciation.

36. In the previous year, 1849, Forbes reported paying subsistence of only 2 strings/80 cowries per day ([1851] 1966, 1:52); it is not clear whether this reflects imprecise reporting, or an increase in rates already in 1849–50.

37. Likewise, in the Yoruba kingdom of Ijebu to the east, when the king in 1859 complained that "the price of provisions had increased greatly," he attributed this to the development of the export of palm oil, and consequent diversion of energies away from food production (PP: Correspondence Relating to the Slave Trade, 1859–60, ii, no.3, Consul Campbell to Earl of Malmesbury, 5 March 1859).

38. Vallon (1860–1, 1:357); PP: Correspondence Relating to the Slave Trade, 1857–8, 1858, ii, no.4: Consul Campbell to Earl of Clarendon, 4 April 1857.

39. A similar explanation of rises in taxation in late nineteenth-century Kano is suggested by Fika (1978:55).

Sources
Archival

Great Britain
Parliamentary Papers (PP)

1842. Report of the Select Committee on the West Coast of Africa: Minutes of Evidence.

1852. Papers Relative to the Reduction of Lagos, 1852, incl.3 in no.13: Journal of Lieutenant Forbes, 2 July 1850.

1850-1.Correspondence Relating to the Slave Trade, 1850-1, Vol. 1, incl.3 in no.198: Lieutenant Forbes to Commodore Fanshawe, 6 April 1850.

1858. Correspondence Relating to the Slave Trade, 1857-8, ii, no.4: Consul Campbell to Earl of Clarendon, 4 April 1857.

1859. Correspondence Relating to the Slave Trade, 1859-60, ii, no.3, Consul Campbell to Earl of Malmesbury, 5 March 1859.

1875. Report from the Select Committee on the Western Coast of Africa, 1865: Minutes of Evidence, W. McCoskry.

Public Record Office, London

FO.84/1141: British and Foreign Anti-Slave Trade Conference, 15 June 1861.

France
Archives Nationales, Paris (AN)

C.6/25, Levet, Whydah, 26 Aug. and 21 Nov. 1733.
C.6/25, Levet, Whydah, 1 Feb. 1746.
C.6/25, Pruneau and Guestard, Whydah, 18 March 1750.
C. 6/25, Conseil de Direction, Whydah, 18 Dec. 1752.

Books, Dissertations, and Articles

Atkins, John. [1735] 1970. *A Voyage to Guinea, Brasil and the West Indies.* London: Frank Cass.

Barbot, Jean. 1992. *Barbot on Guinea: The Writings of Jean Barbot on West Africa*, ed. Paul Hair, Adam Jones and Robin Law, 2 vols. London: Hakluyt Society.

Bosman, William. [1705] 1967. *A New and Accurate Description of the Coast of Guinea.* London: Frank Cass.

Bouche, Abbé Pierre. 1877. "Le Dahomey et les Peuples Nagos." *Revue du Monde Catholique,* 50:161-84.

Bouet, Auguste. 1852. "Le Royaume du Dahomey." *L'Illustration, Journal Universel,* 20, nos 490, 491, 392:39-42, 59-62, 71-4.

Bowen, T. J. [1857] 1968. *Central Africa: Adventures and Missionary Labours.* London: Frank Cass.

Burton, Richard. [1863] 1991. *Wanderings in West Africa,* 2 vols. New York: Dover Publications.

———. 1864. *A Mission to Gelele, King of Dahome,* 2 vols. London: Tinsley Brothers.

Chaudouin, E. 1891. *Trois Mois de Captivité au Dahomey.* Paris: Hachette.

Clarke, William H. 1972: *Travels and Explorations in Yorubaland 1854-1858,* ed. J. A. Atanda. Ibadan: Ibadan University Press.

Clapperton, H. [1829]1966. *Journal of a Second Expedition into the Interior of Africa from the Bight of Benin to Soccattoo.* London: Frank Cass.

Cornevin, Robert. 1962. *Histoire du Dahomey.* Paris: Editions Berger-Levrault.

Crowther, Samuel, and John C. Taylor. [1859] 1968. *The Gospel on the Banks of the Niger.* London: Dawsons of Pall Mall.

Cruickshank, Brodie. [1853] 1966. *Eighteen Years on the Gold Coast of Africa,* 2 vols. London: Frank Cass.

Dapper, Olfert. 1676. *Naukeurige Beschrijvinge der Afrikaensche Gewesten,* 2nd ed. Amsterdam.

Delbée. 1671. "Journal du Voyage du Sieur Delbée." In *Relation de ce qui s'est passé dans les Isles et Terre-ferme de l'Amérique,* Vol. 2, ed. J. de Clodoré, 347–558. Paris: G. Clouzier.

Doublet, Jean. 1883. *Journal du Corsaire Jean Doublet de Honfleur,* ed. Charles Bréard. Paris: Perrin and Co.

Duncan, John. [1847] 1968. *Travels in Western Africa,.* 2 vols. London: Frank Cass.

Dupuis, Joseph. [1824] 1966. *Journal of a Residence in Ashantee.* London: Frank Cass.

d'Albéca, Alexandre. 1889. *Les Etablissements Français du Golfe de Bénin.* Paris: G. Clouzier.

Fika, Adamu Mohammed. 1978. *The Kano Civil War and British Over-rule: 1882–1940.* Ibadan: Oxford University Press.

Forbes, F. E. [1851] 1966. *Dahomey and the Dahomans,* 2 vols. London: Frank Cass.

Guillevin. 1862. "Voyage dans l'Intérieur de Dahomey." *Nouvelles Annales de Voyages,* 6e série, 8/2:257–99.

Henige, David, and Marion Johnson. 1976. "Agaja and the Slave Trade: Another Look at the Evidence." *History in Africa,* 3:91–126.

Hogendorn, Jan, and Marion Johnson. 1986. *The Shell Money of the Slave Trade.* Cambridge: Cambridge University Press.

Hopkins, A. G. 1966. "The Currency Revolution in South-West Nigeria in the Late Nineteenth Century." *Journal of the Historical Society of Nigeria,* 3: 471–84.

———. 1973. *An Economic History of West Africa.* London: Longman.

Houstoun, James. 1725. *Some New and Accurate Observations . . . of the Coast of Africa.* London.

Hutchinson, T. J. [1858] 1970. *Impressions of Western Africa.* London: Frank Cass.

Iroko, Félix Abiola. 1987. "Les Cauris en Afrique Occidentale du Xe au XXe siècle," 2 vols. Thèse de Doctorat d'Etat, Université de Paris I.

Isert, Paul Erdman. 1992. *Letters on West Africa and the Slave Trade,* ed. Selena Winsnes. London: British Academy.

Johnson, Marion. 1966. "The Ounce in Eighteenth-Century West African Trade." *Journal of African History,* 7: 197–214.

Law, Robin. 1990a. "The Gold Trade of Whydah in the Seventeenth and Eighteenth Centuries." In *West African Economic and Social History: Studies in Memory of Marion Johnson,* ed. David Henige and Marion Johnson, 105–118. Madison, Wisconsin: African Studies Program, University of Wisconsin.

———. 1990b. *Correspondence from the Royal African Company's Factories at Offra and Whydah on the Slave Coast of West Africa in the Public Record Office, London, 1678–93.* Edinburgh: Centre of African Studies, University of Edinburgh.

———. 1991a. "Computing Domestic Prices in Precolonial West Africa: A Methodological Exercise from the Slave Coast." *History in Africa,* 18: 239–57.

———. 1991b. *Correspondence of the Royal African Company's Chief Merchants at Cabo*

Corso Castle with William's Fort, Whydah, and the Little Popo Factory, 1727–1728. Madison, Wisconsin: African Studies Program, University of Wisconsin.

———. 1992. "Posthumous Questions for Karl Polanyi: Price Inflation in Precolonial Dahomey." *Journal of African History*, 33: 387–420.

Le Herissé, A. 1911. *L'Ancien Royaume du Dahomey*. Paris: Emile Larose.

Lovejoy, Paul. 1974. "Interregional Monetary flows in the Pre-colonial Trade of Nigeria." *Journal of African History*, 15: 563–85.

Manning, Patrick. 1982. *Slavery, Colonialism and Economic Growth in Dahomey, 1640–1960*. Cambridge: Cambridge University Press.

M'Leod, John. [1820] 1971. *A Voyage to Africa*. London: Frank Cass.

Newbury, C. W. 1961. *The Western Slave Coast and its Rulers*. Oxford: Clarendon Press.

Norris, Robert. [1789] 1968. *Memoirs of the Reign of Bossa Ahadee, King of Dahomy*. London: Frank Cass.

Nørregård, Georg. 1966. *Danish Settlements in West Africa: 1658–1850*. Boston, MA.: Boston University Press.

[Pennington, James]. [1848] 1967. *The Currency of the British Colonies*. New York: Augustus M. Kelley.

Peukert, Werner. 1978. *Der Atlantische Sklavenhandel von Dahomey: 1740–1797*. Wiesbaden: Franz Steiner Verlag.

Phillips, Thomas. 1732. "Journal of a Voyage Made in the Hannibal of London." In *Collection of Voyages and Travels*, ed. Awnsham Churchill and John Churchill, vol. 6, 173–239. London: n.p.

Polanyi, Karl. 1966. *Dahomey and the Slave Trade*. Seattle, WA: University of Washington Press.

Quénum, Maximilien. 1983. *Au Pays des Fons: Us et Coutumes du Dahomey*, 3rd ed. Paris: Maisonneuve et Larose.

Reid, John. 1986. "Warrior Aristocrats in Crisis: The Political Effects of the Transition from The Slave Trade to Palm Oil Commerce in the Nineteenth-Century Kingdom of Dahomey." Ph.D. dissertation, University of Stirling.

Relation [anonymous]. n.d. "Relation du Royaume de Judas en Guinée." Ms. in Archives Nationales, Section d'Outre-Mer, Aix-en-Provence: Dépôt des Fortifications des Colonies, Côtes d'Afrique, ms.104.

Repin. 1863. "Voyage au Dahomey." *Le Tour du Monde*, 1: 65–112.

Ridgway, Archibald. 1847. "Journal of a Visit to Dahomey." *New Monthly Magazine*, 81: 187–98, 299–309, 406–14.

Serval. 1878. "Rapport sur une Mission au Dahomey." *Revue Maritime et Coloniale*, 59:186–95.

Skertchly, J. A. 1874. *Dahomey As It Is*. London: Chapman and Hall.

Snelgrave, William. [1734] 1971. *A New Account of Some Parts of Guinea*. London: Frank Cass.

Staudinger, Paul. 1990. *In the Heart of the Hausa States* (trans. Joanna E. Moody), 2 vols. Athens, Ohio: Ohio University Center for International Studies.

Vallon, A. 1860–1. "Le Royaume de Dahomey," 2 parts. *Revue Maritime et Coloniale*, 2: 332–63, 3: 329–58.

Van Dantzig, Albert. 1978. *The Dutch and the Guinea Coast 1674–1742: A Collection of Documents from the General State Archive at The Hague*. Accra: Ghana Academy of Arts and Sciences.

Verger, Pierre. 1952. *Les Afro-Américains*. Dakar: Institut Français d'Afrique Noire.

PART II

CURRENCY REVOLUTIONS REDESCRIBED

In their lived reality, revolutions are cliff-hangers. The bold find new fields of operation because it is so difficult to differentiate with certainty between the plausible and the impossible, the creative innovation and the scurrilous fraud, the foundation stone of a new order and the temporary high ground in a swamp of alternative possibilities. In some parts of West and Equatorial Africa, there was no clearly discernible shape to colonial rule until the third decade of the twentieth century, so that many of the changes taking place must have seemed more like intensified improvization than definitive structural change. Much of the uncertainty eventually settles out in the subsequent restructuring and retelling of the history. But just as Victor Turner suggested that liminality defines imaginable alternatives to current structures so perhaps people's memories of the alternatives that they experienced during the course of change contain a sense of the fragility and contingency of orders.

Dupré (Ch. 3) describes a mystery, an exotic and ephemeral creation of the early colonial currency interface when lines between the "real" and the "false" were unclear and where even those categories themselves might be inapplicable. Currencies were being created in Africa throughout the period of the Atlantic trade, but without the governmental surveillance of early colonial rule we have no record as precise as this one of the entire life-cycle of a single currency invention. Certain Western museums hold vast collections of what were once termed "primitive currencies." Dupré's analysis makes one wonder how much of those collections are made up of goods that have returned home—from Brussels to Tervuren by way of the Congo, from Birmingham to London through Calabar. The singular case of *mandjong* must stand for what we do know was a major commercial activity of Western merchants, often and increasingly in defiance of their own governments, namely the invention of "primitive money." And the empirical fact of local domestication, imprinted on this object, can stand for what we also know to be a major African cultural and political process with respect to currency innovation. Similar receptivity and active domestication come up in other chapters, especially expressed in language: the terms for new monetary units (Guyer, Ch. 5), words to describe savings (Shipton, Ch. 11), and vernacular appropriations for new kinds of financial crime (Ekejiuba, Ch. 6).

Arhin (Ch. 4), like Law (Ch. 2), addresses a case for which popular innovations all take place in relation to an established centralized power. Unlike Dahomey, however, Asante kept commercial exchange on the fringes of political life. In spite of high levels of production and exchange, and the existence of currencies, he argues that major domains of social life were not commercialized before the early colonial period. Barriers were personal status barriers, not moral injunctions against the convertibility of goods. Colonial monetization did indeed, then, constitute a fundamental challenge, but political rather than moral. In response, the chiefs mobilized a series of policy initiatives to try to contain the damage to a hierarchical order. Here, as in the chapters by Guyer (Ch. 5) and Mikell (Ch. 10), explicit policy is made within African societies to control social payments or to define their entailments because, under commercial and colonial currency conditions, they threaten to escape the political order altogether. These chapters warn against a straightforward populism or individualism in the understanding of people's responses to the more deeply commercialized economy of the early colonial era. In fact, policy was made at many levels, and probably much more than is recorded. We know very little about any policies that communities may have developed about prices, although there may well have been more than we know. For the moment, colonial prices are usually described as if there was no possibility to affect them. The indigenous policy debate about money was shifted then, as Arhin argues, into the sphere of consumption and into social payments. It is the very much higher possibility of local control and innovation that makes social payments—as distinct from narrowly financial or economic provisions—such a critical component in the study of African thought and practice with respect to currency during the colonial period.

Thus is the narrative of currency revolution as it unfolded in communities transformed from a *pris en charge* at the top and responsiveness of various sorts (including both moral erosion and political resistance) from below, to one of multiple policy interventions: some officially sanctioned and others invented on the spot, some with lasting implications and others tying up time and imaginative energy with no achievement except to distract attention from other matters. And all of these measures, we suggest, arose out of a long and varied African experience with currency innovation and management.

3

The History and Adventures of a Monetary Object of the Kwélé of the Congo: Mezong, Mondjos, and Mandjong*

GEORGES DUPRE

It was E. Andersson who first drew our attention to the object that we now refer to as *mandjong*: "a measure of value the Kwélé had, at least in the past, a strange piece of iron in the form of an anchor serving above all in the payment of lobolo" (1953:103). Leon Siroto then wrote of an "anchor-shaped piece of iron, *paazong,* that served as a unit of bridewealth" (1959:77). And it is under the term of *mandjong* that J.-F. Vincent later described these objects that until recently entered into the constitution of marriage payments among the Kwélé of northern Congo. These *mandjong* "look like pieces cut out of flat sheets of iron, of much greater dimensions than the *bitchie*: 50 cm

*I would like to thank Dr. Hans-Joachim Koloss, conservator of the Africa Department at the Museum für Volkerkunde of Berlin, for valuable information concerning a sample collected in 1899. I thank Josette Rivallain, maitre de conference at the Museum d'Histoire Naturelle, who gave me access to two samples owned by the Musée de l'Homme and who gave me benefit of her knowledge of African currencies. I also thank the following people for information that they have shared with me and for their suggestions, without which this chapter could not have been written: M. Bernard Denis, Marie-Claude Dupré, Professor Jean Le Coze, Professor Allen Robers, Jacques Schoonheyt, and M. Varillon. The association EUCOPRIMO gave me important support, and in particular Rolf Braun, Dr. Rolf Denk, Karl Ludwig Ehrbächer, C. de Boer, Dr. Herbert H. Hansen, Professor Allen F. Roberts, Karl Schötter and Karl Schädler. Dominique Guillaud was kind enough to draw the illustrations and J.-F. Vincent was willing to reread and improve a first version of the text.

long, 38 to 40 cm long, but only a few mm thick. Made by careful work, they are remarkably identical from one to the other and, very curiously, resemble an anchor" (Vincent 1963:285).

Vincent wonders about the strange form of the *mandjong*, which she finds "more mysterious" than the *bitchie* used by the neighboring Fang. Josette Rivallain, in her turn, speaks of "more or less extraordinary iron monies," and "curious objects" (1987:759).[1] These impressions are shared by all who showed interest in *mandjong* and are due to the difficulty of establishing a relationship between their form— which evokes the image of an anchor—and their use as a means of exchange in an African society. Their shape makes them difficult to place in one of the categories of iron object that are known to have been used in Africa as instruments of exchange. In the classification proposed by J. Rivallain,[2] they can only find a place in a catch-all category of "forms difficult to identify."

Vincent has researched the forms to which the *mandjong* could correspond. We must set aside the connection that she makes with the *mutenzi* of the Kota. Despite having a form that evokes an engraving tool (Vincent 1963:287) or a scissor (Bruel 1918:443; Rivallain 1987:834), these latter objects are incontrovertibly derived from the hammer, whose name they bear—*ntenzi, mutenzi, mutiene*—among the Kota and various other groups such as Obamba, Ngomo, and Ndasa, who use them for marriage payments.

Vincent also puts forward the idea that the anchor form of *mandjong* might have been inspired in the local smiths by the anchors of boats that circulated on the Sangha River from the beginning of the century. This idea, which the author presents simply as a hypothesis, contains the interesting presentiment that *mandjong* might have been influenced in their form by the colonizer. Vincent's informants "were evasive in their responses; perhaps they came form the Coast." In this latter hypothesis, *mandjong* would be imported objects, but this is not certain since "the Bakwele smiths were very skilful artisans capable of reproducing an anchor" (Vincent 1963:286).

Thus was introduced the idea that *mandjong* have a complex history, that they are not simply traditional Kwélé objects, and that the questions raised by their enigmatic form cannot find answers without repositioning them in the context of relations between the traders of the commercial houses installed in the Sangha region and the Kwélé people.

The inquiry that I pursued in the field, and continued in the archives, contributes to this history and dissipates the mystery of *mandjong*. It establishes with certainty that the *mondjos*, which were objects of industrial manufacture and very similar to the *mandjong*, were introduced by the European traders at the beginning of the century. It further establishes that *mondjos* were inspired by the old Kwélé objects, the *mezong* (sing., *zong*). These are the provisional conclusions presented here.

From the Field to the Archives, 1972–1992

In 1972 and 1973, I stayed in Sangha for a cocoa development project. At the sidelines of the main study, I became interested in the iron currencies of the region, in a comparative perspective, because I had already studied the iron currencies of the Nzabi, the Kota, and other forest peoples during previous research in the forest area of Niari.

From the beginning of the study in the area around Sembe, from the formulation of my very first questions, my informant reproved me, noting that the term *mandjong* was French and that the exact term in the Bakwele language was *mezong* in the plural and *zong* in the singular, a term also used for an axe. Could two words signify two different objects, or was it as question of simple correction of the transcription of the word that designated one single object? The informant could not reply, but he assured me that in Ouesso M. Akoul could inform me better. So I met M. Akoul, who willingly agreed to talk to me about the *zong*. He described to me the different parts of the object, which he went to look for in his house. Very quickly he specified that all the information that he was offering concerned the old *zong* that existed before the advent of Whites, who brought in the new *zong*. According to him, one Monsieur Foix, nicknamed Yagha-Yagha, and another White, nicknamed Ngwangbwa, introduced the new zong called *mazong mayo*, which signifies the *"zong* made with a file." Both Monsieur Foix and Ngwangbwa lived in Sembe and bought rubber and ivory. Akoul saw them in person at an age when he was already married. To get *mezong,* one had to give the best quality rubber. Those who brought *"medebe"* rubber, of poor quality, sticky because poorly coagulated or containing foreign bodies, could not receive *mezong*. In the eyes of M. Akoul, the introduction of new *mezong* by the Europeans was nothing out of the ordinary, and another White of the name (or nickname) of Ebabi, who came after M. Foix, also brought new anvils still known today under the name of *ziz Ebabi*. The new *mezong* resembled the originals. They enjoyed such a great success that they completely replaced the old ones, which the smiths made into tools. And the *mezong* made by the smiths from that time on were on the model of the imported *mezong*. All this would explain why it is impossible today to find in Kwélé villages a single example of the old *mezong*.

These data were consistent and lent themselves—if good fortune would have it—to verification in the archives. Elsewhere and at several junctures, the information given by Akoul about the introduction of *mezong* by the Europeans was corroborated by other informants.[3]

The study could not be resumed until much later, and was undertaken in the Archives d'Outre-Mer in Aix en Provence, where in November 1992 the data collected in the field were confirmed.

The study resumed after my discovery of *mondjos* in a file dated December 1st 1910 and established by the concessionary company of N'Goko Sangha to claim indemnities for a pillaging that took place in the autumn of 1908 at several company posts, as well as for an attack on a shipping convoy on the Koudou River and several attacks on caravans, all in the same year. These facts are referred to collectively in the records as "the Djouah events." The file includes the typed inventory of the goods pillaged, post by post, dividing them under four rubrics: "Trade goods pillaged from the post," "Products," "Equipment," and eventually, where applicable "Property burned by the natives." The term *"mondjos"* figures in several of the inventories, particularly those of the posts at Maniene, Godebe, Maniolo, Maza, and Moisi, under the rubric "Trade goods pillaged from the post." In this category figure the objects sold by the company. The following list under that rubric is given here as an example, and comes from the post of Maniolo. It is transcribed exactly as written, shifts in capitalization included:

9 Basins 1/2 strong

11 filigreed knives

9 leather belts

7 large hats

7 P. Fall Check

4 Long guns

13 Large hand Mirrors

11 Small hand Mirrors

13 Kilo iron wire

7—brass wire

6 Old iron spears

84 Files

58 Large machetes

10 Small machetes

17 Manilla arm-rings

1 Trunk

5 New mondjos

5 Old ditto

4 Enamel bowls

5 Neptunes

4 Large wrappers

9 Swiss wrappers

35 Boxes of powder 0K500

5 ditto 2K

1 ditto 3K500

51 Razors

5 Kilos of salt

2 pieces of guinea

7 Folding knives

Obviously, the goods that figure under this rubric are the trade goods sold by the traders. Under the rubric of "Products" are found the goods bought locally by the company, particularly rubber, ivory, and also chickens. Finally the rubric of "Equipment" comprises things used by the company, such as roman scales, Gras rifles, and various tools.

The objects designated under the name *mondjos* in the inventories and sold by the Company are described several times in administrative reports because they are at the heart of the conflict between the colonial administration and the concessionary company: the introduction of legal colonial currency. The administration wanted to impose French currency in all transactions because the taxes that they were beginning to exact had to be paid in coins. The company, on the contrary, wanted to continue to practice barter, which permitted them to impose exchange rates favorable to themselves.

Several passages in the administrative reports leave no doubt: the *mondjos* clearly had the form of the *mandjong* that we know:

The currencies of the area are of two sorts: the *midjoko,* a copper bracelet worth two francs (real value) and the *mondjo* anchor made in sheet iron worth 5 francs (real value 1 Fr. 50).[4]

The trade goods most appreciated by the natives are salt, palm oil, knives, cloth and above all forged articles in iron and copper, worked in any kind of fashion. In this order of idea the *'mondjo,'* sheet iron, 1mm5 thick, cut in the form of a ship's anchor 60cm tall and whose points are worked with a hammer, is the good most prized.[5]

The *mondjo* is an object of exchange, in iron, having the form of an anchor, stamped out of sheet metal, 50cm. long, of a real value of 0F.25 or 0F.50, given against two to three kilos of rubber.[6]

To judge by these reports, the N'Goko Sangha Company considered the diffusion of specie to be an obstacle to the development of its commercial activities.

But obliged to execute the prescriptions of the Governor General, the company officially instructs all its agents to use coins for the purchase of rubber and ivory. This measure is evidently insufficient to spread the use of this money because the old currencies of the company continue to arrive regularly in the factories.

This money has neither value nor use.

1. The "Mondjo," iron anchor, of a value of 0fr50 (transport paid) is exchanged against 10 kg of rubber.
2. The "Neptune," small plate of brass is exchanged against 5 kg of rubber.
3. The "Machete" a kind of bush-knife in sheet iron worth 5 kg of rubber.
4. Brass wire worth 20 to 30 kg of rubber per kilo.[7]

The archives brought another even more unexpected confirmation of the data gained in the field. M. Akoul had given me the name of M. Foix as that of one of the two Europeans who had introduced the new *mezong*. It seemed clearly to be a French patronym, in contrast to the name of the other European, Ngwangbwa, which was obviously a nickname. I had noted Foix, identifying by ear a quite common French family name. The name of M. Frois, also written Froix, appeared several times in the archives. In the list of personnel of the N'Goko Sangha in Sembe, by status, for the year 1909, the name of Joseph Frois came in second position immediately after the name of M. Gaboriaud, the director. In a document of August 28th 1910, M. Frois was put in charge of the current affairs of the N'Goko Sangha at Sembe. Finally, Frois, Joseph Alexandre was, in 1913, director of the N'Goko Sangha at Sembe.[8]

This ethnological mystery study resulted first of all in settling in striking fashion the credibility of informants and particularly that of M. Akoul. This result is important because it encourages us to have confidence in them on other points that are not confirmed by the archives.

The confrontation of oral and archival information permits us to establish, without possible doubt, that *mandjong* of industrial manufacture were certainly introduced by the traders of the N'Goko Sangha Company, at the beginning of the century and exchanged with the Kwélé against rubber and ivory.

This confirmation, however, even if it makes progress on the question of the *mandjong*, poses new problems in its turn. If one considers the objects themselves that we find today in Africa or in the collections, it is very difficult to see them as objects of industrial manufacture, or at least as objects straight from the press. None of these objects is rigorously symmetrical (Figure 3–1). The "ears" are forged by hammer work;

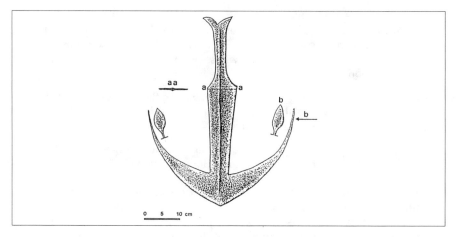

FIGURE 3-1   A mandjong.

no two ears are strictly alike. The contours present irregularities. The median ridge is also irregular in its tracing and often is placed only approximately down the symmetrical axis. The thickness varies from one end of the object to the other. Furthermore, the 15 mandjong for which I have precise information present with appreciably different dimensions, which translate into important weight variation. The weight of the object varies, in fact, from 478 grams to 678 grams. The conclusion is inescapable that all these objects were made by artisanal methods, which is—in its own fashion—in agreement with the field information. According to Akoul and others, the old *mezong* were completely replaced by the new ones obtained from the factories, and the smiths started to make more on this model while all the old ones were transformed into tools. All the objects for which I had information would therefore be *mandjong* made by the smiths after the introduction of the industrial *mondjos*. It is surprising, meanwhile, that none of them has, in any indubitable way, the mark of industrial fabrication. The spectacular success of the inquiry, if it dissipates the mystery of the *mandjong*, leads to a whole series of new questions. One must then take up the question of *mandjong* again, on the basis of new information.

In the text that follows, in order to avoid confusion, the following terms are used. The term *zong* (plural *mezong*) applies to the ancient object existing among the Kwélé before the arrival of the European traders. The term *mondjo* (plural *mondjos)* designates the objects of industrial manufacture, indicated in the factories' stocklist, but of which no single sample has yet been observed. The term *mandjong* (no plural) designates the objects that we now find in the museums and collections.

Mezong in Matrimonial Circulation

It is fitting here to have confidence in the informants, whose credibility has already been demonstrated on other points, and to affirm with them that before the introduction of the industrial *mandjong* there existed among the Kwélé an object of a form quite comparable to the *mandjong*. Without assuming the pre-colonial existence of the *zong*, it would be difficult to see what might have inspired the traders to introduce an object with such a singular form and such a geographically limited use,[9] if there was not already an comparable object before their arrival. Not only are the *mezong* limited to the Kwélé, but according to Siroto and cited by Roberts (1992:18 n. 19) their use was limited to the western Bakwele, in the present day Congo. Moreover, the *mondjos* do not seem to have been diffused by the traders outside of their area of origin. Likewise, the inventory of the factory at Etoumbi, situated outside of Kwélé country, which figures in the file on the indemnities of the "Djouah events," include no *mondjo*. *Mezong* have to be considered as objects specifically Kwélé.[10]

In the 1960s, the Kwélé numbered about 13,000 people (Robineau 1971:36) for the most part spread over the circumscriptions of Sembe and Souanke and the north of the Congo, to which total must be added about 1,500 people who live in Gabon (Vincent 1963:273).[11]

According to the description given by Robineau (1971:83–5), Kwélé society is segmentary. Its organization may be depicted as the result of the dovetailing of different patrilineal groups. The patriclans, or *mbiak*, are divided into segments, the *melenemengia*, in their turn divided into patrilineages. Locally, the residential communities, the *bwoberuk*, group into a village the men of the same patrilineage. Robineau counted 55 *mbiak* for a population of 11,000 individuals, giving an average of 200 individuals by *mbiak*, which then implies an extremely small size for the smallest units, the *bwoberuk*. This very small size of groups is accompanied by a dispersion and intermingling of the *mbiak*. "One can find components of the same *mbiak* from one extremity to the other of the Bakwele territory" (Robineau 1971: 103). In this situation, in which the small size of groups is associated with their extreme spatial dispersal, marriage, "the key to traditional institutions . . . weaves relations of alliance and organizes the exchange of goods" between clans and lineages (Robineau 1971:92). Matrimonial circulation—understood as circulation of persons, goods and information—plays an essential role in constituting and maintaining Kwélé society as an entity with a certain coherence in the absence of a centralized political infrastructure. It must be understood, of course, that this description of Kwélé social organization was made in the 1960s. According to Robineau, the extreme dispersal of the groups that organize Kwélé society is due to "the successive rearrangement of environment imposed on the Kwélé" (Robineau 1971:92) by colonization. Because of this, the clan and lineage structure of the society, maintained during the colonial period, plays today more than ever a political role in matrimonial circulation.[12]

At the beginning of the century an anonymous author, C.C., collected a narrative that he attributes to the Boumoali, a vague designation that applies in general to the people who inhabit this region:

> The Boumoali therefore believe in the existence of a God, who has the body of a man and whose wife Andi is albino. He lives on a high mountain that touches the sky, located, it seems, far away near to the source of the Boumbo, tributary of the Ngoko. . . .
>
> Bembo and Andi had a daughter Dielo and a son Djoumaka, whom they sent to earth to make a village and plantations. But they had sexual relations together, *in spite of their father's interdiction*, from which was born Boumoali. Grown up, Boumoali had a son Lino, by his mother, who then followed the example of his older brother and had two sons of his own, Gouamboko and

Issolo. Nevertheless, Djoumaka was not jealous of his sons because he was aiming at the growth of his race: he even authorized Boussiele, son of Issolo, to replace him with Dielo. From this union was born Boumama, a boy, and Mamo, a girl.

Next came Mokaka, Boquiba, Ossyeba, M'boko, etc., whose tribes still exist.

The God Bembo relented meanwhile and taught the sons of his children to make spears and *manjos*, a kind of large iron knife that serves as currency; then he sent them two Babinga pygmies to hunt elephants.

They were a brother and sister; and they had sexual relations between them, which Bembo no longer tolerated between kin and they were driven out of the village, condemned to live in the forest (C.C. 1909:74).

In this narrative of the beginnings of human society, there are two successive periods. In the first period, the group issuing from the primordial couple reproduce by a cascade of incestuous relations, in particular by brother–sister and mother–son unions. The acquisition of iron goods—spears and *manjos*—brings this period to an end. The incest, even though forbidden initially by the God Bembo, was tolerated because it contributed to the growth of the group. But looking more closely at the narrative, the incest of the first period could not help but be tolerated, because the humans had no means of bringing it to an end. With the metallurgy that God taught to humans, things changed. The acquisition of *manjos* by humans institutes a break. It brings to an end the period of turpitude at the beginning of the world, and the Babinga Pygmies who had not understood this saw their incestuous conduct sanctioned by their definitive relegation to the forest. From then onwards, humans have, in the *manjos*, the means and instrument for life in society. Because they are a means of matrimonial exchange, the *manjos* that the narrative designates as "money," without further explanation, put an end to the previous period.

We find in this narrative something close to the interpretation given by Levi-Strauss to marriage payments. This "operating technique" (Levi-Strauss 1967:539) not only renders matrimonial exchange possible, but implicates a certain type of matrimonial exchange, namely generalized exchange. The compensation obtained by the group that has ceded a woman allows it to acquire another in an open system of exchange. This clearly corresponds to the Kwélé case, because out of 336 cases of matrimonial alliance, only 16 represent alliances internal to the clan (Robineau 1971:103). All the other alliances bring together two different *mbiak*, and because these *mbiak* are dispersed throughout the entire Kwélé territory, matrimonial exchange is a general circulation affecting the entire population of Kwélé. The operation of marriage payments is linked organically to this sort of political configuration.

In fact, marriage gave in the past—and still gives today—occasion for multiple prestations[13] that can be grouped into two assemblages: the prestations termed *egual* furnished by the man and his kin, and those termed *mongo* given by the wife and her family. The *mongo* prestations, which the francophone Bakwele call the "contre-dot" (the counter-dowry), were essentially made up of prepared food, hunting dogs, poultry, mats, and various basket-woven goods. These prestations began long before the marriage and played out during the entire duration of the union.[14]

Marriage compensation, that is the entire ensemble of *egual* prestations (the "dot" or "dowry" of francophones), was constituted by a great number of diverse goods. Amongst local products figured hunting nets, pieces of woven raphia, bark-cloth clothing and a great number of iron objects. Amongst these latter, there were *dupa*, a farm implement used before the introduction of the machete (see Figure 3–5); throwing knives; double bells; iron collars; leg rings; ankle rings; hatchets; anvils; sledge-hammers—*ziz*—of which a great variety existed (*ziz gomak, ziz medul, ziz amuko*); mallets (*egwek*), another hatchet (*zong ekwal*); and the objects that interest us here, the *mezong*. Among the trade goods, there were blue beads mounted as neck-laces on fiber strings, neptunes, manillas, and *midjoko* (a spiral copper bracelet). Finally, elephant tusks could also be given for a marriage. This list was given to me as the list of goods that could enter into marriage payment at the end of the last century. It was given without a chronology and it is therefore difficult to establish any sequence that might indicate any evolution in marriage payments, such as Vincent has established (1963:278–82). One might say in any case that certain objects such as the farm implement, the *dupa*, seem to have disappeared very early as a component of marriage payments.

In the great diversity of objects eligible to figure in matrimonial compensation, it was the bride's family that made the choice. What they demanded depended on their needs, that is to say, on the requests that had been made by the men for whom it needed to find wives. But it was also the requirements of the maternal uncle of the bride that determined the composition of the marriage payments. He could, for example, evoke an old dispute between the two clans and demand a particular object to bring it to an end. It works in the same way as Tessmann established for the neigh-boring Fang at the turn of the century, where there existed "the custom of never demanding for the price of a woman only one kind of item, but to ask for particular items determined from a vast series of diverse goods" (Tessmann 1992:301).

The Form of the Zong: From Use Value to Exchange Value

One could say that the *zong* is " a means of exchange," to use the terminology of J. Schoonheyt (1991). In fact, this is one way of saying that it is not altogether a money, even though it fulfills most monetary purposes. It is also a way of saying that it is more than a money because it is the object of practices that are not monetary alone. The *zong* is more a unit of account than a means of exchange in itself. Most often, *mezong* are in packets of 10, attached together by fibers. It is in this form that they were given in the prestation called "*mbwanza emwas*" that the Kwélé term the "prin-cipal payment." And it is these packets of *mezong* that are the object of strict account-ing, using sticks.[15] But in other marriage prestations, the *mezong* are presented differ-ently. Thus, several *mezong* can be given by the fiance to the kin of the bride at the time of the first visit. By this opening prestation, the future husband indicates his choice; the word used, *esumedor*, originally designates the mark made on a forest that is to be cleared. After the marriage takes place and the bride has been secluded in the home of her husband for some time, she goes to pay a visit to her kin. She is deco-rated, colored black, and dressed with a civet-cat skin. And the *zong* that she holds in each hand shows to all whom she encounters on her way and to her kinsmen, her new status as a bride. Thus, the *zong* is not only on the order of something that can be accounted; it is a sign of social meaning in itself.

On this topic, it must be made clear that *mezong* were not those famous goods referred to as "prestige goods," that are ostentatiously displayed and which abound in the ethnographic literature. The *mezong*, as well as all of the goods given for marriage payments, were stores of value. Metal goods were often conserved in mud that had reducing qualities at the edges of rivers, or carefully packaged and placed above the cooking fire. They were not shown in public except when they changed hands, during the presentations of marriage. As stores of wealth, the *mezong* are modes of action in the marriage circuits, and by virtue of this, they are political instruments. They contribute at one and the same time to the maintenance of a certain order over the sum of alliances, co-extensive with Kwélé society, and also to the power of men over women and the elders over the young. The acquisition and retention of goods that enter into marriage payments are socially controled.

The Kwélé produced no iron. They had to procure it from their neighbors and particularly from the Kuta, who produced it from local ores. The Kwélé obtained unworked iron, but also a certain number of objects that were given in marriage: the anvils and hammers, the *dupa* that came from around Mouloundou. But the *mezong* had been "invented" by the Kwélé, as informants said in order to signify that they had been made and used only by them. To obtain *mezong* from a smith, raw iron and charcoal had to be brought and he had to be compensated for his labor.[16] This means that the acquisition of *mezong* presupposed the capacity to take part in the commercial circuits of the day to obtain the iron, and then the capacity to remunerate the local Kwélé smith who produced the *mezong* with the iron brought to him, and finally, the capacity to mobilize a labor force to produce the charcoal. *Mezong* were clearly not objects that just anybody could acquire. Also, as Vincent says, "the monetary circuit of the Djem and Bakwele was a limited circuit, only existing amongst powerful personages. Our informants in fact remarked that it was exceptional that any ordinary person should possess *bitchie* or *mandjong*; only the clan chiefs were competent to keep them, and to decide about their eventual use" (1963:290). Mary Kingsley similarly described a trade that was entirely under the control of "chiefs and important men" (Kingsley 1898:254).

The form itself of the *zong* contributes to this political control. The present text was almost completed when I received information that allows the description, with quasi-certitude, of the shape of the *zong*. I learned that the Museum für Volkerkunde de Berlin possessed an object purchased in 1899, coming from the Upper Sangha, that presents certain formal similarities to the *mandjong*. The object (Figure 3–2a) is smaller and at 393 g clearly lighter than all the *mandjong* studied, but presents a striking similarity with the *mandjong* in the shape of the shaft. This similarity is perhaps insufficient to affirm that we are really in the presence of the *zong*. But this information was an encouragement to search again amongst the objects already catalogued and published for any that might be linked to the *zong*. It was Rivallain's thesis (1987) that put me on the track and particularly plate LXXXV that presents two objects of which one is altogether comparable to that in Berlin. These two illustrations are taken from Cureau (1912) and Bruel (1918). The examination of these works and especially that of Bruel allows us, in my own opinion, to suspend all hesitation. The object in the Berlin museum and the object presented by Bruel are certainly the *mezong* that existed among the Kwélé before the arrival of the traders. The object I present here in Figure 3–2b comes from a plate, page 444, of Bruel's book, entitled: "Fig. 25— indigenous currencies of the Congo." In this plate, figure f carries the legend:

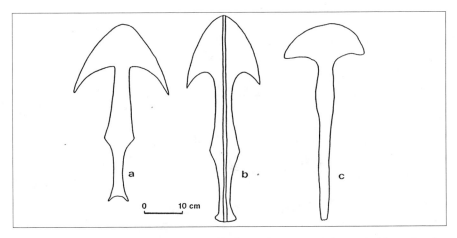

FIGURE 3-2   The *Zong:* a) example from the Berlin Museum; b) Copied from Bruel 1918:444; c) Copied from Cureau 1912:7, plate XIV

"Monzio (Middle Sanga) 1/10 of life size." The text where different currencies are enumerated is a little more explicit: "Monzio (hoe) in the middle Sangha (see figure no. 25-f)" (Bruel 1912:445). The object presented by Cureau, plate XIV, 7, also originating from the middle Sangha, is perhaps linked to the *zong,* but with less evidential support (Figure 3-2c).[17]

How can we interpret the shape of the *zong*? Informants give two interpretations, the first zoomorphic (Figure 3–3), and the other functional (Figure 3–4). The *zong* has a head, a chest, two ears and a body with a tail. The informants' interpretation of the *mandjong* could be valid for the *zong,* putting aside the fact that the latter had no ears.

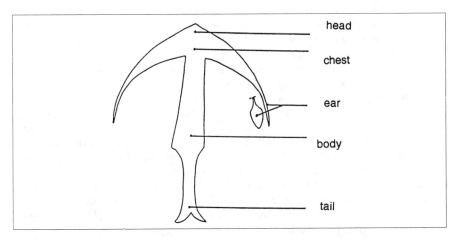

FIGURE 3-3   Zoomorphic Interpretation of the *Mandjong*

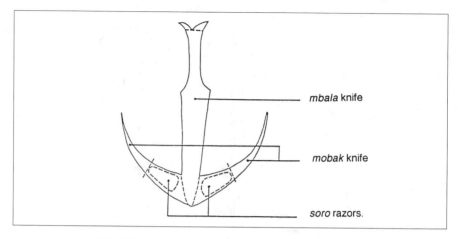

mbala knife

mobak knife

soro razors.

FIGURE 3-4   Functional Interpretation of the *Mandjong*

In the functional interpretation the *mandjong* can be deconstructed into the rough shapes of several tools: a large knife, two small knives and two razors. I have held in my hand one of the small razors that serves to cut hair, but I could not collect any information on the uses of the two knives. The interpretation is difficult to transpose from the *mandjong* to the *zong*. The part they have in common is the shaft or shank (if one uses the terms applied for an anchor), so that the *zong* should first be the rough shape of a knife. This interpretation does not take into account the many other transformations that might be inflicted on the *zong* after it had been withdrawn from exchange and became an ordinary piece of iron. It could be made into a machete (Vincent 1963:288) or into any other tool. One interpretation of *zong* that must be dispelled from the outset is that proposed by Bruel himself. The form of the *zong* cannot be considered as derivative of the hoe because this tool did not exist among the Kwélé, any more than among most of their forest neighbors (M.-C. Dupré 1993), where agricultural work was done with the aid of a multipurpose tool, the *dupa*, that could itself figure in marriage payments (see Figure 3–5c). Neither can the *zong* be identified with the hatchet whose name it bears, because the hatchet also figured as it was—or at least in a derived form—in the *egual* goods.

Whatever the interpretation one gives to the *zong*, the question of its shape remains. Before we knew for certain what shape the *zong* had, we might have imagined that—like the *mandjong*—it took the form of a ship's anchor. And we could wonder why such a singular form had been given to an object used for marriage payments. In fact, the form turns out to be less singular than imagined and actually finds its place at the heart of the esthetics of the Kwélé universe.[18] This, at least, is the sense given by Roberts (1992:9–10) of the similarity between *mandjong* and the form of Kwélé horned masks. And one could multiply similarities of this kind, particularly with the famous horned dance mask in the Barbier-Mueller Collection (Perrois 1985:81). Schoonheyt (personal communication, Dec. 28, 1992) suggests that "The original *mandjong* might be related to the form of the cross-bow used by the Fang."

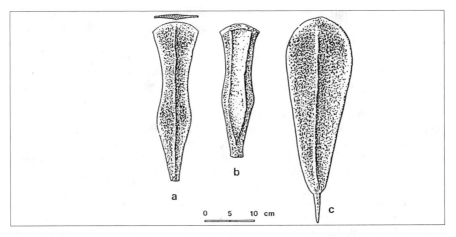

FIGURE 3-5 Monetary Objects: a) hatchet for marriage payments; b) hatchet for work; c) agricultural implement, *dupa*.

This idea is interesting because the weapon also exists amongst the Kwélé, and I was able to see one used in 1972 in a hunt for monkeys.

Now that we know that the *zong* did not have the form of an anchor, but that it was the traders who developed the form from the *zong*, keeping only the shaft the same, a problem remains, but it is of more managable size. It can be posed as follows: how can an object that is interpreted as a knife have the form of the *zong*? This question cannot have a single answer; rather it demands taking into consideration the general situation with respect to metal currencies. Metal currencies have at the same time a use value and an exchange value, and different means can be used to separate these two kinds of value. It can be as simple as a reduction in the size of the object that makes it unfit to be used as a tool. This is the case with the spades and knives used for monetary purposes in ancient China (Thierry 1992). In other cases, it is the form itself that creates the separation. The form of the currency evokes its use value and at the same time renders impossible the realization of that use value. Thus, the hatchets used for marriage are lighter and have a shorter cutting edge than the tool itself, and in any case are never sharpened (see Figure 3–2a and b). Then again, the transformation of the form can be so great that the original tool is not recognizable in the form of the monetary object. This is the case as we have seen for the hammer, and it is the case for the *zong*, which—although developed from the knife—is made completely useless in this capacity by the addition of two laterally fixed razors; at least, this accords with the interpretation given to me.

From the Zong to the Mandjong

As we have seen, it is in the archives for the years 1908 to 1913, concerning the company of N'Goko Sangha, that we find the proof of the introduction of industrially made products that are called *mandjos*, which, according to the description, have a form very comparable to the objects that we know under the name of *mandjong*. But nothing precise is known either about the conditions under which these objects were introduced or about the date of their first introduction.

Jacques de Brazza, the brother of the explorer, was probably the first European to come to the Sangha in 1885 (Vincent 1964:68–9). Later, in 1890, Cholet went up the Sangha River for the first time (Fourneau 1932:268–9). The following year, Fourneau continued the exploration up the N'Goko; the post at Ouesso was created in that year, 1891. At that date there was already a trader of the house of Daumas on the Sangha, at Bonga. But it was probably not until later that the territory attributed to the N'Goko Sangha would see traders really installed. The concessionary company of N'Goko Sangha was formed between 1905 and 1907 by the fusion of three companies: the Produce Company of Sangha-Lipa Ouesso, the Company of N'Goko Sangha Ouesso and the Company for Colonial Explorations.[19]

The N'goko Sangha was one of the 40 concessionary companies created in 1899, which divided up 70 percent of the territory of the Congo with a view to its development. In the event, the concessionary system did not manage to supplant the former trading system and limited itself to the extraction of natural resources. "In sum," as Coquery-Vidrovitch writes, "the Companies lived from *la traite*[20] . . ." (1977:169).

The N'Goko Sangha, situated on the border of German Cameroon, knew multiple vicissitudes linked to Franco-German tension before the 1914 war. Meanwhile, it maintained a dense network of factories and trading posts that brought in ivory and wild rubber.[21]

According to Coquery-Vidrovitch, the concessionary companies, "little disposed to make an effort at adaptation started from the principle that the Africans were brutes susceptible of accepting anything" (1977:153-4). This statement is a remarkably poor summation of the attitude of the concessionary companies toward their African clients. The traders' lust for gain was great,[22] but it went together with a very real, practical knowledge of the local economies and societies. The Europeans' interest in African economies was not new; it had been manifest from the very first contacts with Africa. As evidence, one can point to all the manipulations of which the local currencies were the object.[23] The imitation of objects considered as currency was a common practice among European traders in the region, as in all of Africa and during different periods of history. It constitutes the recognition, well before economic anthropology mixed in, of the importance of local currencies. At the time when the concessionary companies were active not much had changed. The traders established in the North Congo and Southern Cameroon manifested their interest in monetary objects, evidently for commercial purposes.[24] So the narrative of the invention of marriage payments (C.C. 1909) was probably not collected out of simple ethnographic curiosity. The author did not miss noting in passing that the *mondjo* is a currency and it is evident that its role in the matrimonial circuits did not escape him.

These were not just any objects that were reproduced by European manufacture, but those that served as means of exchange. We have seen that there were anvils introduced by the famous Ebabi, the *ziz ebabi*. There were also knives for farming, *dupa*, in every way comparable to that of Figure 3-5 of which Rivallain (1987:802 and 802) has discovered three samples, two in the Pitt-Rivers Museum in Cambridge and one in the Museé de l'Homme. The samples in the Pitt-Rivers Museum are classified as "bride-money" made in Germany and collected in 1932 among the Maka in French Cameroon. The sample in the Musée de l'Homme was found in Sangha in 1904.

This practice that tended to perpetuate the barter economy was obviously strongly criticized by the colonial administration. And the management of the N'Goko Sangha replied by justifying the exchange of *mondjos* against rubber under the name of *marchandise monnaie* ("commodity currency"). Several passages from the administrative reports indicate the conflict:

> Barter is the only commercial procedure practiced by the Company in its transactions with the natives . . . We have to manage to suppress what the director refers to as 'commodity currencies.'

> The concessionary company commits a double delict: 1. In striking money (since certain special goods are considered to be commodity currencies); 2. In refusing the national currency when a native wants to use it to buy *mondjos* or machetes.[25]

> The concessionary company resists as much as it can because it sees only advantages in remaining devoted to barter while refusing to admit it. But we must manage to suppress the goods privileged by the company, "commodity currencies," that they refuse to deliver to the natives against specie currency.[26]

In meeting the expression "commodity currencies" in the administrative reports, I thought at first that it was restricted to the N'Goko Sangha Company and that it was due to the imagination of a trader who was replying, by a formula, to the reproaches of the administration. After all, this expression appeared logical to describe a good that, when used by the local population, became a money. Then I noticed that the expression was in more general use in the colony, and that it took its place in a general theory of monies: evolutionary, as appropriate to the time. "One can then grasp in action," writes Cureau on the topic of barter, "the origin of money. At the moment of the European invasion, progress in the system of exchange had only reached the stage that I have just described. It was not yet money; it was already more than a good" (Cureau 1912:300). Bruel describes the following stage of evolution: "The arrival of European traders on the coast and in the interior provoked the introduction of commodity currencies that were used concurrently with the goods used for barter. They were used to value the object sold or bought, and after the native had chosen a series of diverse goods in the factory, he took the remainder in commodity currency that served in reality as a money to make up the balance" (Bruel 1912:445–6). Evidently, the next stage would be the use of specie, if one took the necessary measures to hasten its arrival.

Bruel and Cureau belonged to that generation of colonials who were explorers, administrators, and ethnographers. How would this theory be explained by the traders of the Sangha?

This returns us to another question that could be posed about the *zong*. It is not surprising that the *zong*, in the same way as other monetary objects of the region, should be reproduced by industrial methods. What is more extraordinary is the transformation of *zong* that becomes *mandjong* in acquiring the undoubted form of a ship's anchor. Omnipresent emblem in the colonial universe, insignia of the Marine Infantry, the anchor would figure on the uniforms of the colonial army and the colonial administrators until African independence. The anchor in the North Congo was at this time the symbol of colonial power.

How did a local monetary object, the *zong*, become transformed by the *traders* into a symbol of the colonial power? How was it that the use of *mondjos* could be justified by the *traders* by a theory that was the theory of the *administration*?

For the moment, I have no other response to offer to these two questions except a name: Gaboriaud. Gaboriaud had been administrator in Upper Sangha and was director of the N'Goko Sangha Company from 1907 (Coquery-Vidrovitch 1977:277, 319). He became director of the N'Goko Sangha, living in Sembe, during the period when the *mondjos* were introduced by the concessionary company. There is no proof of the responsibility of Gaboriaud in the introduction of *mondjos* in the form of an anchor. But who was better placed to do it? Fugitive from the administration, and knowing their methods and language well, Gaboriaud might take a certain pleasure in modifying the *zong* in order to make it the symbol par excellence of the colonial power. He copied a local money, giving it the mark of colonial power and thus became a double money forger. One should note that most of the inventories of the N'Goko Sangha, and particularly the one from Maniolo that I have reproduced, list two sorts of *mondjos*, the old and the new. Could it be that the "old" *mondjos* were copies of *mezong*, and the "new" were the *mezong* transformed into an anchor? We are now in the domain of speculation.

To complete this history, two questions need to be asked: Why did the new *mondjos* have such a success? And why are the *mandjong* that we find today all artisanal products?

At the heart of the reply that one can bring to these questions is the problem of the relationship between marriage currencies and commerce. We can agree with J. Guyer that there is nothing automatic about this interaction (Guyer 1986:604), and that there may be numerous different cases. The present case brings its own contribution to the problem, by showing first of all that this relationship was established among the Kwélé at the initiative of the traders, by means of the copies that they made of the marriage currencies. One can envisage in what follows a type of interaction generally little invoked, that comes from the pressure on the labor force exerted by commercial production.

A great deal of labor was done by the local populations, who exploited the natural resources for the profit of the N'Goko Sangha. To give an idea of the scale involved, I take the year 1907 as an example. The production of the N'Goko Sangha for that year represented, *grosso modo*, 15 tons of ivory and 110 tons of rubber.[27] We can estimate at about 750 the number of elephants killed and at 3,600,000 the number of hours devoted during that year to rubber production.[28] It should be understood that these numbers are only put forward to give some idea of the labor contributed by the population and to show that the activities of the N'Goko Sangha competed with local production and in particular with metalwork, which is a major consumer of labor time. One gathers the sense, from a few remarks made here and there in the administrative reports, that it was less competition with European tools that provoked the demise of metalwork than the pressures on the labor force. Thus, the factories became the principal source of metal of the time. By this logic, one could imagine that *zong* ceased to be produced by the Kwélé blacksmiths and that the *mondjos* obtained at the factories against rubber and ivory penetrated the marriage-payment system. In fact, however, it was not the *mondjos* directly off the presses of the German mills that entered into the marriage circuits, because the objects that we find today under the name of *mandjong* do not look like industrial products.

The *mondjos* were probably produced at the lowest possible cost and arrived in the factories unfinished after the stamping out. The industrial object is likely to have been modified by the local smiths at two points. The medial ridge has clearly been forged by forcing the metal out from the center. This action accounts for variations in thickness that we see in the samples, and also produced irregularities in the contours that were filed off, from which we understand the phrase used by M. Akoul: "*zong* made with a file." The ridge seems to be characteristic of other monetary objects such as the *dupa* and the hatchet used in marriage (see Figure 3–5). Furthermore, the *zong* as it presents in the museum in Berlin or in Bruel's illustration, has the same central ridge, which may be in some way the distinctive sign of Kwélé monetary objects. The other modification that the smiths inflicted on the *mondjo* as it came from the factories concerned the ears. All the informants insisted on the ears, without which the *mandjong* could not be given in marriage payments. Either the ears were added to the industrial object in the blacksmith's fire, or they were hammered on at an angle.[29] These two operations account for the artisanal properties of the *mandjong*.

Through this modification, the Kwélé blacksmiths imposed their own mark on the *mondjos*. They appropriated the industrial object and authenticated it as an instrument for marriage exchange. In so doing, they acted politically, in every way comparable to the ancient Greek practice of placing "counter-marks by a city on foreign coins" (Servet 1984:123). At that moment, Kwélé society gave itself new monetary norms corresponding to the conditions of production introduced by the trade in rubber and ivory. This, at least, is the hypothesis that could be verified in a further stage of the research.

Notes

1. I cite, for the record, the confusion made in a recent work between *bitchie* and *mandjong*: "the shafts of the Djem *bitchie* are tied in packets of 5 that are attached 10 by 10. The Bakwele call them manjong, long, flattened rods of 12 to 15 cm" (Maniongui 1989:159).
2. J. Rivallain (1987:759) proposes the following classification: "1. Ingots and forms difficult to identify; 2. forms derived from instruments of cultivation; 3. forms derived from arms." To this classification, one should add the tools of the forge and metallurgy, such as the hammers, anvils, and sledge-hammers that are found among the Kota and among neighboring groups, and also among the Nzabi (G. Dupré 1982:133–36; Denk 1987).
3. This was particularly the case with M. Bioung and M. Loutou at Sembe. Elsewhere, other information collected in the field came from M. Alphonse Ngiel, village chief of Kéto near to Ouesso, M. Paul Métoul of the same village, M. Béguégyina of Séka, M. Marcel Mbioum of Sembé, M. Andre Zamébé of Elogo, and M. Jean Abessouolle of the village of Alat, Souanké.
4. Report of the Inspector of Administrative Affairs, Circumscription of Sangha, n.d.
5. Report of N'Goko Sangha for 1910, Soufflay, February 1st, 1911.
6. Report of N'Goko Sangha for 1911, M'Vahdi, December 15th, 1911.
7. Report of N'Goko Sangha for 1912, Kemboma, January 31st, 1913.
8. Report on N'Goko Sangha for 1912, Ouesso, February 15th, 1913.
9. " . . . to our knowledge the Bakwele are the only populations of Congo-Brazzaville to present a use object in the form of an anchor" (Vincent 1963:286).
10. According to information collected by J. Rivallain (1987:503–4) from C. Bouet, one could find *mandjong* "among the Bendjabi and the Nzabi of the Ogooué Basin," who used them until recently as marriage payments. I consider these data, without specific localization, with

great reservations. Having myself worked over a long period among the Nzabi and having studied marriage payments particularly (Dupré 1982) as well as on long-distance commerce (Dupré 1972), I have never observed *mandjong*. Furthermore, the Kwélé had no commercial relations with the Nzabi before colonization. If *mandjong* really existed among the Nzabi, it could only concern erratic cases. But one cannot swear to anything in these topics!

11. In 1972, on the basis of the administrative census, B. Guillot estimated the Bakwele population at 12,705 (Guillot and Diallo 1984:19). Taking account of a very weak demographic dynamic and a relatively low emigration rate, one might conclude that these estimates remain *grosso modo* the same today. Siroto (1959:64) suggests the number of Bakwele enumerated by the French administration as 16,200.

12. Leon Siroto insists on the social nature of the strategies permitted by marriage: "Another determinant of the cultural focus on marriage was a political system without hierarchy or ascribed status: the field in which social status could be won was open" (1959:103).

13. Robineau describes the ritual of marriage during which these prestations were made (1971:127-9).

14. *Mongo* prestations are important according to the number of objects of different categories that are furnished, to the point where today—as in the whole Congo—when marriage has become the object of an accounting, they are taken into account and deducted against the *egual* goods furnished by the husband.

15. The goods of the marriage payments were counted with the aid of sticks (*baz*) of two different lengths.

16. One informant estimated the payment at 1 goat for 5 *me zong* that could be made in two days.

17. Several other examples of *zong* have been brought to my attention: one in a private collection, a second in the Museum of Berlin and others published in the literature, in particular: Westerdyk 1975, Thilenius 1921, Quiggin 1949, Schmeltz and de Jong 1904-1916.

18. And not only of the Kwélé. Fang masks describe similar curves. For example, on the Fang mask of Ngontang type, the straight line of the nose as it joins the lines of the brows describes an upside down anchor (Perrois 1985:181). The Fang and the Kwélé, neighbors by geography, speak languages that come from two different language groups of Guthrie's Zone A: A22 and A66, respectively (Guthrie [1948]1967:74).

19. Report for 1911, on N'Goko Sangha, 4 (2) D8.

20. *La traite* refers to the older form of commerce, based on barter, that the concessionary companies were supposed to replace.

21. For example in 1912, the personnel of the N'Goko Sangha Company included 22 Europeans and 18 traders.

22. As witnessed by the report of the Inspector of administrative affairs 4 5(2) D16 "at M'Bio, January 26th 1911, the manager of the factory of N'Gali paid for 5 kg of rubber with a felt hat costing the Company 3F," whereas dried rubber is bought at 1f.50.

23. For example, the *zimbu*, shell monies current in the kingdom of Congo before the arrival of the Portuguese, were imported from Bengela and from Brazil by the Portuguese (Randles 1968:137), which contributed to their devaluation. It was the same story with the raphia cloths in the kingdom of Congo, which were imported by the Portuguese from Loango (Hilton 1985:77), where they were less expensive. They served to pay Portuguese soldiers' salaries until 1694 (Randles 1968:179).

24. Rivallain reports that "in 1906 in the Upper Sangha, sector of Berberati, the Commercial Society of the Upper Sangha procured different sorts of spear heads made in the region of Gaza for the purchase of rubber in other regions. Gaza had no rubber, so M. Chapas collected money. Every day the native brought him one or two pieces of iron and this is his only work" (Rivallain 1987:995).

25. Commercial Bulletin, Circumscription of Koudou, July 1911, 4 (2) D8.

26. Commercial Bulletin, Circumscription of Koudou, September 1911, 4 (2) D8.

27. The precise numbers are respectively 14,843 and 109,56 5, according to the report on the

concessionary companies in 1909, 4(2) D4. I chose 1907 first of all because there are available figures and also because from 1907 production fell by a large amount, reduced by a half in 1912.

28. This estimate is founded on a measure made in 1912 of the amount of work required to produce one kilo of wild rubber, namely 33 hours (Coquery-Vidrovitch 1977:66).

29. The *mandjong's* ears pose a problem. There are none on the *mezong*. They come from the anchor model, and perhaps were made locally by blacksmiths working on the N'Goko Sangha payroll.

Sources

Archival

Archives de la France d'Outre-Mer, Aix en Provence

Les documents utilisés proviennent du Fonds A E F, cartons 4 (2) D8, 4 (2) D12, 4 (2) D16, et 8 Q 20.

Books, Dissertations, and Articles

Andersson, E. 1953. *Contribution à l'Ethnographie des Kuta,* vol 1. Studia Ethnographica Uppsaliensa 6.

Bruel, G. 1918. *L'Afrique Equatoriale Française.* Paris: Larose.

C. C. [pseud.]. 1909. "Dans la Sangha. Mœurs et coutumes." *Bull. Soc. Géogr. Com. du Havre,* 72–89.

Coquery-Vidrovitch, C. 1977. *Le Congo au temps des compagnies concessionnaires.* Paris, La Haye, Mouton.

Cureau, A. D. 1912. *Les Sociétés primitives de l'Afrique Equatoriale.* Paris: Librairie Armand Colin.

Denk, R. 1987. "Otiene-Barrengeld der Kota und Teke." *Der Primitivgeldsammler,* 8:44–47.

Dupré, G. 1972. "Le Commerce entre sociétés lignagères: Les Nzabi dans la traite à la fin du XIXe Siècle, Congo-Gabon." *Cahiers d'Études Africaines,* Paris 12: 616–58.

——— . 1982. *Un Ordre et sa Destruction.* Paris: ORSTOM.

Dupré, M-C. 1993. *L'outil agricole des essartages forestiers: Le couteau de culture au Gabon, Congo et Zaire.* Cahiers de l'Institut de la Méthode No. 2. Bi enne: Association F. Gonseth.

——— . (In press). "From Field to Kitchen: Women's Tools in the Forest of Central Africa." In *Transformation, Technology and Gender in African Metallurgy,* ed. S. Ardener and I. Fowler. Oxford: Centre for Cross-Cultural Research on Women.

Fourneau, A. 1932. *Au Vieux Congo.* Paris: Edit. Comit. Afr. Franç.

Guillot, B. and Diallo, Y. 1984. *Systèmes agraires et cultures commerciales: L'exemple du village de Boutazab (région de la Sangha au Congo).* Atlas des Structures Agraires au Sud du Sahara no. 20. Paris: ORSTOM.

Guthrie, M. 1967. *The Classification of the Bantu Languages.* London: International African Institute.

Guyer, J. I. 1986. "Indigenous Currencies and the History of Marriage Payments: A Case Study from Cameroon." *Cahiers d'Etudes Africaines,* 104:577–610.

Hilton, A. 1985. *The Kingdom of Kongo.* Oxford: Clarendon Press.

Kingsley, M. H. 1898. *Travels in West Africa: Congo Français, Corisco and Cameroons*. London: Macmillan and Co.

Levi-Strauss, C. 1967. *Les Structures élémentaires de la Parenté*. Paris: PUF.

Maniongui, M. 1989. "Les Monnaies traditionnelles congolaises: Les mécanismes de substitution et leur dynamisme socio-économique (1886–1925)." Thèse de Doctorat, Ecole des Hautes Études en Sciences Sociales.

Perrois, L. 1985. *Art ancestral du Gabon dans les collections du Musée Barbier-Mueller*. Genève: Musée Barbier-Mueller.

Quiggin, A. H. 1949. *A Survey of Primitive Money: The Beginning of Currency*. London: Methuen.

Randles, W. G. L. 1968. *L'ancien Royaume de Congo des Origines à la fin du XIXème Siècle*. Paris, La Haye: Mouton.

Rivallain, J., with the collaboration of F. Iroko. 1986. *Paléo-Monnaies Africaines*. Les collections monétaires no. 7. Paris: Administration des Monnaies et Médailles, Imprimerie Nationale.

Rivallain, J. 1987. "Etude Comparée des Phénomènes Prémonétaires en Protohistoire et en Ethnoarchéologie Africaine." Thèse Doctorat Etat Lettres et Sciences Humaines, Paris.

Roberts, A. F. 1992. "The Uncommon Currency of Masks." Paper presented at the Ninth Triennal of African Arts, Iowa University, Iowa.

Robineau, C. 1971. *Evolution Économique et Sociale en Afrique Centrale. L'Exemple de Souanké (République Populaire du Congo)*. Paris: ORSTOM.

Schmeltz, J. D. E. and J. P. B. de Jong. 1904–1916. *Ethnographisch Album van het Stroomgebied van den Congo*. Gravenhage: Martinus Nihoff.

Schoonheyt, J. 1991. "Résumé concernant l'arbre de décision présenté au Congrès International de Numismatique." Bruxelles.

Siroto, L. 1959. "Masks and Social Organization among the Bakwele People of Western Equatorial Africa." Ph.D. dissertation, Columbia University.

Servet, J. M. 1984. *Nomismata: Etat et Origines de la Monnaie*. Lyon: Presses Universitaires de Lyon.

Tessmann, G. 1992. *Les Pahouins. Monographie Ethnologique d'une Tribu d'Afrique de l'Ouest. Résultats de l'Expédition "Pangwe" de Lübeck, 1907–1909, et d'Explorations Antérieures, 1904–1907*. Paris: Musée Dapper.

Thierry, F. 1992. *Monnaies de Chine*. Paris: Bibliothèque Nationale.

Thilenius, G. 1921. "Primitives Geld." *Archiv für Anthropologie*, 18.

Vincent, J. F. 1963. Dot et monnaies de fer chez les Bakwélé et les Djem. *Objets et Monde*, 273–92.

————. J. F. 1964. "Traditions Historiques chez les Djem de Souanké (République du Congo-Brazzaville)." *Revue Française d'Histoire d'Outre-Mer*, 178:64–73.

Westerdijk, H. 1975. *IJzerwerk can Centraal-Afrika*. Rotterdam: Museum voor Landen Volkenkunde.

4

Monetization and the Asante State

KWAME ARHIN

The Meaning of Monetization

This chapter examines the relations between monetization and the Asante state before and after the establishment of British colonial rule in the territories that today constitute the Republic of Ghana. The argument of the chapter is that the operation of the cowry and gold currencies in different areas in the territory controled by the Asante state was, in part, due to the state control of the distribution of gold. On the other hand, because, under colonial rule, the Asante state could no longer impose constraints on the accumulation of wealth, it sought to control the patterns of consumption in those aspects of social and political life that embody symbolic statements about rank and authority.

Goody (1968:22) makes the point that in several parts of Africa, in the period before colonial rule, the tag "subsistence" did not fit the economies. Specifically on "pre-colonial" Ghana, Kay (1972:5) writes: "In many parts of pre-colonial Ghana the social division of labour was quite advanced and the petty commodity production, exchange and monetization were all firmly established." This was particularly true of the Asante "empire" or Greater Asante (Arhin 1967; Wilks 1975), where monetization expanded with the expansion of trade and the evolution of the imperial system.

"Monetization" may be understood in two senses: in the technical sense of a generally accepted medium of payment, either by virtue of customary usage or legal enactment, within the domain of a political authority; and in the substantive sense of the extent to which the accepted medium of payment forms the basis of transactions or interactions in areas of the economy and in the social and political sectors. Monetization advances with the marketability of farm produce and labor, and of land and money (Bohannan and Dalton 1962:20-2). Concerning the "social sector," I have in mind such rites of passage as marriage and death; and the "political sector" includes the relations of allegiance and service, and the forms of tribute and taxation. It is suggested here that, just as in the economic sector the absence of barter in the marketplace argues a high degree of monetization, so also in the social and political sectors, the substitution of monetary payments for gifts in kind at marriage and funeral ceremonies, and for the rendering of service in kind, or of allegiance in person, signifies an advanced degree of monetization.

Lastly, the chapter shows that monetization in the area covered by the precolonial Asante political system was, in the past, of limited and varying character, in contrast with monetization in the period following the imposition of colonial rule; and that the near-total monetization in this century has been the result of external factors that, therefore, have induced distortions and conflicts in social and political values.

Currency in Greater Asante

In nearly two centuries of effective existence (1700–1896), three types of media of payment circulated within the territories controled by the King of Ashanti, Asantehene, collectively called the Asante empire, or Greater Asante. These territories consisted of most of modern Ghana and the eastern parts of the Ivory Coast (Wilks 1975; Ch. 2). But for the purposes of this chapter, the relevant areas were the modern Ashanti, Brong-Ahafo, and the eastern parts of the Northern Regions, and the region in east-central Ivory Coast of which Bonduku is at present the capital. So defined, Greater Asante included "metropolitan" Asante and the northern areas, within which were situated the transit markets of the savannah-forest fringes: Begho, Bonduku, Gbuipe, Salaga, Kintampo, and Atebubu (Arhin 1979).

The earliest medium of exchange recalled by Asante informants, was pieces of iron or iron rods, *nnabuo* (Reindorf, 1895:47; Rattray 1923:324–5; Daaku 1961:13–14; and personal information from Nana Gyebi Ababio, Ex-Essumegyahene). Nana Ababio states that the pieces often circulated in the market of Asantemanso, the largest Asante pre-Kumasi settlement, which was situated near the site of present Esumegya town (Rattray 1923:122), and attracted traders from the north. The north, *Sarem,* was the area, including the middle Niger, from which Muslim traders came to Asante. Garrard (1980:3-4) was informed that "pieces of iron were widely used as medium of exchange in the forest areas and on the savannah-forest fringes"; and that their acceptability was due to their "practical value as objects of barter for they could always be beaten into the form of weapons or agricultural implements" (Garrard 1980:3).

The sources do not make clear the extent and manner of use of the pieces of iron. But they were apparently similar to copper rods, which Hopkins states "were valid for all goods and services, and were split into small denominations . . . in order to facilitate exchange" (Hopkins 1973:69). It is unlikely that the inhabitants of Asantemanso called the iron rods *sika*, which originally meant gold, but has since British colonization additionally meant money, in the sense of both legal tender and wealth. Iron rods were suppressed or ceased to be current by the eighteenth century, when Kumasi became the seat of the expansionist Asante kingdom, and Asante kings felt the need to regulate the distribution of gold dust. Before the slave trade, gold dust was the means by which the Asante obtained European armament: muskets, powder, and shot.

In the eighteenth and nineteenth centuries, two currencies circulated in Asante. These were cowries, *sedee,* and gold dust, *sika futuru* (Bowdich 1819:330; Dupuis 1824:xl). Cowries were in use in the markets of the savannah-forest fringes, the Brong district of modern Ghana, and in the slave marts of the Gold Coast (Metcalfe 1964:22; Garrard 1980:4; Hogendorn and Johnson 1986:101–57). The co-existence of the two currencies was widespread in large areas of West Africa (Hopkins 1973:67–72) and the significant thing about the Asante situation was the operation of two different currency zones within Asante; cowries in the northern and southern peripheries of Greater Asante and gold in Kumasi and the capitals of the other states of the Asante Union (Rattray 1929; Wilks 1975: Ch. 2). In the latter places, cowries and gold were not mutually convertible. Asante traders obtained cowries from the Gold Coast (Metcalfe 1964:22) and the northern markets and kept stocks of them for trade in the north. This explains why Manuh[1] learnt (see Ch. 8) in the Sekyere district of northern Asante, that traders kept hoards of cowries well into this century. The people of Sekyere traded mainly with the north. Visitors to Kumasi in the nineteenth century, among them Bowdich (1819), Dupuis (1824), T.B. Freeman (1843), and Ramseyer and Kuhne (1875), did not report the presence of cowries and bartering in the Kumasi daily markets.

Garrard (1980:4) explains the ban on the use of cowries in Asante, "at least in the nineteenth century," as an attempt to prevent them from becoming disincentive to gold production. That may be so, but it is only one possible explanation. The more probable explanation is the attempt to conserve and regulate the distribution of gold. On the abolition of the slave trade in 1807, gold replaced slaves as the means for obtaining armament and an assortment of European goods. There were circumstances, such as occurred in 1818, when the Asante kings were prepared to pawn items of gold-plated or gold-worked regalia for ammunition (Hutchison's *Diary* in Bowdich, 1819:401). On the other hand, Asante trading at the northern markets did not require gold, but necessitated kola nuts, salt from Ada on the southeastern Gold Coast, and an assortment of European imports (Arhin 1979:Ch. 1).

Gold was valued as much for its political as for its economic uses. It was used in making the symbols of office: the Asantehene was and is known as the one who sits on gold, *ote kokoo so,* an allusion to the Golden Stool, the physical symbol of the Asante supreme political authority, which is also the greatest national shrine. Asante political ranking was regulated by means of the amount of gold with which an authority-holder was permitted to adorn his regalia; and the regulated ranking system, *dibea,* was the legitimizing basis of Asante authority-holding. Either hoarded in jars or cast in the form of items or regalia, gold was the supreme embodiment of wealth as well as the measure of authority (Ramseyer and Kuhne, 1875:304–7; Rattray 1923:301; Arhin 1983, 1990). Hence, it was necessary to control the internal distribution and the outflow of gold. Gold exports were taxed. It was also significant that visitors to whom the Asantehene dispensed hospitality in daily or periodic gifts of gold dust, were obliged to make their purchases in gold dust so that the sums expended in hospitality were not exported, but found their way back into the Asante internal distributive system.

Regulation on the distribution of gold dust extended as well to expenditure on funerals and marriages: it varied with rank as between the rulers, and between royal and commoner lineages (Bowdich 1819: "Customs"; Rattray 1923:82–102).

Gold dust was measured in units based on weights, *mmramuo*, (sing. *abrammuoo*) and cast in forms representing, in Rattray's summary (1923:302):

> The human form, animals, fishes, insects, birds, etc., alone or depicting certain ceremonies and rites, or illustrating some saying or story connected with the object depicted.

> Inanimate objects, plants, seeds, fruit, weapons, articles in daily use.

> Those in which designs appear geometrical and were perhaps once symbolical.

Ramseyer and Kuhne (1875), war-captives in Kumasi for four years, stated the following units of Asante measure with their English values:

Unit	£	s	d
1 peswa			1 ¾
I dama			3
1 kokoa (3 peswas)			5 ¼
1 taku (4 peswas)			7
1 sua		6	9
1 suru	1	0	3
1 asia	1	7	—
1 osua	2	0	6
1 once (1/2 benna)	3	12	—
1 benna	7	4	—
1 peredwane	8	2	—

Rattray (1923:303) gives the following list of greater values:

Unit	£	s
Osoa ne suru		60
Asoanu		80
Asoanu ne suru		100
Asoanu ne dwoa		110
Asoasa		120
Benna		140
Peredwan		160
Peredwan asia		186
Peredwan soa	10	
Tasaunu	12	
Ntanu	16	
Ntanu asuanu	20	
Ntansa	24	
Perequan anan	32	
Perequan num	40	
Perequan nson	56	
Perequan nwotwe	64	
Perequan nkron	72	
Perequan du	80	

Garrard, who has concluded that the Asante–Akan weight system evolved in the course of trading with the Mande-Dyula from the north and the European traders on the coast (1980:213–245), presents lists from the other Akan groups and Asante (1980:Appendix III).

The units presented by Ramseyer and Kuhne were mainly those of the market place, and in daily use; those of Rattray had more to do with loans for trading purposes, and judicial transactions at court.

Generally, as I have stated elsewhere (1976/77), money had limited uses in Asante society before the colonial period. Kumasi residents and visitors to the city needed money to live off the markets and for the purchase of imported items in and outside the marketplaces (Arhin 1990:524–539). But the majority of the Asante people lived on distant or backyard farms (*afuo* or *mfikyifuo*). All Asante, including descendants of slaves, (*nnokofoo*) had access to land for cultivation purposes. Exchange of parcels of land was made between political units and was either a consequence of litigation (Rattray 1929) or of the conferment of subordinate office (McCaskie 1980:189–208). Long-distance traders employed an unknowable amount of paid labor, (*bo paa*) in addition to the use of domestic slaves (*fie nnipa*). Otherwise labor on the farms or on buildings was in the form of self-employment, reciprocal labor, *nnoboa*, service to authority-holders, or to in-laws, or as an element of bridewealth payment. In the terminology of Bohannan and Dalton (1962), the factors of production had barely entered the market, which therefore did not structure productive activities.

In the areas of social relations, there was little need for money. There were no educational expenses. As noted, marriage payments were regulated by the system of social and political ranking that embraced, not individuals, but the corporate matrilineages and their segments (Rattray 1927:77–85). For most individuals, marriage payments consisted of labor for in-laws on buildings and farms, and a couple of pots of palm wine. Funeral rites for ordinary Asante cost little in monetary terms; there was, normally, a balance between funeral debt, *ka*, and donations, *nsa*, (Arhin 1992).

In the political sector also, money was not much in use. Much of taxation took the form of service to the stool occupants in kind, *som*, in the provision of labor on buildings or farms; of elements of regalia, in the case of the craft villages; food, meat and fish, from specified villages; or personal service at court or on the king's person, in the case of palace attendants (*nhenkwa*), or of obligatory military service. A variety of taxes and levies were due in gold dust (Wilks 1975:64–71). Some ordinary Asante may have incurred judicial costs; but the Asante educational system, which emphasized to the young the necessity of keeping one's mouth shut, (*mua w'ano*) and minding one's own business (*nkoka obi asem bi*) was effective in reducing the incidence of court cases. Taxes and levies were corporate, not individual, obligations. In order to meet their obligations, Asante adults engaged in gold-winning or obtained gold with kola nuts at Bonduku, Gbuipe, Yendi, and Kintampo (Arhin 1979).

One may speak, then, of different media of exchange in different parts of an area dominated by one political authority. The basis of the differentiation was not the moral evaluation of goods and services obtainable in exchange (Bohannan 1959). Its basis was the Asante political economy, the set of considerations that prevented the markets of central Asante from becoming parts of the long-distance trading networks that embraced the forest and savannah areas of Western Africa (Arhin 1979:Ch. 1). R.A. Freeman, a British official of the late nineteenth century, suggested that the Asante confined their regional markets to the eastern and western forest-savannah fringes—Salaga, Bonduku, and Kintampo—in order to insulate Kumasi from the socially and politically disruptive effects of international trading (Freeman 1898:241). Locating the termini of the regional long-distance trade away from central Asante was also consistent with the Asante state policy of discouraging commercialism in favor of militarism (Bowdich 1819:335–6; Arhin 1990:533–4).

The basis of the differentiation of the cowry and gold currency zones in Asante was, therefore, political. Because, particularly in the nineteenth century, the state saw gold as the basis of both its expansionist process and the preservation of its integrity, it attached more than economic value to it. It saw its real value in political terms and subjected its distribution to state regulations.

Monetization in the Twentieth Century

Against the nineteenth-century background, the process of monetization in this century means:

1. The removal of political controls on the production, distribution and use of money or wealth
2. The entry of the factors of production into the "market"; and consequently
3. The penetration of money into the social and political sectors, i.e., the rites of marriage and death, and the substitution of cash payments for the rendering of personal service and allegiance

Monetization, as here defined, was the economic concomitant of British colonial rule, which was formally established in the territories of modern Ghana, the Gold Coast Colony, Ashanti, and the Northern Territories between 1874 and 1901. The colonial presence formally established itself in Asante in 1896, when it exiled the Asantehene, Prempeh II, and announced the internal autonomy of the separate states of the Asante Union. But it acquired substantive meaning in 1902 after the British had suppressed an Asante uprising against them in 1900 (Tordoff 1965:111–128).

Colonial rule, Kay has been at pains to point out, was putting into practice the combined philosophies of William Wilberforce and Adam Smith, the practice of philanthropy at 5 percent (Kay 1972:10–11). The ultimate purpose of colonial rule, masked by the manifest doctrine of spreading enlightenment and salvation to the savage and the benighted, was to satisfy the financial interests of British industry, to whose demands the economies of the acquired territories had to be subordinated. This required, above all, the monetization of the economy, fueled by the enforced acceptance of a currency based on, and at par with, the British pound. The monetization of the economy would result in the monetary penetration of all aspects of life, and the colony thus would become a veritable outpost of the capitalist world. The main instruments for advancing monetization were the various forms of taxation, disguised or indirect and direct (on Asante, see Tordoff 1965:93–98); the supply of new kinds of imported goods, such as, in the case of Asante, gin, salt, gun powder, brass and copper rods, iron and lead bars, cutlasses, and cotton goods (Tordoff 1965:96); and the demands of Christianity and Western-style education. The colonial authorities manipulated, in particular, the system of taxation in the direction of the promotion of trade (Kay 1972:10–12).

In Asante, as in Southern Ghana, and elsewhere in the colonial world in Africa, the colonial authorities promoted trade by encouraging the production of a cash crop which, in this part of the world, was cocoa. Introduced into the Gold Coast Protectorate in the last quarter of the nineteenth century (Hill 1963), cocoa reached Asante in 1902–3. The cultivation and expansion over the next decade were phenomenal; from 8,000 tonnes in 1913, it reached 70,000 tonnes in 1926 (Tordoff 1965:187).

Between 1903 and 1930, cocoa production brought both land and labor into the market, and radically transformed the relations of production (Kay 1972:5–6). Land for cocoa production was leased, pledged, and rented to such an extent that between 1938 and 1947, the Ashanti Confederacy Council[2] ordered a ban on further deforestation for cocoa production, in an attempt to maintain what the Council considered a healthy balance between cocoa and food production (Matson[3] n.d.:23–29; Mikell 1975:9). While there was a certain amount of labor from wife and children, maternal relatives, and friends in cocoa production,[4] the industry was, by 1938, according to the Nowell Commission[5]:

> dependent on migrant labour which comes in from the Northern Territories, where money crops are inadequate, or from neighboring French colonies, where money is a necessity to meet direct taxation. There is normally a great annual ebb and flow of such labourers, who tramp down to the cocoa districts from the north of the cocoa season and return by lorry to their homes and families in the food planting season (Metcalfe 1964:653).

This well known pattern of migrant labour (Rouch 1954) in the cocoa industry remained till 1970, when the Progress Party Government passed the Aliens Compliance Order and got rid of most of the stranger-labourers on the farms (Adomako-Sarfo 1974:138–52).

The Monetization of Social Life in Asante

As the colonial situation developed, it was not only categories of land rights and access to labor that became subject to monetary payments. The requirements for the education of children, such as fees and uniforms, and for membership in the churches of the Christian denominations could be met only with cash, obtained through the sale of crops or labor or receipts on the occasions of marriage or even funerals. All monetary payments were demanded in lieu of direct service at the court, or obligatory labor for the heads of the political community, such as on the making of the palaces, *ahanfie* or stool farms, *akonnua mfuo* (Arhin 1976).

The effects of the increasing monetization of social life have been noted by previous writers. Busia (1951:127) stated as a measure of what the Asante considered to be the disastrous effects of monetization that *"Cocoa see abusua, paepae mogya mu,"* "Cocoa ruins the family, divides blood relations." Following Busia, Tordoff (1965:190) wrote of the effect of monetization that it made the Asante people more "acquisitive," more "money-conscious," more "competitive," and more "individualistic." In a previous paper (Arhin 1976:453–68), I attempted to show the effect of what I called the "pressure of cash" on socio-political relations in Asante in the first phase of the colonial period. I then argued that the progress of monetization was marked by protest movements against the patterns of expenditure, resulting in relatively huge debts, and taxation by stool occupants (chiefs), and that these movements resulted in a striking spate of attempted and successful destoolments of the stool occupants.

The impact of the penetration of monetary values on such institutions as marriage payments, the performance of funeral rites, and the contest for stools or political offices was felt across the social strata and, consequently, the ACC attempted to regulate what the members considered to be as irregularities in the forms of the social institutional expression of wealth, particularly by the Asante *Akonkofo*, the nouveaux riches (Arhin 1986:25–31).

Before the establishment of the ACC in 1935, the Council of chiefs in Kumasi, which the colonial administration had established to look after customary matters in the Kumasi state under the supervision of the Chief Commissioner of Ashanti, had tried to restrict the accumulation of wealth in private hands. In 1908, the Council unsuccessfully sought the permission of the colonial government to re-introduce death duties, *awunyadie*, because it had previously been the Asantehene's right, and in order to augment the state treasury. In 1930, the Asantehene, Prempeh II (1888–1931), who had been permitted to return from exile in 1924, and to assume the headship of the Kumasi state, Kumasihene in 1926, also attempted unsuccessfully to restore death duties (Arhin 1974). It was the failure to control the accumulation of wealth by non-holders of authority that led to the subsequent attempt by the ACC to regulate the patterns of consumption.

The problem of the ACC with marriage payments was twofold. First, marriage payments tended to exceed the norm, or what was reasonable for the general populace. In the late 1940s, Fortes (1950) understood the basic element of this payment, which legalized the marriage and gave the man entitlement to adultery payments, to be the "head wine" or *tiri nsa*, consisting of two bottles of gin or the equivalent in cash.[6] Second, the Council was concerned that, as in the days before the British, payments should correspond to status; that those for the women of royal families, *adehyee*, should exceed those for commoner families. The Council stated the various ranks and payments as indicated in Table 4-1.

Costs were a minor consideration to the Council in making these regulations. As in the previous century, the source of political concern was lest payments made by the new-rich for commoner women should exceed those for royalty. The absence of distinctions in these payments would undermine the sanction of "custom," the basis of the legitimacy of the customary authority then buffeted between the demands of colonial authorities and those of subjects. It was, really, not a matter of the devaluation of money and the loss of purchasing power. It was that the use of money would destroy the customary status distinctions and subvert indigenous authority. The Colonial Office's report for 1923–24 portrayed the commoners as having, under the colonial administration:

> a feeling of independence and safety which give vent to criticism of their elders, and a desire when dissatisfied, to take the law into their own hands. At the root of most of these troubles lies "money"—either the chief retains what he should not or attempts to levy what the (commoners) think an unfair tax (quoted in Tordoff 1965:204; see also McCaskie 1986).

The Council brought similar considerations to bear on its regulations on funeral rites. The costs of funeral rites were rising. But here, again, it demonstrated awareness

TABLE 4-1   Rate of Marriage Payments Set by the Ashanti Confederacy Council[*]

Rank of Bride	$G[†] (=£.sh.p.)	Gin (no. of bottles)
Asantehene's Female Relations		
royal (*adehye*), i.e., a woman of Asantehene's matrilineage	9.06.00	4
daughter (*Oheneba*)	9.10.00	2
granddaughter (*ahenehaha*)	2.07.00	2
great-granddaughter	1.06.00	2
Relations of Division Chiefs (amanhene) *and the* Kenyasehene[††]		
royal (matrilineal relations)	4.13.00	2
daughter	2.07.00	2
granddaughter	1.03.06	2
great-granddaughter	1.03.06	2
Relations of Sub-Divisonal Chiefs		
matrilineal relations	2.07.00	2
daughter	1.03.06	2
granddaughter	1.03.06	2
great-granddaughter	1.03.06	2

*From Matson (n.d.: 30–4).
†£G refers to the Ghana pound before the Ghana cedi was introduced and tied to the dollar. £G1 was equivalent to £1 sterling.
††Kenyase is very close to Kumasi: the Kenyasehene belongs to the Okoyo, the ruling Asante clan, though members of his lineage cannot succeed to the Golden Stool.

of the meaning of the public funeral rites; that they re-affirmed basic social values and validated social and political status. Therefore, while the Council made regulations to curtail expenditure on the ground that it was wasteful and devalued money, it sought to ensure that the quantitative and qualitative distinctions between the rites for, on the one hand, customary rulers and their maternal kin, and, on the other, commoners were preserved; otherwise the rites for a rich commoner might exceed, in scale and quality, that for the local stool occupant. It was laid down that the expenditure on funeral rites for a "commoner" should not exceed £G10 (Matson n.d.:39–40, 510–52; see Arhin 1992).[7]

The Council was, above all agitated by the penetration of cash into the contest for stools. Already Rattray (1932) had remarked of the areas of the Northern Territories, in particular of the present Upperwest and Uppereast Regions, in which "dynasties" were of recent origin, that the "skins," or "political offices" were for the highest bidder. In Asante, where dynasties were firmly established, there were indications of the danger of the possible sale of stools to outsiders.[8] The Council also reported increasing bribery of the electors by contestants, and the possibility that electors would not adhere to the norms for selections but choose outsiders who had money. The principal norm is that the selectors of a stool occupant must choose from amongst the men of the royal lineage: the right to selection is validated by a clear genealogical matrilineal relationship to the founder of the stool. The departure from the norm could precipitate agitation for the abolition of the customary authority system.[9]

In its discussion of the growing incidence of corruption, the Council made a distinction between "begging" and corruption. "Begging"[10] was described in the following terms:

> A candidate who is anxious to secure election will usually ask some influential person to beg for the stool on his behalf. The person so begging may be in no way connected with the stool and it is not unknown for the Asantehene, through his representative, to beg for the stool on behalf of a candidate (Matson n.d.:6).

The Council did not consider this wrong though it involved payments. But it laid it down that because the Asantehene was or ought to be the final arbiter in constitutional cases, "begging" ought not to be done through him. Bribery, on the other hand, was defined as "the practice of Stool Elders collecting heavy money from probable candidates for Stools before electing them."[11] In addition to a resolution asking the colonial authorities to make the Asantehene "the supreme Arbiter of all matters relating to enstoolments and destoolments of the Chiefs within the Confederacy," the Assembly of the Council further resolved that any Stool Elder who received a bribe in election and enstoolment affairs should be dealt with according to law. Also:

> That Stools should be given to their legitimate royals even though such royals might not be wealthy persons—and not to persons who had no constitutional right to them because they possessed money.
>
> Any youngman also who would receive money from impostors with a view to encouraging them to lay claim to vacant stools should be dealt with according to law.
>
> The punishment for any youngman should be £25 or six months' imprisonment with hard labour or to both such fine and imprisonment.
>
> The punishment of a Stool Elder also should be destoolment.[12]

The royals were alarmed that the nonroyal nouveaux riches might purchase stools. In the absence of the principle of primogeniture, no royal had an automatic right to the succession, while two factors could lead to the manipulation of genealogies in favour of a rich candidate, as is today generally suspected to be the case, particularly in Asante. The first of these factors was the growing pressure of cash, the near total monetization of all aspects of social life that placed the acquisition of money and the social power that it brought to the acquisitor above communal ideas of social and political propriety. The second factor, which re-enforced the first, was the weakening of the magico-religious sanctions for the observance of political norms as the result of the assault on indigenous culture by Christianity and education (Busia 1951:189–94; Arhin 1976/77).

Conclusion

This chapter has focused on the changing perceptions of money at the level of the state, which, till recently, was the organized vehicle for the expression of communal values. Up to the colonial period, in which the colonial situation produced a melting pot of social values, the Asante state subjected the economic to political values, and regarded the gold-dust currency as an instrument for regulating and maintaining the social order and its political instrumentality, the state. The state perceived wealth as the means for strengthening the community as a whole, rather than enriching the individual and thus upsetting the socio-political order.

The colonial regime reversed this. Its total impact was to promote individualism of which the basis was individual wealth. In the colonial situation, the Asante state, which was weakened and itself controled by the colonial administration, could neither regulate the currency nor restrict the accumulation of wealth. It could, in this context, only attempt to restrict consumption in the areas in which the patterns of expenditure had symbolic implications for the maintenance of rank and authority under the colonial authorities. Its attempts were Canute-like: today, the rich, by virtue of conspicuous consumption in marital and funeral observances, tend to exercise more social power and "respect" than formal customary authority-holders. And some stools appear to go for the highest bidder; particularly if those doing the bidding have clan, though not lineage affiliations, with deceased stool occupants.[13]

Notes

1. At the workshop on "Instability and Values: Social Payments in Long Term Perspectives," held at the Institute of African Studies, Legon, June 16-18, 1992. The Asante people used and use today a certain amount of cowries, *sedee*, for ritual purposes; as charms for children and in armlets of priests of diviners/soothsayers. That is why even today one may find stocks of cowries in the Kumasi and the bigger markets in the present Asanti Region.

2. The Ashanti Confederacy Council (ACC) was an assembly of principal Asante customary authorities as an instrument of indirect rule and a local government body. It consisted of the King of Asante (*Asantehene*), the "Queenmother" of Asante (*Asantehemaa*), the heads of the constituent chiefdoms of the Asante Union of States in the present Ashanti and Brong-Ahafo Regions of Ghana, and the principal subordinate authority-holders of the Asantehene as the head of the Kumasi state. It was granted limited jurisdiction, and under the supervision of the colonial government, could make by-laws on economic and social matters and adjudicate on enstoolment or destoolment disputes in Ashanti. It was renamed the Asanteman Council in 1952, and without the paramountcies in the Brong-Ahafo Region, the Ashanti Regional House of Chiefs in 1959.

3. J. N. Matson was a Judicial Adviser to the Ashanti Confederacy in 1949.

4. As I know from my own childhood experiences, having worked in the various stages of cocoa production on the farms of my fat her and maternal relations.

5. The Nowell Commission was appointed in 1939 to investigate the marketing of cocoa after a widespread cocoa hold-up in Ashanti and the Gold Coast in 1937 (Metcalfe 1964:640-53).

6. There were also other gifts and services to in-laws; and this payment was probably the case only in the urban centers. In the rural areas, young men on the eve of marriage were unlikely to be able to afford two bottles of gin. They were more likely to give less and supplement it with labor on the farms.

7. The *Minutes* of the ACC for June 11, 1935, and for 17th June, 1935, embodying the Funeral Committee Report.

8. ACC *Minutes*, 14th June 1935; in particular the Adontinhene's contribution. See also *Minutes* of ACC for 13th June, 1935.

9. It has turned out that, generally, the subjects of a stool would rather remove a particular occupant than abolish a stool or opt for another political system (see Arhin 1991). Today, in spite of what appear to be widely shared suspicions about the sale of stools, the institution marches on a strongly as ever. Stools are sought by the highly educated and the rich. The

explanation for the popularity of the institution may lie in the instability of the institutions of central government.

10. "Begging," according to Brokensha (1966:132) has mainly a judicial meaning among the Larteh Guan of the Akwapim district of southern Ghana. It is an element of the judicial process in which if a man, accused of an offense, admits it, may "either beg himself or arrange for an elder to beg for him: he combines admission of guilt with contrition and a plea for mercy." The Asante, too may beg, *sre,* as a plea in judicial proceedings. But it is used here as part of the ritual of nomination, election and installation of a stool occupant. A prospective Asantehene, himself, has to "beg" for the stool from the Asantehama, and the Asantehene's immediate Kumasi subordinates who are the "king-makers."

11. ACC *Minutes* for 14th June 1935; Matson n.d.:6.

12. ACC *Minutes* for the 14th June 1935.

13. I add that the modern state of Ghan a is not really unlike the historic patrimonial Asante state. The Nkurmahist state of Ghana, 1957–1966, at any rate, like the erstwhile Asante state, subjected economic to political values and pursued the "political kingdom" rather than economic developmen t. It is in this, essentially, that one may find the failure of economic development in Ghana. See the papers in Arhin (1991), especially Asante.

Sources

Archival

Ghana

Ashanti Confederacy Council (ACC)

Minutes   11 June, 1935
            17 June, 1935
            14 June, 1935
            13 June, 1935.

Books, Dissertations, and Articles

Adomako-Sarfo, J. A. 1974. "The Effects of the Expulsion of Migrant Workers on Ghana's Economy with Particular Reference to the Cocoa Industry." In *Modern Migration in West Africa*, ed. S. Amin , 138–52. London: Oxford University Press.

Arhin, Kwame. 1967. "The Structure of Greater Asante, 1720–1824." *Journal of African History,* 8: 68–85.

———. 1974. "Some Asante Views of Colonial Rule: As Seen in the Controversy Relating to Death Duties." *Transactions of the Historical Society of Ghana,* 15:63–84.

———. 1977. "The Pressure of Cash and Its Political Consequences in the Colonial Period." *Journal of African Studies,* 3:453–68.

———. 1979. *West African Traders in Ghana in the Nineteenth and Twentieth Centuries.* London and New York: Longman.

———. 1983. "Rank and Class Among the Asante and Fante in the Nineteenth Century." *Africa,* 56:2–22.

———. 1986. "The Asante Akonkofo: A Non-Literate Sub-Elite." *Africa,* 56:25–31.

———. 1987. "Savannah Contributions to the Asante Political Economy." In *The Golden Stool Studies of the Asante Centre and Periphery,* ed. Enid Schildkrout. New York: Anthropological Papers of the American Museum of Natural History, 56,1.

————. 1990. "Trade Accumulation and the State in Asante in the Nineteenth Century." *Africa*, 4:524–37.

————. 1991. "The Search for 'Constitutional Chieftaincy'." In *The Life and Work of Kwame Nkrumah: Papers of a Symposium Organized by the Institute of African Studies, University of Ghana, Legon,* ed. K. Arhin, 27–47. Accra: Sedco Ltd.

————. 1992. "Transformations in Akan Funeral Rites and their Economic Implications." Unpublished.

Asante, K. B. 1991. "Nkrumah and State Enterprises." In *The Life and Work of Kwame Nkrumah: Papers of a Symposium Organized by the Institute of African Studies, University of Ghana, Legon,* ed. K. Arhin, 257–279. Accra: Sedco Ltd.

Bohannan, P. 1959. "The Impact of Money on an African Subsistence Economy." *Journal of Economic History,* 19:491–503.

Bohannan, P. and G. Dalton. 1962. *Markets in Africa.* Evanston, IL: Northwestern University Press.

Bowdich, T. E. 1819. *Mission from Cape Coast to Ashantee.* London: J. Murray.

Brokensha, D. 1966. *Social Change at Larteh, Ghana.* Oxford: Clarendon Press.

Busia, K. A. 1951. *The Position of the Chief in the Modern Political System of Ashanti.* London: Oxford University Press.

Daaku, K. Y. 1961. "Pre-European Currencies of West Africa and Western Sudan." *Ghana Notes and Queries* 2(May–August): 12–14.

Dupuis, J. 1824. *Journal of a Residence in Ashantee.* London: H. Coulborn.

Fortes, M. 1950. "Kinship and Marriage among the Ashanti." In *African Systems of Kingship and Marriage,* ed. A. R. Radcliffe-Brown and D. Forde, 252–284. New York and London: Oxford University Press, for the International African Institute.

Freeman, R. A. 1 898. *Travels and Life in Ashanti and Jaman.* New York: F. A. Stokes.

Freeman, T. B. 1843. *Journal of Two Visits to the Kingdom of Ashantee.* London: F. Cass.

Garrard, T. F. 1980. *Akan Weights and the Gold Trade.* London and New York: Longman.

Goody, J. 1968. *T echnology, Tradition and the State in Africa.* London: Oxford University Press.

Hill, Polly. 1963. *The Migrant Cocoa-Farmers of Southern Ghana: A Study in Rural Capitalism.* New York and Cambridge: Cambridge University Press.

Hogendorn, J. and M. Johnson. 19 86. *The Shell Money of the Slave Trade.* New York and London: Cambridge University Press.

Hopkins, A. G. 1973. *Economic History of West Africa.* London and New York: Longman.

Kay, G. B. 1972. *The Political Economy of Colonialism in Ghana: A Collection of Docu ments and Statistics, 1900–1960.* Cambridge: Cambridge University Press.

Matson, J. N. n. d. *A Digest of the Minutes of the Ashanti Confederacy Council from 1935 to 1949 Inclusive and a Reviewed Edition of Warrington's Notes on Ashanti Customs.* Cape Coast: P rospect Printing Press.

McCaskie, T. C. 1980. "Office, Land and Subjects in the History of the Manwere Fekuo: An Essay in the Political Economy of Ashanti." *Journal of African History,* 21:189–208.

————. 1983. "Accumulation, Wealth and Belief in Asante History, 1." *Africa,* 52:25–43.

————. 1986. "Accumulation, Wealth and Belief in Asante History, 2." *Africa,* 57:3–23.

Metcalfe, G. E. 1964. *Great Britain and Ghana: Documentation of Ghana History.* London and Accra: Thomas Nelson and Sons.

Mikell, G. 1975. "Cocoa and Social Change in Ghana: A Study of Development in Sunyani." Ph.D. dissertation, Columbia University: New York.

Polanyi, K. 1964. "Sortings and 'Ounce Trade' in the West African Slave Trade." *Journal of African History,*1:381–93.

Ramseyer, F. A. and S. J. Kuhne. 1875. *Four Years in Ashantee.* London: J. Nisbet & Co..

Rattray, R. S. 1923. *Ashanti.* London: Oxford University Press.

————. 1929. *Ashanti Law and Constitution.* London: Oxford University Press.

————. 1932. *Tribes of the Ashanti Hinterland.* Vol. 2. London: Oxford University Press.

Reindorf, C. C. 1895. *History of the Gold Coast and Asante.* Basel: Basel Mission Book Depot.

Rouch, J. 1954. *Notes on Migrations Into the Gold Coast,* trans. D. E. O. and J. G. Heigham. Accra: n. p.

Tordoff, W. 1965. *Ashanti under the Prempehs, 1888–1935.* London: Oxford University Press.

Wilks, I. 1975. *Asante in the Nineteenth Century: The Structure and Evolution of a Political Order.* New York and London: Cambridge University Press.

————. 1979. "'The Golden Stool and the Elephant Tail': An Essay on Wealth in Asante." *Research in Economic Anthropology* 2:1–36.

PART III

COLONIAL SITUATIONS IN LONG-TERM PERSPECTIVE

The previous section suggested how social-payment policy became one of the arenas in which the dynamics of currency instability was played out in West and Equatorial Africa. The present section looks at money availability and social payments over long time frames; the central concern is with the colonial period, but each chapter reaches back into the past and forward into the second half of the twentieth century. Modifications of marriage payments have been made continuously, as far as we know, over several centuries of African history, and they were the object of policy intervention on the part of European (Guyer, Ch. 5) and African authorities (Arhin, Ch. 4), and innovations by kingroup elders (Ekejiuba, Ch. 6; Manuh, Ch. 8; Guyer, Ch. 5). These changes are interwoven in complex and on-going ways with the market, state economic policies (Falola, Ch. 7) and innovations in other kinds of social payments such as title-taking (Ekejiuba, Ch. 6) and funeral prestations (Manuh, Ch. 8). By the period that we reach in these chapters, the mid-century and onward, very little exchange in African community life was mediated by currencies other than colonial cash. A great, and perhaps sudden, new burden was placed on social payments as "transformers," that is, as a medium for domesticating people's earned cash incomes. The instabilities are no longer due to surges and retreats in the availability of particular currencies, or to changing exchange controls, but far more to the vicissitudes of a pervasive price economy that made incomes highly variable from year to year and to the severance of income from assets through the very limited avenues for the development and deployment of African wealth.

The intricate details of transactions covered in these chapters reflect the punctilious attention given to social payments within African communities during this era. All the authors suggest ultimately that there was both an expectation of instability and varied methods of mitigating it, adjusting to it, heading it off, and otherwise buffering or taking advantage of its power. One of the paradoxes, however, of long-term institutions such as social payments is that they can feed into the very dynamic that people intend them to mitigate. One can suggest from the three chapters that look at marriage payments in some detail that—when all sources have been weighed—there seems to have been some semblance of stability over defined periods of time: either conceptually, in response to policy, or in relation to income. Too rapid change in conditions seems to have deterred some people from involvement altogether rather than subjected the payment system to intolerably rapid response. For example, some Igbo postponed marriage in the post-World War II situation, when ex-soldiers brought home large demobilization funds and out-priced their competitors (Ekejiuba, Ch. 6); and there was a hiatus in Beti marriage in the early 1960s, when the cocoa price fell precipitously and no ordinary farmer could afford the level of marriage payment accepted in the better times of the 1950s (Guyer, Ch. 5).

As Falola's chapter (Ch. 7) suggests, however, people also borrowed to meet these payments, getting deeply imbricated in interest-bearing obligations that exacerbated the effects of income inadequacy or fluctuation. African credit institutions were not entirely new in the colonial period, but they were certainly not "traditional." In the absence of capitalist credit structures, even within the nominally "Western" banking sector, such as the Post Office Savings Bank (Mabogunje, Ch. 12), the simultaneous need to raise productive capital in a commercializing economy, meet social payments under changing socio-political circumstances, and smooth income fluctuations in a market price system, encouraged an experimentation in money management that readily fed on the magical imagery of earlier experience.

Of particular interest is the question of how social payments themselves "smooth" the unfolding of social relations over the lifecycle. Guyer and Ekejiuba point out the broad ramification of relations that are now acknowledged in marriage payments, and Manuh describes how marriage payments prefigure funerary expenses. Even with all the historical contextualization each author gives the particular local story here, the general impression is of a stabilizing institution: one that reaches legitimately into the past and constitutes a complex of valued practices that can be "captured" by specific and changing interests. The idea of institutional "capture" suggests a further theme that is indicated in these chapters and by Mikell in the following section (Ch. 10): the place of women in money management and in constituting social payments. Clearly, one of the developments of the colonial era was an increased participation of women in one phase or another of the earning and spending that went into social life.

The long view on social payments and credit sources that is afforded in these chapters elucidates the empirical patterns, but can only indicate possible interpretations. The directions of change in both social payments and informal sector savings seem quite varied in the present world. It may be that the colonial period should be viewed as the era in which these payments were definitively institutionalized in relation to a commercial economy and state power. The chapters certainly show that the question of payments was diligently worked on: within communities, in courts, state regulatory agencies, and chieftaincy councils. Any semblance of order and coherence was the product of a focused ingenuity. It is possible that the instabilities of the present day are too rapid and the controling agencies too unmotivated for the relative coherence in social-payment institutions described by the authors to continue. In her Epilogue, Berry (Ch. 13) interprets the apparently intensified endorsement of temporal and spatial social reach through social payments as itself a function of and contributor to ambiguity and endless—possibly fruitless—negotiation. Once formally recognized, usually in a fashion that creates precedent, but not exactitude, about rights and duties, social relations become an indispensable but also—under present conditions—a vague, labor-intensive and quite unpredictable resource to mobilize.

5

The Value of
Beti Bridewealth*

JANE I. GUYER

Introduction and Summary of the Argument

Change in economic structures or in the value of goods places enormous pressure on the most intimate relationships and day-to-day routines of life. People's own views of the family and past academic models may tend to emphasize the primary domestic relations as a locus of conservatism and resilience, a context in which long-term obligations are honored and the profound meanings of identity are routinely re-enacted (Bloch 1977). The implication is that such commitments and routines are—to use a part of Geertz's (1966) definition of religion—"uniquely realistic." Traditions, however, can be invented outright (Hobsbawm and Ranger 1983). Or in situations of instability, they can be recreated in that interstitial no-man's-land of experience between full conceptualization and felt conviction, between reasoned strategy and raw intuitive boldness (see Comaroff and Comaroff 1991). To keep moving and changing in relation to shifting events demands constant cultivation of the terrain: reconfiguration of the verbal and nonverbal elements of custom, re-phasing and re-ordering of sequences, and avoidance and pre-emptive capture of contested institutions. Persistence may be a near miraculous balance of multiple cross-cutting ingenuities, rather than an expression of the linear momentum of habitus (Bourdieu 1977).

* This idea was originally explored in 1982, and has been through several versions, each unsatisfactory to the au thor. But it is the topic that initially encouraged me to work on currencies and values in more depth, and hence—several papers and research projects later—it has been reworked for this workshop. The field research in Cameroon in 1975-6 was funded by the National Institute of Mental Health (NIMH). Earlier versions of the paper have been read by Pauline Peters and Christine Jones, and presented at the American Anthropological Association Meetings, and several seminars (Universities of Chicago, Harvard, Columbia and Liverpool).

With this approach, I return to what is an old question from the anthropological literature and a pressing question in people's lives: the value of marriage payments. The most devotedly detailed ethnographies of the peoples of the northwest Equatorial region make the astonishing suggestion that over the entire extraordinarily turbulent history of the twentieth century, comprising demographic collapse and recovery (Balandier 1955), religious innovation (Fernandez 1982), and political and economic change, the real value of bridewealth payments has remained stable. Fernandez writes of the Fang of Gabon: " Despite very great fluctuations in the colonial currency, the real value of the woman had remained about the same over the years" (1982:148). Dupré writes of the Nzabi of the Congo: "If we take the part of the marriage payments constituted by local goods, we can establish that taken together they are equivalent to 6 *nzundu* (metal anvils), that is, a pre-colonial marriage payment" (1982:336).[1] The sense of stability surrounding bridewealth is all the more remarkable because in neither case has there ever been a central authority with the legitimacy or the capacity to enforce such interfamilal transfers. But the impression of stable rates is not universal in this region. In Cameroon, as I will discuss in the body of the chapter, the State made pronouncements about bridewealth levels and the Catholic Church interceded with parishioners to avoid bridewealth payment altogether, at least in part because it provided the foundation for the practice of widow inheritance and thereby of involuntary polygyny (Guyer 1986). In the 1920s, the chiefs complained that rates were too low, and in the late 1940s and early 1950s, an outpouring of commentary complained that they were too high (see Owono 1953, 1959). Clearly, even if the *longue durée* may plausibly suggest certain stable, or at least periodically reinstated elements and relationships, the trajectory is not necessarily a steady one.

Data for the Beti suggest four phases to bridewealth (*mevek*) payment over the nineteenth and twentieth centuries. We cannot reconstruct the first—the early nineteenth century practices—with confidence, but the evidence for later inflation in bridewealth and a positive moral judgment on sister exchange suggest that payments of bridewealth in currency may have intensified over the century. During the late nineteenth century, payments in the indigenous iron-rod currency and in small livestock seem to have risen relative to earlier practices, especially along the trade routes for imported goods. In that second phase, newly ambitious headmen created alliances and built up their political and economic bases through polygynous marriage, intensifying competition for wives and using controls over access to goods to keep the rates out of the reach of most young men (Ngoa 1968; Laburthe-Tolra 1981; Guyer 1986). The third phase differs in its macro-political dynamics from the late precolonial period but less in the micro-politics of the transactions themselves. The high rates relative to most aspirants' possibilities were maintained and intensified under early colonial rule, when social payments were monetized into francs. Finally, the late 1940s and early 1950s, mark a qualitative change, when access to cash income broke out of the clientage mold and marriage became a more competitive "market."

Over this history, the following reconfigurations have been put in place. The word itself and the named components of *mevek* remained quite stable over the entire hundred-year history covered here, with a single major addition, while the application, levels, and media of payment all changed. These patterns of change suggest not the four common-sense phases outlined above, but three phases separated by two fairly clear watersheds: one in the latter half of the nineteenth century and the other in the mid-twentieth century. At these moments, changes in the overall level of marriage payments and the internal balance of the components were so large that one can argue for the replacement of one "regime of value" (Appadurai 1986) by another. Within each of these regimes of value, the level of an acceptable *mevek* relates very closely to one particular element in the overall social framework, but a different one in each era. Because the data are very thin for the earliest era, this argument focuses mainly on the two broad time periods of about 1880–1940, and 1945 to the present.

At the most general level of interpretation, these data suggest that monetization and commoditization have not been incremental social processes. Changes in the "cultural topography of wealth" (Ferguson 1992) and the social geography of the channels through which money moves have been both more convulsive and more subtle than the imagery of ordered growth and change can capture. The interwoven histories of the different elements do lend themselves to presentation in the form of two ideal models: one based on the pre-eminence of descent and the other on the pre-eminence of alliance. But at no historical moment were the models completely realized. Shifts of emphasis and the interjection of totally new elements—new crops, new taxes, new markets, and new currencies—entailed whirlpools of debate, incoherence, and unintended consequences. The history of the configurations is really a composite of the history of the elements and their relations to one another, not a narrative history of a single, coherent institution.

To encompass this view, the chapter first describes Beti *mevek* as a set of fairly stable cultural elements. It then tells three narrative histories that are eventually interwoven: a history of the money "price" of the central payment, a history of the separable component gifts, and a history of the social and economic dynamics that might account for both periods of relative stability and moments of rapid change.

Beti *Mevek*: A Description and a History

For the Beti populations, what we call "bridewealth" in English and what the French-language legal system refers to as "la dot," is termed *mevek*. It is a plural noun, and the etymology refers to public valuation. The verb *vek* is used in other ordinary contexts, meaning to think, measure, weigh, or compare, and is used in the active tense in relation to marriage, as in, "The father *vek* a wife for his son." (Tsala 1956:641). It relates in no way to the verbs for purchase, sale, capture, or any other acquisition words, even though by the end of the nineteenth century both marriage and sales, as well as fines and gambling, were mediated by the same indigenous currency: bundles of small iron rods shaped like spears known as *bikie*, (meaning, simply, "metals"; see Guyer, 1985), which were made by local blacksmiths. One paid—*yaan*—fines and eventually taxes and fares, but not bridewealth. Marriage by *mevek* was considered "real marriage" (*mfan aluk*; Laburthe-Tolra 1977:513), by which is implied a marriage of recognized high status.

To *vek* was only one way of creating a union (*aluk*) whose offspring were unambiguously affiliated to their father. The most important other form was through *atud*. The etymology of this term is not known to me, but it referred to the woman herself, when she was given in a type of marriage exchange in which bridewealth either did not figure at all—such as sister exchange and the acquisition of a low-status woman by a high-status man—or was immediately transferred to a linked brother to fund his own marriage.[2]

Ngoa (1968), the Beti ethnographer, writes that marriage was to the pre-colonial Beti a total social fact: the basis for accumulation of wealth and power and for the forging of alliances amongst neighboring leaders in a segmentary polity. Polygyny was competitive and accumulative, so the demand for wives was always acute. In certain places there may well have been bridewealth inflation in the pre-colonial period, a result of increased demand as the trading economy began to intensify (Guyer 1986). But in the last resort, even in the face of customary amounts of *bikie* as *mevek* and the upward pressures from competition, a father had complete rights to set the marriage payments for his daughter as he wished. The option of donating a daughter to an outstanding man rather than holding out for high bridewealth has probably always existed, and was certainly applied to men of great power in the arts and in production as well as in political life. But the emergence of more powerful leadership in the nineteenth century likely made this option more attractive while possibly focusing it more narrowly on political figures.

Because of the wide discretionary powers of the girl's father, and because of the freedom and competition in political life, the *mevek* was relatively simple in cultural terms. The components of a "standard" *mevek* were distinguished from one another, not according to conceptually different rights which the groom and his group acquired in the wife, but rather according to the different relationships that the marriage initiated amongst the families involved. Rights *in uxorem* and *in genetricem* were not distinguished, but the father of the bride and members of particular categories within the family were singled out for their own gifts.

Apart from various gifts of food, game, and so on, which a man could present to his future father-in-law as he wished or as the elder demanded, there were three different destinations for the goods transferred: to the father of the bride for use to acquire another wife (in theory for the matched brother of the bride); to her other brothers, that is the men of the residence group and possibly a wider group of patrikinsmen; and, in some places only, to the wives of the bride's patrilineal kin, including her own mother. The bride's sisters constituted the only category within the local group that had no formal share because they were considered temporary members and in fact might be married and living elsewhere well before puberty. Only the first category of goods, for the father, was in a form to be retained and eventually recirculated. All the others were destined for immediate consumption. The goods presented to the father consisted of iron rod money (*bikie*) and small livestock designated for this purpose as *mimwulu-si*, "those which walk on the ground" (from the verb *wulu*: to travel) thereby distinguished from the livestock presented to the other kin which were termed *bitsiga*, those destined for slaughter (from *tsig*: to cut) (Ngoa 1968:139–42). According to Ngoa, the distribution of the *bitsiga* was a transaction in which the bride's parents took no part whatsoever, and represented a public and collective acceptance of the marriage by the men of the local group.

The range of local group involved seems to have been quite variable in the past, but considerably narrower than at present. The consumption items therefore formed a small proportion of the total payment. An Eton elder gave the example of a *mevek* consisting of twenty spears (*mekon*), seventeen goats and one machete for the bride's father, along with groundnuts and sesame of a much smaller value. Some people also suggested that a component of the consumption items known now as *bidi bi bininga* (food for the wives) either did not exist at all in the past, was not consistently offered, or was only given to the mother herself *in advance of* her daughter's betrothal, as a kind of pledge. The receipts were very narrowly focused on the bride's father and immediate male kin. Correspondingly, the other members of the groom's descent group might make no significant contribution to his *mevek*. A single individual, usually the father of the groom, accumulated the necessary goods and thereby held exclusive and lineally inheritable rights in the woman and her children.

Over the twentieth century, this complex of payments around marriage has been under constant rethinking, renegotiation, debate, and dispute. The first great wave of intensity corresponds to the period of early monetization and French colonial and mission intervention in marriage, when the courts were full of complaints about broken agreements, incomplete transactions, and refusal to repay. The second main wave of debate came in the post-World War II period. The elite, and eventually the ordinary population, started experimenting with adding new consumer goods to the range of gifts given. One outraged published comment writes of a lorry (*"un camion"*; Owono 1953:53), while records from the Okola Tribunal mention medical fees, beds, clothing, and blankets. In response to a series of church-based, state-centered interests and perhaps also popular concern, the new family code of 1966 totally delegitimated bridewealth as the basis for the legality of a marriage, although the bridewealth transaction did retain civil status as an actionable contract (see Melone 1972). Couples married by bridewealth alone were hereafter referred to in law cases as *fiancés*, regardless of how long they had been married. For the few couples who eventually married in civil law yet further payments had to be made, such as a "suit" appropriate for the bride's father to wear when he attended the ceremony in a government office.

In the mid-1970s, when I carried out field research just north of Yaoundé, couples—when they did decide to forge a socially recognized marriage—were still marrying primarily by bridewealth payment. And bridewealth was still a very considerable expense: a central bridewealth payment to the bride's father took about one entire year's worth of cocoa income, and because fathers controled cocoa farms, enormous intergenerational tensions could arise. Only gradually, as school fees have become integrated into personal budgets and housebuilding becomes more expensive, are other destinations for money savings emerging to divert the flow of personal funds away from an elaborated sequence of payments for marriage.

For most of this century, then, marriage payments were rethought and negotiated, as a key institution, in the context of dramatic changes in the money economy. If we look now briefly at money itself, the changes over the same period seem yet more marked than two world wars, two major price crises (1929–34 and mid-1960s), two price peaks (late 1920s and early 1950s), three colonial currency systems (the mark, the franc, and the franc Communauté Financière Africaine [CFA]) can cover. The coins and bills themselves have changed several times, as have people's terminologies for them. In fact, the entire monetary lexicon is a mix of terms and concepts from several sources. Even though based on the German mark, early colonial currencies were always referred to by English (pidgin) terms; money was *moni*, and the coins were *kaba* (copper), *tolafen* (threepence), *silfen* (sixpence), *sinin* (shilling), and *dolo* (dollar). These words were (and some still are) applied to whichever currency is in circulation, without a direct recalculation of value at the going exchange rate. For example, *dolo* was 5 French francs and stayed five francs, even under the CFA system, in which the exchange rate diverged and the purchasing power plunged. For units of one hundred or multiples of a hundred, a numerical concept is used that is based in the old *bikie*-counting terminology. At one thousand, the system refers back to Pidgin. Another source of change in money use and innovation in monetary terminology has been the taxation system, and the variable kinds and levels of tax appropriation (Guyer 1980, 1991). Any stability, therefore, in the real value of the payments referred to then and now as *mevek*—of the kind indicated by Fernandez and Dupré— must be seen as a cultural and social process of some importance and complexity.

A History of the "Price" of Bridewealth

The first exercise worth doing is to test the conclusion of stability, by taking the cost of the simplest and most publicly known component of *mevek*—the central payment to the bride's father—and looking at how it has related to the cash incomes out of which it was paid. The payment of *mevek* was converted very quickly from *bikie* to *moni*,[3] unlike the Igbo case where indigenous currencies circulated until 1948 (Ofonagoro 1979; Ekejiuba, Ch. 6). In the 1920s, the Beti had only two realistic sources of cash, other than receiving it in a prior transaction. They could sell export commodities (primarily palm kernels at that time, but beginning to include cocoa by the start of World War II) or they could work for wages in porterage. Wages and agricultural earnings still represent the major sources of income to the present. Very few rural people are in formal employment, and those few are more likely to be skilled and professional workers rather than bearers. I limit the analysis, then, to agricultural prices. To express the relationship between cocoa prices and bridewealth rates, the returns from the 220 kilos needed to pay the cash component of bridewealth in 1922 has been used as a price index. Figure 5-1 summarizes the results.

The first impression is that the two bear very little relationship. In the simplest terms, the amount of cocoa that a man needed for a bridewealth in the 1970s was three to four times as much as in 1922. In between, there is a sharp break around the 1940s; before this period bridewealth remained quite stable while cocoa prices fluctuated widely, and after it, bridewealth inflated while cocoa peaked in 1954 and then went into a long decline from which it never recovered in real terms.

Is bridewealth, counter-intuitively, unrelated to the sources of income used to pay it? In fact, of course, the relevant figure is not prices alone but income; people grow a lot more cash crop in 1977 than they did in the 1920s. Figure 5-2 plots bridewealth values against estimates and survey results on "household" income (see "Sources on Bridewealth," appended to this chapter, for sources and methods).

The most interesting inference to be drawn from the sequence of income against bridewealth, fraught as its reconstruction is with errors and approximations, is that the same break in pattern is evident in the 1940s. In the 1920s, 400 to 600 francs was way beyond the annual income of the ordinary "household." At that time, the major cash crop was palm kernels, whose price was much lower than the price of cocoa. To come up with 600 francs, a man would have to work possibly two or three years if he spent none of his income on anything else. Even at this time, when purchase of other items such as clothing and building materials was very low to nonexistent, there were other cash commitments that drew on income besides bridewealth payment.

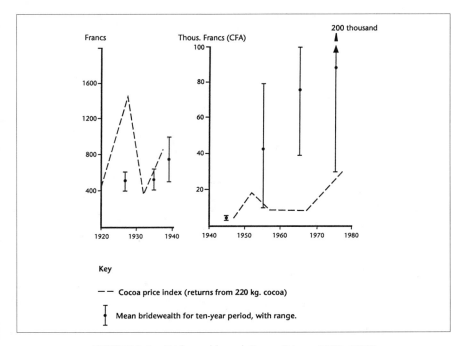

FIGURE 5-1   Bridewealth and Cocoa Prices, 1922–1977

Taxation alone took between 10 percent and 25 percent of the total value of export crops produced in the 1920s and was much higher during the Depression (Guyer 1980).

At 1926 prices, which were very high (see Figure 5-1), a man would have needed 600 kilos of palm kernels to pay a 600 franc bridewealth (CNA APA 11894/A). According to calculations made during the Depression, a family consisting of a man, two wives, and two children could produce 720 kilos if they all worked 30 days a month for the 8 driest months of the year (CNA APA 10904/B). This level of labor input into cash earning is utterly unrealistic for a population that was also producing its own food, fulfilling corvée labor duties of various sorts, and carrying out all the usual nonagricultural activities that people perform when there is little specialization by occupation. If we take, as a rough approximation of the real rather than the hypothetical situation, the total production of palm kernels for the region in 1928 (11,975 tons; CNA APA 11894/A), and divide it by 100,000 (the presumptive number of 5-person families in a population of half a million; see Kuczynski 1939:89), we get a figure of about 120 kilos per family, yielding an income of 120 francs, or about one fourth of a standard bridewealth—before taxes. Wages were somewhat more promising as a source of savings, but not dramatically so. In the same year, wages in the public sector were about 20 francs a month, or 240 francs a year if a person worked full-time, of which 10 percent was taken in head tax. And this was a good year. The Depression was, of course, a catastrophe for cash incomes. People could hardly pay their taxes, let alone entertain a major expense such as bridewealth.

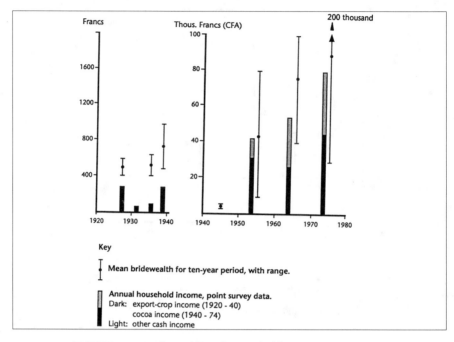

FIGURE 5-2   Bridewealth and Household Income, 1922–1975

The archives and people's memories concur on the inferences one can draw from the figures: that a bridewealth of 400 to 600 francs was very high relative to cash income, even for the years 1926 and 1927, when the gap was somewhat narrowed. A standard marriage payment was probably at least three times the annual disposable income, even of a family let alone an individual. Under the price conditions which prevailed during all but two short peaks (1926-7 and 1936-8) it may have been more. In brief, bridewealth stayed fairly static and high while cash incomes went through a series of convulsions way below its level. One imagines a situation in which cash hardly circulated at all in local communities. Possibly colonial *moni* was an even more special purpose currency for most of the population than *bikie* had been.

Then around 1938, as Owono describes in an early polemic paper on the subject, "a non-customary inflation" began (1953:51). After the war, the evidence becomes much more dependable, and suggests that the cash component of bridewealth began to vary near the level of, or somewhat above, the average annual cocoa income. Instead of a picture of overall *increase* in the real value of cash bridewealth, as suggested in the first graph, one should more realistically see a *decrease* relative to total rural incomes. The level never seems to go above double the average annual income and is only lately seeming to fall slightly below. Above all, the income pattern suggests that commodity incomes and cash bridewealth no longer vary in an unrelated fashion.[4] In fact, two budget surveys done, one in the peak price year of 1954 and the other in the trough of 1964-5, found a change in the proportion of cash income devoted to bridewealth that is comparatively small in relation to the pre-war pattern.

In 1954, bridewealth was 9 percent of global income for the regional sample as a whole (Binet 1956:85) and in 1964/5 it was 12 percent (SEDES 1964/5:73).

In Beti society, some quite rapid change took place in the 1940s which effectively released the valuation process (previously pegged to something fairly static, be it cultural principles or some other factor) and allowed people, in their social practice of negotiating marriage, to re-peg it to variable cash income from commodity production.

The Threshold of the 1940s/50s: The Components of Bridewealth

The price series constructed above is only suggestive. It cannot reveal what the thresholds were or how people changed the referent of the stable, continuing concept of bridewealth. Critiques of the older anthropological literature become useful here, along with a reminder that however straightforwardly Beti people offer a single cash amount when they are asked how much the *mevek* was for a marriage, *mevek* is itself a plural word and the transactions that make it up are plural. In the anthropological literature and in customary law, "bridewealth,"[5] as these transactions were eventually termed, was seen as a single institutional complex for comparative purposes. A whole series of theoretical modifications has been made since then, enough to occupy an extensive review. A few interventions are particularly relevant here, briefly, in order to set the stage for my own contribution. All of them ultimately derive from the simple observation that marriage payments did not seem to be dying out as modernization theories expected. They were, rather, transforming in ways that often were very challenging—not only to scholars but to the people themselves. Marriage payments have had moments in the spotlight of national debate, in addition to creating dramas at more personal levels.

One major thrust in the scholarship that tried to come to terms with these unexpected changes was disaggregation: of the payments lumped together under the bridewealth rubric, the whole series of ceremonial steps by which social adulthood was achieved; and all the various and different institutions of marital transactions in different societies (Comaroff 1980; Tambiah 1989). This disaggregation is the essential basis for thinking about partial and inventive transformations, rather than a single institution either surviving or declining, and "its" cost either rising or falling. Another thrust has been to place the levels and types of payments within larger cultural history. These showed how within a particular society there had been characteristic fluctuations—that is, both rises and declines—in the amounts asked for and paid over the twentieth century that related to other aspects of the economy (Murray 1976; Håkansson 1988). Finally, there has been a set of commentaries on the history of the institution itself, showing how it is at least partially a construct of customary legal procedures, which are clearly related to the politics of the colonial and post-colonial state. Above all in significance is the discovery that in some cases bridewealth marriage was clearly generalized under colonial rule, as the *only* main acceptable form of marriage, whereas in the pre-colonial period other ways had existed for making unions (Chanock 1985; Guyer 1986). These other forms of acceptable marriage, however, may continue to exist in the cultural repertoire and to be mobilized in social life.

The terminologies that people used for the whole range of marital forms may remain in the lexicon without persisting in practice, or the practices may remain accessible without the terminologies being brought forward.[6] We need, therefore, to be very cautious about assuming that terms and practices have been associated with each other in the same way from one era to the next.[7] What we designate as the institution of bridewealth, or marriage payments, is a complex of components and entailments whose nature can be established only by empirical historical study.

We can look, then, at the *mevek* transactions as they were described for the past, and compare them with the 1970s. Certain elements have clearly been retained to the present. Bridewealth still transfers undifferentiated rights *in uxorem* and *in genetricem* in the bride to the husband; it has considerable value; and it still contains the same basic components. There is a cash component, which in theory could acquire a wife for the bride's matched brother, and members of the bride's patrilineage have to be separately provided with consumption goods. The major shifts involve (1) a generalization of bridewealth payment to all marriages, with the elimination of *atud* and all nonconsenting unions, (2) the increased elaboration, expense, and social extension of the consumption component, the *bitsiga* and the *bidi bi bininga*, and (3) the reduction in the central payment relative to the total cost and relative to annual income. In addition, a dowry of household goods, given to the bride by her family, has been instituted on the occasion of religious marriage in the Catholic Church. Because this takes place ten to fifteen years after the first marriage, and only applies to a relatively small subgroup of marriages, it will not be discussed here.[8]

The following is a somewhat expensive rural *mevek* paid in the late 1960s: 69,000 francs CFA (about $350), in cash; 7 goats; 1 pig; 40 litres of red wine; 60 litres of palm wine; a case of beer; a carton of cigarettes; and a carton of matches; 1 woolen blanket; 1 cotton wrapper; 4 other cloths; 7 dresses; 1 pair of shoes; 1 machete and a sharpening file; a tablecloth; and 4 glasses.[9] Other in-kind gifts that I have heard about include medical treatment for the bride, a bed, a radio, kitchen equipment, and farm tools. One of the most extraordinary instances mentioned in the literature was the demand of an automobile (Owono 1953:53); and one of the most interesting that I came across in the field, because it reflected the system of matched siblings from the past, was the payment of secondary school fees for the bride's brother. These purchased items other than the central payment can now surpass the money component by far in total cost. As recorded for court cases, none of these items was designated as destined for one category or another of the bride's kin, but these goods are, in fact, more widely distributed than such payments in the past, as well as being more costly.

At the same time as consumer items have been added to bridewealth, the range of people involved has increased. There are elements now that either did not exist in the past; were token in amount; or only rarely given, such as a payment to the bride's sisters and a lump sum in cash for the bride's mother. The increased importance of women as recipients is recognized in the gifts themselves, but also symbolized by the wives tasting the palm wine, at some length and in front of the assembled company, and choosing the two best dame-jeannes for themselves. The genealogial range of the bride's kin present at the transaction, and therefore sharing in the consumer items (e.g., food, drink, and cigarettes), can include an entire descent segment (*ndabot*) of up to one hundred men and their wives and daughters.

My data are not detailed enough to trace these other components over time with equivalent detail to the central payment, but it is clear that they are now very considerably more expensive than the cash gift to the father. In a recent case in which the father received 120,000 CFA, his wife received 30,000 in cash, the bride's sisters were given 20,000 in cash in return for some chickens, the family received two goats bought for 60,000 CFA, cigarettes and drink cost over 60,000, and there were last-minute "fines" and demands adding up to about 20,000 CFA. The bride also positively pressed her more educated and high-status male kin to ask for a personal gift such as a watch. The food for the wives (*bidi bi bininga*) was negotiated to include two pigs, which would cost about 50,000 CFA each. This last provision, unlike the central transaction, can be postponed for several years. Unlike in the past when the *mevek* was paid at the time of marriage, the addition of these ancillary payments allows parts to be paid over time, even in a system in which there is no conceptual basis for dividing rights *in uxorem* from rights *in genetricem* and transferring them in phases.[10] Important economic repercussions include the diffusion into small shares of most of the capital accumulated for payment, rather than its preservation as an investable lump sum. In social terms, the new practice gives a value to the *ndabot* and to women that they did not consistently have in the past.

Although fairly subtle, these are very powerful changes in the uses of money. Exploration of the sources, and a fortunate spontaneous comment by one of the first Beti local administrators under the French, M. Moise Bengono,[11] suggested that this broadening of the recipient groups began "about the 1940s," in other words, at the same time as the quantitative data suggests a downward shift in the value of the central payment relative to cash income. These two related shifts were made at around the same time: a *reduction* in the central payment of bridewealth that brought its level down from twice or three times the annual disposable cash income of a farmer to about the mean annual cocoa income, and an *extension* of the ancillary payments to more categories of kin and more actual people, always under the rubric of *mevek*. The turning point corresponds to the major changes that began before the war and intensified after it: the rise of cocoa, the introduction of the franc CFA, the influx of metropolitan investment funds, and the abandonment of chieftaincy as the main instrument of colonial administration. Money was newly available to ordinary farmers, and under new conditions.

The fact that one can suggest a watershed around 1950 does not imply that price conditions were stable within either of the eras, before and after. In fact, commodity prices lurched widely. They rose at the end of the 1920s, dropped to one fourth during the Great Depression of 1929–34, rose again briefly before the war, were fixed administratively during the war, peaked in 1954, and then began a long decline into the mid-1960s. In the two eras, before and after 1950, people were guiding their responses and shaping their visions in terms of different components of the situation. One needs, finally to look at the 1940s to explore ways of accounting for the major shift, and reexamine the two patterns of fluctuation.

Toward an Interpretation: Social and Political Dynamics

In the 1940s, the French colonial government was in the process of a policy revolution that some administrators saw as a harbinger of "anarchy" (AR 1938:88). Up to the latter part of the Depression, the state had backed the instituted chiefs in every possible way, including implementing a version of marriage law that the chiefs themselves had formulated. This included high stipulated bridewealth rates, return of the bridewealth *in toto* in case of divorce, and preservation of the inheritance of widows. All these measures supported the control of marriage by the relatively wealthy, who could then mediate marriages as an aspect of patron–client relations. That is, only the wealthy and members of fairly large local groups could come up with a bridewealth fairly easily, and therefore were in a strong position to attract clients. At this time, the only people who could be wealthy in cash were those who had links to the administration, the chiefs, and their personnel, because of close constraints on expanded production by ordinary farmers (Guyer 1984).

In more remote places there must have been many ways around paying such high rates, including resort to sister exchange and possibly a more phased disappearance of *bikie* than I am aware of. The chiefs and the local French government, however, vigorously resisted this situation. In 1927, when commodity prices peaked, Chief Onambele, who himself had over sixty wives, complained that the standard bridewealth rate fixed by the government was too low because it gave dependents a realistic choice of liberating themselves by repaying the total amount. He complained that "this would be a bad example, quickly followed by my other wives." Because their tenuous control over both people and resources depended on the appointed chiefs, the Administration offered to protect them from unruly competitors for their wives through the sanctions of the *indigénat*, that is, a disciplinary puishment of a fine and prison sentence without court procedure (CNA AR APA 11954).

The characteristics of this early period—high central payment, little development of ancillary payments, and concern to keep the payments very high relative to income—can be argued plausibly as due to the way in which bridewealth value was pegged to the power of the chiefs, backed by the government which preserved and institutionalized in the colonial structure the severe traditional constraints on women's marriage options at all stages of their marital careers. This was policy, as well as being a perpetuation of principles developed at the end of the nineteenth century before colonial rule. The legality of *mevek* as creating a marriage became law, along with provisions for the inheritance of bridewealth rights in women, the conditions of divorce, and the amount which had to be returned. And the government acted to support it when it was threatened.

At least, they did so until the mid-1930s. A general disillusionment with the chiefs, the increasing difficulty of controling activities at the local level, and Christian conversion of most of the population, eventually led the government to abandon the rigid policy on bridewealth and many facets of marriage law. This then released the women themselves to pursue options of their own, and they could no longer be forced into arranged marriages for someone else's purposes. Marriage was opened up to becoming a competitive market instead of a rationed market, involving not patrons and clients in a controled economy, but large numbers of income-earning small-holders in an expanding economy. It is this change in configuration of power, at the top as well as the bottom, very briefly outlined here, which must be related to the change in the value of bridewealth and its new structural relationships with other elements in the cultural and economic value system.

One critical component of the shift was the breath of freedom that entered women's lives. A woman might be forced by her father into a particular marriage, but, as the power of chiefs began to wane, the advantages of alliance also began to wane, and the Church offered—in their famous and infamous *sixas* (Beti 1956)—an alternative place to run away and hide in if a woman's father was inhospitable. An extreme example can illustrate the intensity of this historical moment. Zogo Fouda Ngono was Superior Chief of the Manguissa (see Guyer 1984). By 1932, he had 203 wives, and by the time he died in 1939, the number had increased to 583. Under the law, his wives should have been inherited, but according to local oral sources, most of them simply fled, and one took enough money as she went to give her son a medical education in France. Completely contrary to Beti traditions of polygyny, Zogo Fouda had maintained sexual monopoly over his wives, and as a result many of them had been deprived of the possibility of child-bearing. In fact, Fouda's children were enumerated at only sixty five sons, thirty seven daughters, and five widows left pregnant at his death, a total of less than one fifth as many children as wives (Local Archives at Saa). Local oral history tells that the wives' most urgent agenda was to resume a sexual and reproductive life.

As the men reclaimed land confiscated by the chiefs, now slowly but surely being abandoned by the French, and moved rapidly into cash-crop production on their own, women found that the old sanctions against their mobility could no longer be enforced. Indeed their fathers and brothers had no particular interest in trying to prevent them from moving. By the mid-1950s, there were few polygynists with more than ten wives. The majority of the population was settling into much smaller familial and production groupings (Binet 1956), working under the new cocoa regime, in which it was increasingly the agricultural activities of the wives and daughters— rather then the clearing activities of the male lineage members alone—that ensured claims on arable land. In this context, as M. Bengono described to me, the older women who had married into the brides' descent group managed to expand the *bidi bi bininga* to a very substantial payment and to insert the brides' sisters into the category of recipients.

Is there a parsimonious way of understanding the modern configuration of marriage payments that followed this turning point, as there is for the pre-war system? The configuration now includes a lower central payment of about one annual cocoa income, ancillary payments that are high, broadly distributed and recognize women as recipients, and a total that is income-responsive upwards, but apparently quite sticky downwards. Evidence for that latter includes commentaries on the dilemmas of the early 1960s, when cocoa prices plunged. Apparently, the aggregate collective "decision" was to postpone marrriage rather than reduce bridewealth. Many couples started into their reproductive lives without making any payments at all. Why, then, did people start paying again, and at the old rates, when the cocoa price picked up? The answer, I suggest, is the growing importance of legitimacy in claiming access to land. Women gain their best access through their husbands, and can pass on their own plots to their children. Men still want heirs, and brides' fathers do not necessarily want to be forced to improvise a solution to inheritance dilemmas of their daughters' unrecognized children. The past cultural importance of alliance persists in the low status afforded to children not born of fully contracted unions. The mid-1960s experiment with later marriage, then, was seen to create problems that were explicitly debated in the late 1970s and early 1980s as the children born pre-maritally grew up. At the same time, however, women's greater freedom in marriage meant that they had an interest in keeping up relations with their patrilineage of origin, to which they could return. Hence their interest in seeing *all* the members of their home group acknowledged at the marriage, and hence their own use of income to cement those relations (Guyer 1984).

Taken together, all these changes may be seen as concomitants of the shift from a client-based system of resource access to a descent/residence-based system, and from a tribute-based topography of monetary flows, to one in which there is some internal circulation. Men of common patrilineal descent are now represented by village chiefs and *chefs de groupement* in the regional administrative system, and they hold residual rights in one another's land. With economic participation dependent on landholding, and with government based on territorial localities, descent groups have re-emerged and re-configured. This shift toward descent-defined access to resources was accompanied by a gradual limitation in the political importance of marriage alliance in a client-based political system. Interests and constraints have shifted accordingly, although the institutions in which they were embedded and the cultural conceptions that underwrote them have not changed so much. *Mevek* is still presented to the bride's father by the groom's senior kinsman. But the entire ceremony involves a myriad of other recognitions. Each person's share in food and drink is carefully managed and noted. Some people may receive almost nothing in real terms, but they *must* consume wine or take as little as a single cigarette. The bride gains personal prestige from a lavish bridewealth paid for her, but she pays more attention to the details of participation than to the overall amount given, demanding that each and every male kinsman receive something—however small—as a sign of their commitment ("love"). And at a wedding that I attended in 1979, the bride offered herself for a special blessing to the oldest man of the group, a gesture that I have never seen or heard about being essential in the past. A marriage ceremony has become a veritable celebration of kin-group membership in which the bride's interests are far from passive. She stresses her ties to a natal village and actively courts not only her male kin, but also the in-married wives and unmarried daughters, all of whom are acknowledged by gifts. The whole transaction is couched in a moral and spiritual idiom of children's obligations to kin and the group's potential influence on the fertility of the couple, in a situation where the jural control of a father has been greatly diminished.

Conclusion

Seen over the long term, marriage payments appear as a kind of capturable good. They symbolize and mediate both descent and alliance relations; they represent the absolute value of a status marriage; and they constitute a node of cultural elements and definitions that are validated as traditional. The characteristics of each of the different "regimes" of value in practice are consonant with the category of people who have managed to capture the configuration of elements and to elaborate on it: the bride's father in the pre-colonial period, the chief in the early colonial period, and the bride's descent group in the era of cocoa farming. Control by elders and chiefs was achieved by control of the central payment, which was high relative to the total cost and to men's incomes. Control by the descent group resulted in a lateral expansion of categories of gift to accommodate all the categories of people who had to be recognized. Each period had its own currency—*bikie* under the control of elders and headmen, francs under the chiefs' control, and francs CFA under the market—each associated with its own macro-political dynamics and channels of circulation at both the national and the local level.

No major period offered stable monetary conditions, but in each period, dynamics did tend to turn on particular pivotal relationships within the monetized sector of the economy. Throughout the entire history, the Beti people seem to have "rejected" the idea of phasing payments to as a means of dealing with instability, which would have given a lot more play to the range of possible strategies. There is, in fact, little basis in Beti culture upon which to build a system of differentiated and phased payments, although it is now possible, in the last configuration, to offer the *bidi bi bininga* several years later. Instabilities in incomes led to authoritarian interventions in the bridewealth level in the first era, and to popular-level postponement of marriage (when incomes fell) or precipitation (when incomes rose) in the second. In the earlier period of this century, vocal and powerful interests maintained a stable minimum gap between income and marriage payments, intervening and innovating politically when commodity prices, and therefore incomes, began to rise too close to the bridewealth level. In the later period, after 1945, stability lay in a mean or expected balance between annual income and bridewealth. The difficulties under the new regime lay in coping with the income downswings. Rather than political interventions being made to keep these prices in some kind of relationship, people themselves innovated by postponing marriage itself.[12]

In brief, the full breadth of the cultural repertoire has been brought into play to create two different working configurations over this century, each of which has touched off different loci and kinds of responsiveness to the uncontrollable conditions of economic life. The "price" of bridewealth and its fluctutations in each configuration reflect not just an economic response to monetary conditions but a specific cultural and political elaboration of gender relations, social groups, and political hierarchies. Both, however, share certain fundamental and continuing propositions about the nature of marriage.

Sources on Bridewealth

Published figures, archival sources and field cases are used.

—For the period before World War II, the first two sources are more important, although the three field cases documented are also used to indicate the range of variation in the later 1930s.

—For the post-War period, only field cases are plotted, although documentary sources supporting the general picture are quoted below. Exact dates for many of the marriages are unobtainable; because the main argument relates only to major features of the pattern of change, the mean and range for each decade is shown at the mid-decade.

Pre-War Figures

1922 – Annual Report to the League of Nations (AR).
1920s – Interviews in Vincent (1976:94,136).

1930s – Quoted in Bertaut (1935:178).

– Inventory of the property of Zogo Fouda Ngono, Chief of the Manguissa, including the bridewealth value of his widows (CNA Local Archives at Saa).

– Field interviews, four women, one of whom was married in an exchange marriage.

Post-War Figures

1940–76 – Field Interviews.

1940s, n = 3

1950s, n = 6

1960s, n = 5

1970s, n = 8

Supporting sources:

1953 – Owono reports extreme levels up 100,000 francs.

1954 – Budget study reports mean bridewealth given at 31,500 CFA, mean reported received at 40,000 (Binet 1956:85).

1960s – Cases from court records of Okola First Degree Court, reviewed completely for 1973/4. Cases range from 58,000 to 89,000 francs CFA.

1964 – Budget study reports that rural bridewealth "goes up to 100,000 CFA" (SEDES 1964/5:79).

Sources on Prices

Cocoa Prices

1922–37 – AR, freight on board (FOB) prices (not producer prices; these would be approximately two thirds or less the FOB price).

1947–72 – Assoumou 1977: 231, 255, 256.

1976–7 – Field notes.

For simplicity, I have used the cocoa price as an index for prices in commodity production in general. In fact, it has been of changing importance as a determinant of total rural income. Up to the late 1930s, most income was earned from palm kernels. By 1954, cocoa accounted for 70 percent of income (Binet 1956:57), falling to 48 percent in 1964 (SEDES 1964/5:73).

Sources on Incomes

Pre-War Figures

The only budget studies were done during the Depression and were highly impressionistic. However, information about export crop prices, amounts produced in this region, and the tax rate, along with an assumption (unrealistic but necessary) of a "family" size of five people, begins to allow one to piece together a profile. All estimates are based on the sources used in Guyer (1980). The amounts plotted are after-tax income; head tax accounted for the following proportions of total export crop value (FOB, not local prices, i.e., these proportions are considerable lower than they would be if they could be based on consistently reported local producer prices.): 1927: 10 percent; 1932: 48 percent; 1935: 35 percent.

The year 1935 is taken as an example of the calculations involved. Total palm-kernel production for the Beti region, divided by the number of five-person families (i.e., the total population divided by five), gives a per-family production of 162 kg per-annum, with a value of 88 francs. The same calculation for cocoa, gives a per-family income of 57 francs. At a tax rate of 35 percent (at least), this gives a generous estimate of family disposable cash income of 94 francs, rounded to 100.

Post-War Figures

1954   :Binet 1956

1964/5 :SEDES 1964/5

1974   :Reported in Henn 1978.

Notes

1. Very stable prices for certain goods and payments over very long periods of time have, in fact, been noted for other economies, including the western economies. But price persistence is not really well explained since the mechanisms of "custom" (the "moral economy") seem to be quite varied. Bloch 1966 suggests that the exchange rates in kind over the period of the Dark Ages in Europe were implicitly based on a calculus of the defunct Roman currency.
2. *Atud* is described in Laburthe-Tolra (1981) and Guyer (1986).
3. People said that *bikie* were simply thrown away. The currency revolution (Hopkins 1966) was apparently not imposed in Cameroon.
4. As Murray writes of the Sotho calculation of the nominal rates of bridewealth cattle, "it is no longer independent of inflation in other spheres" (1976:110).
5. There was a dispute about the concept of "brideprice" versus "bridewealth" published in *Man* during the period 1929–1931 (Vol. 29:5–8,107, 180, 131; Vol.30: 74, 92; Vol. 31:3–39, 75–76, 163–164, 190–191, 235–236, 284.)
6. See the discussions about Eastern and Southern Africa, where the concepts of the cattle economy continue to form the framework for bridewealth transactions even when all exchanges are in cash: Sansom (1976); Ferguson (1985); Ferguson (1992); Comaroff and Comaroff (1990).
7. See Herzfeld (1980) on the Greek "dowry"; see also Goody (1969).
8. See Moutome-Ekambi (1985) for a discussion of the *"contre-dot"* for the Douala.
9. Okola Tribunal 109/1972-3.
10. As in the Southern African systems, where specific numbers of cattle have to be transferred before a man gains unambiguous rights in the children of the marriage, and where under present conditions this can take up to ten years to achieve (Murray 1976).
11. Interview with M. Moise Bengono, Nkolbisson, July 24, 1979.
12. Håkansson (1988) has developed a parallel argument for the Gusii of Western Kenya that could be compared profitably point by point with the present analysis. He points out that under present conditions poverty postpones marriage but not necessarily cohabitation. The demographic implications of this response were played out in Cameroon in the 1970s:

in the villages in which I worked, 25 percent of all children were technically *père inconnu*, a result—I felt convinced—of the decline of the cocoa price in the early 1960s. Legal claims with respect to teenage children were just beginning to come to the courts. For example, natural fathers may claim daughters when they come of age to marry. I cannot deal with all the demograp hic and legal implications of this situation, however, in the present chapter.

Sources

Archival

Cameroon

Yaoundé

Cameroon National Archives (CNA)

APA 10904/B
APA 11894/A
APA 11954

Government of Cameroun. Annual Report of the Government of Cameroun to the Permanent Mandate Commission of the League of Nations (AR), Nyong-et-Sanaga.

Okola

Okola Tribunal 109/1972–3.

Saa

Local Archives. [Documents uncatalogued.]

Books, Dissertations and Articles

Appadurai, Arjun. 1986. "Introduction: Commodities and the Politics of Value." In *The Social Life of Things: Commodities in Cultural Perspective*, ed. Arjun Appadurai, 3–63. New York and Cambridge: Cambridge University Press.

Assoumou, Jean. 1977. *L'Economie du Cacao*. Paris: Jean-Pierre Delarge.

Balandier, Georges. 1955. *Sociologie Actuelle de l'Afrique Noire: Dynamique des Changements Sociaux en Afrique Centrale*. Paris: Presses Universitaires de France.

Bertaut, Maurice. 1935. *Le Droit Coutumier des Boulous*. Paris: Domat Montchrestien.

Beti, Mongo. 1956. *Le Pauvre Christ de Bomba, Roman*. Paris: R. Laffont.

Binet, Jacques. 1956. *Budgets Familiaux des Planteurs de Cacao au Cameroun*. Paris: ORS-TOM.

Bloch. Maurice. 1977. "The Past and the Present in the Present." *Man* 12:278–292.

Bourdieu, Pierre. 1977. *Outline of a Theory of Practise*. New York and Cambridge: Cambridge University Press.

Chanock, Martin. 1985. *Law, Custom, and Social Order: Th e Colonial Experience in Malawi and Zambia*. New York and Cambridge: Cambridge University Press.

Comaroff, John L. 1980. "Introduction." In *The Meaning of Marriage Payments*, ed. J. L. Comaroff, 1–47. New York: Academic Press.

Comaroff, Jean and John L. Comaroff. 1990. "Goodly Beasts and Beastly Goods: Cattle and Commodities in a South African Context." *American Ethnologist,* 17:195–216.

————. 1991. *Of Revelation and Revolution.* Chicago, IL: University of Chicago Press.

Dupré, Georges. 1982. *Un Ordre et sa Destruction.* Paris: ORSTOM.

Ferguson, James. 1985. "The Bovine Mystique: Power, Property and Livestock in Rural Lesotho." *Man* (n.s.), 20:647–74.

————. 1988. "Cultural Exchange: New Developments in the Anthropology of Commodities." *Cultural Anthropology,* 3:488–513.

————. 1992 . "The Cultural Topography of Wealth: Commodity Paths and the Structure of Property in Rural Lesotho."*American Anthropologist,* 94:55-73.

Fernandez, James W. 1982. *Bwiti: An Ethnography of the Religious Imagination in Africa.* Princeton, NJ: Princeton University Press.

Geertz, Clifford. 1966. "Religion as a Cultural System." In *Anthropological Approaches to the Study of Religion,* ed. Michael Bantan, 1–46. New York: Praeger.

Goody, Jack. 1969. "Normative, Recollected and Actual Marriage Payments."*Africa,* 39:54–61.

Guyer, Jane I. 1980. "Head Tax, Social Social Structure and Rural Incomes in Carmeroun, 1922–37." *Cahiers d'Etudes Africaines,* 79:305–329.

————. 1981. "The Depression and the Administration in South-Central Cameroun." *African Economic History,* 10:67–79.

————. 1984. *Family and Farm in Southern Cameroon.* Boston University African Research Studies no. 15. Boston, MA: African Studies Center, Boston University.

————. 1985. "The Iron Currencies of Southern Cameroon." *Symbols,* December issue: 2–5, 15–16.

————. 1986. "Indigenous Currencies and the History of Marriage Payments: A Case Study from Cameroon." *Cahier d'Etudes Africaines,* 104:577–610.

————. 1991. "Taxation and Currency in Colonial and Postcolonial Cameroon." Paper presented at the African Studies Association Annual Meeting, St. Louis, MO.

Håkansson, Thomas. 1988. *Bridewealth, Women and Land: Social Change Among the Gusii of Kenya.* Studies in Cultural Anthropology No. 10. Uppsala: University of Uppsala.

Henn, Jeanne Koopman. 1978. "Peasants, Workers and Capital: The Political-Economy of Rural Incomes in Cameroun." Ph.D. dissertation, Cambridge, MA: Harvard University.

Herzfeld, Michael. 1980. "The Dowry in Greece: Terminological Usage and Historical Reconstruction." *Ethnohistory,* 27:225–41.

Hobsbawm, Eric and Terence Ranger. 1983. *The Invention of Tradition.* New York and Cambridge: Cambridge University Press.

Hopkins, Anthony. 1966. "The Currency Revolution in South-West Nigeria in the Late Nineteenth Century." *Journal of the Historical Society of Nigeria,* 3:471–83.

Kuczynski, Robert R. 1939.*The Cameroons and Togoland: A Demographic Study.* London: Oxford University Press.

Laburthe-Tolra, Philippe. 1977. *Minlaaba.* Paris: Honoré Champion.

————. 1981. *Les Seigneurs de la Forêt.* Paris: Publications de la Sorbonne.

Melone, Stanislas. 1972. *La Parenté et la Terre dans la Stratégie du Développement.* Paris: Editions Klincksieck.

Moutome-Ekambi, J. 1985. "La Contre-dot chez les Dwala du Cameroun." In *Femmes du Cameroun: Mères Pacifiques, Femmes Rebelles*, ed. Jean-Claude Barbier, 63–72. Paris: ORSTOM/Karthala.

Murray Colin. 1976. "Marital Strategy in Lesotho: The Redistribution of Migrant Earnings." *African Studies*, 35:99–121.

————. 1977 "High Bridewealth, Migrant Labour and the Position of Women in Lesotho." *Journal of African Studies*, 21:79–96.

Ngoa, Henri. 1968. "Le Mariage chez les Ewondo." Thèse, Troisième Cycle, Paris: Sorbonne.

Ofonagoro, W. I. 1979. "From Traditional to British Currency in Southern Nigeria: Analysis of a Currency Revolution 1880–1948." *Journal of Economic History*, 39:623–54.

Ogbu, John. 1978. "African Bridewealth and Women's Status." *American Ethnologist*, 5:241–62.

Owono Nkoudou, J.-R. 1953. "Le Problème du Mariage Dotal au Cameroun Francais." *Etudes Camerounaises*, 6, 39–40; 41–83.

————. 1959. *Tante Bella: Roman d'aujourd'hui et de Demain*. Yaoundé: Librairie "Au Messager."

Parkin, David. 1972. *Palms, Wine and Witnesses: Public Spirit and Private Gain in an African Farming Community*. San Francisco, CA: Chandler.

————. 1980. "Kind Bridewealth and Hard Cash: Eventing a Structure." In *The Meaning of Marriage Payments*, ed. J. L. Comaroff, 197–220. London: Academic Press.

Poulter, Sebastien. 1976. *Family Law and Litigation in Basotho Society*. Oxford: Clarendon Press.

Quinn, Frederick. 1980. "Beti Socie ty in the Nineteenth Century." *Africa*, 50:293–304.

Sansom, Basil. 1976. "A Signal Transaction and its Currency." In *Transaction and Meaning*, ed. B. Kapferer, 143–161. Philadelphia, PA: Institute for the Study of Human Issues.

SEDES (Société d'Etudes pour le Développement Economique et Social). 19 64/5. *Le Niveau de Vie des Populations de la Zone Cacaoyère du Centre Cameroun*. Paris: Secretariat d'Etat aux Affaires Etrangères Chargé de la Cooperation.

Tambiah, Stanley J. 1989. "Bridewealth and Dowry Revisited." *Current Anthropology*, 30:413–35.

Tsala, Abbé Théodore. 1956. *Dictionnaire Ewondo-Francais*. Lyon: Imprimerie Vitte.

Vincent, Jeanne-Francoise. 1976. *Entretiens avec des Femmes Beti du Sud-Cameroun*. Paris: ORSTOM and Berger-Levrault.

6

Currency Instability and Social Payments Among the Igbo of Eastern Nigeria, 1890–1990*

Felicia Ekejiuba

The evolution of the Nigerian monetary system from 1890 to 1990 has been character-ized by simultaneous and successive use of diverse currencies, instability in their val-ues, and over seven switches from one state-issued currency system to another. The centuries-old, indigenous, multicurrency exchange systems were replaced in East-ern Nigeria by the British Pound sterling system from about 1900. By 1952, they were completely demonetized and retired from the exchange system (Ofonagoro 1972:123–172; 612–645; Jones 1958:48–57). The West African Pound sterling currency replaced that of the British from the 1920s. The regional currency was in turn replaced by the national Nigerian pound in 1961, and by the Nigerian decimal cur-rency, its present *naira* and *kobo,* in 1973. The number of successive generations of currencies in Eastern Nigeria was compounded by two additional currency switches. The Biafran pound/shilling currency replaced the Nigerian system in 1968 as part of Biafran efforts to safeguard what turned out to be a short-lived sovereignty, and sur-vive economic strangulation by Nigeria, which had changed its currency in 1968 as part of its economic blockade of Biafra. In 1970, defeated Biafrans were compelled to

* This paper was first read at the African Studies Association meeting of November 1991 in St. Louis, Missouri. It has benefitted greatly from comments and criticisms from panel members. I am particularly indebted to Jane Guyer who not only encouraged me to write this paper but has made many useful suggestions which have helped to improve it

switch back to the Nigerian pound. They were forced to exchange whatever quantity of Biafran pounds that they had accumulated for a paltry sum of twenty Nigerian pounds, thus losing decades of accumulated savings or capital. In 1984, old *naira* bills were turned in throughout the country and re-issued with another color and graphic designs in a space of one week. This was an attempt to save the already weak *naira* from collapsing under the weight of massive illegal importations and the laundering of counterfeit *naira* . In 1990, new coins of five denominations–one *naira* , fifty *kobo*, twenty five *kobo* and one *kobo*—were introduced. These were meant to replace the easily mutilated bills in 1992 when the circulating one *naira* and fifty kobo bills ceased to be legal tender. A new unit, the fifty-*naira* note, was brought into circulation in September 1991, six months later than scheduled. The earlier date was frustrated by the discovery that counterfeits of the original design had been widely imported from outside Nigeria even before the original bill had gone into circulation (*Concord*, July 14, 1991, page 14).

These frequent changes in the form and value of currencies, as well as the changes in the economic structures and sources of income/capital, had considerable impact on people's attitudes to the use and stores of wealth. For as this chapter argues, wealth is used not just as sources of economic capital, but in culturally defined processes of social capital formation, that is: processes of increasing prestige and social status; and creating, maintaining, and reproducing social relationships through gift giving, marriage payments, elaborate funeral expenses, and title-taking.

The data presented below demonstrate the relationship among fiscal policies and changes, capital accumulation, and the creation of social capital. Also indicated are the adjustments that the people of eastern Nigeria had to make in the face of changes in types and values of currencies and also changes because of the economic structure within the processes of creating and maintaining social relationships through transforming accumulated wealth. In general, there are two components of the process of creating social capital. On the one hand, a cash payment is made to the major actors—parents of the bride, the traditional ruler, former title holders, and close kinsmen. The amount is often fixed, relatively small, and often symbolic. There was also a statutory in-kind payment of goods for immediate consumption or for circulation, transferred in the process of creating social capital. This category appears to vary with changes in the value of currencies and sources of income. The nature, size, and quantity of goods has become more varied, and expensive; the process of transferring the goods has become more elaborate, the circle of kinsmen and women who share the goods have widened. As cash incomes have increased, or became relatively easier to acquire, so has the cost of goods, and the range of commodities has become more innovative (including for instance, cars, refrigerators, gas/electric cookers, household furniture, pots, and pans). The range of goods also varies with the degree of affluence of the central actors and with the value of currencies.

This chapter demonstrates the relationship between currency instability, sources of income, stores of wealth, and the social payments through which social capital is created, extended, and maintained. It is shown that as the value of currencies widely fluctuated between 1900 and 1992, social payments have been characterized by what Guyer (Ch. 5) shows to be a combination of stability, flexibility, innovation, and elaboration. Processes of commercialization and currency instability thus have exerted greater pressures on some aspects of social capital and relationship than on others. The creation of social capital and currency switches presented different degrees of crisis to each of the sexes, and the strategies for dealing with the instability differed according to gender.

In addressing these issues, this chapter presents empirical data that describes the socio-political context of the major currency switches from 1900 to 1990; it analyses the socio-cultural dynamics of currency switches; people's reactions to value instability, to official policies that dictated radical changes in value or led to complete collapse of the state-monopolized currency and the pragmatics of policy implementation. The processes through which traditional currencies were de-monetized, retired, and replaced are highlighted. This chapter examines the stages and agencies through which public acceptance and widespread use of the succeeding currencies were established. It also analyses the impact of the de-monetization of old currencies and the related value fluctuations on the processes of capital accumulation and social payments.

A pertinent question is: what strategies of financial management emerged at different levels—personal, group, and official—to enable currency users to cope with problems of wide fluctuations and meet numerous social and economic obligations? What practices and institutions emerged to ensure stability and continuity in social payments—for marriage, funerals, title-taking, political homage, and tributes—which are essential for maintaining social and ideological systems? Are there parallels between processes, patterns, and behavioral responses to currency switches and value instability of the period 1890–1959 and 1951–1990? This chapter concludes by sketching theoretical and comparative implications of transitional instability characteristic of the switch from indigenous to colonial currency for the currency switches from 1951–1990.

The Regional and Economic Context

Although Nigeria became amalgamated into a political entity in 1914, Eastern Nigeria, the regional focus of this chapter, constituted, and will be regarded in this study, as both a geographical and economic unit even before 1914. Before colonial rule, the region had a well developed monetary system and policy, with accepted standard of payments for commodities and social services. Its geographic area is demarcated by the Bight of Biafran coast to the South, the Niger, Benue, and Cross Rivers—to the west, north, and east, respectively. The region was linked by professional traders, of whom the Aro are the best documented in the literature. Other pre-colonial trading groups came from the Efik, Idoma, Igala, the Ijaw ethnic groups, and such other Igbo groups such as the Awka, Abiriba, Aku, and Nkwerre. Up to the beginning of the twentieth century, these traders dominated the regional commerce within Eastern Nigeria, Igboland, as well as the long-range trade that linked the Igbo with their neighbors. They traversed numerous river and land trade routes that straddled across several ethnic frontiers and currency zones, moving from one market to another in search of trade and commerce. These indigenous professional traders diversified the range of commodities that were available in well established networks of local markets by ensuring a supply, even though sporadic, of mainly locally manufactured prestigious, luxury, and imported goods.

The trade in these commodities was superimposed on centuries-old regional commerce in local manufacture and agricultural produce. The diversified production base reflects ecological differences, as well as immense diversities in regional, human, and material resources of Eastern Nigeria. Multiplicity of currencies reflected the trade policies and practices of the professional traders. As middlemen, the traders established and maintained exclusive economic spheres of influence. They often protected their monopoly of the waterways and land routes leading to the markets by exacting tolls on all transit traffic and backing their demands by force (wrestling or fighting) (Ukwu 1967; Ekejiuba 1972; Northrup 1978). They resisted encroachments by other traders, Europeans and Africans, whom they saw as a threat to their exclusive rights: to fix prices of commodities; to determine exchange value of currencies; evacuate the local produce; distribute exotic goods; and link the area to other middlemen, Africans and Europeans, in the relay trade of the region. Thus, the middlemen from the Delta States controled the labyrinth of creeks and rivers that form the Niger Delta (Dike 1956; Alagoa 1970). Efik and other traders controled the trade of the Cross River and the Rio Del Rey (Forde 1956; Latham 1971, 1973). Abo, Brass, and the Igala traders controled trade along the River Niger, while the Tiv/Idoma groups controled that of the River Benue (Ogedengbe 1980). The Awka, Nkwerre, Abiriba and the Aro, mostly Igbo speaking, were land traders par excellence. Awka dominated iron-smithing and trade in parts of Northern and Western Igbo (Neaher 1979; Dike 1956), while the Abiriba dominated that between the Cross River and the Cameroons (Ekeghe 1956). The Aro established several commercial settlements in strategic locations among all ethnic groups in Eastern Nigeria—the Efik, Ekoi, Ibibio, Idoma, Igala, Igbo, and Ijaw (Umo 1952; Ottenberg 1958; Dike and Ekejiuba 1990). The Aro colonies, over one hundred and fifty of which still exist today, were the main avenues and channels for the regional, long-distance, relay trade. As well known traders and agents of the widely famed Ibinukpabi oracle, the Aro enjoyed unrestricted travel privileges; other Igbo ritual specialists, doctors and blacksmiths, enjoyed travel privileges over more restricted areas.

Traditional Currencies: The Multiple-Currency System

The diverse policies of, and the ethnic and regional background of, traders partly explain the multiplicity of currencies used simultaneously or successively in Eastern Nigeria up to the early decades of the twentieth century. Existing archeological studies (Shaw 1970) indicate that the use of money as a medium of exchange, standard, and store of value in Eastern Nigeria has a long history, dating at least, to the ninth century A.D. Shaw's rich Igbo Ukwu archeological finds indicate that by this century, exchange of slaves and ivory for horses, beads, metals, and bronzes from Northern Nigeria was already taking place. Trade between Ijaw and their neighbors was established firmly before the fifteenth century. Through this trade, salt, and fish from the coastal Delta were exchanged for agricultural produce—mainly yams and palm oil—of the hinterland (Alagoa 1970; Northrup 1972). Trade along the Niger River highway between Abo, Igala, Ijaw, and Northern Igbo towns was also established by the fifteenth century (Northrup 1972). Historical accounts of this trade indicate that the rich and diverse crafts and agricultural produce of the upland were traded for fish and salt products of the Delta, as well as for salt and cloth from Ohaozara (Uburu/ Okposi), eastern Savanna region. Salt and cloth served both as currency and commodity. Salt produced from brines was molded into cones of different sizes and used in exchange transactions (Ekejiuba 1972:10–21). Other local products—iron artifacts and tools—were also used as currency. Apart from iron bars and the agricultural tools (hoe and machete) iron products used as currency are referred to in local terminology, as *anyu, apa,* and *umumu.* Basden (1921:198) described the last as "Y"-shaped, about one inch in length. They were produced by Awka/Lejja blacksmiths in northern Igboland, an area endowed with iron deposits.

As professional trading groups emerged in Eastern Nigeria and as trade with Europeans developed, more specialized currencies were imported and used simultaneously with the locally produced "primitive" money. These later currencies consist of cowries of different sizes, brass rods, copper wires, and iron rods. Five different sizes and shapes of copper manillas have been identified, each differently valued and used in specific parts of the region. Cowries and the locally produced currencies were preferred as subsidiary currencies for exchanges requiring payments for small purchases lower than one tenth of a penny. The smallest denomination of the cowry currency comprised of six single cowry shells (*isiego, ibego* or *nkpulu ego*). By 1901, cowries were valued at the Delta at 6d per 1000 cowries, i.e., 1 British penny was worth 167 cowries in 1901, although it had been worth 125 cowries in the 1890s (Basden 1921:198–199; Ofonagoro 1972:137). By 1920, one medium-sized fowl cost 1/4d or 90 cowries at Onitsha. The other imported currencies were used for large or medium purchases because their exchange rates were higher than the others. Indivisibility of the larger units, such as brass rods, created problems for their use as a means of exchange for smaller payments. (Table 6-1 indicates the exchange values of these currencies from 1890 to 1945).

TABLE 6-1 Exchange Values of Traditional Currencies Recognized as Legal Tender, 1890–1952 (Value of one unit of currency in British penny [d])

Year	Traditional Currency						
	Umumu	Cowry	Copper Wire	Manilla[**]			Brass Rod
				a	b	c	
1890	1/50	1/127	1/10	1/2	3	3/4	2 1/2
1900–1902[*]	1/45	1/167	1/8	1 1/4	2 1/2	5/8	2 1/2
1906[†]	1/40	1/120	1/8	1 1/4	2 1/2	3/4	2 1/2
1912	—	1/90	1/8	1	1 1/2	1	2
1920[††]	—	1/60	—	—	1/2	—	—
1948[§]	—	1/60	—	—	1/2	—	—

[*] British colonial presence established in Igboland through miliary action.

[**] a , b, c refer to three different sizes of manillas, which were imported in large numbers, recognized as having different values and given different names in the local languages. The largest (c) was often used for larger purchases, for bride-wealth payment and for payment for initiation into social clubs.

[†] Further imnportation of cowries prohibited in 1904 through British legislation.

[††] Importation of manillas prohibited in 1918.

[§] Operation Manilla: to collect all manillas and therefore force them out of use.

Sources: Compiled from Basden 1921, Ofonagoro 1972, Jones 1958.

Jones (1958:43–54) has demarcated Eastern Nigeria into currency zones. According to him, from 1890 to about 1952, brass rods were the main currency and copper wires the subsidiary money in Calabar and Upper Cross River. Gin and tobacco, which were easily subdivided, were also used as subsidiary currency in the Calabar region. In the Niger Delta, among such Delta States as Bonny, Opobo, and Anang, as well as in southern and eastern Igboland, manillas of five different sizes, shapes, and values were used as the major currency. Cowries were used in these areas as well as in northern and western Igboland; the tiny arrow-shaped iron currency was also used as subsidiary currency. In the Tiv/Idoma areas in the Benue River basin, brass rods, iron rods, and cowries were the medium of exchange (Bohannan 1955). The Aro traveled and traded across existing currency zones. It is therefore not surprising that they used all these currencies, thus making possible exchanges across the zones. They also featured prominently in the management of currencies, particularly in the switch from indigenous multiple-currency systems to the British single currency (1900–1930). Aro connection with various currency zones also lend credence to Afigbo's assertion, in reaction to the demarcation of currency zones by Jones, that "although zones may have existed, each of the currencies was recognized as money in every part of Eastern Nigeria, although one or two might be dominant in one part" (Afigbo 1980:15).

It is clear that by the end of the nineteenth century, Eastern Nigeria had well developed, multiple-currency systems. A variety of currencies were adopted simultaneously or successively. The monetary system was developed with the aid of imported artifacts—shells, metals, and even such silver currencies as the silver dollar (from Brazil, Mexico, Chile, Spain, and the U.S.A.) superimposed on local currencies. The transition from local to modern money economy was thus mediated by several currency forms. From his more than eleven years of firsthand knowledge of Eastern Nigeria, Basden recorded that there was no bartering of commodities (Basden 1921:199).

Values of currencies with different exchange rates varied seasonally, the variation corresponding with seasonality in the production and the volume of trade. Values also depended on the quantity of the imported currencies in circulation, the efforts of the African and European traders to monopolize the trade in their sphere of influence by fixing prices and rates of exchange so as to maximize their profits. The periodic fluctuations in the value of the currencies (Table 6-1) were, however, small by comparative and historical standards. Over the years therefore, people developed enough confidence in the relatively stable currencies as to transact, save, and accumulate stocks of wealth in them. It is however important to note that most currencies had other uses and were often used as raw materials for the manufacture of tools and trinkets.

It is thus feasible to conclude that a monetary system and policy existed in Eastern Nigeria prior to British colonial rule. There were accepted standards of payments for commodities, as well as for social services, across currency zones—payment for consulting the Aro oracle, head-loading or ferrying goods from the hinterland to the coast, paying tolls at the numerous toll gates, bridewealth, and so forth. The huge quantities of manillas and cowries that were collected or abandoned in the storehouses as late as forty eight years into colonial rule are clear indications that various communities in eastern Nigeria had sufficient confidence in the currencies to hoard or invest in them. The high level of confidence in the currencies would explain why the people of eastern Nigeria successfully resisted, until 1952, the coercive legislative measures and sanctions imposed by the British colonial government in their effort to abolish the resilient, centuries-old, "indigenous" currencies.

In addition to being mediums of exchanges, most of the currencies were imported, accumulated, and stored in large quantities: they were often displayed as a sign of prestige (Ofonagoro 1979; Garrard 1980:188–192). The famous architecture of one Chief Mbonu of Ndikelionwu referred to as the "maze" (*Ogbaburuburu*) was, like many others with similarly impressive architecture, designed to protect the cowry/manilla storehouses from being invaded or damaged. Part of the stored wealth was periodically transformed into social capital and personal allegiances (Miller 1988:43, 47; Vansina 1990:251; Guyer 1992:14) in particular, wealth was deployed for bridewealth payment, for financing funerals, title-taking, etc. These payments had cash and in-kind components. The former was modest and often symbolic payment to parents of the bride or to core members of title societies. The cash gifts were considerably smaller than money expended on consumer and personal or household goods for immediate/deferred consumption or circulation to a defined circle of patrikinsmen and kinswomen as well as a narrower circle of matri-kinsmen and kinswomen. The range of goods has become progressively more elaborate and expensive, and now it often includes cars, fridges, bedroom/sitting sets of furniture, and school/college fees for siblings in addition to the more basic and traditional items such as alcoholic beverages, cigarettes, tobacco, wrappers, shoes, soap, salt, and other food items. Obviously, wealth expended on these purchased items surpass the cash gifts, and the total cost varies with the value of the currency and the income level of the central actors. As Guyer (Ch. 5) also notes for the Beti, the circle of those to whom purchased goods were circulated has widened over time to include the bride's brothers and patri-kinsmen, classificatory sisters, and in-married wives. The goods for immediate consumption—meat, food, drinks, tobacco, and cigarettes—serve as medium of public and official announcement and celebration of the marriage (or funeral, title-taking, etc.) transaction by the men and women of the local group. Cash payments may be negotiated and payment spread over time; on the other hand, items for distribution or consumption, though fixed in kind and quantities, have shown the greatest variation in range, cost, and elaboration. They often reflect degrees of affluence, fluctuations in prices, sources, and the nature of income. They have tended to become more elaborate with increase in wages/salaries, income from agricultural earnings, or from petro-dollars. Increase became more noticeable from 1945 onward, when the end of World War II brought the influx of ex-servicemen and their allotment money. It peaked in the 1990s, with fast capital from oil money, the drug trade, and so forth. The process of transferring the goods has also become more elaborate with all-night dances, band music, expensive costumes, and prolonged negotiations and feasting. It is thus obvious that each time the state changed currency or adopted deliberate policies of limiting the currency in circulation, people had to make specific adjustments not only in terms of acquiring, storing, and expending wealth, but also in the process of fulfilling their cultural and social agendas, especially in creating and reproducing social relationships. A picture of how the pattern of acquiring, storing, investing, expending, and transforming money into social relationships changed through the colonial and post-colonial periods, as Nigeria was incorporated into world economic and cultural exchange systems, will emerge from the analysis below of the role of the state in dictating changes in fiscal policies as well as the response to these imposed changes.

Political Determinants of Values: Imposition of
the British Sterling Currency

From about 1900, the British pound sterling, which had been in restricted circulation at the coast since 1880s, began to trickle into the Eastern Nigerian hinterland. The British pound followed the British flag, which moved inland through military expeditions that aimed at subjugating recalcitrant "natives" and at removing all obstacles to "free legitimate trade" in the region. In the process, the British colonial government introduced an all-purpose, single currency, the issue and control of which it monopolized. Although the British currency replaced the existing system and laid the foundation of the contemporary Nigerian national currency, it ran into problems *ab initio*. There seems to have been a deliberate policy of limiting money supply, hence, only very limited quantities of the new currency was in circulation at any given time. This posed problems of cash flow and accessibility to the currency by the users. By 1896, only 60,000 pounds worth of British coins and a few bank notes were in circulation, as compared with trade worth over 522,081 pounds (Ofonagoro 1972:621). Circulation was, by this date, restricted to the coast, where it competed with both traditional and other foreign currencies such as silver and other dollars.

British currency consisted of the Bank of England notes, as well as gold, silver, and copper coins, which were produced by the British mint specifically for use in the colony. In terms of the price levels of the Nigerian market, the gold and silver coins were over-valued. While the highest denomination of the older currencies was worth 2.5 U.S.A. cents, and the lowest about 1/167 cent in 1900, the British coins were worth 20 cents, (the florin or two shillings), 25 cents (half crown), 50 cents (the crown) and $2 (the sovereign). One silver coin was worth 10 cents (1 shilling), while the smallest unit was made from bronze in denominations of 5/12, 1/12, and 1/24 U.S.A. cent, respectively. The aim of the lower denominations was to suit the low price levels of the African market and make the units competitive with and eventually an effective replacement for the indigenous subsidiary currencies, especially the bulky and low-valued cowries.

The high-valued, often scarce gold and silver coins were used, however, at first as restricted currency by traders to pay for revenue to the colonial government. The government used them for paying their employees: laborers, civil servants, and those in the armed forces. Nigerians also melted gold and silver coins to manufacture trinkets.

Between 1902 and 1948, the British colonial government pursued more vigorously the task of delegitimizing and retiring the older multipurpose currencies in eastern Nigeria to make room for the all-purpose, single-currency system. The policies and processes of demonetization were influenced by the colonial government's ambivalence towards African currencies, and their goal of devising the most cost-effective way of introducing British money with minimum inconvenience to British traders and tax payers. There were also mixed reactions from currency users. The traders, Europeans and the Aro, at first ignored the successive legislations. European firms, for instance, realized that their economic survival as traders demanded that they must continue to recognize and use traditional currencies. Besides, they made double profit as they imported, on demand, quantities of cowries, manillas, and brass rods as currencies while imposing barter arrangements on trade with Africans whenever possible. Barter was a creation of the European commercial community import/

export sector and moved inland as European preference advanced. In transactions between Africans and European traders in the local economy, therefore, local currencies continued to be used.

From about 1910 and 1920, therefore, there was a dual monetary system. European firms preferred barter transactions as they exchanged imported goods for the produce of the interior. This increased the opportunity for double profit on both quantity and quality of goods because there was no fixed rate of exchange between British and traditional currencies. African traders naturally preferred their time-tested currencies in all transactions. The colonial administration however, continued to insist on imposing British currencies as the only unit of value and medium of exchange. As the Chronology at the end of this chapter shows, the imposition became more systematic and aggressive between 1920 and 1948.

Delegitimation and Retiring of Indigenous Currencies

Demonetization of the indigenous currencies took place in two stages. The main currencies—manillas and brass rods—were highly devalued and demonetized; at a much later date, the subsidiary currencies, cowries, and so forth were retired. The colonial government at first treated the traditional currencies as barter items, not as currency. It prohibited the barter system, especially in European–African transactions. The government also established a bank through which it extended the use of British currency in Southern Nigeria and banned further importation of "traditional" currencies to force artificial scarcity and to prevent unfair exchange by European traders. Further, the colonial government introduced the British coins, to be controled by the British mint. The West African Currency Board was created in 1912 to replace the British currency and African consumers were expected to accept full liability for the loss of accumulated savings in local currency.

As the Chronology at the end of this chapter shows, periodic currency switches through state legislation or decrees continued beyond the Colonial Era up till 1990. In reaction to the slow rate of acceptance and use of British currency, the colonial government arrived at a compromise and, at first, connived at the continued use of manillas and brass rods in transactions between Africans. It also fixed the rate of exchange between British coins and traditional currencies in African markets in such a way as to limit the extent to which local currencies were legal tender.

However, because British currency under free market conditions could not compete with the time-tested "traditional" currencies in the local economy, the colonial government used its political power to introduce coercive legislations aimed at retiring older currencies and forcing acceptance of British coins as the sole currency to mediate exchange transactions. The Chronology indicates the range of such coercive legislations. These prohibited further importation, use, and circulation of manillas, cowries and brass rods. Each legislation however produced the effect of enhancing, in the short run, the value of locally available stocks of traditional currency, forcing them out into circulation from where they were hoarded—in sacks, hidden in the ground, or in treasury rooms. Although the separation of Gresham's law would dictate that the British currency would be preferred over the local currency because of "at the very least, retaining the value of the metal it is made of" local informants and indigenous logic appear and contradict this classical economic law. It would appear that indigenous currency users at first preferred the long-established values of familiar "indigenous" manilla and cowry currencies with their proven purchasing power. They also preferred the relatively easy access to large quantities of the older currencies, which as a result could be hoarded, so one required only a fraction of the total wealth be used in order to gain social relation and recognition. Moreover, gold, manillas, and cowries, the common currencies, had another established value: counterfeits were easy to detect and losses from fraud impossible because as people could identify the counterfeits. On the other hand, there was a long history of counterfeiting of colonial state–issued currencies, counterfeits that are much more difficult to detect and which cannot be used in other ways. Thus, confidence in the popularity of indigenous currencies as medium of exchange and store of value increased while the value of British currency was at first rejected. As the Chronology shows, it required over fifty years of coercive legislations for the older currencies to be fully retired. The last nail on their coffin was the "operation manilla" of 1948 that enforced collection of the existing stock.

The operation was only a partial success because of the lukewarm cooperation of the local population, resulting from their suspicion and mistrust of handing over accumulated savings to British colonial government officials. It is therefore not surprising that manillas continued to circulate up to 1952, forty one years after they ceased to be legal tender. Traditional currencies thus proved to be resilient despite legislations, economic incentives, and coercive measures aimed at getting Africans to accept British currency.

Reaction to Currency Switches

Africans resisted British coins for several reasons. They were too high in value for the level of monetization and exchange in African markets. They were often in short supply and were thus not as easily accumulated and hoarded in unlimited quantities as cowries and manillas. Africans controled the value and flow of these currencies into the hinterland, which was not true of the new coinage. The lower units of English currency made of bronze pennies were heavy and easily tarnished while cowries were light and never changed their color. European and African traders were also in the habit of counterfeiting currencies or passing on to local producers, a new or polished bronze penny as a florin (i.e., one penny for 24) in purchasing livestock (Ofonagoro 1972:620–630). It should occasion no surprise that time-tested traditional currencies continued to be preferred because they were not easily counterfeited. Also, even when they were too old to be used as currency, they could be used to manufacture ammunition, tools, or ornaments. Only limited quantities of British silver and gold coins, especially new and unused, were accepted and melted down for use as trinkets rather than for payments.

The continued attachment to the centuries old manillas and cowries can also be linked to the level of confusion, distrust, and amazement of the eastern Nigerians at contradictory British policies. Europeans, they argued, had introduced and periodically imported large quantities of manillas to facilitate trade. Generations after the currencies were accepted, and used for the flourishing trade, the British were pushing for them to be retired with the same vigor as they had imported the currency. Many Aro and non-Aro believed that British presence in eastern Nigeria would be short-lived. As Uku (1945:1265) put it, quoting his grandmother, "the British will soon go away, leaving the Aro and the people of eastern Nigeria to manage their affairs as before." In the face of such policy inconsistencies and the wish that the British would soon go away, the level of confidence in the British, their policies, and currency was very low indeed. However, when the British did not go away, the Aro became one of the first groups to switch over to the colonial currency. They capitalized for profit on the diffidence of other groups, quickly replacing their stores of manillas by trading them to non-Aro producers, replacing them with British paper currency, or investing them in purchase or lease of land which was then converted into cash crop plantations. Ultimately the Aro replaced the stores of manilla with other forms of wealth: new British currency and coffee plantations. In this, they facilitated the ultimate acceptance of the colonial currency.

After years of avoiding the British because of the unfounded belief that they would soon go away, the Aro began to respond to the demands of the colonial economy for cash crops. They established plantations of cocoa, rubber, and plantains in several of their colonies. They cashed in on the insistence of the colonial government that British currency be used for exchange transactions and on the reluctance of local producers to accept the new currency, especially the paper currency. The Aro eagerly exchanged for local currencies at half their value, the British coins and bank notes that local producers and traders refused to use. Influenced by the prosperity brought about by their long association with trade, Aro traders also doubled as moneylenders for producers and the emerging class of new traders, who were eager to participate in the increasingly monetized economy. Money was needed as capital to initiate trading ventures; finance the growing number of court litigations; pay tax and school fees; and purchase imported commodities, many of which were needed for marriage and other social payments. The Aro charged exorbitant interests, often up to 80 percent and usually insisted on land as collateral. Because repayment of loans with their high interests often proved impossible within the stipulated time, the Aro were known to have developed the land of their debtors as plantations of cocoa and rubber. The period 1902 to 1940 of the transition to British single, all-purpose currency was marked by increase in tensions resulting from an ever-increasing number of court litigations instituted by families or communities who were eager to retrieve their land and side-track the loans for which they served as collateral.

The story of Omu Okwei, Queen of Osomari (Ekejiuba 1967:633–646), provides an insight into the role of other twentieth-century African factors or commission brokers who augmented the old generation of African traders. The new generation of independent traders or commission brokers exploited the "credit" or barter system of trade between European firms and Africans. Through these, African factors as intermediaries between producers and European firms were issued with "tickets." The tickets were used to collect assorted trade goods, which they sold to the producers in local currency; and then, with the proceeds the factors bought palm oil and kernels, which they sold to European firms either for British currency or for more tickets.

The new generation of independent traders who operated mainly in the urban centers gradually came to rely on British currency for their transactions because it was less bulky, more suited to the new, non-slave-based transportation system and was more readily accepted by the banks. Established from 1910, banks encouraged transactions in the new currency by giving credit facilities to "every native who is able to save a five pound note to import merchandise direct from England and thus flood the town with cargoes" (Stuart-Young 1916:254).

Queen Omu Okwei, like the Aro, was anxious to replace her store of cowries and manillas with the British currency. She thus traded her manillas for paper currency brought by the producers, who were happy to accept half its value in exchange for the older currency. Smith (1921:318), writing about trade in Onitsha, records that the £1 sterling note (20 shillings) was sold freely for 8 and not more than 10 shillings: 1s. silver coin (12 pennies) could be bought for 3 pennies in cowries. Silver and gold coins, which had other practical uses, continued to be preferred to the bank notes; manillas, brass rods, and cowries were preferred to the coins for exchange transactions. Traders such as Omu Okwei invested in importing merchandise directly from overseas or in her trade with British firms. The Aro invested mainly in land, cash crops, and in establishing other businesses.

Acceptance, transactions, and savings in the British-controled West African currency increased phenomenally only at the end of World War II, from 1945 onwards. By this date, the number of African factors or traders who accepted only British money had increased tremendously. Educated Africans working as colonial government servants or functionaries of trading firms received their monthly pay in British currency and thus narrowed the circle in which local currencies were accepted. Syrian firms and the volume of trade they controled had increased. They also preferred British currency in all commercial transactions as this facilitated bank credits and transfers of profits to their home banks. Above all, African war veterans from Burma and India came home from 1945, loaded with British money as "allotment" payment; that is, the accumulated savings from their military service was given to them on discharge. The war veterans increased the colonial currency in circulation thus alleviating the chronic scarcity of the currency, which had been made worse by the depression of the 1930s and the second world war.

The impact of the allotment money on the Eastern Nigerian economy was phenomenal. Prices escalated as commodities, land, and even bridewealth were paid for in British money. Many more European firms became more fully converted to dealing in the British medium of exchange and so started accepting the coins and notes when purchasing produce from African traders and producers. As fewer and fewer people accepted local currencies and available stocks depreciated in value, further depreciation of the African currencies resulted. By 1948, acceptance and use of British-controled currency had become widespread enough to make effective the legal prohibition of manillas and cowries, thus, ending the two parallel currency systems. Steep rises in the price of commodities, and therefore in the quantity of currencies needed to pay for commodities, the artificially induced value depreciation during the "Operation Manilla" of 1948, and the increasingly narrow circle of acceptance created the conditions favorable for the total eclipse of cowries and manillas in favor of the British medium between 1952 and 1954. Stocks buried in sacks, treasury rooms or underground were abandoned as junk. Thus about half a century after "free legitimate" trade was established and eastern Nigeria was incorporated into international capitalism, people, who for centuries had developed expertise for commodity trade, had their stores of wealth and accumulated capital decimated. How did the emerging entrepreneurs deal with the resulting problem of credit and capital accumulation, as well as that of storage and access to wealth for future social payments?

Currency Instability, Storage of Wealth and Capital Formation

Available literature indicates that people of eastern Nigeria devised several strategies to deal with the above problems. Scarcity of capital impeded the entry of the emerging young professional Igbo traders into the increasingly lucrative "free" trade in the first decades of the century. These young traders began by taking loans with very high interest rates from the more established traders like the Aro and non-Aro traders like Omu Okwei. Okwei also lent money to litigants (land litigation became a regular feature of the law courts because land acquired a greater economic value than before). Her interest rates ranged from 60 to 100 percent. Farmers often pledged their land until they had completely paid the loan. So high were her interest rates that her clients often preferred taking her to court to paying the interest. Okwei also lent money to young traders or acted as the guarantor for retailers and litigants. The new class of traders with very limited capital thus gained from Okwei's loan facilities.

As the class of traders swelled in numbers and as the volume of their transactions increased, they also evolved a new system of capital accumulation that has survived till this day. This was a kind of the "people's bank," and involved voluntary but daily savings from one's daily takings from the market. A trusted "local banker" went round each day to collect, from each person willing to participate, whatever sum she wanted to save for the day. In contemporary times, this sum is recorded in the trader's "pass book" as well as in the records of the local "banker." The accumulated savings can be withdrawn by the depositor as capital to increase her volume of trade; it can also be lent to other participating traders in need of capital, at interest rates much more modest than those charged by the bank or big-time trader/money lenders. The accumulated interest is shared by all participating traders, the share being proportional to one's contributions. The daily banking through trusted bankers not only facilitated capital accumulation but avoided the time-consuming, highly bureaucratized, impersonal banking system. It reduced the tension caused by the high interest rates and the coercive, brutal method of debt recovery of "professional" money lenders. It provided a regular banking system for people who could hardly read and who therefore did not have the skill, contacts, or time to operate regular banks. It gave loans with no elaborate collateral and provided saving and capital-pooling services where there were few banks, many of which were not accessible to prospective bankers. The system is widely used today not only by traders but also by various artisans—carpenters, motor mechanics, and so forth. Only occasionally did the "collector/banker" prove to be unreliable enough to abscond with the accumulated savings, as was reported in the daily newspaper *Concord*, in August 1991. In this report, the first to be published in several years, a "banker in Lagos absconded to an unknown destination with over N40,000 savings from various depositors. The savings per depositor ranged from N1,000 to N2,000" (*Concord*, August 18, 1991, page 2).

The absence of any banking system in its modern form, (given the numerous and logistical problems of modern banking) as well as the multiple currency zones in the pre-colonial era gave rise to multiple and individualized forms of storage of wealth. In the pre-colonial era, individuals aggregated human dependents and followers: wives, children, and slaves. In addition, material wealth was stored in various forms. Ofonagoro (1979:630–635) records that storerooms existed in many Igbo compounds for manillas and cowries. The stores were either separate from or part of the main dwelling-houses. Several Aro and Delta State compounds also stored brass rods and manillas in special rooms, both in the main communities and in their settlement/ market centers. (Ekejiuba 1972:12–16). One of the many functions of special porters and slaves was to transport bags or baskets of these currencies from one transaction arena to the other. Many long-distance traders accumulated and stored several types of currencies to be transported and used in and across different currency zones.

Wealth was also stored during this period in the form of various trade commodities: slaves, coral beads (*nkalari* or *aka*), ivory (*odu*) and gold trinkets; locally handwoven *akwete* cloth, imported India Madras (*jioji*), cloth pieces of six to eight yards, which eventually became the "national" attire for the Igbo, Ijaw, Itsekiri, Uhrobo Ibibio, and Efiks. The imported six-to-eight yard cloths, known as the Dutch hollandais (or wax print from Holland) or *abada* in the Igbo vernacular, were also in great demand as part of marriage payments. *Jioji* was also a very important part of the repertoire for funeral payments. In addition to these luxury items, pewter pots, brass, silver, and enamel basins as well as agricultural produce such as yams were important as stores of wealth (Ekejiuba 1967, 1972; Njoku 1990). Just as currencies, brass rods, wires, and manillas can be converted into raw material for the manufacture of trinkets, tools, and other commodities for sale, the commodities that served as stores of wealth can be lent, leased, pawned, exchanged, or sold for cash. They can also be used for social payments for funeral, marriage, and other social transactions. In place of flower wreaths, mourners were given two, four, six, or eight yards of *jioji* cloth by in-laws, and other well wishers. These were used for building canopies for the dead to lie in state. The canopy was left on display for up to forty days after the burial. Mourners were expected to reciprocate the gift of *jioji* and livestock donated by sympathizers on similar occasions. *Abada*, *jioji*, gold, brass, ivory, and coral trinkets were also part of the assortment of gifts by grooms to their future brides, mothers, and sisters-in-law. *Abada* and *jioji*, imported fabrics, replaced local handwoven cloth *okwelike* and *akwete* for marriage payments.

Apart from slaves, which are no longer held, wealth is still stored in contemporary times, through the commodities enumerated above. Gold bullion and diamonds (stored both at home and in banks) have been added to the variety of commodities for storing wealth. Such natural resources as land, plantations of fruit trees (especially the oil palm and raphia palm trees, cocoa, and even cassava) are readily used to improve cash liquidity in times of need by either outright sale or through pawning, leasing, or direct exchange. These holdings can be inherited.

Initiation into title and secret societies such as the *ekpe* and *ozo*, as well as rotating credit societies (*esusu*), are also other forms through which wealth is stored and accessed for future use. As Okonjo (1979) and others have fully documented, old initiates regularly shared the entrance fees of new members; contributors take turns in using the total takings of contributing members in rotating credit associations. Marriage payments were often used to finance marriage of brothers of the bride or used as capital for their training or trading ventures. Investing in social relationships through social payments was thus a significant store of wealth for future use.

Through various forms of social payments, through a system of apprenticeship, or through direct lending, people also transformed wealth into multiple obligations and social credits to be reciprocated at the appropriate time. For instance, a family who donates a six-yard piece of *jioji* or a cow at the funeral of an in-law or family friend, expects the gift to be reciprocated exactly at the appropriate time. Because the actual cash value of the commodity is likely to have changed over time, the original donor gains. A cow donated at a funeral in 1981 at the cost of 600 *naira*, is expected to be reciprocated in 1992 during a similar occasion even though the price of a cow of similar size and sex may have appreciated to 7,500 *naira* (i.e., twelve and half times). A gift of 600 *naira* in 1992 is not regarded as an equivalent of the cow, neither is the gift of 20 *naira* , the cost of a six-yard piece of *jioji* in 1981 accepted as the equivalent of the cloth, which may cost up to 1,000 *naira* in 1992.

Converting commodities into cash was a particularly useful way of dealing with, for instance, the highly unstable (in value) and limited circulation (temporally and geographically) of the Biafran currency used in most parts of Igbo land and other eastern Nigerian communities during the Nigerian civil war. Biafran leaders had rather hurriedly issued Biafran currency to avert total economic strangulation when it became clear to them that Nigeria was withdrawing its old currency and issuing a completely different one in its effort to ensure the success of its economic sanctions as a weapon of war against Biafra. Because the Biafran currency was regularly in very short supply, and price of essential commodities (usually imported) very high, people survived by turning into the much needed cash, their accumulated stocks of cloth—*jioji*, (India Madras), *abada*, locally handwoven cloth, and especially the very expensive *akwete* cloth. Gold, coral, and ivory trinkets, and even imported goods such as bicycles, sewing machines, cars, and radios were also sold, either in the Biafran markets, or in markets located behind "enemy lines" (Nigeria) to raise money with which to purchase food and goods for resale to the economically strapped Biafrans. Today, many Nigerians beat the inflation and hardships imposed by the limited circulation of Nigerian low-value *naira* by smuggling such commodities as petroleum products, livestock, cocoa, and even stolen cars across the Nigerian borders in an attempt to access foreign currency to finance international trade and transactions.

The past eight years have witnessed an increase in rather innovative but illegal modes of fast access to capital as a way of reducing the constraints of extreme currency instability. The periodic reports in the media of embezzlement, smuggling, and of massive importation of counterfeited money challenge state monopoly of the mint and its ban on importation of various commodities. These illegal modes can also be interpreted as a protest against the increasingly difficult access of the younger generation of businessmen to legitimate sources of capital or credit, a reaction to runaway inflation that has skyrocketed the cost of living while decimating job opportunities. Other forms of illegal access to capital in the past five years include the hard drug trade, the infamous "419,"[1] that is, fraudulently obtaining an advance contract fee with no intention of executing the contract; "OBT,"[2] defrauding people of small or huge sums of money by false pretenses; and car snatching and armed robbery of passenger buses along the highway. These combine with other well known forms of "white collar" crimes, such as inflating contract fees, insisting on taking 10 to 30 percent of the value of contracts and purchases and embezzlement, to create a false impression of unprecedented economic boom despite the tight access to legal sources of credit and cash flow problems experienced by most Nigerians.

These sources of capital have increased the number of "millionaires," whose wealth is often conspicuously displayed on occasions for social payments, such as title-taking, funerals, and marriage. In addition to inflating the quantities of various categories of goods for social payments, these *noveaux riches* "spray" higher denominations of both local and foreign currencies on key actors (such as brides and chief mourners). Expensive souvenirs imprinted with the donor's photographs and names are given to all guests. It is mainly the *nouveaux riches* who have established or invested in the biggest industry of the past decade—merchant banks and finance houses—through which the money is laundered, stored, and legally circulated. Huge sums of money are also invested in importing flashy, expensive luxury cars; in building huge homes (often euphemistically referred to as "white houses"); and above all, in social relations through generous donations, especially during the numerous "launchings" of development projects at local and national levels, as a way of increasing one's status and social acceptability.[3]

The Impact of Multiple-Currency System and Value Instability on Social Payments

In the face of the multiplicity of currencies, periodic loss of stores of wealth, and fluctuations in the value and quantity of money in circulation, it is hardly surprising that commodity production, social life, and social payments were only partially monetized, despite the impressively long history of currency use in Eastern Nigeria. Even factors of production—land, labor, and tools—became increasingly monetized only after the introduction by the British of a uniformly and widely accepted currency system in the process of incorporating the Nigerian market into the world capitalist exchange system. Consequently, up till 1954 and even to date, social payments for marriage, funeral, title-taking, and political prestation were made both in-kind and in cash. The combined payment in cash and in-kind can also be seen as a strategy for ensuring continuity in social payments and the related social relationships in the face of wide variations and value fluctuations in the media of monetary exchange.

Marriage Payments

This is the commonest form of social payments, central to various social institutions and the kinship system, and thus important, for reproducing social and ideological systems. Agriculture and even trade were supported by the marriage system, which favored polygyny, because many farmers and traders depended on the labor of their wives, adult children, and sons-in-law.

Although the debate in the anthropological literature on the functions and morality of marriage payments in Africa has not abated, and although there are significant regional variations, one can safely assert that marriage payments, in recognition of the nature and significance of marriage, consist mainly of reciprocal exchange of goods and services: only a small fraction, often a symbolic part of the payment, is made in cash. Focus in academic debates has been more on this fraction of the payment than on the much more elaborate reciprocal exchange of visits, goods, and services between the families of the groom and the bride.

These reciprocal exchanges initiate an alliance and exchange that are characteristic of not only marriage relationships, but of those between individuals, families, villages, and even towns. Unilateral payment of some money (bridewealth) was made as symbolic compensation for the transfer of sexual and other services of the bride from her family to that of the groom. These payments also legitimized the marriage and defined the membership of the off-spring in the patrilineage of the groom. It is noteworthy that commodities which had to be accumulated for marriage payment remained the same even after more advanced and uniform monetary units had been adopted for commercial exchanges. We indicate the various exchanges and payments with illustrations from the Aro group, among whom economic exchanges long had been monetized. Some variations exist in Igboland, especially in the actual amount of cash payment.

Among the Aro, marriage payments and related reciprocal exchanges are made during several stages of the marriage process. They are preceded by lobbying, through visits and presents to key relatives of the prospective bride, by the groom and his family who negotiate through a neutral party (*onye akpa* or *aka ibe*). This go-between oversees the long negotiations to ensure cooperation and minimize conflicts or disappointment throughout the period of negotiation (Okoroafor 1986:289–304). The stages and payments are indicated in Table 6-2.

TABLE 6-2   Marriage Payments in Arochukwu

Stage	Payments
1. Knocking at the door (*iku aka*). Introductory appointment to introduce the topic.	1 bottle of schnapps, given to the father of the prospective bride. Schnapps were extensively used as trade currency until the 1930s.
2. Exploratory visit to obtain permission to initiate negotiation.	4 kola nuts (kola accuminata) 1 bottle of schnapps 1 gallon of palm wine (to be shared by the bride's family and the negotiating team.)
3. Initial Enquires (*ajugu na ububo*) to obtain girl's consent in public.	4 kola nuts 1 bottle of schnapps (to the father, for "treasure" spotted) 1 bottle of schnapps (to be shared by the family, to obtain permission to initiate discussing the "treasure" 2 gallons of palm wine 1 bottle of whisky 1 leg of dried bush meat or goat, 1 forearm of dried bush meat or goat (These four items are to be shared and consumed by the bride's family and negotiating team while the enquires on the "treasure" are going on.) 2 more bottles of schnapps (for general negotiations).
4. Wine Carrying (*ibu mmai*), the traditional marriage ceremony	**A. Gifts of the bride's family to the groom's:** 4 kola nuts 4 gallons of palm wine cooked food (with at least one goat)

TABLE 6-2 Marriage Payments in Arochukwu *Cont'd.*

Stage	Payments
	B. Gifts of the groom's family to the bride's:

(i) 8 kola nuts
24 gallons of palm wine
2 bottles of schnapps

(ii) 6 yards of India Madras cloth
jumper/blouse
hat
3 yards for head scarf
walking stick
shoes (for each parent of the bride)

(iii) For the bride-to-be (after her initial visit to the groom's family, following her public consent) (*nkuru*)
1 bag of salt
1 bag of rice
bars or carton of washing soap
bath soap, powder, pomade, bucket, trinkets, bath towel.
dried fish
corned beef
decorated mats

(iv) For the members of the male patrilineage:
24 gallons of palm wine
packets of cigarettes, size specified
1 bottle of snuff
2 heads of tobacco and natron

(v) for the female relatives:
6 gallons of palm wine
bars of soap (1 carton of 12 bars)
1 bag of salt
1 bag of rice
1 can of groundnut oil
5 big yams
1 big stick of dried fish
6 yards of India Madras cloth (for each of the closest relatives only)

The bride-to-be gives her consent to the marriage proposal and authorizes negotiations by sipping a cup of palm wine and handing the rest to her suitor.

(vi) Bridewealth
Though arrived at after prolonged but humorous negotiation, bridewealth is still officially pegged at Arochukwu for N25.20 (*okwa [akpa] isii*), six bags (see Table 6-4).

TABLE 6-2   Marriage Payments in Arochukwu *Cont'd.*

Stage	Payments
	only official payment in cash, on which many families insist (N30.00 at Onitsha, another long-standing commercial community), but in many other parts of Igboland families have adjusted the bridewealth to reflect currency types and fluctuations. This has introduced instability and the phenomenon of "high bride price" in marriage payments that is the subject of media protests and legislation at the state and local level.
	(vii) The various payments are followed by periodic gifts of food items—yams and fish— to the bride's mother; and tobacco, cigarettes and palm wine to the father, especially during festivals.
5. Final Ceremony (*Nkuru*)	1 gallon of palm wine 8 kola nuts 6 yards of India Madras cloth (*jioji*), tobe draped on the bride as she crosses the threshold of her new home.

These gifts are essential for obtaining permission to transfer the bride finally to the groom's home.

At the existing rates of exchange, marriage payments in cash and kind at Arochukwu added up to £2 sterling in 1900; £10 sterling in 1930; £40 in 1945; £300 in 1960, £1,000 in 1980, and about £5,000 in 1990, of which only a small fraction (N25.20 or $3.00 in 1990) was paid in cash. Up till the end of World War II, the cash payment continued to be made in the traditional currency, until the allotment of veterans popularized British West African currency for such payments.

It is important to stress the reciprocal nature of marriage payments. A substantial part of the bridewealth is returned to the bride by her family in the form of valuable household furniture for starting the new home. In recent times, this furniture has included deep freezers, refrigerators, gas/electric stoves, and even cars and houses, especially among the very rich. It is also necessary to view the cash payment as symbolic of the husband's ability to accumulate wealth and play an instrumental role in the family. Although these payments confer rights *in uxorem,* that is, rights in the woman as a wife, including access to her labor and sexual services, the bride's kingroup retains the rights to monitor the welfare of their daughter including taking her back in the event of repeated abuse, after a divorce, or even after death (a woman's corpse often is claimed, to be buried among her kinsmen). Although Arochukwu and Onitsha communities had succeeded in pegging the actual cash payment to a token 25 or 30 *naira* , many other eastern Nigerian communities constantly adjust the payment to the current cost of commodities and value of currency. In parts of Idoma (Benue), cash payments in 1973 were as high as N1,800 (*New Nigeria*, September 3, 1973), while among the central Igbo (Mbaise) the scandalously high cash payment of N5,000 was in vogue. Between 1960 and 1982, excessively high marriage payments discouraged many young men from contracting marriages and this resulted in a glut of marriage-able young girls. This situation prompted many local communities and state legisla-tures to peg cash payments at N60[4]; a few communities were more realistic in pegging *all expenses*, including cash payments at N1,000 (*Concord*, October 14, 1987).

Other Social Payments: Funerals, Homage and Title-taking:

As is the case for marriage payments, payments for funerals, advances in politico-ritual or social hierarchies, and political payments in the form of either tax, tributes, or homage to social superiors in a patron–client system are still made both in cash and kind. The 1956 Aro native law and custom in Ndizuogu, one of the biggest of the Aro colonies, apart from Arochukwu, stipulated that homage must be paid to any senior person in a family, village, or clan by dependents (patron–client system) or jun-ior persons; that homage should be paid by all persons to the chief on various occasions—the annual Ikeji festival, at funerals, when a daughter is married, before the sod is turned for building a home, and during other major festivals. Homage is paid with the following goods:

1. The ribbed part of a slaughtered goat (cow for burials)
2. 8 large yams
3. 1 gallon of palm wine
4. 4 kola nuts
5. £3 sterling (which now translates into six *naira* or 3 dollars in 1984 or 60 cents according to 1991 exchange rate)

Homage is also paid during the annual Ikeji festival, during first and second burials (during the anniversary of death) of a deceased who is a client of a patron or a chief: the death of such a person is announced and the patron is invited to be at the funeral only after homage has been paid. Payment is completed through the prescribed cash equivalent of £3 sterling ($6) for the most senior, half of this amount for the next in rank, and one quarter for the third in rank.

Social payments to a deceased father's patrilineage and the mother's patrilin-eage or to a deceased wife's patrilineage are similarly made with subsistence consum-able items. These consist of at least the following:

1. 4 kola nuts
2. 1 cow (or at least a goat) to be slaughtered and shared
3. 24 gallons of palm wine, two cartons of beer and 1 bottle of schnapps, gin or whisky
4. 1 bag of rice
5. Processed cassava (both the dried tapioca and the fermented cassava used for foofoo)
6. Dried fish

Similarly, a combination of payment in kind and cash also characterizes entrance fees for title-taking and initiation into social clubs and secret societies. Payment in kind demonstrates the ability to successfully accumulate money through transient economic transactions and to translate the currency or wealth into social prestige, influence, and honor through social transactions essential for "the reproduction and maintenance of long term social and ideological systems concerned with enduring social order that transcended the individual" (Parry and Bloch 1991:18). Both consumable goods and the cash payments are shared by old members. Initiation into title and secret societies was additionally a form of capital pooling and investment; an old-age mutual insurance, and a source of future capital and payments for marriage and initiation. Title-taking thus provided opportunity to save and earn prestige (Uchendu 1965:82).

During a recent initiation ceremony into a club of titled women (*Nze Nwanyi* or club of women chiefs), a young female initiate and civil servant provided the items listed below as part of the initiation fee to the club in her village of marriage.

Items	Approximate Value in Naira (July 1991)
1. 100 cash	100
2. 100 kola nuts	300
3. 100 coconuts	300
4. 100 big yam tubers	800
5. 50 medium sized smoked fish	750
6. 10 goats	3,000
7. 1 cow	6,000
8. 4 crates of soft drink	96
9. 20 gallons of palm wine	300
10. 4 bottles of alcoholic beverage	320

Total cost is approximately N11,960, of which only N100 (i.e., approximately 1/119) is cash payment. The above items were shared by the twenty nine initiated members of the club. In addition, they were entertained with dances, expensive band music, and the following cooked food items:

1. 1 big basin of yam porridge
2. 1 big basin of jollof rice
3. 1 big basin of cassava/yam foofoo, with very rich sauce
4. 1 goat, slaughtered and stewed
5. 50 moderate-sized (1 kg) roasted chickens

The cash payment of one hundred naira, less than half percent of the total payments, has remained constant over the years: so have the various categories of the payment in kind. It is also clear that over the years, components of payment in kind to ritual specialists, native doctors, for advancement in title-secret societies or in political-ritual hierarchies have remained the same despite changes in the value of currency and the escalating costs of such transactions. Stability of the categories of payment ensures conceptual and ideological stability in the reproduction of long-term social order and social relationships.

Discussion and Conclusion

An impression is thus created of relative conceptual stability as many units of accounting for modern currency (e.g., bag-*akpa*, 400-*onu*, bundle, and *afai*) have been carried over from the cowrie/manilla lexicon. Basic commodities for personal use and distribution to groups remain the same over the years, thus giving a false impression of relative stability in social payments despite wide fluctuations in forms and values of currencies. As Guyer (Ch. 5) notes, old values, categories, institutions, and cognition frameworks were not abandoned, but rather reworked, elaborated, and transformed. The conceptual stability veiled price changes. However, because the cost of these items has spiralled through the years, the actual value of these social payments has been correspondingly on the increase (see Table 6-3). The unchanging nature of the categories of in-kind payment should therefore not be confused with the great elasticity of the contents.

In addition to these continuities, many aspects of social attitudes to official currency, which can be traced back to the period of transition from traditional to British currency, persist in contemporary times. Only a sketch of the parallels can be made here. Details will be complete only after more exhaustive research has been made. As Table 6-4 indicates, the system (decimal) and idiom of counting in multiples of four and ten have persisted. The practice of accumulating and melting down metal currencies for use as trinkets (manillas, copper wires, gold, and silver coins) seems to have continued through the present day. The *Concord* (October 25, 1991; May 15, 1992) reports that the practice has spread into the Republic of Cameroon. Hoarding and storage at home of currency (local and international dollars, pound sterling, yen, Deutschmarks, etc.) appears to be part of the socio-cultural context of the changing monetary system. Distrust and low respect for banks and currency are also indicated by the high rate of mutilation of the currency in circulation, as well as by the quest for newly minted currency. These issues have been of major concern to the Central Bank and the subject of organized campaigns through various media. Finally, in spite of the near complete monetization of many aspects of social life, commodity production, and exchange, social payments continue to be made mainly in kind. Units, number, symbolism, and vocabularies of accounting mirror those of the lexicon of traditional currencies.

The discussions above clearly indicate that evolution of the Nigerian monetary system, with its eight currency switches from 1890 to 1990, has been characterized by wide value fluctuations and artificial currency restrictions. Devaluation and periodic demonetization or decimation of stores of wealth in existing currencies have brought about economic instability and financial hardship as old accumulations are abandoned or exchanged at arbitrarily fixed uneconomic rates that render the stocks worthless. Consequently, the development of the Nigerian monetary system has engendered low confidence in the official, single medium of exchange that replaced the multiple-currency system, which was controled for so long by its users. As the British imposed the single-currency system on the traditional currencies, and as all aspects of production and exchange became monetized, prices spiralled and inflation became endemic. This resulted in the rejection of the official media (1900–1940s), in the tendency to fall back on traditional currencies either in real terms (1900–1952) or symbolically by using the concepts and number symbolism to calculate the new currency. Often the ambivalent attitude to the official currency has led many currency

TABLE 6-3 Currency Instability and Social Payments: The Changing Cost of One Unit of Selected Items of Payment, 1890–1991

Year	Cash Components of Marriage Payment (Arochukwu or Onitsha)	Cow	Goat	Chicken	Wine (1 gallon)	Kola nut	Cash Payment for Initiation into the Highest Ekpe Gade
1900			6 1/4d or 5 bags (6,000) cowries	1/4d or 240 cowries	1/16d or 60 cowries (10 isiego)	1 isiego or 6 cowries 1/28d	41 boxes of brass rods (= £100.00; 1 box = £2.10)
1920	30 bags of cowries	£5	£1.10/-	540 cowries	1/4d or 240 cowries	2 isiego or 12 cowries 1/14d	41 boxes of brass rods (= £100)
1945	30 bags of cowries	£10	£2.00	9d or 8,100 cowries	6d	8 isiego or 1/2d or 45 cowries	£100
1973	£30 (Onitsha)	£20 or N100	£4.0	5 sh	1sh	6d	£100 or N200
1981	N30.00 (Onitsha) N.25.20 (Arochukwu)	N500	N45	N5	10sh or N1	50k or 5sh	£100 or N200
1985	N30.00 (Onitsha) N.25.20 (Arochukwu)	N700	N80	N7	50sh/pr N5	N1 or 10sh	£250 or N500
1987	N30.00 (Onitsha) N.25.20 (Arochukwu)	N800	N90	N15	60sh or N6	N1 or 10sh	£250 or N500
1990	N30.00 (Onitsha) N.25.20 (Arochukwu)	N2,000	N200	N45	100sh or N10	N3	N1,000
1991	N30.00 (Onitsha) N.25.20 (Arochukwu)	N5,000	N350	N80	250sh or N25	N4	N1,000
1994	N.30.00 (Onitsha) N.25.20 (Arochukwu)	N12,000	N2,200	N240	N120	N5	N20,000

TABLE 6-4   Igbo Cowrie Arithmetic

Isiego*	Ukwu	Cowries	Ogudo	Akap	Nnu
10	1	60	(Ego Iri)		
10	2	120	(Ogu ego)		
30	3	180			
40	4	240			
50	5	300			
60	6	360			
70	7	420			
80	8	480			
90	9	540			
100	10	600	1		
200	20	1,200	2	1	
400	40	2,400	4	2	1
800	80	4,800	8	4	2
1,200	120	7,200	12	6	3
1,600	160	9,600	16	8	4

*One *Isiego* (also called *ibego;* or in the Onitsha dialect, *ekpiti*) is equivalent to 6 single cowry shells (*nkpulu*).

Note: These concepts and equivalences have consistently been taken from the cowry system and applied to other currency systems in Igboland. For example, *isiego* is also used to denote one shilling and ten kobo, the basic units of, respectively, the pound and the *naira*. *Oguego*, i.e., 20 units of *isiego*, is equivalent to one pound or two *naira*. In spite of currency, value and price changes, there has been remarkable conceptual stability in the monetary system.

users to resort to saving/capital accumulation and investments in foreign currency either in their homes or in foreign banks. The foreign currency is perceived as having stronger and more stable value in addition to its wider circulation and stronger purchasing power both within and outside the country. The Nigerian government legitimized this perception when, in 1987, it authorized the opportunity to open domiciliary accounts in Nigerian banks. These could be operated in foreign currency. It also authorized private exchange bureaus. All this was done to stem the flight of capital to European finance capitals.

Endemic instability of the consistently weak national currency has worsened in spite of the above fiscal policies. The current instability, which exists even in the face of Nigeria's petroleum oil wealth, is associated with excessive dependence on oil to the neglect of agriculture and other aspects of the economy, the structural malfunctioning of the national economy, its weak tax base and heavy government spending (especially on social services), and the aftermath of the Nigerian civil war and the current structural adjustment programs imposed by the International Monetary Fund (IMF), which ostensibly seek to redress the structural imbalance. The widely fluctuating value of the *naira* continues to generate low confidence in the currency and seem to encourage recourse to illegal modes of fast access to capital, which in turn further weakens the *naira* .

Changes and value instability in currency have posed numerous problems for users and for the developing Nigerian economy. These problems notwithstanding,

Nigerians regularly, and increasingly flamboyantly, invest some of their savings, and sometimes loans, in creating, strengthening, and maintaining the social relationships from which they hope to derive social, political, economic, and psychological support. A partial, culturally specific, solution to some of the problems posed by the multiple and fluctuating currencies would be a formula for social payments that combines payment in cash and in-kind, the categories of which have remained the same in the last century even though the actual cost in *naira* continues to escalate as its value against the dollar plummets (since most of the categories of payment in kind are now imported from overseas). Clearly, as Guyer (Ch. 5) notes in her study of the Beti, the composition, priorities, and frequencies of social payments were reworked and most often elaborated as prices fluctuated and sources of wealth widened. The relationship between currency instability and social payment was therefore a dynamic characterized, as Guyer argues, by a combination of stability, flexibility, and innovation.

APPENDIX   Chronology of Political Determinant of Values, 1900–1991: Demonetization and Currency Switches through Legislations and Relevant Proclamations

1902   Native Currency Proclamation
Traditional currencies cease to be recognized as legal tender.

1904   Importation of cowries prohibition
Ban on further importation of cowries. Value of cowries appreciates as hoarded cowries circulate.

1906   Nigerian Coinage Ordinance
Ordinance provides for the minting of subsidiary aluminum coins (1d, 1/2d, 1/4d) by the British mint, to supplement imported gold sovereigns (20 shillings) and florins (2 shillings).

1908   Amendment of the 1906 coinage ordinance to replace the aluminum 1d (*anini*) with a nickel bronze coin, because the former was too light and easily lost (1 nickel = 9 to 18 cowries).

1911   Native Currency Proclamation
Manillas cease to be legal tender.

1912   Creation of the West African Currency Board
Board is charged with producing special West African currency (in pounds and shillings).

1919   Prohibition of transactions in manillas by non-Africans.

1935   Nigerian legislative council debates the manilla problem. Native councils are created and used as agents for fixing rates of exchange of traditional currencies.

1948   Nigerian Legislative Council authorizes the withdrawal of manillas from circulation, followed by "Operation Manilla" (1948–49), during which Treasury Department functionaries systematically collected and redeemed manillas at 1/2d each. Thirty two million manillas are recovered at the cost of £153,000 sterling and exported as metal.

1961   West African Currency Board is abolished.
Nigerian national currency (the pound) is established as separate from that of other West African anglophone countries.

1968   The color, graphic design, and units of the Nigerian pound changes as part of the effort by the Nigerians to win the civil war. Biafran monetary system (pounds and shillings) established.

1970   The Federal Military Government decrees that Biafran pounds cease to be legal tender. Each bank depositor is to receive only 20 Nigerian pounds, then worth about $30.00, in exchange, irrespective of the number of Biafran pounds held. The resulting collapse of the Biafran currency results in the loss of accumulated savings by many depositors. It also creates problems in capital accumulation and in access to business capital.

1973   As a result of a decree by the Federal Military Government, a decimal currency replaces the former Nigerian pounds. New units, color, graphic designs, and values are introduced. Many depositors/hoarders lose about 20 percent of their money as gratification payments to bank officials or middlemen, in order to ensure that they meet the deadline for deposits and exchanges of old for new currency.

1984   Federal Military Government decrees that the entire paper currency of all denominations be replaced with new units, color, and graphic designs, in order to forestall further massive counterfeiting, importation of counterfeited currency, and large-scale hoarding, all of which had depleted both the circulating money supply and and the holdings in legal banks. As in 1973, many depositors are willing to pay as much as 20 percent of their total holdings to middlemen or bank officials to ensure that they complete the transaction of deposit/exchange before the one-week deadline.

1987   The *naira* is floated against the dollar.

1990   Federal Military Government decrees that the one *naira* and fifty *kobo* paper currency be replaced with coins. New ten, one, and twenty five *kobo* coins are introduced. To ensure easier access to the scarce coins, many users in remote and rural areas exchange their bills for only 75 to 80 percent of their value in coins.

1991   New 50-*naira* bill is introduced.

1992   In March, the value of *naira* , which has been floating against the dollar, is devalued from 9.75 to 18.75 *naira* to the dollar.

Note: The impact of the legislation outlined here can be seen not only in the changes in the exchange values in traditional currencies (see Table 1), but also in the low level of confidence in the currency discussed in this chapter and in the changing value of the *naira* against the dollar since 1987.

1986	$1 = N0.75
Aug 1987	$1 = N3.00
Aug 1989	$1 = N7.90
Aug 1991	$1 = N10.80
Mar 1992	$1 = N18.70
May 1993	$1 = N34.60

Notes

1. "419" refers to the exploitation, with a view to accumulating capital, of Section 419 of an act of Parliament which stipulates that at least 10 percent of the value o f a contract be advanced to a contractor, to enable him to mobilize material and labor to execute a project. There has been an increase, in recent times, of the number of contractors who deliberately negotiate a contract with a view to collecting the mobi lization fee without embarking on the project. The term "419" refers more to this class of contractors than to those who, for one reason or another, fail to complete the project.
2. "OBT" is short for obtaining money, property or information by impersonating (a poli ce officer, army or government personnel, or a friend or relative) or through any other dubious means. Like "419," it is a "peaceful" means of extorting large sums of money from another person.
3. Many middle-class professionals, such as medical doctors, nu rses, university professors, and engineers now see "migrant labor" as their only chance of earning money legally to supplement their meager income in Nigeria. Consequently, many contract to work for six to twenty months at a time in Saudi Arabia, Kuwait, Britain, the U.S.A, or Canada. Those who can also contract their services to either the national government or to international agencies such as the United Nations.
4. Laws of Eastern Nigeria, vol. IV, 1963 Section 3.

Sources

Legal Records

Laws of Eastern Nigeria, Vol. IV, 1963, Section 3.

Newspapers

Concord
New Nigerian
West Africa

Books, Dissertations, and Articles

Afigbo, A. E. 1980. "Economic Foundations of Pre-Colonial Igbo Society." In *Topics in Nigerian Economic and Social History*, ed. Afigbo, A. E. 1-24. Ile-Ife: Univer sity of Ife Press Ltd.

Alagoa, E. J. 1970. "Long Distance Trade and States in the Niger Delta." *Journal of African History*, vol. 11:319–29.

Basden, G. T. 1921. *Among the Ibos of Nigeria*. Philadelphia and London: J. B. Lippincott Co. and Seeley, Service and Co.

Bohannan Paul. 1955. "Some Principles of Exchange and Investment among the Tiv." *American Anthropologist*, 57:60–69.

Dike, Azuka. 1985. *Resilience in Igbo Culture*. Enugu: Fourth Dimension.

Dike, K. O. 1956. *Trade and Politics in the Niger Delta, 1830–1885*. Oxford: Clarendon Press.

Dike, K. O. and Ekejiuba, F. 1990. *The Aro of South Eastern Nigeria*. Ibadan: University Press PLC.

Ekeghe, O. O. 1956. *A Short History of Abiriba*. Aba.

Ekejiuba, F. 1967. "Omu Okwei, the Merchant Queen of Ossomari: A Biographical

Sketch." *Journal of the Historical Society of Nigeria*, 3:633–52.
———. 1972. "Aro Trade in the Nineteenth Century." *Ikenga*, 1:11–32.
Forde, Cyril Daryll, ed. 1956. *Efik Traders of Old Calabar . . . With an Ethnographic Sketch and Notes, by D. Simmons, and an Essay on the Political Organisation of Old Calabar, by G. I. Jones*. London and New York: Oxford University Press for the International African Institute.
Garrard, Timothy F. 1980. *Akan Weights and the Gold Trade*. London: Longman.
Guyer, Jane. 1992. "Representation without Taxation: An Essay on Democracy in Rural Nigeria, 1952–1990." *African Studies Review*, 35:41–79.
Hopkins, A. G. 1966. "The Currency Revolution in South-West Nigeria in the Late Nineteenth Century." *Journal of the Historical Society of Nigeria*, 3:471–83.
Jones, G. I. 1958. "Native and Trade Currencies in Nigeria during the 19th and 20th Century" *Africa*, 28:43–53.
Latham, A. J. H. 1971. "Currency, Credit and Capitalism in the Cross River in the Pre-Colonial Era." *Journal of African History*, vol. 7 no. 3:599–605.
———. 1973. *Old Calabar 1600–1891: The Impact of the International Economy upon a Traditional Society*. Oxford: Clarendon Press.
Miller, Joseph. 1988. *Way of Death: Merchant Capitalism and the Angolan Slave Trade, 1730–1830*. Madison, WI: University of Wisconsin Press.
Neaher, Nancy C. 1979. "Awka Who Travel: Itinerant Metalsmiths of Southern Nigeria," *Africa*, 49, 253–366.
Njoku, John E. E. 1990. *The Igbos of Nigeria: Ancient Rites, Changes, and Survival*. Lewiston, NY: E. Mellen Press.
Northrup, David. 1972. "The Growth of Trade among the Igbo before 1800." *Journal of African History*, 13:217–36.
———. 1978. *Trade Without Rulers*. New York and London: Oxford University Press.
Ofonagoro, W. 1972. "The Opening up of Southern Nigeria to British Trade and Its Consequences," Ph.D. dissertation, Columbia University, New York.
———. 1979. "From Traditional to British Currency in Southern Nigeria: Analysis of the Currency Revolution, 1880–1948." *Journal of Economic History*, 39:623–54.
———. 1977. "From Traditional to British Currency in Southern Nigeria: Analysis of the Currency Revolution." *Journal of Economic History*, 39:623–84.
Ogedengbe, Kingsley Nwachukwu. 1980. *The Abo Kingdom*: Ibadan: Longman.
Okonjo, K. 1979. "Rural Women's Credit Systems: The Nigerian Example." *Studies in Family Planning*. 10:326–31.
Okoroafor, Odimegwu. 1986. "Marriage Custom" in *Arochukwu History and Culture*, J. Okoro Ijoma, 284–306. Enugu: Fourth Dimension Publishers.
Ottenberg, S. 1958. "Ibo Oracles and Inter-group Relations." *Southwestern Journal of Anthropology*, 14:295–317.
Parry, J. and M. Bloch, eds. 1991. *Money and the Morality of Exchange*. New York and Cambridge: Cambridge University Press.
Shaw, T . 1970. *Igbo Ukwu, An Account of Archaeological Discoveries in Eastern Nigeria*. Evanston, Il: Northwestern University Press for the Institute of African Studies, University of Ibadan.
Smith, S. R. 1921. "The Igbo People." M. A. thesis, University of Cambridge, Cambridge, MA.
Stuart-Young J. M. 1916. "The Coaster at Home." *Typical Trading Conditions, 1900–1915*. London: G. W. B. Whittaker.

Uchendu, V. 1965.*The Igbo of Southeast Nigeria* New York: Holt, Rinehart and Winston.

Uku, K. 1945. "Seeds in the Palm of Your Hand," *West Africa*, 43: 1246–1265.

Ukwu, I. Ukwu. 1967. "The Development of Trade and Marketing in Iboland." *Journal of the Historical Society of Nigeria*, 3:647.

Umo, K. 1952. *History of Aro Settlements*. Lagos: n.p.

Vansina, Jan. 1968. "The Use of Ethnographic Data as Sources for History." In *Emerging Themes in African History*, ed. T. O. Ranger, 97–124. London: Heinemann.

7

Money and Informal Credit Institutions in Colonial Western Nigeria

Toyin Falọla

This chapter deals with the mobilization of credit against the background of colonial changes. Indigenous credit institutions have been dismissed or ignored in a number of economic texts (see, for instance, Seidman 1986). Also, there was once a misleading suggestion that they are recent inventions (see Bohannan and Bohannan 1968) despite the massive data that supports the conclusion that their basic templates are quite old, predating the colonial currencies. Drawing from a large body of oral data, I discuss first the value system that justified and promoted credit organizations in southwestern Nigeria during the colonial period.[1] A number of the noneconomic and so-called irrational behaviors in the indigenous practices can best be explained by the value system underlying money and lending. At the core of the value system was the cultural view on money and its uses. To the rich, a credit institution did not just provide an opportunity to obtain money for consumption, but also for investments and capital formation. To the poor, it provided a slim opportunity for accumulation, although its major function was to raise loans to meet urgent socio-economic demands and avoid the embarrassment of poverty. Next, I describe some of the available credit options of this period in order to point out the varieties and differences in their operations. The third section examines the attitude of the colonial government through its major policies, in order to address the impact of perhaps the most important factor of change during the period. The conclusion generalizes the data on credit with respect to the region under study. The topics in this chapter are important, providing the issues with which to contrast indigenous institutions with the formal and modern sector of banking during the same period. They also hint at the appropriation of elements of the formal sector by the indigenous credit institutions. The mobilization of credit brings to

162

the fore the social values of money and the several ways through which members of society relate to one another in debt relations.

The study is situated in colonial southwestern Nigeria in the first half of this century. This was a period of great changes, which included, among others, the establishment of a new political authority, bureaucracy, and an economy that revolved around export crops (Ekundare 1973; Falọla 1987; Atanda 1973). The tempo of the economy was accelerated, as more people migrated to the cities to seek employment or to places where export crops were grown. A better transportation system, based on the new railway and roads, among other factors, aided massive rural–urban migrations (Oṣoba 1964). The basis of the economy was agricultural production both for export and domestic consumption. The region became successful in the production of cocoa, palm products, kola nuts, and timber. The export–import trade was dominated by foreign firms with large capital and connections with markets in Europe. There were hundreds of agents who connected these firms with local markets. Internal trade was dominated by Nigerians, falling on the age-old organization of market and trade practices (see Marshall 1964; O'Hear 1986; Awẹ 1973; Falọla 1992b, 1991; and for the more recent period, see Hodder and Ukwu 1969). Long-distance trade with northern Nigeria continued as in the past, and the Hausa trading network endured, with impressive skill and adaptability, in both the profitable cattle and kola nut businesses (Cohen 1969). Internal trade benefitted from the roads and railways, which increased trader's mobility, enabling them to cover larger areas within a shorter period of time, while the region itself became the gateway to eastern Nigeria.

The modern sector of the economy expanded in such spheres as financial houses and the service sector in various forms such as medicine, law, architecture, and catering. Most of the sectors were competitive in access to market and demands for capital and skilled labor. For instance, the indigenous entrepreneurs were jealous of Asian and European traders who had a larger control of the market and who were able to use their branches and agents in the region to partition the market. The African "merchant princes" of the 19th century with power and control over the hinterland market became subordinate agents, brokers, or storekeepers during the colonial period (Nwabughuogu 1982). To these entrepreneurs and indeed other Nigerians, their biggest handicap was limited access to finance for expansion. It was not until after World War II that they were able to challenge foreigners with the capital supplied by the regional governments and boards and the opportunities opened by the decolonization process (Schatz 1974, 1977). There were fewer complaints about labor supply. Slavery was abolished during the century, but pawning of people as workers continued, in addition to the use of available relations and dependants. The use of wage labor was popularized by the colonial state.

The discussion that follows encompasses both the changes of the colonial period and the survival of indigenous practices. There was a formal sector of savings and credit, but side by side with it ran a parallel system. A new elite emerged, but there existed still an older one with its own beliefs and aspirations. Wage labor was established, but other forms continued to sustain indigenous production and distribution. While the educated people formed new visions, many still drew from the indigenous culture to organize their lives and relations with others in the society. The colonial bureaucracy made use of these educated Nigerians to build a "formal-sector" public office. While these wage earners benefited from new financial institutions, there were, in addition, many spin-off values beyond their income and connection to the formal sector. Their wages were conceptualized as valuable assets by the indigenous money-lenders who accepted them as collateral. Wage earners also became reliable guarantors to other loan seekers who did not have regular income and who relied upon the informal sector. Thus, some of the changes initiated by the colonial state for its own specific economic and political uses were applied by the people to other goals that enabled them to either adjust to the changes on their own terms or to connect to a past that they better understood.

The Value System

Money played an important role in the implementation of the policies of the colonial administration. A first step was to legitimize the new colonial currency. The precolonial currency, the cowry (Hogendorn and Johnson 1986), was cleverly manipulated out of circulation,[2] without compensation and consideration for old debts.[3] In the late nineteenth century, working out a standard of comparison and an acceptable exchange rate was the major concern until a head of cowry (2,000) was fixed at 6d (Johnson 1921:119;*The Lagos Weekly Record,* May 26, 1894). However, the cowry was thereafter demonetized and replaced with the British coins and paper currency (Tamuno 1972; Ofonagoro 1979; Hopkins 1966). At the turn of this century, English coins had become recognized and accepted in many places, and foreign merchants were rejecting the cowrie.[4] The introduction of coins of smaller denominations in the first decade effectively drove the cowry underground by 1920.[5] After World War I, paper currency was introduced to most areas; at first, it was rejected and criticized for causing inflation (Ajisafẹ 1964:204–5.), but it became widely popularized in the 1920s (Loynes 1962:19).

A related measure to the spread of the new currency was to monetize society in a way that the use of money would regulate labor relations and the exchange of goods and services in the colonial society. The new currency was used to pay salary, tax, and to organize domestic and external markets. Imported items became more and more popular, pushing up the "index of want," which had to be paid for with new currency. The society became monetized more than ever before, especially with the creation of a labor force that received monetary wages.

Both the old and new currency can be compared and contrasted in several ways. The units of accounting varied and the new currency was easier to carry and transport. The new currency did not service the relay of information as *aroko,* which had relied on the cowry and other objects to pass coded messages from one person to the other (Falọla and Lawuyi 1990). As the new currency spread, however, people got used to it and invested it with the same qualities of *owo* (money) as the cowry.

After an initial skepticism, the value system built around *owó ẹyọ* (cowry money) was imposed on the new currency.[6] As *owó,* the new currency shared with the old similar functions in the transactions of business. Second, the sources of the new and old currencies were shrouded in secrecy to the majority of the population. The process of acquiring *owó* was expressed as a search for the "sources" of money (*wá owó*).[7] Evidence relating to the nineteenth century, in such highly urbanized places as Ibadan and Lagos, show that most people did not know where the cowry came from, just as they did not know the origins of the British currency during this century.[8] There was a factual basis for the ignorance on sources: the cowry was not produced in Nigeria, while the British controled the supply of the new currency. The search for money was futile: many myths and folklore warned that it was a chance find, sometimes in some hidden pots in a grove or by the pathway in the forest or as a surprise gift from a wandering ghost or spirit. The talk about the search for the "source" of money (*ilé owó*) tended to frighten many people.[9] A successful search was not dependent on the use of brute force (*fi ipá wá owó*), wisdom (*ọgbọ́n*), or talent (*ẹbùn*), as many proverbs and popular sayings emphasize.[10] To be rich was to have discovered this source. In cultural terms, such a discovery was an act of destiny.[11] In real life, because only a few could discover this "source," others must either give up on the search or depend for assistance on those who had. To depend on those who had was to seek loans, accept the leadership and generosity of the rich—and the abuse of moneylenders. Thus, in a sense, social stratification was partly rationalized in the cultural ideology of *ilé owó*, that is, the "source" of money, so too was borrowing and the problems that accompanied it.

A third element in the value system derived from currency instability. Like the cowry, the new currency was not immune from instability. In the nineteenth century, the value of the cowry rose and fell, depending partly on the laws of supply and demand (Hopkins 1966). During this century, currency stability was dependent on the state of the economy. For example, the changes brought about by the global depression of the late 1920s and early 1930s and of World War II spurred inflation and reduced the value of money (see Brown 1989). One consequence of this instability was to encourage the conversion of raw cash to lasting assets (e.g., land and homesteads), which were less immune to instability and much more reliable as a store of wealth.[12] The conversion of money to houses and land became more widespread during the colonial period. In the pre-colonial society, such a conversion would have taken the form of additional wives, children, and followers. In the colonial society, the conversion process was ongoing as people used their money to build houses and buy land, and to continue the tradition of polygamy.[13] However, there was a reverse process of converting property to money (e.g., the *paro* discussed below) either to negotiate credit or acquire new items.

Whatever the form that the conversion from money to asset took, it was a delicate exercise in risk management. To have and retain money over a long period of time was a big achievement, because a loss was expected at any time without warning.[14] Just as a poor person could become rich, so too a rich person could become poor. The possibility of rich-to-poor downward mobility was a source of agitation—and the rich were continually seeking the means to prevent it. To some extent, preventing a fall was used by a number of rich moneylenders to justify usurious lending practices.[15]

A fourth aspect of the value system was that money had mystical powers (*ọwọ̀* and *agbára*[16]. The rich person, with knowledge of the "source" of money, could harness this specific power for other ends. To be sure, the items that money acquired (e.g., property, good food, adequate medicine, and followership) conferred their own mystique because they placed the rich well above others in the community. The description of money as *ẹ̀mí* (spirit), *ọṣùpá* (moon), *àléjò* (visitor/stranger) or *ájè* (witch)[17] is to underscore the magical/mystical, strange, and erratic behavior of money to "travel" in mysterious ways to certain people and also to abandon them without notice. In this mystical characterization, someone with the appropriate ritual power could "manufacture" money through magic by "inviting" it to visit.[18] A whole routine of such magic did develop; the most extreme was ritual murder to make money. That the magic that "produced" the cowry in the nineteenth century also "produced" the British currency in colonial Nigeria showed the extent to which the new currency acquired the value system of the old. The belief in ritual power for money was, in a sense, to diminish the role of hard work and luck in becoming rich. Wealth could be acquired by tapping the unseen power of the human body. Indeed, the wealth of an individual who did not show evidence of hard work or any legitimate or flourishing business was associated with the use of magic, if not of theft.[19]

The prevention of downward mobility involved not just rational investments in assets or in business, but control of the magic of money.[20] The rich person or someone aspiring to be rich must not offend the gods. More than this, as money was a "visitor," it must be honored with generous hospitality so that it would not depart in anger. One way of pleasing money was to avoid àgbàná, an extravagant lifestyle that destroyed a rich person to the extent that all of his savings and assets were depleted. A rich man could be destroyed by a manmade charm of àgbàná, an invocation of the magic of money to turn against him. A rich person attained his ultimate goal when he became immune from àgbàná, despite all attempts by his enemies to destroy him.[21] Many wage earners joined in seeking the means to avoid àgbàná not because they were insecure about their jobs,[22] but to prevent poverty. While many avoided àgbàná through rituals and religion, in real life, the problems attributed to àgbàná were probably no more than the inability of an individual to manage his resources, the failure to sustain an avenue for regular income, or ruination brought by a succession of misfortunes. A good number of wage earners with high incomes, who did not acquire property or who were always struggling to make ends meet were included in the list of the victims of àgbàná.[23] Àgbàná in this latter context was usually spelt out as the weakness of the person in lavishing money on women and entertainment. However, it was not the pressure and type of demands on money income that needed to be controlled, but the unseen forces of àgbàná—which prevented the individual from being rational and prudent.[24] The failure to profit from credit could also be attributed to àgbàná, especially when a person took a loan for business purposes but met with disaster.[25]

Another point of the value system was that money was one of the determinants of social stratification. Even if money was not the only criterion regarding social status (others were royalty, age, sex, and titles), it did provide information on social standing (Bascom 1951). The olówó (rich person) was contrasted with the oloṣi (the poor) in material and derogatory terms. The olòṣì had no power, little or no influence, and was expected to rely on the olówó for support. One form of support was to approach a lender for credit, in less than generous terms. Although the lender might cheat, the poor must not grumble too loudly. Àyànmọ́, a philosophy of destiny (Idowu 1963), was a perfect ideology with which to rationalize status and minimize intra-class tension: instead of fighting with an olówó over such an issue as high interest on loans, the olòṣì should strive to alter his bad destiny, that is, if it was not already too late to do so.

In the pre-colonial society, access to money was largely through power and trade. Power was the ideal agency, as it guaranteed avenues to gifts, tributes, labor and land to exploit or with which to generate rent (Law 1978). However, the desire was not limited to having liquid cash but assets—a compound, wives, children, horses, clothes, and jewelry. A distinction was made between a person with raw cash (olówó) and one with assets (olórò); the latter was superior. Where òró was com-bined with power, the *olówó* was very inferior. Indeed, what a clever *olówó* would do was to seek a title, to be able to combine the dignity of political office with raw cash and also to use his money to acquire tangible assets.

The post-1850 changes, brought about by missionary activities and colonial rule, broadened the criteria of stratification and the conception of influence. Western edu-cation, good wage incomes, and access to the colonial state became important crite-ria. The avenues to make money and accumulate assets were affected equally. For the entire duration of the colonial period, the traditional elite continued to manipulate their offices and control of land to obtain rents, gifts, salaries, and so forth, as a way of obtaining money (Atanda 1973; Falola 1983). For instance, they justified the reten-tion of pawning because they benefitted by being able to recruit labor.[26] Like the other members of society, the traditional elite also benefited from the credit institutions.[27] For instance, for those with land and farms, the *paro* described below, provided a source of credit. This elite suffered a decline in some aspects: they no longer could make booty from wars because there was peace; tributes from the colo-nies stopped as areas fell under the British rule; and they lost many slaves on their farms because of the decline in slavery. Also, hundreds of palace officials and free-born with significant social connections in the pre-colonial society witnessed severe losses or decline in their ability to appropriate the surplus of others during the colo-nial period because such opportunities were either gone or minimized. Conse-quently, they had to look elsewhere, usually to the new sectors that the colonial soci-ety opened up. If wage employment was not possible, cash crop production provided a second-best alternative. To the new generation of youth, the products of a new age, the acquisition of Western education was more rewarding than anything else, because it brought an income and influence. Through good jobs and connec-tions, education provided an additional access to a large network of contacts and to corruption.[28] From the point of view of the contemporaries, education broke down the rigid traditional class structure based on ascription. A good wage income was an avenue to good living, and to creditors a secure collateral with which to negotiate loans. Trade and other forms of business were equally as important as education. Although the competition in trade was rather intense, with the Lebanese and the Europeans dominating the key sectors, the ambition was to participate in the export-import and transport trade.

The definition and uses of assets were to see significant changes, too, again under the influence of Western education and colonial rule. The horse as a status symbol gradually gave way to the car, beginning from 1906 when a motor car trav-elled for the first time from Lagos to Ibadan (Elgee 1914:20); a house in the town became more important commercially than one in the village as towns became cen-ters of colonial administration and commerce; land in the new town centers and rail-way stations, the hub of economic activities, became highly prized; and big com-pounds gave way to smaller one-story houses as individuals acquired resources to build personal houses for their nuclear families and smaller number of dependants.[29] The taste for foreign food, clothes, drinks, and fashion spread, but this cultural expansion was yet another way of assessing progress and status for those who were able to participate. Imported goods like jewelry, radios, televisions (after 1957), wrist watches, books and newspapers, suits, shoes, and so forth, entered into the organiza-tion of credit simply because they were highly valued.[30] Whereas land and houses were collective property in the pre-colonial society and were hardly used as collateral, this was to change in the colonial society as individuals acquired property of their own. There were cases of conflicts over family land and houses used as collateral,[31] but in general, individuals with personal houses and land exercised the right to use them for credit.[32]

There was a general aspiration for abundant wealth. Southwestern Nigeria had always been a prestige-conscious society, in which the individual needed money to demonstrate success and victory over real and imaginary enemies. Avoiding sickness, prolonging life, acquiring wives and children, and eating well were all desires that consumed much money. In spite of the respect for age, it was better to combine it with some wealth: as one proverb sums up elegantly: "An elderly man without money is unwise, whoever has money is like a king in the village." As in the pre-colonial society, money could be used and wisely managed to purchase *iyí* (fame), *ọlà* (honor), and *agbára* (power). The ideal was to have all: *owó, ọlá, iyí*, but above all *ọlà* (wealth).[33]

However, even to those who did not have such a passion for wealth, there was occasional need for "bulk" money for a variety of reasons such as paying medical bills, school fees, and raising capital to start or expand a business.[34] For most of the time, social expenses, notably of funerals, marriage, child naming and title-taking provided strong justification for seeking credit. The desire for large families and honor, and a strong social requirement to bury the dead in a dignified manner, including lavish entertainment of guests, all encouraged not just savings but applications for instant loans.

To conclude this section, the main point to be remembered is that the conception of money and the search for it were ideologically well connected by an elaborate but integrated value system: there were reasons to seek money (*wá owó*), the mystical object (*àjè, àléjò, òṣúpá,* etc.) with a difficult "source" (*ilé owó*). In what follows, I explain one "source" of money through credit (*gbèsè*) and its attendant complications.

Credit and Accumulation: The Informal Options

The avenues to borrow, save, and accumulate were available, and were diverse and expanding in their operations during the colonial period. The scope for the individual to enrich himself widened more than in the pre-colonial society, for reasons of education, wage labor and the cultivation of export crops. As in the pre-colonial period, the people were still prestige-conscious: money glorified a person and the god whom he or she worshipped. The demands for credit were economic and social. Whether for small-scale or large-scale business, there was a need for money to start, expand, risk, and invest. Social reasons were wide ranging, including the celebrations of birth, marriage, and funerals. So scarce was capital for most people and so severe could the pressure become that it was considered a problem next to the infertility of a woman: *ail'ówó / 'ọwó, baba ijaiyà* (literally, poverty is the father of fear). The worst evidence of poverty was the inability to raise credit at short notice.

Individuals in need of credit had the option of either exploring the formal or informal institutions in a dualistic money market. The formal ones came with British rule, beginning with the establishment in Lagos of the African Banking Corporation in 1872 to service the government, large business organizations, and an emerging army of salary earners (see Mars 1948; Fry 1976; Nwankwo 1980; Okigbo 1981). The stability of the formal sector was assured by government control and the supervision of the Nigerian branches by their head offices in Europe. The limitations of modern banking were, however, many. The banks avoided the hinterland, mainly confining their services to the seats of administration (Loynes 1962:6). For the banks to have established in the villages and small towns would have been to push their luck too far, because there was no evidence that these areas could generate sufficient money to justify returns and operation cost. In general, the banks were not designed for those without education, given all the paperwork involved in opening and running accounts. Even long after independence, those without education still find modern financial houses impersonal and complex (Geertz 1962:42). When it came to loans, it was clear that the preference was for the Europeans and Asians. Nigerians were often denied because the banks believed that their business experience and practices were limited or shoddy, that they could not come up with acceptable assets to use as collateral, and that they would not repay the loans (Akeredolu-Ale 1976; Akintola 1975:Ch. 1). This discrimination forced the Nigerian entrepreneurs with assets and ideas to fall back on the informal institutions.

The indigenous entrepreneurs, however, saw the formal sector as the ideal. They endeavored to create formal structures of their own along the European model. They, too, established banks, such as the Industrial and Commercial Bank and the Nigerian Mercantile Bank, which collapsed in the face of capital shortage and lack of experience. The first success story was the National Bank of Nigeria, established in 1933. Four more banks were established between 1945 and 1947 and another eighteen in the famous bank "mushrooming" of 1950–51. Again, only two, the Agbonmagbe and the African Continental Bank, survived not for their efficiency but because the regional governments diverted funds to them to keep them alive (see Brown 1963). The successful indigenous banks were instruments of manipulation used by an emerging political elite and political parties to consolidate power and accumulate money at a fast rate.[35] To the majority of the population, the banks generated little confidence and failed to benefit people without education and connections.

With all these problems, most people depended on traditional practices that were sustained or modified to keep up with the changes of the colonial era. Apart from the need for credit, many people tried to save a part of their income, while the indigenous lenders, behaving like modern banks, sought the means to collect and use other people's money for their own investments. Unlike modern banks, however, indigenous lenders gave no interest on savings. Other reasons worked to sustain this informal sector. The colonial system imposed some financial burdens on everybody by way of taxation introduced to most areas after 1918. By rejecting payment in cowrie, the taxation forced many people to seek ways to obtain the new currency. By disallowing payment by installment, it compelled them to look for a "big" sum. Taxation was linked with migration, wage employment, and credit institutions, all in the attempt to seek the means to be able to pay.

The informal sector comprised indigenous practices that were continued either in their original forms or in modified ways. In the description that follows, I categorize the credit institutions into three options that reflect the continuity with the past and the changes of the century. From the records of the nineteenth and twentieth centuries, there is a strong element of continuity in the descriptions of the practices, which is a warning that the impact of colonial rule upon them should not be exaggerated.

However, there were changes in practices to reflect urbanization, literacy, and lack of trust, although such changes are poorly documented in official sources. The categorization is for analytical convenience: individuals in search of credit did not think in terms of the boundaries that I have erected here and crossed them to benefit from whatever was available at a minimum hardship.

Option A: The Traditional Practices of *Eṣusu* and *Ajọ*

Ájọ and *eṣúsú* were practiced in the nineteenth century and also survived the colonial period. These two are the best reported of all the indigenous credit institutions, as part of an emerging global synthesis on "roscas"—rotating credit associations—found in Asia, Africa, and the Americas. Improving upon an earlier definition by Clifford Geertz, Shirley Ardener describes them as "an association formed upon a core of participants who agree to make regular contributions to a fund which is given, in whole or in part, to each contributor in rotation" (Ardener 1964:201; see Geertz 1962:243).[36] *Eṣúsú* and *ajọ* were two forms to build capital as saving devices, without obtaining interest on it.

The operations of both during the colonial period were reported upon in official documents of the 1920s and in the writings of contemporary Nigerians (see, for instance, N.A.I., *Report on Native Organisation of the Ife Division* by J. A. Mackenzie Esq., D.O.; Partridge 1910;[37] Fadipe 1970; Delano 1937). An excellent study in the early 1950s yielded additional data (Bascom 1952). In *eṣúsú*, a number of people who trusted one another formed a small savings club, under the leadership of a leader, the *Olori Eṣúsú*, who kept and disbursed the funds. The club had a definite life span, at the end of which all the members would collect their share (Johnson 1921:119). At the beginning, the members decided on the amount, duration, and regularity of contribution (daily, weekly, or monthly), the three issues known as the *ọwọ́ kan*, that is, "one bulk." *Ọwọ́ kan* was the minimum contribution for every participant, but one with the means could increase the "bulk" to two or more, to add to the savings. A member could not pull out until *eṣúsú* ran its course. On the last day, usually in the night when members were free for the day and in the house of the collector, everybody received his contribution (Adeoye 1979:157–8). A person could belong to more than one *eṣúsú* to increase his savings. One advantage of *eṣúsú* was to encourage compulsory savings.

As at the time of Bascom's description in the 1950s, *eṣúsú* was still in vogue. He indicated that an *eṣúsú* could be large, the leader had subordinate lieutenants who ensured collection, these lieutenants behaved like apprentices with the aspiration of becoming *eṣúsú* leaders in the future, the leader received some limited pay for his services, and that the club could collapse. It is not clear whether some of these observations on size, ambitions, and problems were products of the colonial age or surviving aspects of older practices. Some of the changes that can be associated with the colonial period were the need to take precautions on members who might default and to document transactions. Contemporary sources show that *eṣúsú* flourished more in the villages and cocoa-growing areas, which would tend to indicate that members knew one another very well before they decided to associate. In cases where *eṣúsú* was mentioned in the towns, the members shared other things in common, such as the membership of a trade guild, church, or neighborhood. Underlying this convergence of interest with *eṣúṣú* was the need to build trust so that no member would cheat. In many *eṣúṣú* examples mentioned in the 1940s and 1950s, recordkeeping became a way of management. Apart from making collection more tidy, the issue of trust was also mentioned as a reason for documentation. The fact that trust was mentioned would suggest that there were cases of embezzlements, although we have no archival evidence.

The *àjọ* was different in a number of ways from the *eṣúṣú*.[38] First, a contributor received less than the entire savings, because the collector would take a day's savings as reward for his services. Second, contribution could be on a daily basis, but would be terminated after a short period already agreed upon, at which point everybody would collect his savings. Third, there was a long-range plan, a rotating saving association called the *olówó-ìkó*, lasting at least a month. There was a club, with a leader and a clubhouse to serve as an office. Contributors knew one another, and decided as to when every person would receive his share. The rotation could be adjusted to help a member in trouble by giving him his contribution on demand.

The *àjọ* saw some changes during the colonial era, too. Unlike *eṣúṣú*, which drew members that were known to one another, a collector (*alájọ*) was enough to run an *àjọ*, by attracting clients scattered in location and who had nothing to do with one another. Indeed, the *alájọ* became a profession by itself. A person with an education adequate to keep records and credibility could take to the trade. He would start in a small way, using a small number of initial clients to recruit new ones. With a small catchment area, all he needed was a small notebook and a bag, and of course a secure place in his house to keep money. The use of bicycles and later of motorcycles enabled the *alájọ* to widen the territory of operation in order to connect a number of small villages or cover a large town. The *alájọ* was a person of good humor, and had to take an interest in the trade and children of his clients to improve rapport. He must be trustworthy with money and he must live an exemplary life, displaying prudence and wisdom. Unlike in *eṣúṣú* where a circle had to be completed, the contributor to an *àjọ* could demand his savings at any time, as in a modern bank. The power to withdraw was the check on the *alajọ*'s ability to risk collections. If an *alájọ* failed to return money on demand, his credibility was lost. What a wise *alájọ* did was to invest only a small portion and live by his charges so that he could always meet requests for withdrawal.

While the modernization of *àjọ* sustained its continuity, the changes also provided the main reason for its problems. A collector could run away with other peoples' money, or he could risk it in an unprofitable venture. He could cheat, by failing to record the correct amount of contributions, especially as most clients relied on their memories to keep records.

Option B: Modified Traditional Practices

The use of cash crops as a pledge to raise credit was common in areas suitable for cocoa, kola nut, and palm production. As leading products in domestic and international trade, there was always the assurance that the products would find a market, thus making them valuable assets.[39] A debtor would pledge all or part of his valuable farmland to a creditor for a loan. The lenders were smart enough to determine possible yields over a certain number of years. The debtors, realizing that a great asset had been mortgaged, struggled to repay their debts in order to recover control of their farms. In general, it was a risk-free option to a lender who multiplied his investments in a very clever way: the debtor had to tender the farm and could not profit from price increases or favorable harvests. As in pawning, the farm was both a collateral and an interest: as long as the principal was unpaid, the creditor controled the farm (Galletti, Baldwin and Dina 1956:Ch. 14). It was an arrangement that cost little to maintain because the lender did not have to spend time and resources pursuing the debtor. The limitation was that the land did not belong to the lender, only the crops. What the lender had to check was that the farms were productive enough to recover his money.

A more generous contract was to limit the interest to the sale of the crops in one annual harvest. This was like obtaining credit, with a promise to pay later with the crops. Produce dealers engaged in this type of deal to out-manoeuvre their competitors by preventing them from buying from the same person. The trouble was that if the debtor did not pay the principal, the term extended over to the next harvest.[40]

In whatever form, exchanging farm crops for a loan was exploitative. As in pawnship, the creditor controled a substantial part of the labor of the debtor, thus making it hard to have the resources and time to liquidate the principal. The creditor made more money by selling the mortgaged crops because he negotiated at a price below that of the market, while this also prevented the debtor from reaching out to other traders.

Another modified practice was that of the òṣómáló which involved the use of goods as credit in a system of hire purchase.[41] The word, òṣómáló, of Ijesa origin, captures only an aspect of the trade on debt recovery: òṣó ni ma a lo kí mó fi a gbo o mi (I will stoop until I recover my money). The òṣómáló was a trader who encouraged clients to buy on credit and settle later, similar to the trust system established by the European merchants in their relations with their African collaborators during the nineteenth century.[42]

The òṣómáló relied on aggressive advertising to sell their products, especially at a time when their clients were low on funds. They went to the farms and villages before harvest and annual social events in order to advertise imported clothes, cheap jewelry, cosmetics, and other retail items. The art of persuasion was the key to the trade. The òṣómáló had to seek those who required credit, and then used all the means, tricks, and peer connections possible to convince a client to purchase on credit.

Through hard work, aggressive marketing, and a consummate desire for profits, the òṣómáló penetrated the nooks and corners of the region, moving to areas with cocoa, timber, and other principal products. If their clients did not have much money or were not interested in clothes, the òṣómáló promoted minor articles such as cosmetics. Because the products were sold on credit, high interests boosted their regular profits.

The distinctiveness of the òṣómáló was their ruthless ability and designs to recover debts. Strict rules were set at the beginning on recovery. Some accepted installment payments, as long as service charges were added, and some requested bulk payment on a certain day. Should the client pay as agreed, the òṣómáló would lure him to another purchase. To those who refused to pay or who sought a new date, the òṣómáló turned nasty. At first, relations and friends of the debtors were requested to collect the debt. When this failed, the òṣómáló resorted to intimidation and force. Before dawn, the òṣómáló, in company of apprentices and others, would lay siege on the debtor's house, to prevent him from attending to his daily duties and needs. The *òṣómáló* became a nuisance: he could threaten to commit suicide; he would use violent language in great anger; and he harassed the debtor and the other members of the household. The use of force and intimidation were usually effective, although the most successful among the *òṣómáló* would attribute debt recovery to the use of charms. Through powerful charms, the debtor was allegedly hypnotized or turned into a fool to turn over his/her entire purse.

As a shrewd trader, the *òṣómáló* would immediately renew friendship with the humiliated client after collecting his money. "Life is too short to fight" became the new slogan, to again trick the client into buying another product with a generous extension of time to pay. The *òṣómáló* would also make up with the aggrieved neighbours, again to coax some of them into buying and to repair damaged relations.

The *òṣómáló* established a specialized trading practice. While they did not constitute a united trade network, each individual relied on a team of family relations and apprentices to sell and buy. They were itinerant traders for most of the time, traveling to the major trading centers like Lagos and Ibadan to buy in bulk, later to retail. They were good at monitoring prices and predicting economic changes. An *òṣómáló* began the career with a small amount of money, gradually built capital and reinvested in more trade.

Like the Lebanese trade rivals (Falola 1992b), the *òṣómáló* engaged in a skillful interaction with the political authority and prominent people in their areas of operation. They befriended the powerful with gifts and prudent extension of credits, just to ensure their cooperation when it came to debt collection and the public humiliation of bad debtors. Unlike the Lebanese, however, the *òṣómáló* could not use skin color to advantage. Rather, they sought an identification with the community by making one or two friends, choosing a likeable nickname, and refusing to be drawn into local politics. The use of a friend in the community was to gather information and ensure that an eye was kept on the debtor.

To the buyer, the advantage was the ability to live on credit for upwards of three months. When the good was textiles, debtors were satisfied that they could keep up with the taste and trend and had something new to use for important social engagements. To the *òṣómáló*, the advantage was to use credit for trade and capital accumulation. An *òṣómáló* calculated his assets in tangible possessions such as land or house, trade goods, liquid cash, and the totality of uncollected debts. The long-term ambition of an *òṣómáló* was to use profit to educate his children, build houses, and eventually retire to a big store after a life of extensive and exhausting trade.

Option C: New Forms

Two new forms emerged during the century. The first, *pàrò-olówó*, was the use of assets to raise money or to exchange one property for another.[43] The need for money forced loan-seekers to use their property as collateral even if property was held superior to money. Only a well-to-do person or a salaried person could use assets to raise this type of loan. Unlike pawning, the poor could not resort to this action, because the article demanded by a creditor was usually expensive and equivalent or more to the loan. The most common assets were gold ornaments, radios, expensive *dandogo* cloth made of velvet or wool, wristwatches, leather shoes, and so forth. It was expected that the debtor would repay the loan in order to retain his goods. The gain to the lender was the high interest. The lender must not use the collateral, but could sell or confiscate them if the debt was unpaid.

The use of assets for loan in the *pàrò ólowó* was more of a feature of city life, where a concentration of people earned regular incomes and possessed negotiable assets. It was a sign of trouble to give up an asset for money. The practice is well remembered in oral traditions with respect to those who sold off their inheritance for money—the *arungún*. While the use of inherited assets for loans could be justified in economic terms, it was condemned as a moral failure, the betrayal of the ancestor, and an inability to manage and build upon inherited property.[44]

There was a more widespread practice of *pàrò ẹlẹru,* which was to exchange one item for another or for cash.[45] There is no nineteenth century reference to it; neither is the origin of the practice known because there is little reference to it in archival records until the 1950s.[46] The organizers of *pàrò* were itinerant traders who made profits on secondhand items. The business was very simple and not at all risky: the trader offered money or an article to a client who wanted to dispose of an asset. Durable assets, such as land and houses, were excluded in the transactions. Household wares, clothes, ornaments, shoes, cosmetics, and books were the notable ones used. The *pàrò* trader carried new items to bargain for used ones, with a skill that made it possible to bargain one new item for many old ones, which then could be resold or renegotiated for profit. The profitability of the trade rested on seeking clients who needed secondhand items. Although the trade continues today, the limitation to it was the distance that had to be covered with goods carried on the head. The successful *pàrò* traders were able to make use of apprentices or hired labor for human porterage. The *pàrò* traders concentrated their activities in urban areas, where there was a largepool of people with assets and the urge to acquire additional ones.

A second new form was an usurious practice known as the *sogúndogòjí* ("convert twenty to forty"), whereby a debtor would be charged a very high interest rate of between 100 and 300 percent (Falola 1993). In addition, the surety collected a fee, while the lender could cheat by a false recording of the principal collected by the debtor. No one wished to resort to this, except in desperate situations. Spending the loan on consumption, as many people did, caused regret later because the repayment called for hard work. To spend the loan on a business was to calculate on a profit of over 300 percent, be able to pay the principal and its huge interest, and still break even. In spite of the high interest, money-lenders were not without clients, especially in the towns where strangers had no other avenues to raise credit, and for people in urgent circumstances that required money. Of the latter cases, funeral and sickness pushed many people to the money-lenders.

From the point of view of lenders, they could not operate without the high interest. Apart from the consideration of profit, the cost of collecting debt was high. Available collateral by most debtors was limited indeed, while problems always attended the confiscations of such collateral in cases of default. There was an additional risk that debtors might relocate elsewhere to avoid payment. To minimize their losses, the lenders obtained information on their debtors, preferred salary earners with fixed addresses, and insisted on reliable guarantors.

The debtor required a guarantor, the *onígbòwó,* who provided a testimony on character and assumed responsibility for loan repayment. The *onígbòwó* was more of a witness because it was rare of them to assist in loan liquidation with their own money; rather they would collaborate with the lender to put pressure on the debtor.

For his services, the *onígbòwó* received a fee from the debtor, usually deducted from the principal. The debtor was not required to give up his labor to service the debt; rather he paid the interest in money. What the lender wanted was money, instead of labor, because he did not invest in farms but in trade or real estate. Urban-based, with some good financial standing and large aspirations, moneylenders were tough, calculating, and brutal. A debtor knew that he must pay at all cost to avoid trouble.

Because of the high interest and draconian debt-recovery methods, moneylenders were unpopular, in spite of their services. They suffered a lot of bad-mouthing, their children were cursed, and their misfortune was a cause of joy to many people.

Colonial Policy: Tolerance And Opposition

The colonial government adopted three approaches in dealing with the informal sector. The first was a policy of noninterference in customs that it did not find repugnant or which did not constitute an obstacle to the running of the administration. The government was either silent or approved of those options such as *àjọ, eṣúsú,* and *òṣómáló.* The general argument was that without them, trade and production would suffer. In this argument, colonial officers were supported by the missionaries, the Yoruba- educated elite, and "scholars."[47]

The second policy was to seek the means to prohibit the practices that the government did not approve of. The colonial administration fought only pawning, a custom whereby an *ìwòfà* (pawn) rendered service to a creditor to pay the cost of interest on a loan until it was repaid (Johnson 1921:126–130; Fadipẹ 1970: 189–93). Pawning was an established credit institution in the nineteenth century, next to slavery in the procurement of labor, and was further promoted by the warfare of that age (Oroge 1985). It continued well into the colonial period (Falọla 1994). Indeed, pawning increased during a period of transition to wage labor, from the 1880s to the 1920s, as many people remained unsure as to whether or not to work for wages.[48] At the same time, slavery was declining, due to the cessation of wars in the country and the attack from the colonial administration. The demand for labor was high, both in the traditional economies such as farming which was expanding, and in the modernizing sector of the colonial society. While the colonial administration resorted to wage labor, the local elite chose pawning. Chief I. Delano, a notable cultural nationalist, listed pawning as part of the "soul of Nigeria" early in the century (Delano 1937:71–77). Pawns were counted in thousands in such towns as Ibadan, Oyo, Abeokuta; those of Ibadan alone were estimated at 10,000.[49]

The colonial administration did not like many aspects of pawning, such as the indefinite nature of the use of labor in lieu of interest, the involvement of children (notably girls), and the alleged brutalities against debtors. While the early administrators in places like Lagos, Abeokuta, and Ibadan complained about the practice and discussed its abolition with the chiefs, nothing significant occurred (Akinyele 1911:132; NAI Abe Prof. 9/2). Indeed, the Governor in Lagos told his subordinate colleagues that he was not opposed to pawning.[50] Pawning, however, began to move to the center stage in 1916 when the Lugard administration enacted the famous Ordinance No. 35, whose concern was to abolish slavery, but which touched on pawning. Pawning was allowed, but the high interest rate was to be controled. The pawn should not serve for an unlimited time, and was advised to seek redress in court after a certain period. The ordinance stipulated the accepted interest rates to be used by the administrative officers and courts in determining cases referred to them: the value of a day's work should be calculated at "threepence per diem, if the pawn is fed and housed, and 6d if he is not" (Lugard [1918] 1970:236).

The 1916 Ordinance was ineffective, and no significant number of cases reached the court. Lugard and the other administrators were themselves not convinced that the time was right to strike a blow on pawning if they did not want to disrupt agricultural production. Lugard cautioned against interfering with the contracts entered into by those who pledged themselves, as long as they were not cheated by too high an interest.[51] The Yoruba elite and missionaries cautioned them against any policy of abolition, arguing that the life of the economy depended on this custom.[52]

There was one major reason in the 1920s to review the liberal position on pawning. The Nigerian government was embarrassed by the international attention focused on pawning by the League of Nations which was opposed to it and which demanded reports on the state of its abolition.[53] The pressure by the League forced Nigeria to embark on some "tough" measures, although the colonial officers were divided on the course to pursue.[54] In 1927, the Ordinance of 1916 was modified and publicized in many towns. Cited below is that of the Oyo Province, which actually was reproduced elsewhere, with minor changes to names of districts and provinces:

1. It is His Majesty the King's wish that the present system of IWOFA shall cease as not being in accordance with the principles of civilization particularly where children are concerned.

2. No boy or girl under the age of 16 years shall be engaged as an IWOFA after the 28th February, 1927.

3. With effect from 15th August, 1927, the labor of an IWOFA shall be paid for a fixed rate per 100 heaps, and the value of the labor shall be calculated towards the extinction both of the debt and the interest thereon.

4. All debts are recoverable in the Native Courts or Provincial Court.

5. The rate of pay will be as follows:
   In Oyo Division 2d per 100 heaps
   In Ibadan Division 3d per 100 heaps
   In Ife Division 3d per 100 heaps.[55]

The public interpretation of this notice was that the government allowed pawning as long as children were not involved. Adult self-pawning went virtually unchecked in the 1930s. There were cases of prosecution that involved children, but many contracts could not have been detected by the government. To the indigenous elite and those who supported them, adults were free to do whatever they liked with their labor. The Lagos elite, annoyed with the discriminatory lending practices of the modern banks, justified pawning as the only available means for "an illiterate man" to raise credit if he did not want to sell or forfeit his land.[56]

Such an argument found little favor in small official circles, where pawning had come to be regarded as an encroachment on individual liberty. In 1938, the penal code prohibited all forms of pawning, the use of labor as interest on loans, and child marriage. The central government instructed the provinces to be active in suppressing pawning.[57] By the late 1930s, the colonial government had consolidated itself: wage labor was in place and there was a large pool of peasant producers to make a success of the export economy. Cases of prosecution were reported throughout the 1940s which suggested that pawning continued despite the prohibition (Delano 1937:71-72; Greenidge 1958:70). The cases reported in the 1950s were few, and indicate a decline in the practice (Falọla 1994). While the government enacted anti-pawning legislations, it showed less commitment to enforcing them, a good signal to those who needed pawns to go ahead with the practice.

A third policy adopted by the colonial government was to fight usurious lending practices. When the first ordinance on money lending was passed in 1912, the motive was to regulate interest rate in such a way as to make pawning less attractive. This ordinance was a complete failure for the simple fact that the government that framed it did not know that it was dealing with a century-old practice. Pawning was likely to have offered the most generous interest rate during the nineteenth century. In transacting other loans, an interest rate known as the *ẹdà* was applied, a periodic payment of a fixed sum of about a thousand cowries until the principal was repaid. The other one was the payment of *ele*, a bulk sum as an interest paid along with the principal.[58] Bishop Crowther who observed both in the 1880s described the rates as very high.[59] Methods of debt recovery were harsh, resulting in enslavement and the use of force to seize the debtor's property.[60]

After 1912, fighting usury focused on the regulation of the activities of the *sogún-dogóji*, professional moneylenders. Money lending by the *sogúndogóji* produced many conflicts and complaints that reached the tables of colonial administrators. Among the issues that created problems were the attempts to cheat borrowers by giving them less than the amounts stated in the records as the principal, payment of service charges which cut into the loans, the brutal methods of debt recovery, and the high interest charged.[61] Of all these problems, the one that worried the administration the most was the high interest rate. There were cases reported in the mid-1930s of the payments of such interests of £15 on a loan of £10 over a thirty-day period and for "a loan of £20 for 12 months a Promissory Note for £32 ha(d) to be given."[62] Moneylenders, always careful not to reveal their huge profits, justified the high interest rate by pointing to the high risk involved in the trade and the complications of debt recovery.[63]

The first ordinance to control the lenders was enacted in 1917. This turned out to be a weak response to the problems, as there were no means to enforce the rules and many people were in fact not aware of the ordinance.[64] It was not until 1938 that another ordinance was enacted to take care of wide-ranging issues of defining who a lender was and determining appropriate interest rates.[65] The lenders were forced to register their businesses and obtain licences from the government. The interests on various types of loans were pegged below 30 percent per annum. To some, including colonial officers, the approved rates were too high. The lenders were not too happy with the ordinance and they were cunning in finding the ways to circumvent the laws. Desperate borrowers were themselves too willing to ignore official interest rates because the lenders insisted on operating without respect for the ordinance.[66] The advantage to those who were ready to fight the lenders was that they had the law and the government to support them. However, as the cases that reached the courts were few, the only possible conclusion that can be made is that the 1938 ordinance was not as successful as the government had anticipated.

Conclusion

I bring this chapter to a close by reflecting on the major characteristics of the indigenous credit institutions in southwestern Nigeria. While the primary concern is to elaborate upon access to wealth in a colonial society, I point out in the first segment of the chapter that the local value system, which arose originally around cowry money was later imposed upon the British currency. This value comprised a conception of money in which the source and origins of money were shrouded and mystical. The cultural understanding of money affected in many ways the organization of the credit system.

I characterize the indigenous credit option as "informal" because there was a new "formal" money market that accompanied colonial rule. The informal options were many, including the traditional, modified, and new ones aforementioned. Many people also fell back upon their network of family and friends, while the European and Asian firms continued the much older practice of providing advances on export crops (Galletti, Baldwin and Dina 1956; Berry 1975:71–87). New institutions were introduced to assist members in trouble, such as the co-operative societies, ethnic, and Progressive Unions in the cities, and social organizations within the Christian churches. Some practices, such as the sogúndogójì, borrowed extensively from traditional and Western practices to create innovative methods of transactions. For instance, moneylenders tried to operate mobile banks, while the òṣómálò adapted the established trust system of trade between the Europeans and Africans in the nineteenth century. As the demand for labor as interest on loans declined, more emphasis was placed on the use of assets such as land, farm crops, houses, jewelry, and clothes.

Whereas the basis of indigenous savings and credit was located in the moral concept of ìrànlọ́wọ́ (help), which was why the influential sociologist, Dr. N. A. Fadipe, called them "mutual help associations" (1970:256), this was hardly the case in most of the organizations already described. The alájọ, for example, operated his business in order to make a living, while the òṣómálò and sogúndogójì were shrewd and calculating investors. The current attempt to return to indigenous practices as appropriate models of credit organization tends to portray them in idealistic terms, ignoring that their practices had undergone substantial modifications and that there were ruthless manipulators and risk bearers among the members (see, for instance, Stiglitz 1990; Oyejide 1977; Geertz 1962; Kurtz 1973; and Ardener 1964).

In all the avenues for credit, the poor were able to interact with the rich, even if their motives differed. Such interactions had an economic motive for both classes, but were justified by a value system that demanded that the poor should look to the rich for support, information, and assistance. One hidden agenda in the value system was exploitation, as lending practices were not presented as exercises in accumulation and access to liquid cash for investments. However, through the ájọ and eṣúsú, a person, irrespective of class, could build up small capital over time. In these two cases, neither savings nor loans attracted an interest. In explaining the origins of their capitals, many traders and cocoa farmers mentioned the ájọ and eṣúsú as their sources. Although the eṣúsú and ájọ were generous and not usurious, they had their own problems. They did not meet all demands for money, especially for quick capital mobilization. The eṣúsú and ájọ assumed that a contributor had a regular income and that his main interest was to save for small capital or for anticipated consumption.

The need to meet the contingent demands of those without any reliable network or those who required large amounts of money enabled other forms to flourish and develop into professions despite their harsh terms. The lenders were drawn from a pool of successful traders, produce dealers, and merchants, who were smart in manipulating the needs of others to build and consolidate their own capital. The desire for mobility, passion for money, and prestige consciousness of many people assured that the lenders had clients. Money was scarce but demands for it were many because aspirations for consumption and trade were too high.

The use of assets for transactions was an evidence of change in collateral and property rights during the colonial period. In the process of raising credit or accumulating capital, many items constituted key assets. In pawnship, it was the use of direct labor. In òṣómáló, debt had to be repaid by selling the products of labor or using one's salary. When money did not change hands, commodities were used, as in pàrò. Crops were pledged for loans. Whereas land and compounds could not be used to raise loans in many parts of the pre-colonial society, the individual with sole rights to these in the colonial era used them for whatever reasons chosen. Those who inherited property could also negotiate them for money, in spite of the cultural objections. Thus, land commercialization and the idea of individual property were to encourage the use of assets for credit during a period that witnessed a decline in the use of human labor as collateral. Similarly, many wage earners turned their earnings to advantage in raising loans because they could borrow against their income. To moneylenders, those with regular jobs already had reliable collateral.

The conditions imposed by lenders, in particular high interest rates, made loan repayment very difficult. The power of the rich, the support by political authorities, and the survival of indigenous debt-recovery methods, all ensured that debts were collected. Rather than use the formal public agencies of the police and the courts in debt recovery, lenders chose alternative means. As in the pre-colonial era (Johnson 1921:130-1), they employed force and intimidation, and in cases when the debtor died, they insisted on payment before the body could be buried (Fadipe 1970:164-5).

In all forms of lending, the sore point was the debt-recovery methods. The lenders did not want to use the police and the modern courts, because they tended to be slow and they allowed debtors the opportunity to present their plight, thus making them equal before the law with their creditors. A big problem could arise if a debtor had no relation or friend who could help to repay a debt when the lender resorted to threats and force. All sources agree that a debtor could be abandoned by his relations and friends, unlike in pre-colonial society, in which assistance was more forthcoming. Indeed, there is abundant evidence that the isolation of a debtor did happen, especially in the towns where an individual did not have the contacts to fall back upon. When a debtor felt cheated or embattled, the opportunity to seek redress was usually private, by calling upon influential people and guarantors to appeal to the creditors for more time. In the 1950s, when Bascom noted fraudulent practices in eṣúṣú, he also noted that high litigation cost prevented members from using the court in conflict resolution (1952:66).

The complication of debt recovery was one reason that limited reliance on kin-groups for credit. While it is true that a lot of money changed hands between relations (and friends) as loans, the difficulty of using force to collect unpaid loans served to caution those who did not want to risk their wealth. A source of protection among the Yoruba was not to talk much about the extent of wealth or savings, not only to quell their enemies, but also to limit what they could give away as gifts or advance as loans. A person with resources to give would avoid strangers and relations on whom he did not have adequate information or whom he did not trust (Berry 1975:78).The preference was still to lend to those without ties to the creditor so that he could use force to obtain his money. An informant who described himself as wealthy in the 1930s and 1940s said that he rather would serve as a guarantor to his relations or asked his friend to accept them as pawns to protect his money.[67] Whether this was a common strategy is unclear, but it was sound in that this person had the opportunity to pressure his relations to pay, without commiting himself to help. Another informant of the same generation said that he lent what he could afford to lose should the loan be defaulted.[68] Again, this sounds like a prudent strategy to enable the rich person to maintain clout with his relations and dependants without destroying his own financial base. To combine these two opposing strategies, it would appear that both were careful not to destroy relations and patronage and at the same time guarded against downward mobility.

It was also the debt-collection methods that destroyed the character and image of most lenders. Lenders were tough and ruthless people. Thus, a lender might not meet all the criteria of an ideal "big man." He could not be an *onínú rere* (a good hearted person), or a *gbajúmọ* (a gentleman), although he could still occupy the upper strata identified by Bascom as *ọlọ́rọ̀ olówó*, which did not necessarily embrace the virtues of good character. As most of them avoided advancing huge loans to people with power, whom they would not be able to intimidate in order to recover money, moneylenders also ran the risk of not enjoying a close identification with power. Hated by the poor and derided by the power elite, a moneylender was a victim of success: he acquired money, lent it to others, but found it difficult to use it to acquire *iyí*, *ọlá*, and *oyè*, the aspiration of the leading members of his society.

The colonial factor had three major consequences on the informal organization of credit. First, the colonial state was tolerant of many of the practices, only condemning pawning and high interest rates. This liberal attitude was dictated by the need to protect the agricultural production sector from disruption. Pawning, for instance, enabled the use of labor by farmers. An efficient indigenous money market also freed the state from the pressure of having to manage tension between the modern banks and Nigerians, who would have grumbled about dispossession and deprivations if they had no where else to turn to for assistance. Second, in modifying the indigenous institutions, "modernity" provided key lessons: printed documents were introduced to explain practices, contracts were prepared to be signed by the parties, lenders kept registers, interest rates by modern banks provided the lead to follow, and so forth. Third, the state itself interfered in some of the practices by showing its opposition to pawning and enacted ordinances to prohibit it. However, the state was cautious not to accelerate the end of pawning because it will destroy an easy access to labor. To minimize the conflicts arising from moneylending and to check excessive interest rates, the government enacted ordinances to control the trade. However, most of the measures by the state were subverted by many people who, out of ambition or desperation, had to seek credit—an important "source" of money, the "mystical" object with the power to "visit" only a selected few.

Notes

1. To the best of my knowledge, this is the first discussion on the value system as it relates to money in this region. In general, cultural values at the root of historical events and institutions have been ignored by historians of Nigeria.
2. Public Record Office, London, CO 520/8 Sir Ralph Moor to Colonial Office, No. 156, 12 June, 1901.
3. To date there is no major work on the crisis of cowry devaluation and demonetization in spite of many references to such problems in oral data. The problem has been mentioned briefly elsewhere, but without an adequate analysis (see Ofonogaro 1979).
4. *Lagos Annual Report*, 1899, p. 85.
5. National Archives, Ibadan (NAI), Iba Prof. 3./10, Correspondence Book, Letter No. 103/09, 30 April 1909.
6. Oral Interviews: Local historians at Ibadan (J.A. Ayọrinde, E.O. Adeyẹmọ, S.A. Babalọla; various times).
7. Oral Interviews: ibid.; and A.A. Ọlọkọ, H.A. Ọjẹrinọla, both of Ibadan; various times.
8. Oral Interviews: ibid.; and also S.O. Ladipọ of Ibadan; various times.
9. Oral Interviews: ibid.; and also S. Lasẹbikan, local historian, Ẹdẹ.
10. The theme of seeking the "source" of money is predominant in many songs and plays, including many recent popular dramas. In presenting alternative routes to the "source," an aggressive person is portrayed as a loser. There is, however, a general failure to explain success. The rich person is presented as gentle and generous, but there is a silence on what the rich do for a living or how his or her substantial wealth has come about. In large part, such a silence may reflect the reality in modern Nigeria, where it is always difficult to explain how wealthy people came about their wealth, or it may be a legitimization of corruption and the privileges of power as sources of wealth. See for instance Barber (in press).
11. Oral Interviews: Informants mentioned above and T. Ladele of Ibadan. Poverty, too, can be similarly constructed, as in the case of Pauper, father of Wretchedness, the prodigous character in the respected novel by Amos Tutuola, *Pauper, Brawler and Slanderer* (1990).
12. Oral Interviews: local historians at Ibandan, O. Oyewole and S. Siyanbola.
13. Oral Interviews: ibid; and Chief S. O. Ojo, the *Bada* of Saki.
14. Oral Interviews: ibid; and K Adebiyi of Ibadan.
15. Oral Interviews: P. Olunlọyọ and P. Ladapọ, both local historians based at Ibadan.
16. Oral Interviews: ibid; and A. Fatoki, Lalupọ/Ibadan.
17. Oral Interviews: ibid.
18. Space does not permit an elaboration of how the people attempted to discover the various "sources" of money. Discussions on the "sources" of money and power occupy much space in cultural literature written mainly in Yoruba, with a leadership enjoyed by D.O. Fagunwa in almost all his classics, such as *Ogboju Ode Ninu Igbo Irunmale* (1950) and *Aditu Olodumare (1961)*.
19. Oral Interviews: A Adeyẹmọ, Ile Ifẹ; O. Oni, Ilẹsa. It was common to accuse rich people of magic.
20. Oral Interviews: ibid.
21. Oral Interviews: ibid. Even today, such a view is widely held. For instance, in a number of praise songs for Chief M.K.O. Abiola, one of the richest Yoruba men, his wealth is said to be secure from the "machinations of *àgbànà.*"
22. Separate magics developed on job protection. This and other aspects of the new value system constructed on wage labor need to be studied.
23. An allowance was made for inflation in the application of *àgbànà* to an individual.
24. Oral Interviews: O. Faniran and J. Olubukun, both of Ibadan; W. Oyebami, Ijẹbu-Ipẹru.
25. Oral Interviews: ibid.

26. NAI, C.S.O.26/2/11604, "Pawning of persons."
27. Oral Interviews: Chief Bada, *Olubadan* Akinbiyi.
28. The connection bewtween education and corruption has yet tobe investigated.
29. The process and consequences of the urbanization process are discussed by Mabogunje (1968).
30. For instance, the *pàrọ̀* credit mentioned below relied mainly on these imported items. The *osomalo*, too, relied on the use of these imported items in trade and credit transactions.
31. NAI Ije Prof 4/956 vol. 1, Money Lenders' Ordinance, Cap 147.
32. Oral Interviews: O Adesanya, trader and local historian, Lagos; O. Laja, Abẹokuta.
33. For the differences in terms and overlaps, see Bascom (1951).
34. Oral Interviews: Adesanya and Laja.
35. The link between the indigenous banks and the power elite deserves a separate investigation.
36. For another useful description of the same practice in another culture, see Nwabughuogu (1984) and Amogo (1956).
37. Notes for Partridge's article were prepared in 1906 by an Egba man, Sholanke, but this was revised by Partridge, the Resident of Abeokuta.
38. Oral tradition and history are rich on *àjà*. Valuable data was obtained from those already mentioned and K. Morgan, author and local historian, Ibadan; F. Faseun, Ile-Ife; O. Akinbola, trader, Ondo.
39. A recent World Bank publication (Udry 1990) suggests that the pledging of crops as collateral and interest is very widespread in Asia and Africa. There is an older, somewhat neglected study (Firth and Yamey 1964). For another description of the practice in the Nigerian region, see Abasiekong (1981).
40. Oral Interviews: Akinbọla, Ondo; O. Mubo (ex-Produce Dealer, Esa Oke); F. Ali (Farmer/Produce Dealer; Ondo).
41. Oral Interviews: ibid.
42. See the extensive literature on the organization of the slave and "legitimate" trade, including Dike (1956).
43. The description here is based on information obtained from many informants.
44. Oral Interviews: T. Adeniyi [extrader, Ilesa]; O. Oke [extrader, Osu]; O. Bello of Ilorin (in fieldnotes of K. Abiọla; cited by permission).
45. Oral Interviews: ibid.
46. NAI, C.S.O. 26/30315.
47. See for instance, PRO CO 147/133; evidence of James Johnson.
48. On this uncertainty about wage labor in the early years see CMS G/AZ1/4 Enc. 125, Statement by the Rev. D. Williams.
49. *Church Missionary Gleaner,* 37, 1910, 74; The Native Races and the Liquor Traffic United Committee, *The Liquor Traffic in Southern Nigeria as set forth in the Report of the Govenment Committee of Inquiry of 1909; an Examination and a Reply.* London, 1910, pp. 41–42.
50. NAI, Abe Prof 2/1, Letter from William MacGregor, January 20, 1903.
51. Ibid., 236
52. See, for instance, NAI APP 3/1/47, Egba Custom, Memorandum by A. Edun, Secretary, Egba Native Administration.
53. NAI, C.S.O. 26/1/06827 vol. I, League of Nations, *Advisory Committee of Experts on Slavery,* Third (Extraordinary) Session of the Committee, Geneva, April 15–24, 1936.
54. NAI, C.S.O. 26/1/06827 vol. II (see the memo to the Secretary, SP of June 2, 1926.
55. National Archives, Ibadan, Oyo Prof 1028/989, Public Notice.
56. See, for instance, *The West African Pilot,* July 5, 1938.
57. NAI Abe Prof 341/63.
58. CMS G/AZ1/1. Encl. 25, Paper by Bishop Crowther.
59. Ibid.

60. See, for instance, a document introduced by A. G.Hopkins (1969:88ff).
61. NAI, C.S.O. 30315 vol. 1, Money Lenders' Amendment Ordinance 1935.
62. Ibid.
63. Ibid.
64. NAI Ije Prof 4/J.679 Money Lenders' Ordinance Cap 147 Corresp. in re. 1929/44 and Ijaw W. 4/W.1 167 vol. 1 Money Lenders' Licence-Matters Re 1937/48.
65. NAI, C.S.O. 26/30315 vol. II.
66. See, for instance, Ije Prof 4/956 vol. 1.
67. Oral Interview: informant wants anonymity.
68. Oral Interview: Chief Bada of Saki.

Sources

Archival

Great Britain

Public Record Office, London (PRO)

C.O. 147/133; evidence of James Johnson.
C.O. 520/8 Sir Ralph Moor to Colonial Office, No. 156, 12 June, 1901.

C.M.S (Birmingham

C.M.S. G/AZ1/1 Encl. 25, Paper by Bishop Crowther
C.M.S. G/AZ1/4 Encl. 125, Statement by the Rev. D. Williams.

Nigeria

National Archives, Ibadan (NAI)

Abe Prof 2/1, Letter from William MacGregor, January 20, 1903
Abe Prof 341/63.
APP 3/1/47, Egba Custom, Memorandum by A. Edun, Secretary, Egba Native Administration
C.S.O. 26/1/06827 vol. I League of Nations, *Advisory Committee of Experts on Slavery,* Third (Extraordinary) Session of the Committee, Geneva, April 15–24, 1936
C.S.O. 26/1/06827 vol. I, Memo to the Secretary, SP of June 2, 1926, 236.
C.S.O. 26/30315 vol. I, Money Lenders' Amendment Ordinance 1935
C.S.O. 26/30315 vol. II.
C.S.O. 26/2/11604, "Pawning of persons."
Iba Prof. 3./10, Correspondence Book, Letter No. 103/09, 30 April 1909.
Ije Prof 4/956 vol. 1
Ije Prof 4/956 vol. 1, Money Lenders' Ordinance, Cap 147.
Ije Prof 4/J.679 Money Lenders' Ordinance Cap 147 Corresp. in re. 1929/44 and Ijaw W. 4/W.1 167 vol. 1 Money Lenders' Licence-Matters Re 1937/48.
Oyo Prof 1028/989, Public Notice

Government Documents

Lagos Annual Report , 1899

Interviews

Abẹokuta

O. Laja Ẹdẹ.

S. Laṣebikan

Esa Oke

O. Mubo

Ibadan

K Adebiyi, E.O. Adeyẹmọ, J.A. Ayọrinde, S.A. Babalọla, O. Faniran, P. Ladapọ, S.O. Ladipọ, T. Ladele, K. Morgan, H.A. Ojẹrinọla, A.A. Ọlọkọ, J. Olubukun, P Olunlọyọ, O. Oyewole, S. Siyanbola

Ijlebu-Ipẹru

W. Oyebami

Ile Ifẹ

A Adeyẹmọ, F. Faseun

Ileṣa

O. Oni

Lagos

O Adesanya

Lalupọn/Ibadan

A. Fatoki

Ondo

F. Ali, O. Akinbọla

Elsewhere

Adesanya; Laja; Chief S. O. Ojo, the *Bada* of Saki; Chief Bada, *Olubadan* Akinbiyi.

From the Field Notes of K. Abiola, Cited by Permission of K. Abiola

T. Adeniyi, *Ilesa*; O. Oke, *Osu*; O. Bello, *Ilorin*

Newspapers

Church Missionary Gleaner

The West African Pilot

Books, Dissertations, and Articles

Abasiekong, E. M. 1981. "Pledging Oil Palms: A Case Study on Obtaining Rural Credit In Nigeria," *African Studies Review*, 24: 73–82.

Adeoye, C. L. 1979. *Aṣa Ati Ise Yoruba*. New York and Ibadan: Oxford University Press.

Ajisafẹ, A. K. 1964. *History of Abeokuta*. Abeokuta: Fola Publishing Co.

Akeredolu-Ale, E. O. 1976. "Private Foreign Investment and the Underdevelopment of Indigenous Entrepreneurship in Nigeria." In *Nigeria: Economy a nd Society*, ed. G. William, 106–122. London: Rex Collings.

Akintola, J. O. 1975. "The Pattern of Growth in Manufacturing in Southwestern Nigeria 1956-1971 and the Role of Direct Public Policy in that Growth." Ph.D. dissertation, Boston University, Boston, MA.

Akinyele , I. B. 1911. *Iwe Itan Ibadan, Iwo, Ikirun at Osogbo*. Ibadan: I. B. Akinyele.

Amogu, O. O. 1956, "Some Notes on Savings in an African Economy." *Social and Economic Studies*, 5.

Ardener, S. 1964. "The Comparative Study Of Rotating Credit Associations." *Journal of the Royal Anthropological Institute*, 94.

Atanda, J. A. 1973.*The New Oyo Empire: Indirect Rule and Change in Western Nigeria*,

1894-1934. London: Longman.

Awẹ, B. 1973. "Militarism and Economic Development in nineteenth Century Yoruba Country: T he Ibadan Example." *Journal of African History,* 14:65-77.

Barber, K. (In press). "Petrol and Popular Drama." In *Oil and the Nigerian Society,* ed. Toyin Falọla. London and New York: Longman.

Bascom, W. R. 1951. "Social Status, Wealth and Individual Differe nces Among The Yoruba." *American Anthropologist,* 53:490-505.

―――. 1952. "The Esusu: A Credit Institution of the Yoruba." *Journal of the Royal Anthropological Institute,* 82:63-69.

Berry, S. 1975. *Cocoa, Custom And Socio-Economic Change In Rural Western Nig eria.* New York and London: Oxford University Press.

Bohannan, Paul and Laura Bohannan. 1968. *Tiv Economy.* Evanston, IL: Northwestern University Press.

Brown, C. V. 1963. *Government and Banking in Western Nigeria.* New York, Oxford, and Ibadan: Oxford University Press.

Brown, I., ed. 1989. *The Economies of Africa and Asia in the Inter-war Depression.* London: Routledge.

Cohen, Abner. 1969. *Custom and Politics in Urban Africa: A Study of Hausa Migrants in Yoruba Towns.* Berkeley, CA: University of California Press.

Delano, I. 1937. *The Soul of Nigeria.* London: Laurie.

Dike, K. O. 1956. *Trade and Politics in the Niger Delta, 1830-1885.* Oxford: Clarendon Press.

Ekundare, R. O. 1973.*An Economic History of Nigeria, 1860-1960.* London: Methuen.

Elgee, C. H. 1914.*The Evolution of Ibadan.* Lagos: Government Printer.

Fadipe, N. A. 1970.*The Sociology of the Yorubas.* Ibadan: Ibadan University Press.

Fagunwa, D. O. 1950.*Ogboju Ode Ninu Igbo Irunmale.* Lagos: Nelson.

―――. 1961.*Aditu Olodumare.* Lagos, Nelson.

Falọla, Toyin. 1983 "Power, Status and Influence of Yoruba Chiefs in Historical Perspective." Conference Paper, University of Ibadan.

―――, ed. 1987. *Nigeria and Britain: Exploitation or Development?* London and Atlantic Highlands, New Jersey: Zed.

―――. 1991. "The Yoruba Caravan System of the Nineteenth Century." *The International Journal of African Historical Studies,* 24:111-132.

―――. 1992a. "Warfare and Military Alliances in Yorubaland in the Nineteenth Century." In *Warfare And Diplomacy in Precolonial Nigeria: Essays in Honor of Rob ert Smith,* ed. Toyin Falọla and Robin Law, 26-30.. Madison, WI: African Studies Program, University of Wisconsin.

―――. 1992b. "The Lebanese in West Africa." In *People and Empires in Africa: Essays in Memory of Michael Crowder,* ed. J. F. Ade Ajayi and J. D. Y. Peel, 121-142. London: Longman.

―――. 1993. "My Friend the Shylock: Moneylenders and Their Clients in Southwestern Nigeria." *Journal of African History,* 34:403-42.

―――. 1994. "Pawnship in Colonial Southwestern Nigeria." In *Pawnship in Africa: Debt Bondage in Historical Perspective,* ed. Paul Lovejoy and Toyin Falọla. Boulder, Colorado: Westview: 245-266.

――― and O. B. Lawuyi. 1990. "Not Just a Currency: The Cowrie in Nigerian Culture." In *West African Economic and Social History: Studies in Memory of Marion*

Johnson, ed., D. Henige and T. C. McCaskie. Madison, WI: African Studies Program, University of Wisconsin.

Firth, R. and B. S. Yamey, eds. 1964. *Capital, Saving and Credit in Peasant Societies*. Chicago, IL: Aldine.

Fry, R. 1976. *Bankers in West Africa: The Story of the Bank of British West Africa Limited*. London: Hutchinson.

Galletti, R., Baldwin, K. D. S. and I. O. Dina. 1956. *Nigerian Cocoa Farmers: An Economic Survey of Yoruba Cocoa Farming Families*. London: Oxford University Press.

Geertz, C. 1962. "The Rotating Credit Association: A 'Middle Rung' in Development." *Economic Development and Cultural Change*, 10:241–263.

Greenidge, C. W. 1958. *Slavery*. London: Allen & Unwin.

Hodder, B. W. and Ukwu, U. I. 1969. *Markets in West Africa: Studies of Markets and Trade Among The Yoruba and Ibo*. Ibadan: Ibadan University Press.

Hogendorn, Jan and Marion Johnson. 1986.*The Shell Money of the Slave Trade*. New York and Cambridge: Cambridge University Press.

Hopkins, A. G. 1966. "The Currency Revolution in Southern Nigeria in the Late Nineteenth Century." *Journal of the Historical Society of Nigeria*, 3:471–83.

———. 1969. "A Report on the Yoruba, 1910." *Journal of the Historical Society of Nigeria* 5:67–100.

Idowu, E. B. 1963. *Olodumare: God in Yoruba Belief*. New York: Praeger.

Johnson, Samuel. 1921. *The History of the Yorubas*. Lagos: C.M.S.

Kurtz, D. V. 1973. "The Rotating Credit Association: An Adaptation to Poverty." *Human Organization*, 32:49–58.

Law, R. 1978. "Slaves, Trade and Taxes: The Material Basis of Political Power In Precolonial West Africa." *Research In Economic Anthropology* 1:37–52.

Loynes, J. B. 1962. *The West African Currency Board, 1912–1962*. London: West African Currency Board.

Lugard, F. D. [1918] 1970. *Political Memoranda*, 3rd ed. London: Frank Cass.

Mabogunje, A. L. 1968. *Urbanization in Nigeria*. London: University of London Press.

Mars, J. 1948. "The Monetary and Banking System and the Loan Market of Nigeria." In *Mining, Commerce and Finance in Nigeria*. Vol. 2 of *The Economics of a Tropical Dependency*, ed. M. F. Perham. London: Faber and Faber, under the auspices of Nuffield College.

Marshall, G. 1964. "Women, Trade and the Yoruba Family." Ph.D. dissertation, Columbia University.

Native Races and the Liquor Traffic United Committee. 1910. *The Liquor Traffic in Southern Nigeria as set forth in the Report of the Government Committee of Inquiry of 1909; an Examination and a Reply*. London: Native Races and the Liquor Traffic United Committee.

Nwabughuogu, A. I. 1982. "From Wealthy Entrepreneurs to Petty Traders: The Decline of African Middleman in Eastern Nigeria, 1900-1950." *Journal of African History*, 23:365–79.

———. 1984. "The Isusu: An institution for Capital Formation among the Ngwa Igo: Its Origin and Development to 1951." *Africa* 54: 46–58.

Nwankwo, O. 1980. *The Nigerian Financial System*. London: Macmillan.

O'Hear, Ann. 1986. "Political and Commercial Clientage in Nineteenth Century Ilorin." *African Economic History*, 15:69–84.

Ofonogaro, W. I. 1979. "From Traditional to British Currency in Southern Nigeria:

Analysis of a Currency Revolution, 1880-1948." *Journal of Economic History,* 39:623-54.

Okigbo, P. C. 1981. *Nigerian Financial System.* London: Longman.

Oroge, E. A. 1985. "Iwofa: An Historical Survey of the Yoruba Institution of Indenture." *African Economic History,* 14:76-86.

Oṣoba, S. O. 1969. "The Phenomenon of Labour Migration In The Era Of British Colonial Rule." *Journal of the Historical Society of Nigeria,* 4:515-538.

Oyejide, T. A. 1977. "A Structural Analysis of Some Institutionalized Saving Patterns in Nigeria, 1961-73." *Journal of Business and Social Studies,*1.

Partridge, C. 1910. "Native Law and Custom in Egbaland." *Journal of the African Society,* 10:422-433.

Schatz, S. P. 1974. *Development Bank Lending in Nigeria: The Federal Loans Board.* London: Oxford University Press.

————. 1977. *Nigerian Capitalism.* Berkeley, CA: University of California Press.

Seidman, Ann. 1986. *Money, Banking and Public Finance in Africa.* London and Atlantic Highlands, NJ: Zed.

Stiglitz, J. 1990. "Peer Monitoring and Credit Markets." *The World Bank Economic Review,* 4:351-66.

Tamuno, T. N. 1972. *The Evolution of the Nigerian State: The Southern Phase 1898-1914.* London: Longman.

Tutuola, Amos. 1990. *Pauper, Brawler and Slanderer.* London: Faber and Faber.

Udry,C. 1990. "Credit Markets in Northern Nigeria: Credit as Insurance in a Rural Economy." *The World Bank Economic Review,* 4:251-69.

8

Changes in Marriage and Funeral Exchanges Among the Asante: A Case Study from Kona, Afigya-Kwabre

TAKYIWAA MANUH

In this chapter, I explore some changes that have occurred in marriage and funeral exchanges among the Asante over the past half-century. The link between marriages and funerals may be seen from casual observation in Asante social life. In particular, this is true at funerals, where the fullest expression is given to the reciprocal relationships and obligations established between the kinfolk of a man and a woman upon marriage, arising from what Levi-Strauss (1969:60–61) termed the "total phenomenon, total exchange . . . comprising food, manufactured objects, and that most precious category of goods, women." (cited in Comaroff 1980:26).

Extant accounts of Asante marriage (Rattray 1923, 1929; Fortes 1950; Busia 1951) have depicted marriage as a process, characterized by ongoing negotiations between the two parties. Marriage rites were simple and the payments small; the sums of money paid did not serve to enrich the parents or family of the bride, but were distributed among witnesses (Rattray 1929:78). There appeared to be considerable flexibility in marriage arrangements; divorce was relatively easy, and could be initiated by either party at any time. Fortes' account in the 1930s describes the conjugal relationship as a bundle of separable rights and bonds rather than a unitary "all or none tie" (1950:280). All accounts agree that marriage transferred little to the husband, save the exclusive right to the wife's sexual favors, which entitled him to collect *ayere fa* , (the fine imposed in the case of the wife's adultery) (Rattray 1929:78; Fortes 1950; Odudoye 1981). Indeed, the wife's uncle could compel her to reside with him and to provide him with her labor (Rattray 1929). Apparently only a woman who was also a pawn was obliged to render labor services to her husband, while free women had greater control over their labor and engaged mostly in food production for the needs of the households in which they resided.

This was to change with the advent of cocoa in Asante at the turn of the century, when all were drawn into commodity production, and the labor of wives, children, and other family members became crucial to the successful operation of a cocoa farm (Okali 1983). This was also a period of momentous social change (see Arhin, Ch. 4; Field 1960), which was played out at the level of social relations by the definitions and redefinition of roles, rewards, and expectations, as attempts were made by chiefs, elders, and husbands to assert greater control over the labor and sexuality of women (Roberts 1987; Clark 1993). Many informants speak of a "hunt" for wives during this period, which resulted in a rise in the levels of bridewealth payments. Fortes mentions payments of 10 shillings with an additional 6d. for rum or wine as *tiri nsa*, or *aseda*, for a commoner in the 1920s. By the 1940s, this had increased to £3, although most descriptions refer to "spirits" (alcohol) and a few shillings (Fortes n.d.; see Rattray 1929:81 for a scale of *tiri aseda* before the 1920s). Similar increases in funeral payments as well as an expansion in the actual ceremonies and performances in connection with death were noted, and were the subject of discussion and legislation by traditional authorities.

The theoretical framework for this chapter is derived from Comaroff's analysis of the meaning of marriage payments, which locates such payments centrally within socio-cultural systems. As noted by Comaroff (1980:33),

> Marriage alienations derive their meaning by virtue of their location in the embracing logic of cycles of reciprocal giving and taking. . . . Prestations cannot be understood except in so far as they are elements in total socio-cultural systems. Any such system may be analyzed at two levels. On the one hand, it exists as a set of related principles which give form to the socio-cultural universe. On the other, it is a lived-in, everyday context which represents itself to individuals and groups in a repertoire of values and contra-dictions, rules and relationships, interests and ideologies.

This view of prestations appears useful in exploring changes that have occurred over time in the levels of payments at marriage and for funerals, and the variations within each, including the greater significance ostensibly accorded some categories of relations. It may explain also the outstripping of marriage payments by funeral payments; and the ways in which they are perceived by members of a society. The Asante have been chosen because marriage payments have never been large, in comparison with other Ghanaian ethnic groups (see Nukunya [1969] for the Anlo Ewe), while their expenditure on funeral payments appears now to exceed those of all other groups. The choice of a rural town, Kona, is also deliberate, because of the belief that change is usually slow in rural communities and they may therefore show more adherence to "traditional" practices and usages. However, Kona is not very far from Kumasi, the metropolis, and is thus subject to its influences. The question may be posed then: in light of their more limited access to wealth, how have rural communities dealt with change and currency instability, and how is this reflected in marital payments?

A related issue concerns changes in the value of expenditure for funerals, the observance of which is arguably more important to the Asante than any other practice, bringing together kin, affines, and associates in increasingly more elaborate and widespread ways (Arhin 1993). Indeed, there appears to be little to equal or surpass the celebration of funerals in Ghana generally, and in Asante in particular, where funerals become a means to *poatwa* , pull rank, or cast insinuations through a display of wealth (Arhin 1983). The elaborateness of the funeral ceremony attests to both the wealth of the family and the esteem in which the deceased was held; it becomes a means by which the performers are in turn esteemed by society. The funeral of important maternal relations, such as the mother, uncle, or grandmother of an Akan person, and to a slightly lesser extent, of his or her father or spouse, becomes a means of valuation according to customary norms.

Rather than seeing these expenses on funerals and other social observances as wasteful, it might be more useful to see them from the perspectives of their practitioners. Berry (1988) characterizes these expenditures and others as a diversification of options in a period of stress, and investing in social institutions as a strategy for gaining access to productive resources. Similarly, Arhin (1993) sees high expenditures on funerals as not only cementing existing social relations and creating new ones, but as having a positive economic impact through the boost that it gives to service industries and micro-enterprises.

Marriage Rites

Marriage typically proceeded through stages in Asante, beginning with the *kokooko* (knocking) rite, performed with palm wine in the past, and later with a bottle of schnapps or *akpeteshie* (a local brew), and having no money involved.[1] The "knocking" signifies interest and makes the family aware of the intentions of the suitor. It also permits the man to pay nocturnal visits to the woman and not be branded a thief. Premarital sex and childbearing are permitted at this stage, as long as puberty rites have been performed for the woman. However, it does not confer any rights upon the man with regard to the freedom of the woman. Where there is a funeral or litigation between the woman and another member of the house, there is no obligation to invite the man, even if he has had children with the woman. Normally certain outsiders will be invited to litigation hearings if they are not of a sensitive nature because they can serve as witnesses, but an outside man who is otherwise treated as the intended husband of a daughter of the family has no particular rights to participate.

The next stage in the marriage ceremony is the *ahunu animu* (showing your face) rite. By this rite, the prospective groom is introduced to the family of the woman as someone who is about to marry a woman in the house. This rite is sometimes called *nkotoagyan* (a useless bottle). On any occasion or event within the house, the man may or may not be invited, depending on the decision of the family members. Where they believe that the man's behavior towards them is extremely cordial, they may invite him to participate in their deliberations. He is always invited on issues concerning the prospective wife. *Ahunu animu* is also called *atumpan hunu* (another term for "useless bottle") because if the wife commits adultery, the family may refuse to back the husband's claim to the adultery fine. During this stage, the family collects some money as custom demands, which is distributed among members of the matrilineage to serve as a witness to the marriage. The brothers-in-law charge their *nkonta gye*, a symbolic amount for allowing their sister to go, according to how much they can extract out of their in-law.

The final stage is the *etiri aseda* (thanks offering for the giving of the head), thanking the maternal family and father of the bride for allowing the suitor to marry the woman. This is the climax of the marriage and once this rite is performed, it is recognized by all and sundry that the woman is married. The husband may also give presents to his wife, consisting of cloths and headscarves and other items for her personal use. Such gifts are not required, but reflect the status or means of the parties. No special gifts appear to be made to the mother and other female relatives present, beyond their share of what is given to the matrilineage. A part of the *aseda* fee is sent to the father, if he happens to be elsewhere. The husband is also directed to go and see his father-in-law.

The significant results of this rite are several: the man becomes the recognized husband of the woman; the husband, supported by the woman's family, has the right to collect *ayere fa* (the adultery fine) from any man who makes an attempt to flirt or actually flirts with the woman; the husband acquires the right to take the woman to a shrine for clarification as to whether or not she has been flirting; when there is a funeral in the wife's family, the husband is counted as a member of the family and he pays what other members of the family pay; and, finally, the husband or wife is allowed to perform all rites pertaining to the death of the other and she or he is allowed to bring *ade sie die* (burial items) when the mother-in-law or father-in-law dies.

In Kona, throughout the first part of the twentieth century, many husbands chose to perform all the rites at the same time under the rubric of *aseda* fees. This procedure reduced the cost of marriage considerably, because the *aseda* was always fixed to some extent, and consisted of two bottles of gin, one of which was sent to the father of the bride with a part of the *aseda*, where the marriage was contracted before the wife's matrilineage. The rest of the *aseda* was distributed within the matrilineage. The reverse was also true, so that where the marriage occurred before the father, he had to transmit a part of the *aseda* payment to his daughter's matrilineage.

In the event that the wife was related to a shrine—either because she was conceived through the intercession of the shrine, or because the shrine was located in her family—a bottle of gin and a specified amount had to be paid to the shrine. The husband would also approach the father-in-law for an assessment of other "customary" fees to be paid.[2] These fees were made up of the costs of *danta* (loin cloth); *Nyame dwan* (God's sheep), and *taa* (tobacco), all specifically meant for the father of the bride. These were not fixed, but were a bargain between father-in-law and groom. The sheep or its equivalent in money was to be used by the father to offer a libation to his guardian spirits, and was given to him in gratitude for the care and guidance devoted by him to his daughter during her childhood (Fortes 1950: 212). *Danta* is a long piece of cloth, roughly 2 m long and 10 cm wide, which is used to cover the waist of a dead man about to be buried. Custom expected *danta* to be provided during the burial of a father-in-law. According to informants however, experience had taught fathers-in-law to collect their *danta* as early as possible for the following reasons. First, some fathers-in-law wanted to see the quality of the loin cloth to be used for their burial—usually, they preferred the type woven in Northern Ghana. More importantly, if they did not collect the *danta* at the time of marriage and there was a break-up, they might never get it. A father might have as many *danta* as possible, depending on the number of daughters whom he had, and the number of times they married. With the advent of British coins in circulation and the European silk yarns on the market, it became easier to value *danta* in monetary terms, and it was possible to commute it to a cash payment.

Funeral Rites

Unlike marriages, funerals are much more elaborate and highly ritualized. Particular ceremonies and observances such as fasts, avoidances by some categories of persons, and wailings occur, and funeral ceremonies involve the participation of many people because death is regarded as a matter of public concern. Rattray (1929) describes the funerals of ordinary people from the moment that the last rites have been administered to them, and the description that follows is drawn from his account. The body is washed and dressed in fine clothes, and various forms of what is regarded as "ghost" or "soul" currency is tied to the wrists, while packets of gold dust are also tied to the loin cloth. Burial objects (*ade sie die*) are presented by particular relations, including the head of the political unit to which the deceased belonged, paternal relations, children, widowers or widows, and close friends. These obligatory and reciprocal exchanges are commented upon by Rattray (1929:155) as follows:

> So essential and rigid were the unwritten laws that certain . . . persons must perform certain acts and give presents at the funeral, that proof of this kind of cooperation is even now held in the courts of law as evidence that a certain relationship between the deceased and the person who took a particular part in the rites must have existed.

The burial gifts are for the benefit of both the deceased and the living, and while the deceased is believed to require them for his journey to and residence in the land of ghosts, those making presents stake claims for the attention of the family in order to validate a status or a right, or to fulfill a reciprocal obligation. The bulk of the gifts are retained by relatives of the deceased. The quality and quantity of burial gifts paraded before assembled mourners enhance or diminish the social standing of the lineage.

The *ade sie die* include presentations of sponges and towels for bathing the deceased, mats, pieces of cloth, gold dust, and sometimes a small nugget of gold.[3,4] Food and sheep for performing particular rituals and for provisioning mourners are also provided. Some of the cloth, rings, and gold dust are buried with the deceased, accompanied by messages to dead relatives in the land of the ghosts and prayers to the ghost of the deceased. In earlier times, coffins were not much in use, except for persons of high rank, and dead persons were buried in mats. The use of coffins has become more common, and they are now provided by the children. The family itself, the *abusua*, provided gunpowder for firing guns; apparently, the quantity of gunpowder expended was a measure of the wealth, number, and position of a family. In addition, they provided food and several pots of palm wine.

The actual funeral celebration generally occurs on the third day after death, when the corpse is buried to the accompaniment of drumming and dancing and ostensible merrymaking. The proceedings vary according to the rank of the deceased. Thus, funerals for chiefs or office-holders would be much more elaborate than those of "commoners." It is a community event, when donations (*nsa*) of money and pots of wine are made by specified relations and friends. However, it is the *abusua* that is liable for any debts arising from the funeral.

Legislation on Marriages and Funerals.

The more generalized invasion of wealth into the Asante economy with the development of cocoa production, new avenues for the acquisition of wealth accompanying
colonial rule, and the absence of the Asantehene and his court led to the dissolution
of former rank and class gradations in Asante (Arhin 1983). One of the ways in which
this was manifested was in the increase in expenses connected with both marriages
and funerals. In the case of funerals, this was accompanied by changes in scale and
quality, and became the subject of some official concern.

Table 8-1, which lays out the costs of *aseda* during different periods in the past at
Kona, illustrates some of these changes.

TABLE 8-1   Changes in Marriage Payments in Kona, 1900–1955

Period	Commoners			Royals		
	Nhunu-animu	Aseda	Father's Portion	Nhunu-animu	Aseda	Father's Portion
1900–1905		£0/3/6			£0/7/0 **	
1920–1925		£0/13/0	£0/7/0		£1/0/0	
1930–1935	£0/7/0			£0/13/0	£1/1/0	
1936–1940		£1/1/0	£0/13/0		£1/1/0	
1941–1945	£0/10/6				£2/7/0	
1946–1950	£1/1/0	£1/1/0			£2/7/0	
1951–1955		£4/13/0	£4/13/0 plus		£4/13/0	

As is evident from the table, marriage payments increased with time, and payments for women of royal birth were almost twice as much as for commoners. A similar process occurred in the case of funerals, with changes in scale noticeable from the
1930s and 1940s.

The restoration of the Asante Confederacy Council in 1935 led to attempts to
regularize matters in Asante and was also the occasion to attempt to restore status
differentiations. In 1941, the Council came out with a declaration on marriage,
divorce and funerals. The reasons for the new enactments were as follows:

1. To eliminate customs thought to be outmoded
2. To unify marriage payments throughout Asante
3. To prevent extortion from unscrupulous parents
4. To generate revenue for the Council through the collection of registration
   fees
5. To categorize the fees due to traditional rulers and commoners according to
   their status within the Confederacy

The declaration spelled out what was to be paid in performing the *aseda* rite and
funeral payments. The nine divisional chiefs took half of what the Asantehene took.

All other chiefs in Asante received the following fees on the marriage of the following relations:

Relation	Aseda
Royals (i.e., their female relatives—nieces etc)	£2/7/0 and 2 bottles gin
Daughter	£1/3/6 and 2 bottles gin
Granddaughter	£1/3/6 and 2 bottles gin
Great granddaughter	£1/3/6 and 2 bottles gin

Commoners were to receive £1/3/6 as *aseda* fees. If a man wanted to marry any of the "queenmothers," *ahemaa*, who were unmarried, the following was the scale of fees:

Relation	Aseda
Asantehemaa (the queen-mother of the Asante nation)	£18/12/0 and 12 bottles gin
obaahemaa (queen-mother of any division)	£9/6/0 and 4 bottles gin
obaapanyin (senior woman of a sub-division)	£4/13/0 and 2 bottles gin

At the time of the legislation, a bottle of gin was valued at 7 shillings, and husbands could pay the amount involved instead of buying the bottles of gin.

The declaration stated that when a woman divorced her husband, she had to return all articles of dress and valuable trinkets given to her. If, on the other hand, it was the husband who divorced her, then monies given to her for her maintenance and donations were not refundable. Secondly, if a young woman betrothed in her infancy (an *asiwa*) refused to consummate the marriage on reaching puberty, expenses incurred by the husband were recoverable if the *aseda* had been paid.

The 1941 enactment enjoined all and sundry to register their wives at a cost of five shillings, to enable the council to increase its revenue base, and at the same time to give recognition to marriages in the Confederation. The declaration on marriage, divorce, and funerals was concerned to maintain the old distinctions in quality and scale among funeral rites for grades of chiefs, chiefs, and commoners, and members of royal lineages; to curtail the rising costs of funeral rites; to abolish widowhood rites; and to abolish the custom of distinguishing between matrikin and spouses in matter of payments of funeral expenses. It also attempted to curtail the period of mourning and fasts,[5] discontinue the practice of *adosua kyekyere*,[6] and to limit the donations that could be made to commoners.

The enactments in respect to marriage fees appear to have been observed in Kumasi and the areas of the divisional chiefs. The subdivisional areas, a category in which Kona fell, also observed them to some extent for a while, until 1950, when the order began to be disobeyed. For the order to be obeyed, the Asantehene needed the cooperation of all divisional and subdivisional chiefs, who were to educate their subjects on the order. Some towns and villages adhered to the order. They would not collect any marriage fees in excess of the stipulated amounts.

In Kona, between 1940 and 1949, the marriage fee hovered around 1 guinea (£1/1/0). Between 1951 to 1955, however, the *aseda* fee soared, and the probable cause of this was the sharp rise in cocoa prices to 4 pounds sterling per load of 80 lb. of cocoa. This high price led to migration by aspiring farmers, many of whom required wives to go out with them. The increased demand for wives, coupled with the improved incomes of cocoa farmers, accounted for the high *aseda* fees.

Of the men and women interviewed by the author at Kona, only a few knew of the existence of the by-laws, even though they were adults in 1940. According to them, no *gong-gong* was beaten to explain issues to residents. (Beating the gong-gong was the form of public address, giving notice to the populace of all significant events, meetings and declarations.) The regulation on *aseda* fees could be and was slighted; funerals were observed for more than the stipulated four days, and there were observations on the eighth, the fourteenth, and the fortieth day following death, as well as on the first anniversary. According to informants, widows were treated with contempt and made to follow tradition as it existed in the past. Finally, none of the men registered his wife.

In 1949, an enactment relating to the fidelity of wives was made, and set out a scale of adultery fines commensurate with the rank of the aggrieved husband. The following is the scale for the subdivision of Kona.

Rank	Adultery Fees
The subdivisional chief's wife	£37/4/0
The chief's son's wife	£4/13/0
The chief's grandson's wife	£2/7/0
Commoners	£1/3/6

(Adultery with the divisional chief's wife resulted in a fine of £74/8/0.)

The reasons given for the creation of the ordinance included the need to curb immoral practices and to reduce the exorbitant fees charged by some chiefs.[7] But the real reasons were otherwise, and suggest an attempt to control the sexuality of women and to increase the powers and privileges of chiefs. Certain chiefs had several *ayete* (wives by custom), some of whom they neglected, but from whom any man was barred unless the chief had divorced them formally.

Transformations in the Contemporary Period

There have been profound changes in the Ghanaian political economy and social life, particularly beginning in the mid-1960s, arising from a combination of domestic and external factors. The separation of currency from the British pound, the introduction of the new cedi, inflation, and massive devaluations of the currency have affected people profoundly and have created various instabilities in the content of social life. Paradoxically, but perhaps not really so (Berry 1989), the current period coincides with massive changes in the scale and quality of material culture, and displays of wealth in many aspects of social life. Expenses for marriage and funerals provide a window from which to view some of these adjustments, and as Arhin (1993) comments, the essentials of funeral rites have been so altered in scale that they bear little resemblance to the rites remembered by older Asante informants. Similarly, there have been alterations in the size of marriage payments, but they are nowhere near even minimum expenses on funerals, expressing perhaps the Asante view of marriage as transient, compared to the more enduring and almost unseverable links that compose kinship identity. I use data from Kona and Kumasi to analyze some of these transformations.

By 1968, the *aseda* fee at Kona was NC20 (twenty new cedis),[8] and this covered all aspects of the marriage rites. Two decades later, research could not even define the marriage fee. At Kona, some fathers will now "charge"[9] not less than C10,000, for husbands to pay, and some fathers say they would charge not less than C15,000.[10] While in real terms the payments may be more or less equivalent to payments in earlier periods, they are high relative to incomes of rural dwellers. These have barely kept pace with inflation, except perhaps more recently for those farmers in possession of cocoa incomes, who have benefited from raises in the producer price of cocoa.[11]

There seems to be little difference between performing the marriage rites in a rural or urban area, although they would be considerably more expensive, depending on the status (wealth) of the parents, the educational level of the woman, and the income or status of the would-be husband. For example, in Adum, a suburb of Kumasi, some parents said they would not collect anything less than C15,000. However, in the present period, there has been little attempt in Asante to regulate the scales of marriage payments, and a laissez-faire approach is dominant.

What is interesting is the apparent the increase in the prominence of the father in marriage transactions. While the father was always consulted in the marriage of his daughter and had the obligation in Asante for finding a wife for his grown son, in the past, the matrilineage was more active in the marriages of women. This appears to be changing now. In part it may be due to the fact that many fathers now assume direct responsibility for the maintenance of their children, sending them to school, and helping to establish them in a trade or profession afterwards. Such fathers may well feel that they have earned the right to any benefits from a child, especially when marriage payments are now expressed as "charges." In fact, although Asante maintain extreme delicacy in such matters, it is not unusual to detect elements of hard bargaining at marriage ceremonies, with some fathers expressing the feeling that their dignities have been insulted by the paltry sums of money offered in the name of "tradition and custom."[12]

While more attention seems to be paid to not offending the feelings of the father, little appears to have changed in the position of the mother and other female relatives during marriage ceremonies; most end up with paltry sums of money given to the "women in the household." But this may also be changing, and I have witnessed ceremonies of high-status marriages in which the mother received a parcel of cloth for her work in bringing up the young woman. In these types of marriages also, cartons of "soft" drinks (soda) and aperitifs or sweet wine may also be given to the mother and other female relatives, but these are not, as yet, generalized occurences.[13]

What are considered exorbitant charges for marriages have prevented many "husbands" from performing the rites, and may have increased the incidence of people living together in many forms of fluid relations. Of the ten women interviewed who were in a union, none had had the rites performed for her. A man who performed his in 1987 paid as much as C7,000. By 1988, another had to pay C10,000. From interviews, it appeared that much more change was taking place in the area of marriage than just the expenses connected with it, although the expense was used often as a shorthand to express a reluctance to marry. Many young men and women, for example, were not ready to marry. For example, some young women said they were too busy pursuing their business enterprises. Others argued that today's man has nothing to offer his wife and for this reason, they would not commit themselves to any form of marriage. [14] A more extreme view characterized marriage as slavery; this informant refused marriage. Others said that they had married once or twice, and from the experience gained, they would never marry again. Some teenagers wanted to acquire a few possessions before committing themselves to marriage, or needed to learn a trade in order to help their future family. For many men, the expenses connected with marriage were cited as the reason. These views express the conflict that many women, for example, clearly foresee between the demands of their business enterprises and the duties of marriage. Beyond the constraints of time, there is expressed some ambivalence about the perceived security obtained from marriage, as opposed to one's own business, and reflects some of the larger tensions in gender relations in Ghana over the past two decades (Clark 1993).

In the area of funerals, the transformations are much greater, and Arhin (1993) suggests that these may be due to the growth of towns; migration; acquisition of new tastes and outlooks; better communication systems; and, more importantly, changes in religious beliefs.[15] Thus, while Islam, for example, prescribes simple burials for its adherents, Christianity may be seen as weakening the beliefs and practices of traditional religions and advancing the conversion of a predominantly sacred event into a profane one, converting funerals into opportunities for money making (Arhin 1993).

There has been an elaboration of the ceremonies and performances connected with death—and the costs. A typical "programme of events" for a funeral consists of a "lying in state" and wake-keeping, which is usually on a Friday; burial on Saturday, followed by the actual performance of the funeral rites, which are continued on Sunday; "making accounts" (Monday); thanking mourners (Monday); a memorial service, which could take place on the Sunday after burial or some time hence; a fortieth day celebration; and the anniversary, which brings the funeral finally to a close. Financing such an enterprise demands human and capital resources, with people running various errands and seeing to "arrangements," and sometimes making loans or donations of one or another sort of equipment. Loans may be raised from friends or banks in the expectation that the funeral will generate enough revenue to pay off the expenses, if not leave a small sum as profit. What also is interesting to me is that a certain division of labor has arisen in the organization of funerals, with the women more involved in the ritual aspects, particularly on the deaths of nonroyalty. Women buy the cloths, receive the *ade sie die*, get the men's cloths ready for the funerals, decide what is appropriate for their menfolk to wear, and are involved with the preparation of food and refreshments for visitors. Men, on the other hand, typically organize the financial aspects of the ceremony. Such a separation of men and women's roles seems to be fairly recent.

Typical funeral costs include: mortuary storage costs, as bodies are kept frozen for some time to determine the most opportune time for burial and celebration; announcements that are made in various media including the radio, newspapers, and loudspeaker vans in towns and cities; and printed announcements that inform all those within the deceased's social networks—children and affines, within Ghana and abroad. Other fees include transportation of the body; a coffin that denotes the status of the deceased, which is provided by the children; morticians' fees for the preparation of the body for burial; and various materials—flowers, curtains, beddings, hire of bed, cloths, carpets, and ornaments—all of which may cost up to C50,000–C100,000. The wake-keeping and funeral also require getting the house "ready," often involving painting and repairs, renting of a generator (especially in places with no electricity or unreliable power supply), the renting of chairs and canopies for mourners and their transportation to and from the place of hire. These have been estimated to cost between C60,000-C100,000 (Arhin 1993). Additional expenditure on the wake-keeping consists of drinks and sweets, imported and local (e.g., cola, ginger, toffees); musical groups (e.g., gospel band, *nnwonkro, adowa, kete*); and the hire of a video camera. The value and scale of *ade sie die* has become a veritable statement of the esteem in which the deceased was held and the status of the person making the presentation. In addition to the cloths, loin cloths, rings, and handkerchiefs, there may be trays of perfumes, soaps, and powders for bathing the corpse. These presentations create an arena for competition between or among co-wives, or lineage wives, although they also may agree to make a joint presentation, thus saving costs and removing tensions.

At a funeral (which takes place in a public space, usually a park) the donations of cash and drinks by various categories of relations—including the wives, children and other members of the bereaved family—turn the celebration into a veritable spectacle. Wives must make a display of donations or gifts to their husbands and vice versa, made up of cloths, leather sandals, and the *awisia do*, a special necklace hired for the occasion to express condolences. Women borrow cloths to make a display for the occasion, and it is not unknown that the huge bottles of imported drinks sometimes only contain coffee, or water colored to look like the genuine article. Mourners are hired by husbands or wives to carry drinks and other donations around the gathering, and announcements are made through a public address system telling the gathering how much particular people have donated to express their sorrow. By the end of the day or certainly by Sunday, the family has an idea of whether the funeral has brought a loss (*eka*) or paid the costs of the funeral, although it is customary to apportion costs among members of the family.

Conclusion

It is difficult to offer any firm conclusions. I have tried to trace some of the developments and transformations in both marriage and funeral ceremonies and to offer some analysis of people's actions and interpretations of events. Of the two, it is funerals that offer the most spectacular view of change, although the link between the two is clearly established by the reciprocal exchanges and obligations that arise from the marriage relationship. Because it is within marriage that some of these exchanges occur, developments that prevent or delay the formalization of marriage relationships may jeopardize their performance. But it may only be a minority of people who are opting out of or delaying marriage, in which case the essential performances are not affected. From time to time, as I have noted, pronouncements are made about the expenses connected with funerals and the stresses and unhealthy rivalries that they generate. And for a while, local measures may be effective in keeping the expenses and displays within bounds. However, their tenacity may suggest that even these high paynents and displays, which are acknowledged by many to be highly taxing, express particular values that may be too dear to give up.

Notes

1. In Rattray's (1929:84) descriptions of marriage rites, all the stages are merged.
2. Rattray (1929:81) mentions the husband making "the customary gifts of antelope meat, salt, palm-wine, tobacco etc to the parents," in addition to gold dust or cash payments.
3. Some of the gold dust was buried with the deceased, while the rest was kept by the family and converted for the purchase of various articles in connection with the funeral. It is also possible that it served as a basis of accumulation, but I have no direct evidence. In Kumasi, some of the gold may have been used to pay death duties, but this practice fell into abeyance with the absence of the Asantehene, and attempts to reintroduce it were resisted by the newly rich, who found an ally in the colonial state (Arhin 1974).
4. Funeral observances occurred on the eighth, fortieth, and eightieth days after death, and on the anniversary.
5. A practice whereby the widow had to bring a train of articles to her late husband lying in state. Where a widow had faithfully "served" her husband prior to his death, the successor had no right to call on her to repay any expenses incurred on her by her husband.
6. Reference was made to a Mamponghene who had fined a man and his brother £350 for allegedly having had sex with his wife.
7. The Ghanaian currency had been changed in 1965 with the introduction of the new *cedi*, which was originally at par with the British pound. See note 9 for exchange rates.
8. This is actually how informants referred to this transaction, connoting a sale, in contrast to clear Asante views of the nature of these payments. Thus, what is being transformed is not only the scale of payments, but also morals and values.
9. After 1984, following the adoption of a structural adjustment program, the *cedi* was devalued drastically, and its value fell, from US$1.00 = C2.75 to US$1.00 = C200. At the time of the interviews, the rate of exchange was around US$1.00 = C350, a rate that has continued to fluctuate downwards.
10. This refers to the economic recovery program started in 1984, under which a structural adjustment program was adopted with assistance from the World Bank and the International Monetary Fund (IMF). The export sector has benefited through a raise in producer prices following major devaluations of the Ghanaian currency, and specifically in relation to cocoa, a conscious policy of paying producers closer to the world market price.
11. I make reference here to ceremonies that I myself have witnessed in Kumasi, where the quality of the drinks—local versus imported ones—were commented upon, and sometimes rejected, and the *aseda* fee was also renegotiated
12. There is a belief that women should not drink alcohol, although this does not really accord with what occurs in the culture.
13. Some of these themes were picked up at the 1993 African Studies Association meeting, at the panel discussion entitled "Negotiating Space: Religion, Marriage and Women's Autonomy in 19th and 20th Century Ghana." Many of the presenters brought out how onerous women considered the "services" required in marriage (Tashjian 1993), the resistance that women have had to put up against having their labor conscripted by men for cocoa production without pay (Allman 1993), and women's "marriage" to their work to avoid the uncertainties of changing marriage and kinship relations. It is necessary to add that the presenters were conscious of life-cycle changes and of how stages in a woman's life course facilitated the adoption of one or another strategy.
14. Much of what follows is taken from Arhin (1993), although I also draw on my knowledge of these ceremonies to augment the sources and make interpretations of what is occurring.

Sources

Interviews

The data on which this chapter is based was collected from interviews in Kona, Afigya-Kwabre district, Ashanti Region in July to August 1991, with the assistance of Mr. Akwasi Agyeman, and I am grateful to him and my informants for their time and patience.

Books, Dissertations, and Articles

Allman, Jean. 1993. "Rounding up Spinsters: Unmarried Women, Moral Crisis and Gender Chaos in Colonial Asante." Paper Presented to the Thirty-sixth Annual Meeting of the African Studies Association, Boston, MA, December 4–7, 1993.

Arhin, Kwame. "Two Views on Colonial Rule: The Controversy Surrounding Death Duties in Asante."

———. 1983. "Rank and Class Among the Asante and Fante in the nineteenth century." Africa, 56:2–22.

———. 1993. "The Economic Implications of Transformations in Akan Funeral Rites." unpublished.

Berry, Sara S. 1989. "Social Institutions and Access to Resources." Africa 59:41–55.

Busia, K.A. 1951. The Position of the Chief in the Modern Political System of Ashanti. London: Oxford University Press.

Clark, Gracia. 1993. "Working and Marrying: Balance and Divergence in Asante Gender Relations." Paper Presented to the Thirty-sixth Annual Meeting of the African Studies Association, Boston, MA, December 4–7, 1993.

Comaroff, J. 1980. The Meaning of Marriage Payments. London, New York: Academic Press.

Field, Margaret Joyce. 1960. Search for Security; an ethnopsychiatric study of rural Ghana. Evanston, IL, Northwestern University Press.

Fortes, M. 1950. "Kinship and Marriage among the Ashanti," in African Systems of Kingship and Marriage, ed. A. R. Radcliffe-Brown and D. Forde, 252–284. New York and London: Oxford University Press, for the International African Institute.

n.d. "Marriage Prestations" Meyer Fortes Papers, Centre for African Studies, Cambridge University. Cited in Allman, 1993 op cit.

Goody, J. and Tambiah. 1973. Bridewealth and Dowry in Africa and Eurasia. New York and Cambridge: Cambridge University Press.

Levi-Strauss, Claude. 1969. The Elementary Structures of Kinship. Boston: Beacon Press.

Mauss, Marcel. 1954. The Gift; Forms and Functions of Exchange in Archaic Societies. Glencoe, IL: Free Press.

Nukunya, G. K 1969. Kinship and Marriage Among the Anlo-Ewe. New York: Humanities Press.

Odudoye, Mercy Amba. 1981. "Socialization Through Proverbs" African Notes Vol. 1. Ibadan: Institute of African Studies.

Okali, Christine. 1983. Cocoa and Kinship in Ghana: The Matrilineal Akan of Ghana. Boston and London: Kegan Paul International, for the International African Institute.

Rattray, R. S. 1923. Asanti. London: Oxford University Press.

————. 1929 *Religion and Art in Ashanti*. London: Oxford University Press.

Roberts, Penelope. A. 1987. "The State and the Regulation of Marriage:Sefwi-Wiawso (Ghana), 1900–40," in *Women, State and Ideology: Studies from Africa and Asia*, ed. H. Afshar, pp. 48–69.

Tashjian, Victoria B. 1993. "Opting for Autonomy: Menopause and Non-Marriage in Asante, 1900–1950." Paper Presented to the Thirty-sixth Annual Meeting of the African Studies Association, Boston, MA. December 4–7, 1993.

PART IV

LONG-TERM THEMES IN
PRESENT SITUATIONS

This section is devoted to the present: conceptions of wealth, ways of saving, chang-ing and contested definitions of inheritance rights, and a new policy aimed at over-coming the assetless condition of Nigeria's rural population in the credit market. The themes of multiplicity, constant re-creation, and innovation recur. Shipton (Ch. 11) analyzes the extraordinary range of savings mechanisms amongst a rural Gambian population under credit conditions not dissimilar to those described by Falola (Ch. 7) for Nigeria. Mikell (Ch. 10) discusses the difficulties for the matrilineal Akan of creat-ing new criteria for valuing a wife's labor in the new Ghanaian family code. The authors stop short of a full-fledged analysis of currency innovation under conditions of structural adjustment, with large-scale smuggling across the borders of currency zones and civil crisis, although Ekejiuba (Ch. 6) describes some of the particular ille-gal innovations common in Nigeria in the 1980s and 1990s.

As the authors show throughout, African communities will come to the eventu-alities of the new financial order with a long history of monetary management under a variety of unstable conditions. By no means all of these experiences have involved an erosion of moral values or a failure of control. In fact, the macro-picture to the contrary, all of the chapters in this section suggest a mobilization of local expertise: an embrace of money in Yoruba culture; the application of a variety of rubrics, including Islam, to savings in the Gambia, the resolution of court cases favoring recognition of wives' contributions in Ghana, and a new banking policy in Nigeria. Each contribution draws out how dilemmas and solutions come out of experience, and—by simply invoking historical precedent and describing the means by which wide repertoires of possibility have been built up and maintained—stresses that these are not communities bereft of resources in the face of new instabilities. Much has been seen and tried out before. But each also tells a story that implicates the state and state institutions. Engagement with the state on monetary matters, either directly or indirectly, is by this time an intrinsic feature of community dynamics, and the state itself is therefore a major—if not *the* major—source and mediator of confidence or instability. Possibly the contributions of Law (Ch. 2) on the monetary dilemmas of a (precolonial) state and G. Dupré (Ch. 3) on idiosyncratic inventiveness at the interface also provide contributions to this section devoted to the newly intensified dynamics of current instability.

We leave unresolved, then, the tension between, on the one hand, Barber's (Ch. 9) and Mabogunje's (Ch. 12) implied positive embrace of monetary originality, and, on the other hand, Berry's (Ch. 13) implied cautions about the systemic implications of local patterns of action. Multiple innovations are happening at once in ways that demand another history and detailed empirical description. We can simply draw attention to African communities' long previous experience with "money magic" (Falola, Ch. 7), with the domestication of foreign elements (Dupré, Ch. 3), with outright counterfeit (Ekejiuba, Ch. 6) and with currency instabilities of all kinds.

9

Money, Self-Realization and the Person in Yorùbá Texts[*]

KARIN BARBER

Money as Enabler

"Mo mò ón bí ení mowó": "I know her (him/it) as one knows money."

Money, in this Yorùbá proverb, is taken as an instance of the most intimate and familiar relationship that a person can have. Nothing can be better known to you than money. It is what is closest to you; the starting point, in comparison with which other relationships and other knowledge can be assessed.

Marx, in *Capital*, and Simmel, in *The Philosophy of Money*, both represented money as an ambiguous force, at once liberating and alienating. The "ancients," according to Marx, "denounced money as subversive of the economic and moral order of things" ([1887] 1954:132), because it dissolves personal bonds and corrodes traditional institutions. As commoditization proceeds, "everything becomes saleable and buyable," and relationships formerly based on sacred values become motivated purely by commercial interest. But Marx evokes with visionary intensity the transformational potential of money, which has such power that "The circulation becomes the great social retort into which everything is thrown, to come out again as a gold-crystal. Not even are the bones of saints . . . able to withstand this alchemy" ([1887] 1954:132). Simmel, though he lays much more stress on the positive, liberating and expansive

---

[*] This paper owes its inspiration to Jane Guyer's "Wealth in People and Self-realisation in Equatorial Africa" (1993). I am grateful to her for letting me see the manuscript. I am also very grateful to Richard Fardon and Paulo Farias, for their comments on an earlier draft, and to Catherine Burns for her critique of a more recent one.

propensities of money, also recognizes its negative effects. On the one hand, "money is responsible for impersonal relations between people" ([1900] 1978:297) and this makes possible an "inner independence, the feeling of individual self-sufficiency" ([1900] 1978:298). If freedom can be seen as the articulation of the self in the medium of things—the "Ego" extending itself into its possessions—then money is the best medium through which to experience this freedom, because it alone among possessions cannot resist the will of the owner: it "adjusts with equal ease to every form and every purpose that the will wishes to imprint it with" ([1900] 1978:325). And because money is a *means* par excellence, it enables people to attain to objective thought beyond immediate subjective needs, envisaging purpose and chains of causation; indeed intellectual energy itself is produced by "the specific phenomena of the money economy" ([1900] 1978:429). On the other hand, the impersonality made possible by money may bring with it a loss of traditional rights and voice. The liberated individual is projected into an empty world, where he or she must find or create fresh constraints in order to survive. Money "solves the task of realizing human freedom in a purely negative sense" ([1900] 1978:402).

Anthropological studies of cultures undergoing the impact of monetization have drawn more on the negative than the positive half of such paradigms. Bohannan described the destruction of traditional Tiv moral spheres of exchange by the penetration of money (Bohannan 1959). Peoples who have experienced monetization often apparently have found ways either to contain money ideologically, distancing themselves from its operations (Taussig 1980) or to "launder" money so that short-term cycles of commercial profit can ultimately be converted into long-term spheres of sacred value (Parry and Bloch 1989:23-30).

Bernard Belasco (1980), in the only attempt that has yet been made to reconstruct the cultural history of money among the Yorùbá, likewise takes for granted the negative, devaluing effects of the penetration of money into the Yorùbá coast and hinterland. He postulates, *a priori*, an evolutionary sequence from a sacred and mystical conception of wealth in the pre-contact era to a naked commercialism at the height of the slave trade, postulating "a commodification process . . . in which traditional notions of wealth are reinterpreted . . . divine symbols of value collapse in a passage toward profane standards of exchange" (Belasco 1980:23). This stripping-down process is one that Belasco sees as a form of "pre-adaptation" to capitalism. Yorùbá society, in his view, was evolving in definite stages from a primordial sacred gift-exchange economy to a modern secular money economy.

This argument—despite its surface plausibility—is both speculative and circular. No one can doubt that the slave trade and the resulting huge increase in the circulation of cowries[1] must have had a radical impact on local ideas surrounding money, exchange and value. But there is no evidence—oral or written—to tell us anything about the stages and nature of such ideological transformations in any period before the mid-nineteenth century. The assumption that monetization or commoditization had a specific, well defined, sequence of negative effects is given in Belasco's evolutionist model, not demonstrated by his analysis. He organizes his material in accordance with the paradigm, rather than drawing a paradigm from the material.[2] His achievement, however, was to seize unerringly on the centrality of the idea of money in the many texts and sources that he consulted, and to reveal its productive penetration of wide areas of discourse.

In the oral and written Yorùbá texts with which I am familiar, the image of money recurs constantly. However—contrary to the implications of Belasco's model—what is most striking is the predominantly *positive* valuation placed on it. Even in texts that are clearly of nineteenth-century provenance or later, when commoditization in Belasco's account was at its zenith, the predominant view appears to be not that money strips social relationships down to a bare instrumental skeleton, but that money is what *constitutes* social relationships and indeed social being. Money functions as a powerful organizing symbol, exerting a magnetic force on a whole field of discourse about social values, achievements, aspirations, and relationships. Money, the market, buying and selling, credit arrangements, interest and profit form a complex of metaphors by which the social and spiritual worlds are envisaged. In this view, the world itself is a market; abstract values such as truth and falsehood are bought and sold there; anything that is highly prized—including good behavior or profound thought—is described as being "worth money." Money is what makes things effective: "*A kì í fowó ra òòyì kó má lè kóni lójú*" "When you spend money buying dizziness, it won't fail to make your head spin" as a popular writer wittily remarks (Òkédìjí 1989:38). That is to say, if you paid for it, it will work.

Most significantly, as I intend to argue, money in Yorùbá culture is conceived of as constitutive of individual self-realization. It is the medium in which human potential becomes fulfilled. Energized by money, people can expand and fully occupy the space that they have chosen as their destiny. And this self-realization is, in the texts that I will be considering, conceived of as being inherently social. That is, money is inseparable from the social regard and the social bonds that support the successful individual. To understand the crucial role of the notion of money in Yorùbá thought, then, we need the other half of Marx's, and especially Simmel's, dual paradigm: the characterization of money as a profoundly *enabling* and energizing force.

Marx, speaking of the transformative power of money, quotes a passage from *Timon of Athens* in which Timon evokes the power of gold[3] to "make black, white; foul, fair; /Wrong, right; base, noble; old, young; coward, valiant . . . " (Marx [1887] 1954:132). There is a remarkable resonance in this with Yorùbá evocations of Ajé,[4] the female deity or personification of wealth. Belasco quotes one version of her *oríkì* (attributions or "praises"):

A sọ eníí gbón di eníí gò
A sọ eni í gò di eníí gbón . . .
. . . Ṣe òun ló sọ ọmọdé di àgbà
Ṣe òun ló sì ń sọ àgbà di ọmọdé . . .
. . . Ṣe ìwọ ni o sọ erú di ọba
Ajé o,
Ajé o, olótù ohun rere ayé . . .

One who makes the wise person foolish
One who makes the foolish person wise . . .
. . . She is the one who turns the youth into an elder
She is the one who turns the elder into a youth . . .
. . . You are the one who turns a slave into a king
Wealth, Wealth, the one who distributes all the good things of life . . .[5]

The brazen, uncompromising energy of the *oríkì* is strikingly similar to that of the *Timon* passage so relished by Marx. Both passages proclaim the extraordinary powers of money. Both could be read as an out-and-out denunciation of these powers. But in the *oríkì*, at least, this would be a misreading.[6] The main purpose of the *oríkì* passage is not moral judgment, but the celebration of power itself. Power is most profoundly apprehended by its capacity to transform: a capacity vested in deities, who empower people when they "mount" or possess them; in Death, who transforms a bodily existence into a spiritual one; and in the ancestors, whose power is manifested when they transform themselves to appear in the guise of *egúngún* among their living descendants. On a more mundane level, bodily enhancement is often a sign of enhanced status, as when a person becomes visibly elated and inflated on being praised with *oríkì*, or when a new chief or *ọba* is transformed on installation, by being wrapped in his incantation-saturated regalia. Ajé, hailed in the above *oríkì* as an agent of transformations, is being saluted as one of the greatest forces at work in society, a force that it is essential to capture.

The idea of money presides, in these texts, over the sphere of social differences and equivalences. Money's circulation, passing through chains and networks of people and things, is what makes the notion of pervasive relations of equivalence thinkable. The texts suggest that people are constituted as members of a shared humanity by money, for everyone, from the poorest to the richest, participates in its circulation. A proverb says:

> *Náwónáwó kò ná ṣẹ̀gi, otòṣì kò ná erèé dàgbà; olúpọ́njú tí ń ṣẹ̀gi tà*
> *nígbẹ̀ẹ́, owó ni gbogbo wọ́n n ná.*

> Even the big spender doesn't spend ṣẹ̀gi beads, even the indigent person doesn't grow old spending beans; the poorest firewood-seller—it's money that all of them spend.

In other words, whatever the differences of fortune and status, there are no separate spheres of exchange for the affluent and the indigent. All of them have to participate in the circulation of the same medium: money. Having and spending money renders them equivalent in the fundamental sense of belonging to the same social system. It is striking that abject poverty is rarely signified in Yorùbá texts by the figure of the beggar, who is uninteresting because he is a terminal point in the circulation of wealth, with nothing to offer in exchange for money. The poor person is much more often represented by the *aṣẹ́gità*, someone who goes into the bush to collect sticks to sell as firewood. This is marginal, backbreaking, wretchedly paid, and shamingly low-status labor: but it is nonetheless an element in the cycle of production and exchange. To be part of Yorùbá humanity, it is necessary to take part in this cycle, which is mediated by money.

The Texts and Their Relationship to the Past

There have been some preliminary and tentative studies of ideas about money in the recent past of the oil boom (Barber 1982, Watts, 1994), though these could be developed much further. As far as I know, little has been written about ideas surrounding money in the crucial period from 1900 to 1950, the period during which British currency, taxation, wage labor, and cash crops transformed the local economy, and during which slavery, indentured service, the huge households of the nineteenth century and many ideas about personal obligations gradually faded. What I shall attempt to do in the remainder of this paper is to reconstruct some of the earlier views, those immediately preceding the colonial period. It must be stressed that the nineteenth century was itself a period of extraordinary upheaval and transformation; many ideas, institutions and relationships involving money were already being violently contested. There is no stable base-line, nor should we attempt to install one. Rather, I hope that this reconstruction, speculative as it is, will serve as a prologue to richer and more detailed studies of twentieth-century ideas, which could draw on a much wider range of documentary sources than are available for the nineteenthth century.

The texts that reveal indigenous ideas about self-realization and the person most fully and most revealingly are the oral genres of *oríkì* (attributive epithets or "praise poetry"), *ìtàn* (narrative histories), *ẹsẹ Ifá* (Ifá divination verses), and *òwe* (sayings or proverbs). *Oríkì* in particular are crucial sources, for the performance of *oríkì* actually plays a part in the constitution of the subject's inner identity and public reputation. In this paper, I draw mainly on the personal *oríkì* of nineteenth-century "big men" in the small Ọ̀ṣun town of Òkukù (Barber 1991b). I also refer to the *oríkì* of the war-leaders who ruled Ibàdàn between 1850 and the 1890s (Akinyele [1911]1959), and to *oríkì orílẹ̀*, the "*oríkì* of origin."

Personal *oríkì*—that is, epithets composed for specific individuals to commemorate specific incidents, sayings or qualities associated with them—were almost certainly composed during the lifetime of the subject and addressed to him or her directly.[7] They continued to circulate after the subject's death, both to invoke his[8] powers as an ancestor and to salute his descendants who had inherited his place and identity in the town. Personal *oríkì* of nineteenth-century men were, one can therefore assume, composed in the nineteenth century. The time of composition of *oríkì orílẹ̀*—the *oríkì* of origin that link large scattered groups of people claiming common origins in an ancient, named city—is more difficult to estimate. *Oríkì orílẹ̀* are more highly valued and more carefully preserved and transmitted than any other kind of *oríkì*. In some cases it is clear that accretions have occurred over a long timespan. The majority of the passages in *oríkì orílẹ̀* probably date from the beginning of the nineteenth century or earlier.[9] Thus, they might have already become old texts by the time of some of the nineteenth-century big men commemorated in the personal *oríkì*.

Regardless of when they were composed, none of the *oríkì* I shall be discussing were published until the twentieth century. As with all oral texts, the possibility that they were significantly revised after the time of their composition must be considered. *Oríkì* as a form exhibit a peculiar combination of fluidity and tenacity, giving the performer licence to recombine and amplify her[10] materials, while stubbornly preserving a core of compact, gnomic formulations even when their literal meaning has been forgotten. Despite their fluidity, however, there is good reason to believe that the *oríkì* of men known to have lived in the nineteenth century do still evoke the ethos of that period. They allude frequently to experiences characteristic of the Ìlọrin-Ìbàdàn wars, which affected Òkukù from the 1840s to 1893: war-leaders and war-camps, the capture of slaves, large households of *ìwọ̀fà* (bondsmen and bondswomen), spears, swords, arrows, and the possession of horses. No anachronisms from the more recent past appear to have been introduced. What is interesting is that the *oríkì* of more recent figures—"big men" of 1900-1940, after which few new *oríkì* seem to have been composed—do not speak of any of the huge changes that overtook the town in early colonialism. They do not refer to the church (established in Òkukù in 1905), Islam (given an institutional presence in Òkukù in 1910), taxation (imposed on Òkukù in 1917), wage labor (which involved the majority of Òkukù men from c.1910–c.1950), or mission and government schools; and they refer only very rarely to the railway[11] (which transformed the Òkukù economy from 1904 onwards), cash crops (first yams, then cocoa and kola), and local government institutions.[12] It is as if they continued to speak in an older idiom, hailing contemporary big men for their intransigence, their self-sufficiency, and their command of medicine (all of which were still important), but remaining mute about their activities in the church, their educational achievements, and their position in local government.[13] These more "modern" aspects of experience were commented on extensively in narratives of personal memory, which circulated symbiotically with the *oríkì,* but rarely in the *oríkì* themselves. When modern allusions do occur in *oríkì* chants, they often appear in the passages of prayer, blessing, and popular song which the performer interpolates, rather than in the *oríkì* proper. It thus seems likely that the *oríkì* of nineteenth-century big men have not been revised radically to suit modern concerns. On the contrary, the resources of *oríkì* were not very much adapted even for twentieth-century big men.

Some of the ideas that emerge from these texts are amplified or corroborated by an indubitably nineteenth-century source, Johnson's *History of the Yorubas,* written in the 1890s, though not published until 1921. Johnson's own perspective as an educated Christian informs this work through and through. But his largeness of vision, his enormous curiosity, and his attention to popular views and experiences—as represented in sayings, nicknames, *oríkì* and "ditties"—make it an extraordinarily valuable record of emergent popular consciousness nonetheless. Much of the later part of this great volume is based on firsthand testimony from people involved in the events that Johnson describes, often cited explicitly as eyewitnesses. Indeed, attention to his narrative strategy reveals a quite deliberate siting of exemplary anecdotes as stepping stones through the thickets of the nineteenth-century politics that he describes in so much detail. These anecdotes have all the hallmarks of popular tales of recent and raw experience. Further supplementary evidence will be sought in future stages of this project, in missionary and government records, in early Yorúbá publications (such as the *Ìwé Ìròhìn* of Abẹ́òkúta, first published 1859) and in a wider range of *oríkì* of nineteenth-century personalities. My analysis in this preliminary essay is based on the supposition that while *oríkì* and other oral texts cannot be lined up to represent a definite historical sequence of ideational stages —let alone stages going right back to a "pre-contact" era—many *oríkì* do evoke the values that were in place immediately before the onset of colonial rule.

The fact that discourses such as *oríkì* continue to be valued and performed after they have ceased to register the immediate social changes of the moment is not just a problem about dating oral historical sources. It is a problem about assigning any unitary "belief system" to any single "historical period." For, quite clearly, there were and are multiple discourses circulating, some older than others, some more valued than others, encoded in different genres according to different conventions. The ideas they embody may be different and even incompatible. It would be a simplification to claim that some represent what "the Yorúbá" *really* "believed" at a particular moment while others did not. This would be to under-rate the tendency, pervasive in Yorùbá culture, to value a proliferation of alternatives—a tendency that makes any unilinear account of Yorùbá ideological change as a succession of monolithic world views difficult to sustain. The materials considered in this essay, limited as they are, nonetheless reveal something of the depth, complexity and heterogeneity of the representations of money available in the second half of the nineteenth century. The evidence suggests not only that alternative views were simultaneously available, but also that, in particular social-historical situations, particular configurations and emphases could come to the fore, and later retreat again into the background. The second half of the nineteenth century saw the establishment of new, heterogeneous, expansionist military polities, such as Ìbàdàn (Awẹ 1964; Falọla 1984) and to lesser extent Abẹ́òkúta (Agiri 1972; Biobaku 1957), and Ìlọrin (O'Hear 1983), where the aggrandizement of individual leaders—based on conquest and capture—seemed virtually unlimited. Ideas about money and personal self-realization in *oríkì* texts associated with Ìbàdàn leaders are remarkably divergent from those found in the *oríkì* of big men of other more traditional towns. But by 1893 the British-induced peace had closed off the military avenue of self-aggrandizement. The older style of imagery was taken up again in *oríkì* of successful people in Ìbàdàn, though without completely effacing the new style. This suggests not only that ideas were constantly open to revision, but also that alternative perspectives were kept open, rather than being automatically erased by "structural amnesia" when they did not fit the immediate circumstances of the time.

What I try to do in this paper is to suggest how and why money was so central to the field of ideas about self-realization that appeared to be circulating in the second half of the nineteenth century. I then show very briefly how these ideas were inflected or transformed in Ìbàdàn in its military expansionist phase.

Self-Realization Through Purchase

If participation in the circulation of money was regarded as a necessary condition of humanity, then participating successfully was the means to full self-realization. Money was represented as a principle of individual autonomy. A remarkable passage from a performance of *oríkì*, honouring an Òkukù woman who lived around the turn of the century, bears this out:

> *Bógun bá múni a ó rara*
> *Ekú a rasọ gbájà bí Isòbò*
> *Ò-lòyí-lòyí tí í losọ bí Ègùn*
> *Ìyá Wúràọlá rasọ, rasọ gbájà ròde,*
> *Pọ́nl é ọmọ olówó tí í ru gégébí osẹ*

> If you are captured in war you buy yourself back
> The masquerade costume buys cloth with which to sweep the market like an Isòbò
> One who wears costume after costume, who wears cloth like an Ègùn
> Mother of Wúràọlá bought cloth, bought cloth with which to sweep the market on her outings,
> Pọ́nlé child of the rich person who foams up like soap.

These wonderful lines evoke a process that could be called *self-investment*. They make metaphorical connections in the usual manner of *oríkì*, by simply juxtaposing the objects of comparison. Here the juxtapositions bring together an enslaved war captive, someone who has become a commodity; an ancestral masquerade, that is a spiritual being who periodically comes to the world from heaven; and a woman, the subject of the *oríkì*, for whose benefit these comparisons are being made, who is very wealthy. Each of these beings *makes* himself or herself. The person captured in war performs the most fundamental act of self-redemption: he buys himself back. That is, he substitutes money (or another person, captured by himself) for his person. The masquerade *èkú*—the sack-like costume that makes up the body of an *egúngún*—is conceived as buying its own fabric to build up its volume and impressiveness, so that it may "sweep the market," that is, display its magnificence in the central locus of human interaction. "Mother of Wúràolá" also embodies her splendor in layer upon layer of fabric. She has as much cloth as the Ègùn—a coastal people from Porto Novo who had good access to imported goods. Like the masquerade, she also "sweeps the market" on her social outings. The intensity of her grandeur is clinched in the striking image of the rich person who "foams up like soap"—the black indigenous soap that is used in preparing good-fortune medicine.

Each of these three subjects, then, is seen as consituting its own social self through a process of literal embodiment. The slave gets his body back from his captor; the ancestor builds his physical body—in which he manifests himself to the world—out of cloth; the rich woman creates a magnificent persona by investing her body with sumptuous material. Each builds his or her self onto his or her physical body. They act autonomously—even the slave takes responsibility for regaining possession of his own person. The ultimate goal is to build a visible self, a persona, that will attract the gaze and adherence of others—others whose presence is already alluded to in the image of layers and layers of cloth, always a metaphor for "people." "[T]he Ego is surrounded by all its possessions as by a sphere in which its tendencies and character traits gain visible reality" (Simmel [1900] 1978:322). But what is most remarkable here, and remarkably consonant with Simmel's analysis, is the notion that individual self-realization is achieved through *purchase*, signified by the verb *rà*, the most basic and common word for all forms of buying. The capacity of the autonomous individual to realize him or herself is achieved through the medium of money. The slave buys himself. The ancestor buys the means by which to manifest himself bodily among the living. The rich woman buys the cloth (and the people) who constitute her splendor. The lines of this passage are structured in a way typical of *oríkì*, in parallel sequences that draw attention to the continuity and semantic variations of a repeated key word, which appears each time in the same structural position. In this passage the key word is *rà*; the notion of buying is thus brought to our attention as the central point upon which the passage is built.

The result of such expenditure is inscribed in the very being, the actual existence, of the subjects. The most intense images of human greatness that I have come across in *oríkì* are all images of bodily intensity, often with a hint of menace: the fully achieved big man or woman is said to "quake" (*mì*) with honor or magnificence; or to be dark like threatening stormclouds (*sú bí òjò*), or, as in this extract, to "foam up"—(*ru*), a verb that also suggests the fizzing, boiling energy of blood or a chemical reaction.[14] The physical body is transformed by investiture with *olá* (high esteem, social sufficiency, "honor") just as the ancestor's floating spiritual force is transformed, channeled into the human world when it takes on its bodily realization, and just as the slave's body is transformed into a real person's body when he obtains his freedom.

The passage deliberately spans the widest possible range of personal situations, embracing the slave, who is temporarily almost not a person at all; the ancestor, who is more than a person; and the rich woman, who is the summit of achieved personhood among the living. Each of them is represented as investing (and investing in) himself or herself through purchase. That is, just as everyone participates in the circulation of money, so everyone has the potential of self-realization, self-creation. Money passes through everyone's hands; everyone can "buy" him or her self. What this conception recognizes is a stubborn preservation of the capacity of every individual for initiative, the stubborn resistance to being "written off," the stubborn insistence that everyone has the potential to expand to fill the social space in which they find themself.

Money and People

Why was money such a central image in the discourses of self-realization? In a society whose dynamic was driven by the self-aggrandizement of "big men," social acknowledgement was the key to political success. The individual built up a position for himself by recruiting supporters, his "people." As members of his household, "people" supplied the labor that enabled the big man to expand his productive and consumptive activities and the reproductive capacities that generated further people, making him the head of a "great house." But having "people" meant more than this; at its most extended, it meant being surrounded by people who acknowledged his leadership and patronage. Their gaze conferred authority. Their acknowledgement confirmed status.

People and money were inseparable. The components that made up *ọlá*, the ultimate status aspired to by a big man or woman, were multiple. However, in all texts, their bedrock is the twinned pair: people and money. People (or children) and money were the joint constituents of social well-being. Incantations, invocations, divination texts and *oríkì* all solicit the powers that be for *owó àti ọmọ* (money and children). The voices of women, in *oríkì*, praise their husbands' families for providing them unstintingly "with money and children."

Money and people were inter-translatable and mutually generative at several levels. First, at a literal level, they could be exchanged for each other. People were acquired through expenditure: slaves and *iwọ̀fà* (bondsmen or bondswomen) directly, family members through the laying out of sums on bridewealth and child-rearing. Conversely, people could be cashed in. Even within the family, dependants were regarded as potentially realizable assets. An indebted senior could lend out a junior as an *iwọ̀fà* to his creditor, the junior's labor counting as interest on the loan. In a crisis, people could even cash themselves in; Johnson speaks of patients who could not afford their doctors' fees, and who instead handed themselves over bodily in payment (Johnson 1921:121).[15] Such cash-mediated transference of persons must be seen as part of a vast network of transactions in which people and things could be substituted for one another, in relationships that went well beyond the model of rational agents (people) exchanging commodities (things), posited by classical political economy.[16]

The cycle in which people and money circulated and changed places was celebrated in *oríkì* as predominantly benign and honor-bearing. The money used to acquire people seems to have been regarded as more than a mere medium of exchange. In this *oríkì orílẹ̀*, belonging to the Aláràn-án people whose traditional profession is masquerading, the *origin* of the money used to acquire a wife has symbolic significance:

> *Owó eégún ni wọ́n fi fẹ́ ìyáà mi*
> *Ọmọ adọ́kọ níbi owó gbé so*
> *Wọn ò yóó jẹ̀bà ó hun mí*

They married my mother with money earned from *egúngún* performance
Child of one who has lovers where money is plenty
They will not allow my homage to bring retribution

The speaking voice in this text is claiming that because his or her mother's bride-price was paid for with money earned from masquerading, *egúngún* peformance is in his or her blood, and the "homage" every entertainer pays before embarking on a chant will be accepted by the powers that be. The money is thus pictured as being a value-charged ligature, which ensures the transmission between persons not just of rights and obligations, but of talents, propensities, and capabilities.

Members of the household, acquired with money, participated in productive or commercial activities that generated more money and thus brought in more people. *Oríkì* celebrate the ownership of slaves and bondspeople both as embodiments and as producers of wealth. In this *oríkì orílẹ̀*, for example, the petty transactions of slaves and *iwòfà* are represented as bringing in money which is used by the owner for the grand transaction of purchasing further slaves:

> *Ẹrú Ọlọ́là wọ́n a tẹ̀ẹ́gun*
> *Ìwòfà Ọlọ́là wọ́n a tọ̀gbùngbùn*
> *Ọmọ bíbí Ọlọ́là wọ́n a ràkókó ẹrú wálé.*

The Ọlà people's slaves will sell silk-cotton shoots
The Ọlà people's bondswomen will sell silk cotton sprouts
The true-born children of ọlà will buy well-formed slaves and bring them
     home.

Secondly, at a practical level, a big man's money was manifested in bodily display and conspicuous expenditure which attracted more people to his entourage.[17] The productive interactions between generosity, social salience, and the encircling gaze of admiring adherents are evoked constantly and with great metaphorical subtlety in *oríkì*. For example, one of the principal bodily signifiers of wealth is cloth. Gbángbádé, an Òkukù man famous for trading down to the coast, and for his part in the Ilọrin-Ìbàdàn wars,[18] was saluted, "*Ògírí dáṣọ má lè gbe*" ("Sprightly fellow bought a cloth so huge he could hardly wear it"), and there are numerous similar examples in the *oríkì* of nineteenth-century men. But cloth is at the same time a well established metaphor for people: ọba Oyèkànbi (1861–77[19]) was saluted "*Àlàmú 'lábùta ọ̀rẹ́/ Láníhun baba ló wáá régbẹ bora bí aṣọ*" ("Àlàmú possessor of many friends/ Láníhun the father has companions to wrap himself with like a cloth"). Beads were another great material manifestation of wealth. Olóngbé, chief Ọjọmu during the reign of Oyèkànbi, was evoked buying beads as lavishly as he dispensed cash to his guests:

Alájogún wá n gbọnwó bí ẹní n gbọn omi
Eníkú má mugún
Ó rayùn ra wẹẹrẹ
Ótàgbàdo ra iyùn ẹpà

The generous host scoops out money like someone scooping water
One who doesn't bother to claim his inheritance when his relative dies
He buys coral beads in great quantities
He sells wet-season maize to buy "groundnut" coral.

The link between the personal and bodily display of wealth and the generosity that attracts "people" was made more explicit in the *oríkì* of Ẹnúkónípẹ̀, remembered as one of the early heads of *ilé* Ọlóyàn of Òkukù:

Ọmọ ajímáasín, òsínṣẹgi
Babaà mi ò-jí-n-kùtùkùtù-sínyùn-ẹpà
Ọmọ Òwàrà Àrẹmú tó fọ́n ṣẹgi dàá'gbó
Ó ní torí aṣẹ́wé
Ó ní torí aṣẹ́gi
Ó ní torí ilàpá tí ń làgbẹ́ sùàsùà.

Child of one who wakes to thread, one who threads *ṣẹ̀gi* beads
My father, one who rises at the crack of dawn to thread "groundnut" coral
Child of Òwàrà Àrẹmú who scatters *ṣẹ̀gi* beads in the forest
He said it's because of the pluckers of leaves
He said it's because of the breakers of sticks
He said it's because of the destitute who traverse the bush far and wide.

The splendor of the wealthy is pictured as scattering widely enough to benefit even those who inhabit the very margins of the monetary exchange system. Expenditure of money is thus envisaged at the center of a process of personal enhancement. Money can be invested in bodily display, which attracts the regard of others. Or it can be generously distributed to those others, again attracting their admiration. The interchangeability of people, money, and other "blessings" and appurtenances of high estate is represented in such texts as productive and desirable. Money itself is almost always evoked in images of natural, magical, or vegetative abundance: it is scooped like water, doled out like beans, dug up like weeds, and plucked like fruits from the trees. People generate wealth; wealth generates people; the cycle is represented as proceeding harmoniously, providing abundance of good things, of which even the destitute firewood seller can get a share.

Thirdly, and at a more definitely metaphorical or symbolic level, money represented the support of "people" in a further sense: gifts of money very often betokened social acknowledgement or regard. Sometimes such gifts were purely symbolic—no actual transfer of resources took place—as when the Aláàfin would present his Basọrun,during each of his three state festivals, with "one head of stringed cowries" which the Basọrun would return the next day, "the apparent gift being merely a part of the ceremony" (Johnson 1921:53). More commonly, the handing-over of money was both an actual transfer of resources and a symbolic act of recognition. There were many contexts in which this occurred: as tribute to a ruler, as a token of submission after defeat in war, and as a mark of acknowledgement of a person's claim to a particular status, for instance as a widow or bride. Let me take as an example the act of recognition that was indicated when people handed over a few cowries to itinerant òrìṣà-devotees. J. D. Y. Peel, rightly taking issue with John Iliffe's (1984) depiction of Yorùbá as an alms-giving culture, describes this transaction, recorded in the nineteenth century, as a form of sacrifice (Peel 1990). "Sacrifice," here, however, should in turn be redescribed as a public acknowledgement of the claims of the god, on which the god's continued reputation depended. This meaning is revealed in Johnson's account of the god Kori (Johnson 1921:26–27), who was represented by a string of palmnut shells:

> little children go about with it to the market places begging for alms. The object of worship is then worn by one of their number, who goes before, his companions following behind him, shouting the praises of the ancient god Kori. In this way they parade the market places, and sellers before whom they halt to sing, make them presents of money (cowries) or whatever they may happen to be selling, usually articles of food. Thus the little children perpetuate the memory and worship of this deity, hence the ditty
> "Iba ma s i ewe, Kori a ku o
> (But for the little children Kori had perished)"

The children acknowledged the claims of Kori to recognition by acting as his emissaries and shouting his praises; the market-sellers responded to this demand by acknowledging both the children and the god with "presents of money" or equivalent articles. It seems to have been explicitly acknowledged that only this recognition, solicited by the children, kept the god alive.[20] Furthermore, it was not only the god who was being acknowledged in this transaction. The devotees themselves, for instance the Eléṣù who were "encountered by the missionaries, 'going about in the markets and from house to house ... to bless the people, receiving in return a cowry or two'" (Peel 1990:470) were also receiving recognition in their own right. That is presumably why passers-by would give a few cowries to *each* of the Èṣù devotees encountered in a party on the highway (Johnson 1921:28)—not just a lump sum to be transmitted to the god by any one of them. Their status as individual priests with powers in the community was being acknowledged.

In all these cases, transferences of money represented the acknowledgement, regard, and attention of other people—which was the basis of reputation and influence, and thus constitutive of social being.

These actual and metaphorical equivalences between people and money are foregrounded in poetic texts. *Oríkì* and *òwe* draw parallels between them: people, like money, are slippery, fluctuating and unstable.[21] Both people and money are inclined to drift away from you to a stronger rival. "*Àlejò lowó; bó bá yalé rẹ, o tójú rẹ̀   dáadáa*" ("Money is a visitor; if it calls on you, make sure you treat it well");[22] and by the same token, visitors are like money, with the inherent propensity to move on. Money, like people, has a mind of its own; it decides for itself whose house to visit. In the *oríkì* of Gbángbádé, the nineteenth-century warrior mentioned above, it is said that:

Ajé ló wáá mọlé ẹni tí ń lọ
Wealth knows whose house she's going to

Only a fortunate person can expect it to settle down permanently with him or her:

Mofómikẹ́ owó la fi ṣoge, ó bá ọ gbélé orígun[23]
Mofómikẹ́, it's money that makes one magnificent, it has
    taken up residence with you in your quarters.

The saying *"Odò lowó: bó bá san wá, á tún san lọ"* ("Money is a river: if it flows up to you, it will then flow away again") has an exact counterpart in the observation about people: *"Odò lèniyàn: bí wọ́n bá san wá, wọ́n á tún san lọ"* ("People are a river: if they flow up to you, they'll then flow away again"). Money, which exists to circulate, is inherently slippery, dispersed, and mobile: and this makes it a key metaphor in a society of big men where power rests on the recruitment of people and the acquisition of reputation, which are themselves fluctuating and unstable.

What then, in the view expressed in these texts, makes one person a more successful big man than another? It is often suggested that money is acquired by hard work. *Ọ̀lẹ* means both "lazy" and "poor." But this reason is given within the framework of a more encompassing explanation. It is said that:

> *A à mọbi olówó gbé yanrí*
> *Mbá re yan tèmi*

> We don't know where the rich man chose his head
> Or I'd have gone there to choose my own

In the unpredictable, fluctuating and competitive world of individual self-creation, in the last resort each person must rely on his or her *Orí*: head, fortune, destiny. The *Orí* is sometimes represented as an ineluctable fate, anterior to a person's earthly existence; but it is also the individual's principle of self-realization. It is one's *Orí* that allows one to navigate successfully between unknown forces: deities, ancestors, and human beings, whose intentions can never be fully known, even when they are close blood relatives. *Orí* is closest to one; it is one's most reliable and most intimate companion. A good *Orí* guides one to success, enables one to attract money, people, and reputation, causes these blessings to stick and accumulate, not to drift off to some stronger head.

Johnson describes the personal shrine made by successful men in honor of their *Orí*. The *Orí* is represented by forty one cowries strung into the form of a crown. It is kept in a large coffer covered with as many cowries as the owner can afford, up to 12,000. "The manufacturer who is generally a worker in leather receives as his pay the same amount of cowries as is used in the article manufactured." A rich man, then, would spend (sacrifice) a large sum of money in order to immobilize another equally large sum. The cowry currency would be arrested in the crown and the coffer: an invitation to the endlessly slippery, circulating medium to stay with him, not to desert him for a rival. On his death, we are told, "the image of Ori with the coffer is destroyed, and the cowries spent" (Johnson 1921:27). The cowries were not kept as a shrine to the dead man, as might have been expected; the currency went back into circulation, revealing clearly the understanding that a person's *Orí* could only temporarily freeze the fluidity and fluctuations of a means to greatness which was common to all Yorùbá humanity and which afforded all the opportunity to create social place for themselves. Ultimately, this reflects the fact that the flow of money was never brought under the control of the pre-colonial state, unlike in the Asante case described by McCaskie (McCaskie 1983).

The Pathology of Militarism

The *oríkì* texts discussed so far were recorded in a town that was disrupted by the nineteenth-century wars, but which was never a military state and, indeed, never had an organized army. A strongly contrasting discourse seems to have become prevalent in the expansionist military state of Ìbàdàn in the mid-nineteenth century.[24] Johnson's account of events that radiated out of Ìbàdàn from about 1850 onwards is a vast and conscious narrative of pathology. Strategic anecdotes call attention to self-realization based on massive, indiscriminate accumulation of money and people. Excess in all things—in accumulation, expenditure, and the range of persons and things that can be made equivalent to each other through money—is what these anecdotes exemplify. Johnson does not suggest that it was only in Ìbàdàn that the relations between money, people, and self-realization took this turn. Famine, brutalization, and constant fear of capture were, by his account, pervasive influences. But he clearly situates Ìbàdàn at the center of these transformations, and suggests that that was where they were most radical and most full-blown.

One of Johnson's emblematic anecdotes is the story of a young woman, travelling with her father and mother in the early 1880s after the closure of the Ìjẹbú road, who seized the opportunity of bartering her mother to a trader in exchange for salt. The father, however, turned the tables on her by offering her to the trader as a substitute; the trader was to marry her, and the bridewealth was the salt (1921:453). People who should not be exchanged were exchanged (the mother); transactions which should be social and lineage-based were scarcely distinguishable from entrepreneurial commerce (my daughter for your salt); misbehavior which should be punished within the family was punished by disposing of the culprit to an outsider (the father handed over the daughter to punish her for attempting to sell the mother). The tracks and boundaries that map out the limits of acceptable substitution and equivalence are flagrantly breached; this seems to be Johnson's point.

One of his most striking and ironical anecdotes is of the Ìjẹ̀ṣà who after being defeated by the Ìbàdàns in 1869 sent 400 bags of cowries as a sign of submission, to sue for peace (Johnson 1921:379). The Ìbàdàn chiefs "feared to touch the gift, as it might have been poisoned." However, one of them, Àjàyí Ògbóríẹfọn, was running low on funds and as a result was losing his men to better provided rivals. He therefore personally accepted the cowries, and spent them on recruiting troops. The forces he assembled in this way were then marched out against the very Ìjẹ̀ṣàs who had sent the cowries as a token of submission. In this story several conventions are broken or suspected of being broken. The money, sent as a symbol of acknowledgement, is first converted, in the minds of the Ìbàdàns, into a dangerous, disease-bearing material. It is then adopted by a single individual when it was intended for a collective leadership; and Ògbóríẹfọn treats it as mere cash, without symbolic significance. It is transformed, by Ògbóríẹfọn's expenditure, into "people," that is, warrior adherents; and finally, its original symbolic significance is blatantly cancelled when Ògbóríẹfọn marches his new troops out against the very people who had sent it as a token of peace. The always porous and negotiable boundaries between symbolic, relationship-creating uses of money and pure exchange transactions have been, perhaps defiantly, erased in order to make a more typically Ìbàdàn claim, a claim to unbridled license and what Ògbóríẹfọn called "pleasures bordering on crime" (Johnson 1921:380).

In the oríkì of the Ìbàdàn leaders of this period, wealth as a "blessing" has almost totally disappeared. Money, in fact, is referred to in these oríkì less frequently than in the oríkì discussed above. The Ìbàdàn leaders are commended for military power, conquests, and their ability to strike terror into their enemies (see Barber 1991a for a more detailed discussion). When the oríkì do allude to riches, the language is startlingly different from the language of nurture, generation, and natural abundance that characterizes the Òkukù texts. Rich men's assets are enumerated baldly, as in these *oríkì* belonging to Balógun Àjọbọ:

> Ògúnlérin'ó ni tángānrān
> Òjìlénu ni panù
> Ògédé àwo bí amọ̀ tó ẹgba àwo
> . . . Bí o bá ẹgba àwo nílé
> Ẹran ni nbẹ ninu gbogbo rẹ̀
> . . . Irínwó l'ẹrú Ògúnmọ́lá
> Òtàlúgba ni ti Sùnmọ́là
> Gbogbo wọn ko i ti to
> K'áta kó'yọ̀ lôjọ́ nile Awútutu.
> "Mo ṣebi rínwó ni ìlù ti o nsìn mí"
> "Òdúnrún ọ̀kẹ́ ni wọn nrù wá"
> Oluwarẹ kò le l'ẹran lọ́bẹ̀ bi Ajọbọ . . .
>   Akinyẹle [1911] 1959:85)

He has 420 china plates
He has 440 tin ones
Old-fashioned plates made of clay total 2,000
. . . If you find 2,000 plates in his house
All of them will be full of meat
Ògúnmọ́lá has 400 slaves
Sùnmọ́là has 260
And all of them together are not enough
To fetch the pepper and salt [consumed] daily in Awututu's house.
"I suppose there are 400 chiefs who serve me"
"Each of them brings 500 bags of cowries"
This person [i.e., the person who says this] can never have as much meat
   in his stew as Àjọbọ . . .

When the Ìbàdàn empire, locked in stalemate with the Èkìtìparapọ, submitted to the British-imposed settlement, the acquisition of "people" through wholesale capture ceased to be an option for big men. From around the time of Baṣọ̀run Apanpa (1907–10), the *oríkì* of big men in Ìbàdàn seem to turn again to the resources of the older, and enduring, idiom of money as benign allotrope of social regard, constitutive of social being (see Akinyele [1911] 1959:162ff).

Many of the old parallels and equivalences between money and people are still current in present-day discourses. A popular slogan on mammy-waggons is *"Mo lówó mo lénìyàn, kí ló tún kù tí mi ò tíì ní?"* ("I have money, I have people, what remains that I have not got?"). Handing over money is still an act of social recognition in numerous contexts. Self-realization through purchase is a figure of thought that is still being creatively redeployed (see, for example, Òkédìjí 1989:25-26). At the same time, the convertibility of people into money is being given a grisly new emphasis in the petro-naira narratives of money-magic (Barber 1982), and ironical, bitter new proverbs are being coined which seem to combine contempt for the poor with resentment of the rich—for example, *"Olówó ń sọ̀rọ̀, tálíkà lóun ní idea"* ("The rich person speaks [and is obeyed], the poor person says s/he has an idea").[25]

In any money economy, it would seem likely that money is a means or medium of thought as well as of exchange. In recent Western discourses, money as manifested through the "market" has become a master metaphor for the representation of a modern social ideal: Western capitalist democracy (Dilley 1992). This is an appropriate moment, therefore, to consider the way in which Yorùbá people took the metaphor of money into domains that would even now be considered immune from it in Euro-American culture: "going further" than Simmel himself, just as in a certain sense the Asante could be said to go further than Gadamer (McCaskie 1989) and *oríkì*-composers go further than Derrida (Barber 1984). A deeper analysis of the ideological conjuncture of money, the body, people, and self-realization in Yorùbá thought would enable us to understand aspects of the culture that have been hitherto neglected.

Notes

1. According to Hogendorn and Johnson, cowries were being imported southward across the Sahara into the African states on the upper and middle Niger as early as the eleventh century A.D., and there is definite evidence of their use as money in the Mali empire in the fourteenth century (1986:16–17). On the coast, the first Portuguese expeditions to arrive in the 1480s found a diferent type of cowry, probably of Angolan origin, already in use in the Gulf of Guinea (1986:18–19). Portuguese imports of Maldive *Cypraea moneta* to the West African coast began around 1515 A.D., and imports increased steadily as the Dutch and then the British joined the trade, until a climax was reached in the mid-nineteenth century with the growth in the palm oil trade. Hogendorn and Johnson are cautious about earliest presence of cowry currency in the Yorùbá area, but state that "By the nineteenth century they [cowries] were in use on the lower Niger, throughout Yorùbá country and in northern Igbo country, and in all these areas they may have circulated long before this" (1986:107). Belasco is surely correct in his assumption that cowry currency was circulating in the Yorùbá speaking area well before the nineteenth century, possibly as early as the sixteenth or seventeenth centuries.

2. What he has done is to sift through materials, almost all of which were recorded in the nineteenth and twentieth centuries, and arrange them in chronological sequence purely on grounds of thematic content. He assumes that texts expressing a "sacred" view come from an early period and that those expressing a secular view are more recent. The texts are then cited as evidence of ideational change—an obviously circular procedure. His interpretation has other weaknesses. He appears not to have realized the significance of tone, or of the difference between open and closed vowels, in the Yorùbá language. He treats a number of distinct words as the same word or as minor variants or "inflections" of the same word (e.g. *ọlá* (honour, high esteem) and *ọlà* (riches); likewise *owó* (money), *òwò* (trade), *ọwọ́* (hand), *ọ̀wọ̀* (respect)). It is because these concepts are distinct that deliberate metaphorical and punning connections can be made between them.

3. Compare McCaskie's account of wealth in Asante history, where he draws attention to the crucial "substantive mutability of gold," a mutability that it shares with excrement, and which explains its symbolic aptness to be a "transferential agent" (McCaskie 1983:27): since gold can be cast into numerous forms, its physical properties mimic money's abstract capacity to convert numerous commodities into each other. However, as Belasco insists, the Yorùbá also made a connection between cowries and excrement, in an important Ifá narrative (Belasco 1980:45, 102). But Belasco does not consider that excrement might be a metaphor for money's power to transmute: he sees it only as a denigration of money as "unsavoury" because "excrement-like" (1980:102).

4. Although Ajé can be translated as "wealth" in contra-distinction to *owó* (money), this distinction is not clear-cut, and I would question whether it is very significant. In many texts, *ajé* is used to refer to the actual means of exchange, (i.e. cowries or coin).

5. Yorùbá text excerpted from Belasco (1980:140); diacritical marks added. The translation is my own.

6. Prawer (1976) points out that in this passage it is "the misanthropist Timon who speaks," and that it is no part of Marx's purpose to discuss how far, if at all, these represent Shakespeare's own views (or, as I would prefer to put it, the views articulated by the play as a whole or by the larger corpus of Shakespeare's plays). Prawer concludes that the representation of cupidity as the root of all evil is "one that remained congenial to Marx even after his economic studies had shown him many of the ways in which a modern money economy serves the cause of progress" (1976:79). However, there is a zest in Marx's treatment of this passage that suggests a relish for the transformative powers of money as much as disapproval.

7. Old people in Òkukù recalled that personal *oríkì* of individuals of their own and their parents' generation were composed at the time of the incidents, actions, or utterances that they celebrate. Rumor, observation, and popular commentary were turned into epithets, which would then be taken up by the praise singers and drummers. There is evidence in J ohnson (1921) that this was equally true in the nineteenth century. Johnson is acutely sensitive to the way *oríkì* emerged and circulated in response to significant or remarkable experiences. He makes it clear (192:242) that new *oríkì* were composed in the immediate aftermath of the events they celebrated: for example, "Chief Kurumi claimed the honour of the victory [in the Erumu war] and hence his bards sang to his praise 'O pa Mayẹ, o pa Ọgini, O pa Degẹsin, O fi ọkọ ti Ifẹ laiya' (he slew Mayẹ, he slew Ọgini and Degẹsin and thrust his spear into the breasts of the Ifẹs)." This war is placed by Fálọlá "early in the 1830s" (1984:19).

8. Women as well as men were saluted with *oríkì* belonging to their lineage or their forebears. Prominent, outstanding women might have new *oríkì* composed for them, but this was relatively rare: personal *oríkì* participated in the dynamics of the creation of "big men," a sphere that was difficult for women to enter. See Barber (1991b:230–6) for more detailed discussion.

9. Some scholars believe the timespan over which *oríkì orílè* were composed to have been very great—as much as 700 years, going back to the early period of city states such as Ifẹ (see Babalọla 1966:12). It is quite possible that certain elements in the accumulated corpus of some cities' *oríkì* are as old as that; other passages are definitely of more recent origin (e.g. those alluding to historical personages of known provenance, such as Àfọ̀njá the ruler of Ìlọrin who rebelled against Ọ̀yọ́ in c. 1817 (Law 1977:248). *Oríkì orílè* are more elaborated in northern Yorùbáland than elsewhere. It seems at least worth considering the possibility that they became most fully elaborated precisely when large numbers of people were being *displaced* from their native cities by the onset of the nineteenth century wars that ravaged the northern and central areas.

10. Professional *oríkì* performers (Johnson's "bards") were as often male as female. However, in Òkukù at least, the much more substantial domestic, local traditions of *oríkì*-chanting were carried on mainly by wives and daughters of the town's compounds.

11. Except in a prayer, in which the performer asks that the addressee's *"wágọ̀nù"* (wagons) "will not come uncoupled" (i.e., that his children will not die).

12. In a survey of approximately 1500 lines of the texts of personal *oríkì* that I recorded in Òkukù, references to objects or experiences that entered the culture in the twentieth century were confined to the following: two-storyed houses (1 instance); prison (1); iron roof (1); mirror (1); matches (1); Europeans (3); lorries or trucks (4); shillings (1); train (1); china plates (1); and Mecca (1). And some of these objects—for example, china plates, matches, and mirrors—could well have been brought into to Òkukù before the end of the nineteenth century.

13. Occasionally, twentieth-century figures are celebrated in *oríkì* for bringing something new into the community: a chief for being the first to roof his house in corrugated iron sheets, an ọba for "bringing" the colonial police to the town. But these instances are very rare.

14. I am grateful to Dr. Akin Oyetade for this gloss.

15. This passage in Johnson is part of his general account of "Manners and Customs," which he represents as having been in place *before* the cataclysmic changes brought by the nineteenth-century wars. This style of bondage, according to Johnson, was called *"Gba mi o ra mi,"* i.e., Help me and appropriate me (1921:121). Fálọlá, however, describes the *"ìwọ̀fà gbà mí o rà mí"* system as a tough new Ibàdàn variant of the old *iwọ̀fà* institution (1984:63).

16. Miers and Kopytoff (1977) point out that in a slave-taking and slave-owning culture, when persons are bought and owned they are not simply transferred from one clear-cut category (persons) to another (thing-like commodities). Rather, such transactions must be seen in the context of a network of rights in people and things that encompasses all people of whatever status. Kopytoff (1986), furthermore, argues that commoditization is a process rather than a once-and-for-all ascription of status; commodities (both people and things) have biographies in which they may move in and out of a state of commodityhood in various degrees and stages. This analysis, applied to the Yorùbá material, could be taken much further. Again, Simmel's work suggests the direction that investigations might take. The "rigid demarcation" between property "and the self, between internal and external life, is quite superficial . . . " (1978:322), and the extension of the Ego into people is equivalent to its extension into things: "striving for sons" is equal to "striving for possessions." In Medieval England, if you had the power to give away your daughter in marriage and sell your ox, you were free; otherwise, you were in bondage (1978:323-4). Self-realization ("freedom") is here conceived in a way that seems profoundly relevant to understanding the significance of *ẹrú, iwọ̀fà* and *ọmọ* (slaves, bondsmen, and "children," i.e., free members of a lineage) in 19th-century Yorùbá culture.

17. A proverb says *"Àìlówólọ́wọ́ ni ẹbí kò sí; bá a bá lówó lọ́wọ́, tajá tẹran ní í maa kíni ní baba"*: "Without money, you have no family; if you have money, man and beast (lit. dogs and goats) will call you father." People, that is, go where money is. Rivals may actively deploy their money to deprive you of your people: *"Bí iyàwó ọlẹ bá dàgbà, olówó ni yóò gbé e"*: "When a lazy/poor man's affianced wife grows up, a rich man will marry her."

18. One of his *oríkì, "Ìjẹbú ò kóyọ̀ wá mọ́,"* "The Ìjẹbú don't bring salt here any more" suggests an association with the salt famine which followed the closure of the roads by the Ìjẹbú in c.1881 (Johnson 1921:452).

19. Dates supplied by the official king-list of the present ọba.

20. For a discussion of present-day devotees' responsibility to maintain their *òrìṣà*'s reputation, and thus its continued power and even existence, see Barber (1981).

21. An Ifá verse tells of a destitute man, Ọ̀bàrà, disconsolately roaming the bush and suddenly being met by thousands of people swarming towards him, their original town having been disbanded. They make Ọ̀bàrà their king and found a new settlement on the spot (Wande Abimbọla, personal communication). An Ifá story in Yemitan and Ogundele, conversely, describes the situation of an ọba whose "people" suddenly abandon him for no good reason (Yemitan and Ogundele 1970:23-7). There is a proverb that captures the sense of the unpredictable and fluctuating adherence of "people": "Kì í burú burú kó má kẹnìkan mọ́ni; ẹni tí yóò kù la à mọ̀" (Things are never so bad that not a single person remains with one; but you can never tell who it is who will remain).

22. Again, I thank Dr. Akin Oyetade for telling me this proverb.

23. *Oríkì* of Olúgbẹdẹ, father (or senior brother) of Mofómikẹ́. Olúgbẹdẹ was "a great man, a hunter, in the time of Oyèwùsì," the Ọba who reigned c. 1888–1916. See Barber (1991b:17–19) for a discussion of the passage in which this line occurs.

24. One avenue for future research would be the investigation of oral texts associated with leaders of the other nineteenth-century military cities that shared some, but not all, of Ìbàdàn's unusual political features: e.g. Ìjàyè, Abẹ́òkúta, and Ìlọrin.

25. Thanks to Bísí Adéléyẹ-Fáyẹmí for this proverb.

Sources

Oral Sources

Those *oríkì* quoted in the text that are not drawn from Akinyẹle 1959 [1911] were recorded and collected by the author in Òkukù, Ọ̀ṣun district, between 1974 and 1984.

Books, Dissertations, and Articles

Agiri, Babatunde Arẹmu. 1972. *Kola in Western Nigeria, 1850–1950: A History of the Cultivation of Cola Nitida in Ẹgba-Owode, Ijẹbu-Rẹmọ, Iwo and Ọta Areas.* Ph. D. Dissertation, University of Wisconsin at Madison.

Akinyẹle, I. B. [1911] 1959 *Ìwè Ìtàn Ìbàdàn.* Exeter: James Townsend and Sons..

Awẹ, B.A. 1964. *The Rise of Ibadan as a Yoruba Power.* D. Phil. thesis, Oxford University.

Babalọla, Adeboye. 1966 *Àwọn Oríkì Orílẹ̀* Glasgow: Collins.

———. 1975. *Àwọn Oríkì Bọrọkìnní.* London: Hodder and Stoughton.

Barber, Karin. 1981. "How Man Makes God in West Africa: Yorùbá Attitudes Towards the Òrìṣà," *Africa,* 51:724–745.

———. 1982. "Popular Reactions to the Petro-Naira," *Journal of Modern African Studies,* 20:431–450.

———. 1984. "Yorùbá *Oríkì* and Deconstructive Criticism," *Research in African Literatures,* 15:497–518.

———. 1991a. "*Oríkì* and the Changing Perception of Greatness in 19th-Century Yorùbáland," in *Yorùbá Historiography,* ed.Toyin Falọla, 31–41. Madison: University of Wisconsin Press.

———. 1991b. *I Could Speak Until Tomorrow: Oríkì, Women and the Past in a Yorùbá Town,* Edinburgh University Press for the I.A.I.

Belasco, Bernard. 1980. *The Entrepreneur as Culture Hero.* New York: Praeger.

Biobaku, S. O. 1957. *The Ẹgba and their Neighbours, 1842–1872.* Oxford: Clarendon Press.

Bohannan, Paul. 1959. "The Impact of Money on an African Subsistence Economy," *The Journal of Economic History,* 19:491–503.

Dilley, Roy. 1992. "Contesting Markets: An Introduction." In *Contesting Markets,* ed. Roy Dilley, 1–34. Edinburgh: Edinburgh University Press.

Falọla, Toyin. 1984. *The Political Economy of a Pre-colonial African State: Ibadan, 1830–1900.* Ile-Ifẹ: University of Ifẹ Press.

Guyer, Jane. 1993. "Wealth in People and Self-Realization in Equatorial Africa." *Man* (n.s.), 28:243–265.

Hogendorn, Jan, and Marion Johnson. 1986 *The Shell Money of the Slave Trade.* Cambridge: Cambridge University Press.

Iliffe, John. 1984. "Poverty in Nineteenth-Century Yorubaland." *Journal of African History,* 25:43–57.

Johnson, Samuel. 1921. *The History of the Yorubas.* London: G. Routledge & Sons.

Kopytoff, Igor. 1986. "The Cultural Biography of Things: Commoditisation as Process," in *The Social Life of Things,* ed. A. Appadurai, 64–91. New York and London: Cambridge University Press.

Law, Robin. 1977. *The Ọ̀yọ́ Empire c.1600–c.1836.* Oxford: Clarendon Press.

Marx, Karl. [1887] 1954. *Capital*, translator, Samuel Moore and Edward Aveling, ed. Frederick Engels, vol. I. London: Lawrence and Wishart.

McCaskie, T. C. 1983. "Accumulation, Wealth and Belief in Asante History, 1." *Africa*, 53:23–43.

McCaskie, T. C. 1989. "Asantesεm: Reflections on Discourse and Text in Africa." In *Discourse and its Disguises*, ed. Karin Barber and P. F. de Moraes Farias, 70–86. Birmingham, AL, Centre of West African Studies Publications.

Miers, Suzanne, and Igor Kopytoff, eds. 1977. *Slavery in Africa*. Madison, WI: University of Wisconsin Press.

O'Hear, Ann. 1983. *The Economic History of Ìlọrin in the Nineteenth and Twentieth Centuries: The Rise and Decline of a Middleman Society*. Ph.D. Thesis, University of Birmingham.

Òkédìjí, Ọládèjọ. 1989. *Bínú Ti Rí*. Ìbàdàn: Oníbọnòjé Press.

Parry, J. and M. Bloch, eds. 1989. *Money and the Morality of Exchange*. Cambridge: Cambridge University Press.

Peel, J. D. Y. 1990. "Poverty and Sacrifice in Nineteenth-Century Yorubaland: A Critique of Iliffe's Thesis." *Journal of African History*, 31:465–84.

Prawer, S. S. 1976. *Karl Marx and World Literature*. Oxford: Oxford University Press.

Simmel, Georg. [1900] 1978. *The Philosophy of Money*, translator, Tom Bottomore and David Frisby. London: Routledge and Kegan Paul.

Taussig, M. 1980. *The Devil and Commodity Fetishism in South America*. Chapel Hill, NC: University of North Carolina.

Watts, Michael J. 1994. "The Devil's Excrement: Oil Money and the Spectacle of Black Gold." In *Money, Powe r and Space*, ed. N. Thrift, 406–445. Oxford: Basil Blackwell.

Yemitan, Ọladipọ, and Ọlajide Ogundele. 1970 *Ojú Òṣùpá, apá kejì*. Ìbàdàn: Oxford University Press.

10

The State, the Courts, and "Value": Caught Between Matrilineages in Ghana

Gwendolyn Mikell

Introduction

The transformation of uxorial duties of women from a domestic obligation to a good possessing monetary value has transformed the relations between men and women in rural Ghana and created many problems for the state. The monetization of matrilineal Akan women's labor means that they now create conjugal as well as private property, which is usually under the control of husbands or spouses. Although the movement away from the traditional uxorial uses of women's labor occurred during pre-colonial and colonial periods, it began to create publicly recognized problems as fluctuations occurred in the global, national, and local economies during the twentieth century. Between 1978 and 1985, the collapse of the national economy was accompanied by severe dislocations in family economic relationships, which had the strongest negative impact on women and children. The growing impoverishment of women throughout the country and the Provisional National Defense Council (PNDC) government's felt responsibility to deal with destitute women and children in urban areas have been the determining factor in the state's legal recognition of the "conjugal family" as a social and economic unit. Consequently, the new 1985 laws on intestate succession (PNDCL.111), on marriage registration (PNDCL.112), and the Administration of Estates Act (PNDCL.113) were intended to empower women who were discussed in this legislation as contributing to the resources of the conjugal family.[1]

This legislation reverses the traditional exclusion of women and children from inheriting when a husband and father dies (Manuh 1989). Also implicit, however, in the state's recognition of women's capacity for generating value and their resulting right to inherit a share of a husband's wealth is a challenge to the traditional notion of what constitutes economic value, and the question of whether women's labor has economic value. The effect of the new family and inheritance is to create competing claims on household/domestic and private resources, and to generate a new class of legal cases that cross the traditional *efiesem* (household) level of cases in the minds of matrilineal Akan people, because these were not customarily dealt with through the political system.[2] The grassroot responses to the economic realities and legal pressures involve some unique manipulations of family economic norms, which are revealed in court cases from the Brong-Ahafo region.

In this chapter, I will examine three property cases that involve the changing notions about Akan women's labor and the value that it bestows upon farms and landed property, as well as how the competing claims to this value are made by kinspersons, wives and children of the deceased. Leaving aside the issue of how effective court actions are in changing economic behavior of ordinary people (Mikell 1991) I analyze the claims, arguments, and counterclaims within the cases that illuminate notions of value. These three cases (from among the twenty five cases that I collected in the High Court Sunyani in the Brong-Ahafo Region in 1990) were selected because they seem to represent a continuum of the types of claims and treatment of value created by women that one can find in this matrilineal area. These cases confirm a process that was implicit in the literature and in cases during the colonial period — that of a continual manipulation and negotiation of economic norms and concepts of value as the material conditions of Akan society changed through trade, conquest, colonialism, and modernization. There is every reason to believe that these concepts should continue to change, in response to a volatile market economy in which money is unstable but "value in persons" persists.

Cultural Notions of Women's Labor and Value

Traditional Akan societies (whether Asante, Brong-Asante, Fante, or Kwahu) were based on jural relationships between groups of related persons having both *abusua* (lineage), *mogya* (blood), and kin-ritual (clan) ties to each other (Rattray 1923:21–85). Over time, Akan societies expanded, became more stratified, and developed centralized state structures and relationships that extended and eventually superseded the kinship and ritual ties of the base. As this happened, economic relationships also changed, and more economic control was vested in the state. But the kinship ties among groups within the state were never eradicated; and these with religious ties undergird traditional political and economic legitimacy among the Akan.

Originally, Akan societies were made up of hierarchically arranged groups of persons having free birth as well as slave birth, but the factor that united them was their labor on behalf of aristocrats who controled the land in the area. It is hypothesized that these localized work groups expanded as labor was drawn into the forest zone of Asante and further southward, and that they moved outward and formed localized chiefdoms in which royals had the powers of ritual control over commoner lineages and their members (Kea 1982). The proto-typical Akan culture was thus elaborated with minor variations in different regions among the different subcultural groups. However, royal and aristocratic lineages (*abusua*) thus controled and managed land in this extensive forest zone, where labor, rather than land, was in short supply. Everyone, even chiefs and lesser royals, owed allegiance and some degree of labor to someone or some larger corporate group. Ultimately, it was "rights in persons" that made chiefs and people prosperous as village members continued producing the food and utilitarian products needed for everyday life (Wilks 1977).

Naturally, female reproduction, as well as control over marriage and reproduction guaranteed the well-being and prosperity of the group. This meant that women (who were the central members of the *abusua* because it traced descent through women) were valuable to the group as a whole, filling important domestic, communal, ritual, and political roles (Meyerowitz 1951; Arhin 1983a). Women's subordination to group interests, however, was evident, and polygynous marriage was one mechanism for regulating population to fit groups and resource needs. Marriage, which united a woman's blood (*mogya*) with the spiritual force of the husband (*ntoro*) created a child who belonged to the mother's *abusua* but bore a personality (*sunsun*) that was marked by the father (Fortes 1963). Despite the father's contribution, the new infant belonged to the *abusua* of the mother, and later all its productive energies would be claimed by the *abusua*. Asante and other Akan men paid no real bridewealth, because they possessed rights "in uxorem" rather than rights "in genetricum." Few economic rights were given to husbands, and under normal circumstances only ritual gifts such as the headwine (*tiri nsa*) were exchanged. It was the *abusua* tie that identified a person and marked his or her duties, rights, and privileges vis-a-vis the family and the community writ large. It was also the jural identity of the *abusua* as one of the component kingroups of the area, that gave a person the right to use land resources of the community for family subsistence.

These and other norms regulating family relations and resource use were enshrined in Asante traditional legal principles, which have been identified as *efiesem* (household traditional behavior).[3] These defined the heretofore large range of day-to-day behavior for Akan people in the southern matrilineal areas of the Gold Coast. An understanding of these principles is crucial for understanding the kinship and issues of "economic value" being affected by the changing family law in Ghana, so it would be beneficial to state them in brief. The norms underlying Asante kin/property behavior can be generalized into five sets of *efiesem* principles:

1. *Links between nature, the ethnic group, and lineage rights and duties*: That the natural resources which the kin–ethnic group uses (especially land) were given by the supernatural; that all rights to resources come though membership in a localized lineage (*abusua*) and ethnic group, and outsiders have no claim to local resources; that any male or female of the *abusua* may request land to be used for subsistence; that land always has an owner—its control is vested in the chief (*ohene*), the headman (*odikro*) or other traditional leader, until such time as it is given to a usufructuary; that usufruct rights are extended to members so that they can meet the needs of the group, and that usufruct rights can never be converted to personal property rights; that usufruct rights extended to outsiders must be recognized by the payment of yearly tribute.

2. *Identity and leadership within the abusua*: that lineages are the component jural units within any town or village, and membership in them confers the status of "belonging"; that individual males and females are given jural representation and identity by the lineage and therefore fully under the control of the *abusua*; that slaves can be attached as adjunct members of an *abusua*, but

may not inherit positions that lie with the abusua; that the lineage can give any male or female member as a "pawn" for a debt, with an obligation also to redeem that person; membership in the *abusua* brings a right of residence in the matrilineal compound; that at any generation, the children of sisters of the lineage will be the ultimate heirs to the brothers of the lineage; that both male and female leaders can exist within the family; that the Head of the Family (*Opanyin*) has responsibility for allocating specific uses of lineage land to which usufruct rights have been granted; that becoming Head of the Family confers economic responsibilities that if neglected or abused, will be punished supernaturally; that although individuals can request land or resources, they retain responsibilities for making group contributions from these resources.

3. *Property transmission across generations*: that the matrilineal *abusua* is a corporate group that maintains an interest in the economic and landed estate of the lineage (Ollenu 1962; Asante 1975); that death converts a person's personally acquired property to lineage property, unless it had been otherwise designated publicly; that family (lineage) property must be passed on to lineage heirs; that males have priority in the inheritance and guardianship of family property; that inheritance passes first through brothers and then to sisters' sons (nephews); that the family heir may assume control of farms and land of a deceased person and use it in the interest of the family group; that becoming the heir to a deceased man confers economic responsibilities that if neglected or abused, will be punished supernaturally; that men can designate a specific male heir to inherit their "male" personal property and females can designate a specific female heir to receive their "female" personal property; and that *abusua* members retain the right to leave personal property to someone through a verbal will (*samansiw*).[4]

4. *Separation of the wife's matrilineage from the husband's lineage*: that the *abusua* has the right to arrange marriage, and receive *tiri nsa* (literally, "headwine,") for its women in ritual recognition of legitimate marriage,[5] that in the marriage of an *abusua* woman to other Akan man, the children belong to the *abusua* of the wife; that the wife's brother was and is the natural authority figure for a woman's children; that wives may continue to reside in their matrilineal compound, while husbands reside in their matrilineal compound or their own houses; that, if necessary, the responsibilities of father may be assumed by others of the father's abusua (Fortes 1963); that children of a man do not have a right to inherit property of their father; wives do not have a right to inherit *abusua* property of their husband; that if family members (children) belonging to another *abusua* contributed to building personal property for a man, he is obligated to compensate them for their labor.

5. *Marital and affinal relationships*: that legitimate marriage occurs through the receiving of *tiri nsa* for a woman; husbands have a moral responsibility to contribute to the maintenance and training of their children; that husbands have a spiritual responsibility to recognize their children as members of their *ntoro* (ritual) group, and to seek their well-being in life; that if the offspring of a woman's womb does not bear her husband's *ntoro* and she does not confess her infidelity, she will die in childbirth; that personal or abusua property

of a wife does not pass to the woman's husband; that wives have a responsibility to contribute to the maintenance of their children, whom they own; that wives have a responsibility to contribute labor to their husbands and their families of procreation; that a wife should help bring food and maintenance into the household shared with a husband; that property generated by the wife during the marriage belongs to the conjugal family, and could be claimed by the husband; that a good husband gives "gifts" to a good wife during his lifetime; that personal property that a person desires to give to a family member of another *abusua* must be recognized by the receiver's lineage giving *aseda* (thanks) to the giver in a public ritual; that children must contribute the casket of their father when he dies; that with death, a man's traditional heir has the responsibility to maintain the widow and children of his predecessor.

The above principles provide one with the basis for understanding that for ordinary people, both male and female labor, on land yielding subsistence goods needed by the *abusua*. The day-to-day economic activities of *abusua* members did yield some surplus, but this was primarily agricultural produce and palm oil, as well as game, snails, tobacco, kola nuts, skins, and so forth, needed to feed families and supply the growing towns. Women maintained control over some of the proceeds of their labor by the sale of their agricultural produce, but, unless they were in large towns, the money value accumulated was relatively small. But in general, personal control over labor and its product were not part of these economic relations. The *abusua*'s control over women was maintained even after marriage because Asante women usually married men in the same or nearby villages, and they frequently remained resident within their own *abusua* compound. A husband used the uxorial labor of a wife when she cooked meals for him, raised vegetables for the family on land to which he had usufruct rights, and assisted him in weeding and planting his food farms from which they also obtained foodstuffs.

In the seventeenth and eighteenth centuries, there was little beyond subsistence and reproductive value that a husband could derive from a wife's labor. Because a wife usually lived separately from her husband and sent meals to him in the evening by his children, she performed relatively few household duties. More of these household duties (cleaning, washing clothing) were traditionally performed by sisters than by wives. Most of the food that wives raised on the husband's farms was consumed by the husband, wife, and children. In fact, a wife went from her husband's farm to work on her own or her matrilineage's food farm in the afternoon, before coming home to cook.

On the other hand, people did dig or wash for gold. Gold (either gold dust or nuggets) was the main item that symbolized wealth in Asante, and although ordinary individuals or families could acquire small amounts of gold dust from streams, it usually required the cooperation of more than one person to wash for gold. Here, a husband who was fortunate enough to have a wife living with him might have an advantage in obtaining an item of value, but the amount was relatively small and could purchase only an occasional elite item such as an unusual cloth. It was the exceptional man who was able to migrate with his wife to an area where she could invest all her labor and time on land (or gold washing) from which he and she alone could derive the profit. Because nuggets of gold were supposed to automatically belong to the chief (with portions transmitted through him to the Asantehene)[6] husbands who desired to retain gold were probably better off not using a wife's labor or even informing her.

Because wealth did flow to elites, women among royal groups were often given in marriage to men from the appropriate clans and lineages, so that supernatural relationships affecting politics would be enhanced. Royal women also had the ability to control tracts of land (with the "rights-in-persons" or patronage from those who resided there), and they frequently participated in the "market in towns and villages", (Wilks 1977:20–21), using these purchased rights to enhance their economic well-being. Likewise, Akan women who were given as gift wives to merchants, coastal middlemen, or European traders, also had increased ability to control resources and capital, and generate wealth that might enrich the conjugal couple. This became particularly true among Creole and Fanti families in coastal communities. But this did not affect the economic status of ordinary women. More important was that greater contact with external societies and the increasing centralization within Asante began to change male control over the labor of men and women. Northward and westward expansion brought the Asante greater control over additional resources and slaves, created a larger labor force for agricultural production within the Akan forest zone, and it resulted in an increasing number of relationships with Muslim traders who desired the agricultural produce of the forest. In the 1800s, kola nuts were the main trade items with the northern Muslims, and gold and palm oil were the main local items involved in the European coastal trade (Mikell 1992:39–40).

Prospering men, whether commoners, the wealthy *sikafo*, or the commercial entrepreneurs (*akonkofo*) and other Asante bureaucrats, also tried to enrich themselves as individuals. By hoarding gold, they could invest it in the expanding coastal, European-influenced trade, and enrich the conjugal family under their control. From the 1830s onward, in an attempt to enrich the state, keep the internal economy solvent and retain local allegiance, the Ashantehene pressured the elite and traders by implementing "death duties" (*awunnyade*), which converted a deceased man's property in gold and land as well as his titled offices back to the King, leaving little for his wives, children, or lineage members to control or inherit. So onerous was this form of taxation and the tyranny of Asantehene Mensa Bonsu and others, that many *akonkofo* fled into the coastal Protectorate, further contributing to the collapse of the traditional Asante state.[7] The *awunnyade* did not survive British conquest in 1896, although attempts at personal enrichment using the conjugal family continued. Men particularly desired the booty of war—female slaves who could be wives, produce children totally under the control of a man and his *abusua*, and make large labor contributions to his farms or trading business. Campaigns against the North, and subsequent female enslavement was at its height during the 1800s, and enslavement continued during the civil wars within Asante in the 1870s and 1880s (Aidoo 1975). As the Asante military and bureaucratic structure fell into disarray, and as the commoner leaders (*nkwankwaa*) agitated against an oppressive chieftaincy (Mikell 1992:47–58), female enslavement declined. However, some have argued that female enslavement had a negative impact on the status of ordinary Akan women (Vallenga n.d.).

The manipulation of an elite man's household dependents, landed clients, slaves, and female pawns, could and did enrich men in the late nineteenth century. In fact, in response to fluctuations in the internal Asante economy, families tried to extract themselves from debts incurred by funerals or other misfortunes by pawning female members of the lineage of wealthier men, who treated them as wives and benefited from their labor. Having paid the debt, a patron could retain a woman and any of her subsequent progeny until the family redeemed her, if they could. This movement of women appears to have become the major means by which matrilineages adjusted their financial budgets, and it stimulated considerable anger among British administrators who saw it as equivalent to female enslavement (Aidoo 1975:607–8).

At the turn of the twentieth century, Asante women's labor underwent another important transition. Colonial conquest had posed an internal threat that created tension among Islamicized groups inland from the Gold Coast and Ivory Coast. In the 1890s, in an attempt to forestall French penetration, and to weld the faithful into an Islamic state that could resist the corruptions of the heathen and Christians, the Islamic leader Samory had pushed his jihad, burning Senufo, Diola, Kulango, and Baule villages, across northern Ivory Coast and into the Brong borderland of the Asante state. Samory's jihad failed to halt the French, although it did expand Islam across the Ivory Coast border into Ghana, and it did solidify the Muslim trading communities that had been resident in these areas since the 1700s. However, for women the devastation in the local food economy, and in rotating markets of yams, fruit, and snails that had extended across this area, and new colonial borders with their reorganized political relations, left them without cash and in a more dependent position relative to men.

Asante soldiers who had fought the British, or men had fled their home area during the civil wars, returned after 1900 to find themselves totally dependent upon their food farms for subsistence and more in need of the labor of women. Elderly Brong-Asante informants recalled that in this environment men were desperate for wives: they contracted for unborn infants who "might" be female, and paid what elsewhere would be considered "bridewealth" in order to acquire them.[8] This was significant because the labor of wives was now used more extensively on men's farms, but the competing pull was from a woman's *abusua*, which desired to use her to accumulate surplus by transporting goods over long distances to trading southern points. In fact, the colonially stimulated exploitation of rubber trees heightened the competition for women's labor in transporting the product to collection depots further south.[9] Brong-Asante oral histories recount the *abusua*'s use of mothers and sisters to carry rubber to the coast and bring back salt for sale inland. More importantly, during this period Brong data confirm that there were serious efforts on the part of Asante men to form the conjugal family of co-resident spouses and children. With this conjugal family, a man could migrate and accumulate some capital through sale of produce from land, and then return (Mikell 1992:67–70; Arhin 1983b).

Although these early changes in use of uxorial labor were occurring outside the context of the indigenous village and *abusua* land, and did not initially constitute a direct challenge to the *abusua* principles regulating women's labor, as economic change began within Asante communities in the twentieth century, they quickly infringed on the *abusua* rights, which were embedded within culture.

In a summary of the major changes across time, a number of things appeared to have fueled the early gradual monetization of women's labor: 1) the occasional incentives to control women in conjugal relationships as a means of adjusting to economic fluctuation, instability, and crisis, or as a means to economic stability; 2) the increased monetization of the Asante economy as coastal capitalist influences and imported commodities inflated "wants" within Asante society; 3) the struggle between the Asantehene and his bureaucrats as he tried to control the shrinking gold supply that was creating fiscal and monetary problems; 4) the economic profit generated by slavery and its impact on women's status; 5) the decimation of women's local economy roles with the juxtaposition of jihads and colonial conquest; and 6) British colonial support for Christian monogamy with co-resident spouses, which had its maximum influence in coastal Fante communities.

The early changes were minor in comparison to the monetization of women's labor in response to the expanding cocoa industry in the 1920s and 1930s. Although the *efiesem* principles clarify that, with the exception of uxorial labor, the proceeds from the labor of women belong exclusively to their lineages (*mmusua*), the definition of what constituted uxorial labor was transformed after cocoa production. After colonial conquest, the British attempt to commercialize Asante agriculture began with the introduction of cash crops such as cotton and cocoa, to men rather than to women. When Asante men began cocoa-farming after 1906, more often than before women married men from distant Asante villages and spouses began co-residing. But co-residence had the dual effect of increasing the labor contributions women made to food farms, and generated sufficient surplus food to rebuild local and rotating market networks and bring women additional capital. Women were entitled to retain this money, but living apart as they did, they often used these resources on behalf of the family. Many Asante argue that this new trend fueled later erroneous legal interpretations of Asante women's resources generated while living with the husband as belonging to the husband (Ollenu 1962).

Naturally, with co-residence, women's labor contributions to the *abusua* decreased, and this was met with some anxiety and occasional conflicts between a woman's brother and her husband. Of certainty was that a husband could gain from using a wife's labor on his food farms and cocoa farms. Female labor contributions were crucial in the development of the migrant cocoa farms in southern Ghana between 1910 and 1920 as Hill recounts (1959; 1963), and in the establishment of second farms in the Brong-Ashanti area between 1920 and 1940, as I have earlier described (Mikell 1989). For men who had been patient and long-suffering while working with uncles and hoping to establish *abusua* farms, the labor contributions of wives made it possible for them to achieve relative independence from the tyranny of *abusua* control. I have explored elsewhere some of the economic dilemmas for male and female cocoa farmers during the global depression of 1929 through the 1930s. The externally stimulated machinations of the local economy again had a major impact on women's economic status. As the depression began and the indebtedness of one group of cocoa farmers was evident, many impoverished families used a cyclical tendency to encourage women to reside with husbands; and then, in contradictory fashion, they warned them to be careful to receive compensation for labor on a husband's cocoa farms. Men relied on the labor of wives to maintain cocoa farms while they worked for additional wages wherever this could be found. But we note that for those few women who were able to rally their own resources or the labor of their own children, they could acquire their own cocoa farms during this period, although they became economically vulnerable later (Mikell 1984:195-218).

Herein lay the source of the many conflicts over property in farms and land that surfaced in the 1960s through 1980s. Notions of women's labor value had become monetized as had many other things in Asante life. When wives and husbands lived separately, a husband usually gave the children's maintenance to his wife in *cash* rather than in foodstuff from the farm; when a wife worked on husband's farm, he increasingly tried to make certain that there was a patch of cocoa from which she could derive cash for the children's everyday needs. Prior to 1948, few Asante or Brong-Asante men married according to Ordinance Law, and even today most Akan marry under Customary law. Another trend toward informal alliances rather than customary marriage was also set in force, particularly among men who did not desire co-residence and saw little to be gained from acquiring a wife (Mikell 1992). Therefore, few had any inducements to transfer property to wives, and few made written wills leaving women property. Although neither the symbolism within the marriage ceremony nor any formal agreements reflected the monetization process occurring as husband and wife worked together, the actual and personal relationships between husband and wife recognized it tacitly.

The slowest thing to change was public recognition of the monetization of *uxorial labor*, possibly because oral culture—popular proverbs, *efiesem* norms, and so forth—all denied this. Particularly entrenched was the traditional notion that a wife's contribution was quite small: she provided sexual satisfaction, cooked food, and was the source of a man's children, who were his pride but did not belong to him; she owed a husband domestic service, but household service did not create wealth. However, in the popular jargon of men when joking with each other about the value of wives, men would say: "Yes it's good to have wives; they can be working on the farms, and cooking for you, and working in the market . . . yes, it helps."[10]

In effect, a dysjuncture had occurred between women's economic roles as reflected in traditional culture and their modern economic roles in a capitalist economy. At various points, traditional authorities had been unwilling to address this dysjuncture because of the implied potential to question traditional legitimacy and traditional law.[11] So only those married under Ordinance Law had rights to a share of a deceased husband's property.[12] However, given the economic collapse and its social consequences, the PNDC government was forced to recognize that this contradiction between traditional structures and modern practice was creating "moral injustice" and the "impoverishment of women." In 1985, the courts, by enforcing new laws on intestate succession, marriage registration, and administration of wills, were pushing the state's new interpretation of the economic value of women's labor into the public arena, and casting light on the conflicts between traditional notions of women uxorial labor and current notions of women's cash-generating potential. Cases based on the 1985 legislation were finally represented in substantial numbers in the High Court by 1990. What comes through clearly in the court data that I collected in the Sunyani High Court in 1990, was that women now conceptualized their labor as having monetary value and wanted to reap its benefit for themselves. But how were they to do this without disrupting all the other *efiesem* relationships and challenging local cultural norms—especially those *efiesem* norms that privileged the *abusua* and the males within it?

One stereotypical assumption that many people make is that matrilineal women can control resources and capital in their own interests and pass it on to daughters and sisters as they desire. Some few women successfully pass on to daughters the small food-farms that they establish, but most Akan women have difficulty acquiring and controlling property of the *abusua*. Although Akan women have the right to control their own capital and resources, often generated through their trading of foodstuffs and other market activities, they are expected to distribute it to their children, among whom sons appear more privileged than daughters.

My interviews in the Sunyani District in the 1970s revealed that Brong-Asante women usually hoped that husbands would publicly recognize their contributions on his farm by giving one of his cocoa farms to them, or dividing his farms into a portion that became her own. But most often these hopes did not come to fruition. On the other hand, many of those few women who were successful cocoa farmers had either been given land by prosperous husbands or had his assistance in paying for farm labor. But success and inheritance of a woman's cash-generating property posed other problems. A typical outcome of the inheritance of a woman's property is that sons receive cash-generating resources including land and farms, and daughters receive jewelry, clothing, small moveable items, and personal effects, and only vegetable farms.

During the 1980s one heard rumors about women who had the audacity to make a claim to farms belonging to a deceased husband, but few of these rumors materialized into real court cases.[13] Most Akan do not make Wills; in this area of Brong Asante it was the more prosperous men, having several cocoa farms and and involved with rents from property, profits from businesses, accumulating interest from immovable property, and so forth, who actually make Wills. However, by 1990, a number of cases involving either Intestate Succession, Wills, or Letters of Administration were passing through the High Courts in Sunyani. This provided me with an opportunity to examine twenty five cases, looking at how husbands viewed wives' contribution to accumulating property, how women viewed their contribution, and how *abusua* members viewed it. Presented below are three cases that appear to cover the spectrum of these issues.

Case A: The Estate of Kofi Duro

On 15th May, 1989, Opanyin Philip Kwaku Manu, the son of Kofi Duro presented himself to the court, claiming to be the "head of his family." He applied for Letters Of Administration, which would give him the right to undertake economic transactions on property that had been willed to him, his mother, and his ten brothers and sisters by his deceased father. He presented the Will, executed on the 25th of October, 1988, which stated that Kofi Duro willed to his surviving widow and eleven children one cocoa farm with adjoining scrubland, a second scrubland, his compound house (cement) No. WH14 at Wamahinso, and all his personal effects, including his local gun No. 25582.

However, Yaw Barimah, the representative of Kofi Duro's matrilineal family, entered a Caveat on the 2nd of February 1990, asking for an interim injunction while they investigated the rights of the matrilineal family. Through Yaw Barimah, the matrilineal family claimed that all three pieces of property (the cocoa farm, the scrubland, and the house) belonged to the family, and could not be willed out without their consent.

Philip (son of the deceased) responded that the cocoa farm which was willed to them had been cultivated by his father, together with his farmer wife Madam Nyame and his deceased wife Brempomaa. He claimed that his father had obtained a declaration of title to the seven-room compound house when a dispute had arisen with his matrilineal family, making it necessary to clarify ownership. Philip stated that the scrubland had been obtained by his father in its virgin state, and that his father had authorized his eldest daughter, his wife, and his brother-in-law Kosi Asokiwa to cultivate and care for the land.

Yaw Barimah (*abusua* representative) still objected that all these properties were family properties belonging to the *abusua* of the deceased, but he produced no further evidence to substantiate the claim.

Philip, son of the deceased, then entered an affidavit declaring the date on which the Will had been executed and complaining about the Caveat. He accused the Caveators of seeking to deprive the children of the deceased of any benefits from their father's personal property. He further stated that he, his mother, brothers and sisters had delayed to see whether their father's customary successor would look after them; but because the customary successor had completely neglected them, the children of the deceased had begun to harvest the cocoa from the farm to pay for their necessities. The case was adjourned until the 15th of October, 1990.

In this case, the issue that Philip Kwaku Manu (the son of Kofi Duro) uses as the ultimate bolster for his claim to the property of his deceased father is the role that his mother played in contributing the labor and helping to accumulate the resources that his father needed to build up "personal property" distinct from lineage property. Philip explained that when his father's *abusua* attempted to make an unjustified claim, it prompted his father to seek and obtain title to his material possessions. Note that "maternal labor" was not the first principle he cited to justify his claims; but when the others appeared to be challenged, he resorted to the final factor—the one that most Asante hesitate to publicly recognize—that a wife's labor helped create valuable property. Although there are a number of other normative issues raised in this case (Who can be a "head of family?" Are men manipulating female claims to enrich themselves? What will impel customary heirs to deal honorably with widows and children of deceased men? etc.), the issue on which the case turns is the one of a wife's labor and its implication for male property.

Case B: The Estate of Opoku Gyabaa of Dormaa Ahenkro

On 19th March, 1990, the Reverend George Boaheng and Kwabena Asamoa of Dormaa Ahenkro applied to the court for the Probate of a Will regarding the estate of the deceased Opoku Gyabaa of Dormaa Ahenkro, an Akan man who was former Managing Director of Opoku Gyabaa Timber Company. The applicants were family members of the deceased and were named as Executors of the estate in Will #1, which the deceased signed and dated in 1978. However, a second applicant, Richard Afari Mintah of Dormaa Ahenkro, also presented Will #2, which the deceased signed and dated in 1984. Will #2 dispossessed the matrilineal family of any property from the estate of the deceased.

A Caveat was immediately brought by Kwabena Peprah, the oldest son of the deceased, also residing in Dormaa Ahenkro. During his lifetime, Opoku Gyabaa was married monogamously and had lived with his wife Afua

Afriyie (who had helped him in his business) and had eight children (the ages of the children were not given). His son Kwabena Peprah claimed to file the Caveat as a formality on behalf of this conjugal family, in case any question was raised as to the accuracy or legitimacy of the Wills. This was important because there was no mention of the matrilineal family in Will #2. Kwabena Peprah listed all the deceased's property and declared the titles of each. The judge adjourned the case until a copy of Will #2 could be officially filed with the court.

In Will #1 of 1978, Opoku Gyabaah bequeathed one third of his property to his wife, one third to his children, and one third to his matrilineal relatives. He specified that the children's one third share should be apportioned equally among them, and that the specifics of the Will should be strictly adhered to.

However, in Will #2 of 1984, Opoku Gyabaah revoked all former wills. He bequeathed all his self-acquired properties in his timber-contracting business, both movable and immovable, to his wife Afua Afriyie and eight children. He requested that if he should die before the death of his mother, Madam Adwoa Pepraa of Dormaa Ahenkro, his wife and children should maintain her until her death. The wife and children should also bear his funeral expenses. Third, he declared that "nobody else helped me in my business, so nobody has a share in it. My nephew Kwadwo Poku stole some parts of my timber lorry and bolted to Asankraguaa. My Brother Yaw Gyamfi, who comes after me, did not help me in any way." Finally, he stated that, "I could not build a house to accommodate my wife and children, so this Will is to enable them to have funds to build their own houses so that they could live happily after my death."

As of August, 1990 no further movement had occurred on this case.

In Case B, the deceased husband Opoku Gyabaah is monogamous, and focuses his economic and emotional attention on the conjugal family. However, what is striking is that between the first will dated 1978 and the second will dated 1984 he has apparently altered his views of what his wife and children are entitled to as fair compensation for all that they have shared with him during his lifetime. The fact that he give one third each to the wife, children, and the matrilineal family in the 1978 Will might be traceable to the public discussion about changes in family and inheritance law that was taking place in the capital, and among church members.[14] However, by 1984 he has formulated his views that the contributions of his wife and children were of overwhelming significance. He asserts that his matrilineal family was a negative influence on his acquisition of property and money, and therefore denies them any benefit from it. In this case, the contested property is a business rather than cocoa farms, but the point is that the contribution of the monogamous wife is publicly acknowledged. Having no property in land or buildings, Opoku Gyabaah endows his wife with the business, expecting that she will liquidate it and convert it to permanent property that she and the children will use.

Case C: Estate of Opanyin E. Owusu

On 29th September, 1989, Isaac Adjei and Kwabena Karimu, both male *abusua* members of the deceased Opanyin Owusu, applied for Letters Of

Administration over the deceased's estate. The first applicant was a lawyer and claimed to act on behalf of the matrilineal family. He stated that the deceased had two farms, two other lands, a house, and a two-story building, all totaling C1,600,000, and that these were properties in which the family had an interest.

However, on 19th December, 1989, a Caveat was fined by Abdul Karima and children of the deceased challenging the matrilineage's claims to administer the estate. They claimed that the deceased had been married under Islamic law to three wives, producing fifteen children, five by each wife. They produced a Will written by the deceased. Because their Caveat did not clearly itemize which property they contested, the case was continued until they did so. The Will of the deceased indicated that all the property was to be divided between his wife and fifteen children, but very little mention was made of any *abusua* members except the nephew.

In the Will submitted to the Court, Opanyin Owusu gave a farm stead and two other fallow lands to his first wife Fatima Kisiwaa, and another farmstead to his third wife Halima Yeboah for her dedicated service, but no mention was made of the second wife. He gave his daughters by the above two wives joint farmsteads, each near their mother's farmstead. He gave his sons by Fatima large farmsteads nearby. But the sons by Halima Yeboah received a whole cocoa farm at Nsuta. In addition, the sons by Halima each received separate farmlands. A larger cocoa farm in the migrant area of Sefwi was to be divided equally among his sons, and an orange plantation was also to be shared equally among the children. The deceased's ten-room house was to be divided equally between the first wife and the second wife (five rooms to each). The two-story building was to be given to the third wife and her children, as well as a maize barn and mango tree to them. However, one of his sons and his nephew were to keep the barns that he had made for them. He gave land at Asuasuano to his friends Ahmed Badu and K. Ose. Finally, he required that all his children "should continue in the Islamic faith, and anyone who abandons it forfeits an interest in the house as I already described."

Case C, concerning the estate of Opanyin E. Owusu demonstrates some of the most potent challenges to the traditional legal restrictions on lineal/affinal resources exchanges—i.e., a total rejection of *efiesem* norm accomplished by adopting the patriarchal framework of Islam. While recording this case, my astute research assistant, Betty Akumatey, commented that "it is possible that Akan men become Muslims so that they can enjoy the benefits of patriliny." Goody has noted this tendency for religions such as Islam, Christianity, and Buddhism to "[reach] out into areas that might otherwise have retained features we have associated with the separation of male and female property" by reinforcing paternal family relationships (1976:119). Islam continues to be resorted to in order to accomplish this function, particularly with respect to economic resources,[15] a point that is well demonstrated in this case. It appears that he perceived Islam as negating any other economic norms that were operative within the Akan community. He also appears to want to keep his family together as a patrilineal family group, and uses Islam as a means to accomplishing this end. Although he breaks with Islamic precepts in not treating all three of his wives equally, in doing so he rewards wives who have invested the most time and labor on his land. One might argue that he could equally well justify this using the *efiesem* principles regarding the type of gifts that one gives to the "good" wife, and this would explain the lesser amount given wife number two.

Legal Systems and Reality in Recognizing the Value of Women's Labor

One might say that the economic outcomes of new laws in Ghana are a case of good intentions that will have ambiguous results. The Ghanaian courts do not aim to destroy traditional economic norms that regulate daily exchanges within households, or between spouses and other kin, but they seek to impose new national legal norms that will create justice in the transmission of economic goods across generations. Instead of a variety of different cultural/traditional systems regulating women's economic rights, the new law intends to create a national standard that relieves the economic exclusion that women have faced. However, instead of empowering women economically, the courts may be providing new means by which competing notions of individual and female labor are integrated or countered in contemporary economic behavior. It is noteworthy that in the Sunyani High Courts, it is primarily men who formally bring the family-property cases. Although wives may have been the initiators and they are listed among the primary plaintiffs bringing the Intestate Succession Cases, and although the wife may be the primary beneficiary listed in the Will, those individuals who step forward as Head of Family on her behalf are almost always men.

Allowing women to individualize their labor and its product may constitute a fundamental assault on the coherence of the traditional *abusua* system, which undergirds Asante culture and upon which traditional legal behavior is based. Although historical experience was moving Akan culture in the direction of the monetization of women's labor, the profit was always controled by a larger corporate group or by men (husbands, brothers). One could argue that to allow the structurally important persons in a matrilineage the possibility of economic autonomy would threaten corporate economic responsibility and action—something that has been fundamental in the stability of extensive agriculture (horticulture) in the forest zone.

Of major significance is that these cases demonstrate the instrumentality of alternative normative systems (Traditionalism, Islam, or Western Christianity) with their attendant legal relationships in altering economic behavior. In the Brong-Ahafo area, where Islamic communities extend back at least 200 years, some men have "reclaimed" Islam to achieve their economic purposes. In six of the twenty five cases that I analyzed, Islam among the Akan was a factor, and in another two cases, Christianity or Ordinance Marriage provided the reference system that was used to bolster women's rights to property and offset *abusua* claims to women's labor and property. The remainder of the cases involved interpretation of male and female roles within the context of traditional culture and the *abusua* system. Most of these cases appear to involve attempts to use the new PNDC laws within the context of one of these reference systems. Leaving aside the many important issues surrounding the deliberate manipulation of cultural norms, roles, and responsibilities (Mikell 1992), one can focus on other important theoretical issues raised by these cases. One major issue is why there appears to be greater ease of recognizing and valuing ("monetizing") female labor in an alternative Islamic cultural reference system, or in a Christian cultural reference system, than within an Akan reference system. There are a number of important factors within this issue.

First, the experiences of other West African Islamicized populations suggest that Islam cuts though the traditional lineage construct as the cohesive center for the social group; and it inserts the unity of Islam and the community of believers as the alternative center (Rosen 1984; Eisenstadt, Abitol and Chazan 1988)· But what happens to the rights rooted in the undergirding traditional cultural base?[16] Some would argue that Islam lessens the corporate focus, and the traditional identification of women's rights with group rights. Then, the shallowness of the patrilineal family that appears with Islam and the continued separation of male and female resources presents opportunities for women to exert control over resources and over value created by their own labor. It is implied that the theoretical separation of women's resources from men's resources, and the public honor that is involved in keeping these separate, act as a force that empowers women, although covert attempts to manipulate women's resources often occur (Schildkrout 1978; Coles and Mack 1991). But note that in the cases here, although property is conferred upon women who have contributed to its existence, these women are economically empowered *by virtue of being a wife, or daughter, of an Islamic man, not as an individual.* These men consider the rejection of Islam as constituting a negation of the economic rights that have been conferred.

Secondly, neither is the separation out of women's economic rights in terms of the value they create completely clear nor within the Christian and Ordinance Law based cultural/legal system. In several cases, religion is explicitly mentioned, the couple were married with church blessings, and church personnel are occasionally appointed to see that the wishes of the deceased are carried out. In this case, the religious community provides the social reference point. Women and children are thought to be empowered as legitimate legal dependents of a man by virtue of monogamous marriage, rather than simply as individuals who are economic contributors to an estate that he controled. Frequently, however, the children are empowered more than wives are empowered, thereby beginning or continuing a patrilineal emphasis.

Thirdly, within the context of traditional Akan culture and its reference system, the possibility of women as autonomous economic actors is vague and may be perceived as dangerous, as described above. This leaves open the possibility that as property is conferred upon "wives" by the new laws, their status as empowered economic individuals will be temporary, and that the dynamics will shift back to align themselves with traditional culture. Although any Ghanaian can make a Will, few women have the resources to do so, and family pressures are likely to build up against any woman who attempts to do so. It is generally only those urban, economically prosperous women who do not function within the context of traditional culture, who make Wills.[17] Traditional property succession from a woman's estate, exclusive of formal wills, and emphasizing male inheritance, may again result. But because the new laws have given additional recognition to individual property rights, it may be sons that exercise these individual rights over this property at the next generational level.

Finally, what effect will these female economic rights within the "conjugal family" have on marriage relationships? The data from the late 1970s and my data from the 1980s already suggest that fewer Akan men are marrying because they do not want the increased economic obligations that come with marriage, and that this increases the economic pressures on women. The questions that Oppong raised in 1974 about problems in the separation of resources in the Akan conjugal couple are pertinent today (1974). But it is too early to have conclusive data about the impact of the 1985 laws on marital relationships.

The possibility that husbands who are facing divorce will attempt to use the new family laws to acquire property owned by wives has generated concern among Akan women and the *abusua*. Even prior to the 1985 family laws, there were hints in some Accra High Courts cases that husbands were already legally contesting the right of wives to maintain separate ownership of any property that they had acquired during marriage, and even any property acquired prior to marriage that they may have been better able to maintain as a result of marriage.[18] Expanding the misinterpreted traditional concept of a wife's conjugal labor as belonging to the husband, or arguing that his household contributions enhanced his wife's property, some urban husbands have made legal claims to the property of Akan wives. This process requires additional investigation in light of the new family laws.

For the most part, there is the danger that property rights given to Akan women with one hand may be taken away with the other. Women's increased individual rights to control their labor and its value do not mean that they will be able to control these resources in their own interests. These new rights now become the subject of intense cultural manipulation, as Akan husbands, brothers, heads-of-households, and others figure out how to renegotiate cultural norms and to best position their claims vis-a-vis both traditional culture and the law. In the case of wills, winning the case and obtaining access to property of the deceased may mean that women and their labor come under control of a new group and according to altered principles.

This is not something that judges, politicians, and bureaucrats can easily understand. They do know that the global economic system is affecting the Ghanaian economy in ways that require individual economic recognition, and they experience significant global pressures to respond by "individualizing" and "liberalizing" in order to guarantee external aid. In a disemic fashion,[19] they state that such laws are supposed to "free individual actors to contribute to the economy and to development." But as these leaders respond to external demands and internal crises such as the impoverishment of women, they have little ability to imagine the gulf that exists between new legal economic rights and structures, and what happens in reality as these interact with cultural structures, such as those embodied in Akan *efiesem* principles.

Notes

1. The Memorandum to PNDCL.111 states that: "The growing importance of the nuclear family brings with it its own logic of moral justice. Simply put, this argues that the surviving spouse be compensated for his/her services to the deceased spouse; . . . The customary law conception of marriage did not regard a wife as part of the husband's economic unit. Therefore, the wife's claim on the husband's property was also limited. . . . The provisions of this Law are therefore aimed at giving a larger portion of the estate of the deceased to his spouse and children than is normally the case at present . . . " The force of such ideas and legislation also encouraged wives to take other actions in Family Courts to ensure that fathers provided maintenance to their children, despite divorce (see Mikell 1994).

2. See R.S. Rattray 1923:40–41. These domestic property cases are radically different from the traditional *"oman akyiwadie"* (public/political) cases, which involved swearing oaths, the payment of oath fees, and were heard before traditional courts. The *oman akyiwadie* typically involved incest, treason, or other heinous acts, and people were fearful about being involved.

3. I refer throughout this chapter to traditional legal concepts, as opposed to customary law. Customary law has often been described as a product of colonial creation, representing a system that colonial administrators used to unify legal practices appl ied to "tribal groups." When I use the term "traditional law," I refer to behavior grounded in cultural practices that the people recognize as legitimate.

4. The *samansiw* declaration must be made in public, knowledgeable to the giver's lineage and the receiver's lineage (see Woodson 1974:269–84).

5. However, marriages involving transactions of greater value usually involve absolute sexual rights over a woman, and entitle a husband to higher compensations if a wife is unfaithful (see Rattray 1923; Fortes 1963).

6. Hoarding gold was a crime against the Asantehene and the state, and according to *oman akyiwadie* (political) principles an offender could be put to death (see Rattray 1923. Wilks 1977:20–21).

7. The *awunnyade* were not inhibited by any verbal wills or *samansiw* that a man might make. Because, prior to colonial conquest, written wills had no force in Asante, they also did not inhibit the *awunnyade*. Almost no Asante made written wills until about 1910, when the creole elite who were married monogamously began to do so.

8. This modification of the marriage gifts obligated women to the husband and insured greater servitude, because she could not divorce without being able to return these gifts the value of which over many years might be great (see Mikell 1989:68–69).

9. District Administrative Record Book, Sunyani (1907–1915), #225/07.

10. This paraphrases a line from the film *Asante Market Women*, 1982.

11. This issue of economic justice for women had come before the Kumasi Council of Chiefs, the center of the customary legal structure. The Kumasi chiefs debated whether some modification of Asante inheritance law was not in order, given that matrilineal custom tended to exclude wives from sharing the benefit of farms they had helped husbands to create. However, legal modifications were never passed in Council because of the intensity of support for custom among the Chiefs. At a later point, there was pressure from the clergy, particularly the Presbyterian Churches, to gain public support for their operational procedures of one third of property of husbands going to widows, one third to children, and one third to the customary family (see Busia 1951:125; Busia 1948; and Vallenga 1983).

12. Section 48 of the Marriage Ordinance, 1951, Cap. 128, conferred one third of property under customary law, and two thirds under English law. Therefore, the widow and children were to receive six ninths of a man's property when he died intestate.

13. During the 1960s, some of these land cases involving women's claims for farms were handled by the Labor Department (see Robertson 1986).

14. This type of conflicting opinions was characteristic of the middle-aged men, who had grown up with traditional notions of *abusua* control of property, but who were monogamous and desired to treat the conjugal family in an equitable fashion (see Aboagye 1979).

15. It is undeniable that Isaac Adjei intended that only those connected to him though marriage and therefore to his "family of procreation" should enjoy the benefits of what he considered to be personal property. In keeping with Islamic practice, Akan muslims practice what Goody calls "diverging devolution" endowing both female and male children, but females receive smaller shares than males (no cocoa farms) (see Goody 1976).

16. In some parts of India, despite the attempt by the state to recognize plural legal systems, including traditional ones that allow female property ownership that is not negated by Islam, a process tends to occur in which women's property rights are exercised on their

behalfs by their brothers or other members of the patrilineage. Therefore, women are still excluded as autonomous economic actors (see Gaborieau 1993).

17. The analysis of my 1990 data set from the Accra High Courts is still in process and will be presented in later work.

18. In case D&MC No. 2982.87, the husband (plaintiff) filed for divorce and requested a share of the wife's business which she had maintained during the 1983–1984 recession and in which he claims to have made some investment when he returned from Togo in 1987.

19. According to M. Herzfeld (1989:123–4), "disemia" oc curs when "tutelary outsiders define the criteria of local culture, and insiders find it necessary to disguise those aspects of ordinary social life that conflict with imposed models. [It] is the play of cultural contradictions produced by conditional independence—an independence, cultural or political, that is paradoxically enjoyed only on the sufferance of some more powerful entity."

Sources

Archival

Ghana

Government of the Gold Coast. 1907–15.
    District Administrative Record Book. Sunyani, #225/07.

Laws

Government of the Gold Coast. 1951.
    Section 48 of the Marrige Ordinance, Cap. 128.

Provisional National Defense Council. 1985
    PNDCL.111
    PNDCL.112
    PNDCL.113

Court Cases

Sunyani High Court
    The Estate of Kofi Duro
    The Estate of Opoku Gyabaa of Dormaa Ajenkro
    Estate of Opanyin E. Owusu

Accra High Court

Books, Dissertations, and Articles

Aboagye, Patrick Kofi. 1979. "Modern Attitudes Toward Matrilineal Inheritance." Department of Sociology, University of Ghana.

Aidoo, Akosua Aidoo. 1975. "Political Crisis and Social Change in the Asante Kingdom, 1867–1901." Ph.D. dissertation, University of California.

Arhin, Kwame. 1983a. "Akan Women and Politics." In *Female and Male in West Africa*, ed. Christine Oppong, 91–8. London: Allen and Unwin.

―――. 1983b. "Rank and Class Among the Asante and Fante in the Nineteenth Century." *Africa*, 53:2–22.

Ashanti Market Women. VHS, Grenada Television International. Imprint NY, New York—Filmmakers' Library.

Asante, S. K. B. 1975. *Property Law, 1844–1966*. Accra: Ghana University Press.

―――. 1951. *The Position of the Chief in the Modern Political System of Ashanti*. New York and London: Oxford University Press for the International African Institute.

Coles, Catherine and Beverly Mack, eds. 1991. *Hausa Women in the Twentieth Century*. Madison, WI: University of Wisconsin Press.

Eisenstadt, S. N., Abitbol, M., and N. Chazan, eds. 1988. *The Early State in African Perspective*. New York and Leiden: E. J. Brill.

Fortes, Meyer. 1950. "Kinship and Marriage Among the Ashanti." In *African Systems of Kinship and Marriage*, ed. A. R. Radcliffe-Brown and D. Forde, 252–284. New York and London: Oxford University Press, for the International African Institute.

"The Submerged Descent Line Among the Akan." In *Studies in Kinship and Marriage*, ed. I. Schapera. London: RAIGB.

Gaborieau, Marc. 1993. "Islamic Law, Hindu Law, and Caste Customs: Daughter's Share of Inheritance in the Indian Sub-Continent." In *Juridical Norms and Social Practices*, ed. Hassan Elboudrari, Unpublished ms. Institute for Advanced Study, Princeton, NJ.

Goody, Jack. 1976. *Production and Reproduction: A Comparative Study of the Domestic Domain*. London: Cambridge University Press.

Herzfeld, Michael. 1989. *Anthropology Through the Looking Glass*. Cambridge: Cambridge University Press.

Hill, Polly. 1959. The Gold Coast Cocoa Farmer, London.

―――. 1963. *The Migrant Cocoa-Farmers of Southern Ghana: A Study in Rural Capitalism*. New York and Cambridge: Cambridge University Press.

Kea, Ray. 1982. *Settlement, Trade and Polities in the Seventeenth-Century Gold Coast*. Baltimore, MD: Johns Hopkins University Press.

Manuh, Tekyiwaa. 1989. *The Intestate Succession Law and Children in Ghana*. University of Ghana-Legon, Institute of African Studies.

Mikell, Gwendolyn. 1984. "Filiation, Economic Crisis, and the Status of Women in Rural Ghana." *Canadian Journal of African Studies*, 18:195–218.

―――. 1991. "Legal Change and the Negotiation of Economic Norms in Matrilineal Areas of Ghana." Paper presented in the Law and Ethics Seminar at the Institute for Advanced Study, School of Social Science, December 2, 1991.

―――. 1992. *Cocoa and Chaos in Ghana*. Washington, DC: Howard University Press.

―――. 1994. "Using the Courts to Obtain Relief: Akan Women and Family Courts in Ghana." In *Poverty in the 1990s: The Response of Urban Women*, ed. Fatima Meer, 65–86. Paris: UNESCO and the International Social Science Council.

Meyerowitz, Eva Lewin-Richter. 1951. *Sacred State of the Akan*. London: Faber and Faber.

Ollenu, N. A. 1962. *Principles of Customary Land Law in Ghana*. London: Sweet and Maxwell.

Oppong, Christine. 1974. *Marriage Among a Matrilineal Elite*. New York and London: Cambridge University Press.

Rattray, R. S. 1923. *Ashanti*. Oxford: Clarendon Press.

———. 1929. *Ashanti Law and Constitution*. Oxford: Clarendon Press.

Robertson, Claire. 1986. "Women's Education and Class Formation in Africa 1950–1980." In *Women and Class in Africa*, ed. Iris Berger and Claire Robertson, 92–113. New York: Africana.

Rosen, Lawrence. 1984. *Bargaining for Reality: The Construction of Social Relations in a Muslim Community*. Chicago, IL: University of Chicago Press.

Schildkrout, Enid. 1978. *People of the Zongo: The Transformation of Ethnic Identities in Ghana*. Cambridge: Cambridge University Press.

Vallenga, Dorothy Dee. n.d. Ms. Oberlin College Library.

———. 1983. "Who is a Wife: Expressions of Heterosexual Conflict. " In *Female and Male in West Africa*, ed. Christine Oppong, 144–155. Boston and London: Allen & Unwin.

Wilks, Ivor. 1977. "Land, Labor, and Capital, in the Forest Kingdom of Asante." In *The Evolution of Social Systems*, ed. J. Friedman and M. J. Rowlands, 487–534. London: Ducksworth Publishing.

Woodson, Gordon. 1974. "The Rights of Wives, Sons and Daughters in the Estates of Their Deceased Husbands and Fathers." In *Domestic Rights and Duties in Southern Ghana*, ed. Christine Oppong. Legon Family Research Papers no. 1. Legon: IAS-University of Ghana.

11

How Gambians Save: Culture and Economic Strategy at an Ethnic Crossroads *

Parker Shipton

Introduction

In the background gather the women and children—the women like a flock of gay-coloured tropical birds with their upstanding headties and gay *pagnes* and gleaming gold jewelry. No more beautiful sight can be imagined than a welcome from the Serahuli women and girls at Fattoto, where they wear silver headdresses like small diadems with bosses, the heavy silver bracelets called "manillas," which were once used as currency in West Africa, and silver necklaces and chains. Each Serahuli woman wears a floating silk cloak over her shoulders ranging from red and apricot, purple, pink, and flamingo, through shades of blue and green and yellow—a blaze of colour in the sunlight—which takes away the breath of the newcomer accustomed to the drab crowds of Britain (Southorn 1952:214–15).[1]

*The many Gambian villagers who have so generously given of their hospitality and time during field study deserve lasting thanks. Field research was funded by the U.S. Agency for International Development, for the first two visits as part of a Harvard Institute for International Development (HIID) project in the Ministry of Finance and Trade in The Gambia. My Harvard colleagues and the staffs of the Ministry of Finance and the AID Banjul office provided valuable support. Revisions were generously funded by the Carter Woodson Institute for Afro-American and African Studies, University of Virginia, under a residential research fellowship, and by the World Bank. All this help is gratefully acknowledged. Special thanks are due to C. Baldeh, E. Baldeh, A. Jallow, A. Jammeh, F. Khan, J. Newlands, A. Sillah, and M. Trawally for their assistance in The Gambia, to B. Gilman and P.F. Njie for data processing, and to D. Cole, Y. Dem, C. Elias, F. Janneh, R. Klitgaard, P. McNamara, M. McPherson, R. and P. Mueller, S. Radelet, L. Sanneh, M. Sanyang, B. Sidibe, P. Steele, J.D. Von Pischke, P. Weil, two anonymous referees, and especially J. Guyer, for advice and information. None is responsible, however, for any errors.

The display that so dazzled Lady Bella Southorn in her Gambian sojourn in 1952 was nothing new. Other voyagers up and down the Gambia River since Mungo Park in 1795 had commented with approval or puzzlement on the gold he described upriver as "massy and inconvenient, particularly the ear-rings, which are commonly so heavy as to lacerate the lobe of the ear" (Park [1799] 1971:303–4).[2] Beloved by wearers and photographers alike, precious and stunning jewelry of this type is worn around the country still.

The Gambia is regularly listed in United Nations statistical tables as one of the world's ten poorest countries; and more importantly perhaps, today's Gambians speak as though they *feel* poor.[3] With almost no usable mineral resources, thin and desiccated topsoil that blows out into the Atlantic with the Harmattan each year, and almost no large-scale industry, rural Gambians have grown measurably poorer and more dependent on foreign finance, and international labor migration since the British colonial era that ended with independence in 1965. Wealth in a country like this has to be conserved and invested carefully, whether in jewelry, cattle, bank accounts, or people.

It can also be gleaned from or lost to sources overseas. International relief and development agencies, large and small, public and private, have been active and well represented in the country. From multilateral agencies such as the World Bank to bilateral ones like the U.S. Agency for International Development, to private religious and secular ones such as ActionAid, Catholic Relief Services, and the Islamic Association for Relief, Development, and the Environment, the list is long. Over a dozen of the international and domestic nongovernmental aid agencies have been involved lately in rural finance.[4]

By the beginning of the 1990s, international financial aid for rural Africans was at a turning point. The gradual realization that credit had failed as the main economic strategy of the postwar period was leading many program planners to consider mobilizing local savings as a complementary or alternate approach. One reason for the disappointments of the credit strategy had been that initiatives were planned without adequately knowing what kinds of credit and debt were already occurring among the peoples concerned. The emphasis continues to shift now from credit to saving, and to combinations of both. But some of the most rudimentary questions about how rural West Africans seek to conserve and augment their own economic resources have never been satisfactorily answered: who tries to save what, how, and why?

This chapter describes some rural saving strategies in this small and heavily dependent country. A multiethnic Sahelian farming and trading nation of just under a million people, about 80 percent rural, The Gambia has been traversed by foreigners and open to wider markets for centuries.[5] A feeder route for the Atlantic slave trade from the fifteenth to nineteenth centuries, the nation is nearly surrounded by Senegal, and it shares several languages and cultures with that country and others.[6] Gambian farmers grow sorghum, millet, maize and rice, among other crops, for food, and groundnuts (the country's sole important export crop) mainly for cash. They also raise small and large livestock, and some also trade or migrate for wage work. The country receives rice and other food aid from overseas every year, but while malnutrition and related health problems are major concerns, The Gambia has avoided mass starvation in Sahelian famines of recent decades—whether because of or despite foreign aid.

The simple question, "how do rural Gambians save?" has various answers, some neither simple nor obvious. By describing several indigenous and other saving systems, starting with those closest to a rural home and proceeding outward, the chapter shows farmers resorting to both individual and group methods of saving, many of them convenient, but in some ways costly to them.[7] Some predated colonial currencies, others have arisen partly in response to a long history of currency instability, and most involve local innovation of one kind or another.

These are the main points. Rural Gambians save not just in money, but also in other forms; and one who conceives of saving in terms of money will miss most of the activity.[8] Nor can one assume a liquidity preference, as many economists have done in the past. Gambians often make substantial sacrifices to remove their wealth from their own temptation and from the demands of their spouses and others, suggesting, if anything, a contrary illiquidity preference, or more precisely, a desire to keep their wealth in forms not too easy to fritter away but still accessible in emergencies. Among the biggest goals of saving, in whatever form, is to enable young and middle-aged men to migrate abroad to find work.

Saving is seldom something that individuals can just freely decide to do on their own behalf. It is also, and at the same time, socially structured and culturally conditioned. Successful saving means finding ways to conserve wealth without appearing selfish. The mixture of individual incentives and group norms and controls is often subtle, but worth attention and perhaps also emulation. A lesson is rural West Africans' need for particular kinds of balance in their financial lives.

Research in an Ethnic Crossroads

Research for this chapter was done during three visits in 1987, 1988, and 1992. It involved participant-observation; intensive, open-ended interviewing with a few key informants (usually these are the best research methods on rural African finance) in two villages where I lived; broader, structured surveys; and reading in the Gambia National Archives and other collections in Banjul. For the structured surveys, five randomly chosen villages were studied on both sides of the river, in April and May 1987 and from July to October, 1988.[9] On my third visit from July to September, 1992, I spent most of my time on participant-observation and open-ended interviewing in a Fula- and Serahuli village in Upper River Division, where I had also spent much of my time before.

The ethnic distribution of informants in the surveys, mainly Mandinka-, Pulaar- (Fula, Fulani, or Peul), and Wolof-speaking in that order of frequency, roughly approximated that of The Gambia as a whole.[10] A word about ethnic variation. The Gambia differs from some other parts of Africa south of the Sahara in that members of different ethno-linguistic groups are fairly well mixed in the countryside; while some groups predominate in particular divisions and districts of the country, it is only at the village level, and often not even there, that anything like ethnic uniformity may be found. Interethnic contact is constant and pervasive. Some important differences in economic thought and behavior remain between ethnic groups—and between villages too—but one may speak of general Gambian saving tendencies in a way that would make less sense in many other African countries.[11]

Some Basic Principles

West African farmers are usually not just farmers. Multiple occupations (sometimes intermittent and often missed in questionnaire surveys) cut subsistence risks, even out food and cash income through the year, and put family labor to beneficial use. Real rural people do not live in economic "sectors" as conventionally defined, and these notions, as embodied for instance in the divisions between corridors of large international aid agencies, are not as real or important to Gambian farmers as to some development planners from northern countries. Saved and borrowed resources are exchangeable and substitutable (to economists, "fungible") between agriculture, for instance, and housing, trade, health, or education, in ways financiers cannot and probably should not try to control. Labor migrations and remittances also link country and city dwellers—money, foods, and other resources flow both ways between kin—though not as actively as in some more densely settled parts of agrarian Africa. Most of the saving strategies found in the Gambian countryside can also be found in the city.

There are several social divisions common to the largest Gambian (and southern Senegalese) ethnic groups. All these peoples, with the exception of some of the Jola (or Diola) groups, have *nucleated villages* with elected (though often quasi-hereditary) headmen, whose function is largely consensus-building. All have preferentially exogamous (out-marrying) *patrilineages*, and in most or all, village endogamy (in-marriage) is frequent though not a hard and fast rule.[12] In all, with the exception again of many Jola groups, Gambian peoples also divide themselves into *castes*. These are endogamous occupational categories whose members, recruited by patrilineal heredity, may or may not practice the specified occupations in fact.[13] Different castes and subcastes are represented in different ethnic groups (with some broad similarities) and more importantly, in different villages. Male and female *age-grades*, stages of life that individuals pass through (analogous to school grades) and *age-sets* (groups of specific persons analogous to the class of 1992 or 1993) who pass through them are enormously important organizing principles in village life, for they structure some of the important intravillage associations known in Mandinka as *kafo* (or *kafoo*) groups (and in Pulaar, the Fula tongue, as *dental* or more commonly now, *kompin* —from "company," or the French, *compagnie*). The *kafo*—men's, women's, and mixed—have single leaders, and the leader of a married women's *kafo* is effectively the leader of all women in the village (without negating the headman's at least ostensible authority over all). Other important social organizing principles include socioeconomic classes, Islamic worship groups, and various kinds of voluntary associations beyond the *kafo*, like sports teams, and rotating saving and credit associations. There are also patron--client ties, for instance between land hosts and seasonal immigrants or local land borrowers; and ties between former schoolmates (from government or local Qur'anic schools), trading partners, friends who entrust each other with cattle, and so on. These crosscutting associations (or social divisions, seen another way) give each individual multiple economic resources and obligations within and outside of a village.

There is no single social unit of analysis such as "the household" to consider within villages by and large, but a nested hierarchy of decision fields, including village wards (where they exist), lineages, compounds (sets of houses, often sharing a common enclosure), and work groups and cooking groups within compounds. Decisions about family resource allocation are often not made unilaterally by "family heads". In The Gambia, as elsewhere in Africa south of the Sahara, men and women often make their financial decisions separately, or negotiate and compete about joint savings or investments (See Moock 1986, on other parts of the continent; see also Guyer and Peters 1987).

Saving, consumption, investment, and insurance are often not clearly distinguishable on West African farms. Purchasing a draught animal, for instance, can mean all these things simultaneously, as can contributing labor or grain to a ceremony in which other participants are potential part-time helpers on one's farm. In a sense, lending can also be a form of saving, and an effective one, because it removes property from the constant demands of relatives, neighbors, friends, or tax collectors.

Seasonal and Longer-term Fluctuations

The role of time in Gambian financial and economic life is probably better understood as cyclical than linear. The region has grown groundnuts for export since the early 1830s, and ever since then, the annual boom and bust cycle that follows the single groundnut-growing season has affected nearly all aspects of rural life. The harvest produces an annual spurt of wealth, trade, and other economic activity nationwide from about December (as the main crops are harvested) to about March. Most loans of agricultural inputs are sought around June, at the onset of the rains; food is commonly borrowed as needed between then and the harvest of the first crops (in some areas, early millet in September), though it may be borrowed at any time for ceremonies or other special needs. It is at harvest time that farmers will make most of the loan repayments that they make. Some rotating saving and credit associations among farmers suspend their operations during the rainy season, when cash for contributions becomes scarce, and recommence in the trade season. In rural bank branches, lending may similarly fall off during the year as money for lending becomes scarce. The seasonal nature of credit in The Gambia strongly influences local thought about interest rates.[14] Longer-term cycles matter too, of course. The movement of individuals through their life-cycles, and of domestic groups through their development cycles, governs their propensities to save, and the ways in which they do it.

Saving Without Money: Storage Cycles and the Intrafamilial Walls of Property

The first and most basic point about saving in The Gambia is that most of it does not take the form of money. The most important material forms of saving include animals, stored crops, jewelry, tools, and household goods. To judge by the writings of early European travellers and administrators, it seems always to have been so, though the relative importance of different commodities, and the purposes to which they have been put, has altered somewhat over time.

Livestock

Animals are the most important form of movable property saved in The Gambia. Nearly every rural family keeps some small or large stock, or both.[15] Men claim most of the cattle, and nearly all the donkeys and horses. Sheep and goats are at least as commonly owned by women as by men. Like most other Africans south of the Sahara who possess large and small livestock, Gambians seek to convert grain to small stock, and small stock to large stock (while still keeping at least a few small stock for diversity and liquidity). Large stock, in turn, can be useful to men for marriage and other ceremonies, and thus for obtaining a larger labor force to produce more grain and groundnuts.[16] Men value large stock as a form of savings (among other reasons) partly because it is indivisible and thus more or less removed from the day-to-day claims of their wives and other kin. Few of those who can afford to convert at least some of their sheep and goats to large stock will fail to do so, even though sheep and goats multiply more quickly. Analogies between livestock and cash are common. When I once asked a Mandinko informant why he preferred large to small stock, he asked, "Would you rather have a 10 dalasi note or a 25?"—an argument that he knew was hard to refute without pedantry. Mandinko say their grandparents historically referred to livestock as *fangkanta* (literally, self-guard), or reserve. Gambian Mandinko use the same term now for personal cash savings.[17] Illiquidity is by no means the only reason for converting small stock to large. Also important are draft capabilities and complementary grazing habits. It is only in cases of hardship or special ceremonial needs that Gambian farmers are likely to sell or slaughter cattle.

Although it shelters wealth from the daily demands of kin, livestock is none the less subject to some special family claims that limit its use. Among Mandinko, for instance, stock inherited by a group of siblings cannot be disposed of by any individual for his own self-enrichment without the consent of the others, because it is believed that this would produce "bad money" (in Mandinka, *kodi jawo*): money that ultimately will be wasted or bring a tragedy to the one who sold the family property.[18] In indigenous Gambian religions, the spirits are thought to control the outcome of these events; to the contemporary Muslim majority, it is Allah alone or as an additional force. Today, many Gambians question this kind of knowledge or popular beliefs about alienating family wealth, but most prefer to stay on the safe side.

It is common practice, particularly among cattle-keeping Fula, but among others as well, to lend cattle out to relatives or friends for months or even years. This is done for several reasons. One is to provide needy kin with milk or manure. Another may be to reduce pressure on grazing lands around one's own village. A third is to save labor during particular periods of a family cycle when herdboys or the means to hire a herdsman are lacking. A fourth is to conceal one's wealth from tax-collectors, neighbors, or others. A fifth is to minimize risks of losing one's entire herd through an epizootic disease or a theft. A final reason, not so narrowly economic in nature, is to affirm a particularly strong and trusting friendship. Because herds of different owners are usually mixed, and because Gambians deem it impolite to ask how many cattle a farmer has, it is extremely difficult to assess wealth in livestock.

Farmers give several reasons for preferring to save their wealth in stock, in addition to the subtler considerations of gender noted above. These include the fact that animals breed, the advantages of milk and manure production, the usefulness of animal traction, the ceremonial values of animals, and the mere satisfaction of having herds to watch over. To these one might add what Jane Guyer, in the introduction to this volume, has called "conceptual stabilization." Having complex meanings and use values, and being subject to complex interpersonal claims, cattle are not just something to exchange like money, and they can serve to buffer local people from market forces and price fluctuations over which they have little control, and from moral implications they may deem problematic in one way or another (Shipton 1989). Ecologically, however, an unlimited accumulation of livestock may be hazardous in its soil erosion effects, particularly as the human population and cultivation pressure on land also grow, and this is probably a good reason for farmers to need and seek other savings options.

Propensities to invest in livestock, like propensities to save cash, seem to vary from one ethnic group to another. In The Gambia, the Fula and some Jola have acquired reputations as avid cattle-keepers, and among them, it is the elder men who tend to pay most attention to herd conservation and growth. But seemingly nearly all rural Gambians would rather convert other property to livestock than convert livestock to other property. Therefore, development project planners should not consider cattle as a store of freely usable wealth, expendable for agricultural inputs, such as fertilizer, or able to be liquidated for community projects.

Jewelry

If cattle are a characteristically male preserve of wealth, gold and silver jewelry are a female preserve. They have been so for centuries, as noted earlier; and goldsmithing and silversmithing are historically the preserve of a metalworking caste that also includes blacksmiths. Most important currently are earrings.[19] Necklaces, pendants, bracelets, and forehead plates attached by headbands are common too. The showier ones—twirled and pounded into rings with butterfly-shaped cross-sections, or filigreed— are likely to be worn only for ceremonies, but can be worn at times in marketplaces and even around home compounds in small villages. Earrings provided to a young Mandinka woman by the time of marriage commonly cost, in the late 1980s, 1,000 dalasis ($145) or more.[20] The ornaments may grow in size as a woman ages; gold can be added by a smith as a woman acquires new wealth.

Like livestock, jewelry is something that rural Gambians will not part with easily, and for this reason among others it constitutes a useful store of wealth for times of crisis. In the occasional instances where collateral is demanded for loans by traders or distant acquaintances, it can take the form of jewelry.[21] While the jewelry that a woman wears or keeps in a locked trunk is ordinarily looked upon as her personal property, the truth is not so simple. Her husband may sometimes ask or even force her to part with it for sale or pledge in a family emergency if she does not offer to do so herself. So here, as with cattle, individual and group rights overlap to a degree; but there is an asymmetry, because men claim more power over jewelry than women can over men's cattle. Jewelry also differs from cattle in being just as useful to town dwellers as to country villagers when times get hard.

Stored Crops

A substantial part of the wealth of each domestic compound is its living and stored crops. Standing crops or stored food usually fall under the control of one family member, though other members may complain if they think it is misused.[22] In most of the ethnic groups, men are usually expected to store coarse grains (millets, sorghum, and maize) for family food; women who grow rice store much of it too for family consumption. Gambian women and men are accustomed to storing much of their rice and coarse grains in their houses or compound grain stores, where they may try to keep secret just how much they possess at any time.

Though both men and women now grow groundnuts in most of The Gambia— the gender division of cropping varies somewhat by ethnic group—they are expected to use some of it in different ways. Women are generally expected to store a substantial part of their groundnut crops for family food; men are not. Men, however, are expected to store and provide seed for the family, while women are not. On balance, this means that women store greater proportions of their groundnuts for family use than men do, and that men sell greater proportions than women.[23]

Gambian farmers who sell groundnuts and other food crops tend to do so just after harvest. They know well that withholding crop sales until later in the year, when food becomes scarce and prices rise, might yield them more cash. But few feel they can afford to wait. What some have dismissed as "improvidence," or more sympathetically lamented as a tragedy of poverty, must also be considered more seriously and positively.[24] One reason for this practice, long observed, is that losses in storage can be heavy. Another is that the demands of needy relatives become stronger in the hungry season, and saving one's crops and selling them then may appear anti-social. While maximizing short-term profits, that is, one risks losing a social support network that may have longer-term economic value. A few who can afford to withhold or buy crops at harvest time, and are willing to risk some social disfavor for doing so, serve as a kind of food pawnbrokers for other farmers, selling them back similar foods later in the season at higher prices.

Some villages have central seed storehouses that members of all compounds may use for groundnuts, coarse grains, and other seed. In these, however, sacks or bundles of seeds are usually individualized and may be labeled.[25] The stores are often kept locked, and two or more keyholders may be required to open them. An advantage of this form of storage is the economy of scale in strong construction.[26] A cement house with an iron roof, beyond the means of many individual farmers, cuts down rodent damage. Centralization also makes treatment with storage pesticides cheaper and easier. Another advantage is that the system adds disincentives to consuming one's seed before planting, because doing so requires arrangement with the keyholder(s), and possible embarrassment.

While few are likely ever to put all their crops in central village stores, again for reasons of privacy, rural Gambians have welcomed attempts to help them improve these stores.[27] Village seed store programs of nongovernmental agencies (most notably the Freedom from Hunger Campaign) have been well received, but many villages remain without central stores. Gambian farmers have been losing their resources to rodents, birds, bugs, worms, and molds, while continuing to accrue new and expensive debts for food and seed.

Hitherto, most village seed stores have been built and used for groundnuts. Storage facilities would also be welcome for women's rice—a crop highly vulnerable to rodents and other pests—and perhaps coarse grains. Larger "cereal banks," also tried in recent years, have been designed not for single villages but for clusters of several. Some of these latter projects have included resources for buying and selling crops. The buildings constructed seem to have been more successful than the cash components of these projects, which have suffered graft similar to that in state cooperatives and have soon collapsed. A problem, just as in the cooperatives, seems to have been the absence of a feeling of shared responsibility between members of different, ostensibly cooperating villages. Generally, basing storage facilities on the village unit has worked better.

Linkages Between Storage and Credit

Farmers calculate their seed storage with the likelihood of receiving loans in mind, and they store higher proportions of their own groundnut seeds, for themselves or for "strange farmers" (seasonal land clients) when warned that the cooperatives will not lend seeds at planting time. Early warning can help them plan. When cooperative groundnut-seed credit diminishes, storage facilities for *other* crops become more necessary, because farmers' storing more groundnuts squeezes other crops out of the stores.

Most cash borrowing from unofficial sources is for food, mainly rice; and this is true even after several consecutive good harvests (as in 1988, when there had been three). Cultural and religious pressures favor credit for immediate consumption over credit for immediate production. But the real truth is not so simple. Most informal borrowing of money and food occurs during the rains. This is when hunger, weakness, and malarial disease coincide with the peak labor season, and when most crops need weeding and rice needs transplanting. So credit for food is also a kind of indirect production credit. Because labor is about the scarcest resource in Gambian farming, this function is not to be underestimated. Those who cannot consume cannot produce.

Other Household and Farm Goods

In the brief period of relative solvency after harvests, rural Gambians often buy hard goods that they will use and later resell, whether the resale was part of their original plan or not. These durable goods are an important form of savings. They may include electronic goods such as radios or tape recorders, "luxuries" such as fancy beds; vehicles such as bicycles or carts; or food processing machines such as peanut-butter grinders. In the cities and larger towns, fine clothing is also used and often resold. So when travellers such as Lady Southorn observe the spectacle of fine cloth in a public gathering, what they are witnessing is, among other things, saving.

Saving in Cash, and Coping with Its Volatility

To pinpoint the origins of money in West Africa would be a Sisyphean task, not just because older coins keep being discovered, but also because the conceptual distinctions between cash and other traded commodities are subject to easy redefinition. But the Gambia River, as a long-distance slaving and ivory trade route for centuries before colonial times, has long known money of many kinds, not just European notes and coins (including, at various times, French, British, and Portuguese specie, and Maria Theresia Thalers minted in Vienna) but also cowries, gold dust, salt blocks, iron bars, and specialized currencies and quasi-currencies such as cloth.

When Mungo Park first crossed through present-day The Gambia, Senegal, and Mali in 1795, he observed no coined money in general use. He did, however, find cowry shells used as currency inland, where they were naturally scarcer than on the coast; and iron bars (used for farm tools and weapons) in use on the coast. The latter he found to be "the measure by which the value of all other commodities was ascertained" (Park [1799] 1971:27).[28] He found that "according to the plenty or scarcity of goods at market in proportion to the demand, the relative value would be subject to continual fluctuation," but that the whites insisted on stabilizing the value of a bar of iron (or a bar worth of anything else) at two shillings sterling (Ibid.:27–28). The clash of variable and fixed price systems seems to have caused uneasiness on one or both sides. Park wrote, in a tone rather disparaging of African actors:

> In transactions of this [fixed] nature, it is obvious that the white trader has infinitely the advantage over the African, whom, therefore, it is difficult to satisfy; for, conscious of his own ignorance, he naturally becomes exceedingly suspicious and wavering; and indeed so very unsettled and jealous are the Negroes in their dealings with the whites, that a bargain is never considered by the European as concluded, until the purchase money is paid, and the party has taken leave (Ibid.:28).

The description could be restated otherwise to turn the table of prejudice. It is worth a more neutral consideration, however, because both fixed and variable prices have their pros and cons. One is more precise, the other more predictable. In this as in many other parts of Africa south of the Sahara, local commodity merchants, happy to keep up with floating and negotiable market prices (and to spend the time or enjoy the fun of bargaining), still commonly meet visitors from European and North American countries who feel safer with fixed ones.[29]

Notes, Coins, and Their Shifting Values

Trading Gambians knew British money, as Park noted it, before the colonial administration was set up in Bathurst (now Banjul). It remained in circulation through the subjugation of The Gambia to the Sierra Leone governorship in 1866–8, the reseparation in 1870–76, the division into colony (Banjul and Georgetown) and protectorate (the rest of the territory) in 1888, and the final drawing of the present Gambia–Senegal boundary a year later. The penny and tenth-of-a-penny were introduced in 1907. The West African Currency Board, newly formed in 1913, then issued special coins at par with U.K. money for British West Africa; and in 1917, the 1-pound, 10-shilling, and 2-shilling notes were introduced.[30]

But French currency continued to change hands in the region, as well it might, given The Gambia's small size and the fact that it was nearly surrounded by a French colony. "The currency of the colony is sterling, but the five-franc piece is largely circulated throughout the protectorate," wrote colony Treasurer F.B. Archer in 1906 (1967:123). So it remained. The 5-franc piece (locally known as a dollar) was legal tender in The Gambia until 1922, and it remained in use after no longer being officially recognized. The authors of the 1960–1 *Gambia* Report observed that:

> Notes of the Banque de l'Afrique Occidental circulate freely in parts of the Protectorate and British West African currency circulates across the border in Senegal and Casamance (Colonial Office [CO] 1961:15).

On May 13, 1964, half a year after The Gambia officially became self-governing, The Gambia Currency Board took over from the West African Currency Board, and by October it had printed up the Gambian pound, replacing the West African pound at par.[31] On November 20, 1967, the Gambian pound was devalued 14.2 percent parallel to the pound sterling, from $2.8 to $2.4 U.S. On July 1, 1971, The Gambia's Central Bank broke free of the sterling link, replacing the Gambian pound with a new decimal currency, the dalasi.[32]

Over a decade beginning about 1975, the country experienced increasingly severe balance of payments problems (at the same time as a long-term drought and unstable international groundnut prices). Imports outstripped exports, and the country's store of foreign exchange sank. In international economists' eyes, the currency became increasingly overvalued, even after being officially devalued by 25 percent on February 25, 1984.

With foreign-financed advice as part of comprehensive economic adjustment program, but with a finance minister firmly in favor, The Gambia floated its currency in January, 1986, effectively diminishing its value immediately by about 40 percent.[33] As exchange controls were swept away, the wide gap between official and parallel (i.e., curb) market values of the dalasi quickly closed. The CFA franc circulating across the border in Senegal, however, remained highly overvalued in its official exchange rates, still affording some opportunity to illegal currency traders, who had profited in the past from the overvalued dalasi. In the early 1990s, the overvalued CFA and the very porous Senegalese border were helping the Gambian economy by encouraging a lively re-export trade from The Gambia and an illegal groundnut market with far better prices than farmers could receive at home. International pressure was mounting for a CFA devaluation, very likely to hurt Gambian groundnut farmers and exporters.

Two points emerge from this brief summary. The first is that plural currencies long have been a feature of Gambian economic life. The second is that money in The Gambia, as elsewhere in West Africa, has broadly tended not to hold its value over long periods, whether because of currency switches, official devaluations, or inflation. While animals tend to grow and multiply (albeit with periodic major losses), cash has weakened over time.

Cash and Its Context-Specific Uses

A report on the Gambia Fula, undated but deposited by David Gamble in the national archive in 1968, suggests what the observer now may equally note: that money ebbs and flows seasonally in the countryside, in a way heavily dependent on the single groundnut season; and that it does not pervade all transactions, and particularly not those involving cattle.

Any one may buy or sell, but as a matter of fact cattle who constitute the whole wealth of the Fullahs [or Fulas] seldom change hands. Exchange [apparently meaning barter] is the common method of effecting business transactions.

The selling of milk and butter is nearly always done by the womenkind; as a rule corn is received in exchange which in its turn is exchanged for cows when a sufficient quantity has accumulated.

The use of money is well known and p[l]ays a large part in business transactions, more especially after the groundnut crop has been sold, when the natives are for a time in possession of a certain amount of ready money (Gamble n.d.[a]: section 7).[34]

The difference between countability and uncountability may enter decisions about whether cattle are properly exchangeable for money. Gamble quotes a 1914-5 report from a J.K. McCallum in what is now the McCarthy Island Division, "Fullahs. .- . . are the owners and herders of the majority of the cattle in this Province. . . . they will hardly ever sell their animals and under no circumstances whatever count them" (Ibid.:48).[35] Of course, whether the Fula and others count their cattle privately and publicly are two different questions. And hunger (as a stick) and foreign travel tickets (as a carrot) do tempt some rural Fula, even elder men, into selling. But the point remains that cattle and cash are not considered commensurable in a qualitative sense, no matter what the prices involved.

What Rural Gambians Save For

Throughout the twentieth century, money has been a necessity throughout The Gambian colony and protectorate. In 1895, the British colonial government instituted the "hut and yard tax"—in today's terminology, a tax on all houses and house compounds.[36] The tax outlasted the colonial era and was still recognizable by 1992 in the "rates" collected by the independent government's Area (division) Councils.[37] Unpopular though it may remain, however, taxation is no longer a main reason to save money. A bigger reason is the wide variety of foreign consumer goods— including rice, corrugated iron roofing, imported cloth, and paraffin—that have entered the country in seemingly steady increase over the second half of the twentieth century.[38] Labor recruitment now often requires cash too, whether to pay individuals or *kafo* groups. But these are not the main concern either.

Currently, the biggest reason to save, whether in cash or in other forms, is *to get out of The Gambia*—or to get particular individuals out, temporarily if not permanently. This reason, sad to say, has become steadily more important over the twentieth century as the country's natural resources have dwindled in relation to its population, and particularly since the drought set in and international groundnut prices almost simultaneously began their long decline in the 1970s. By and large, rural Gambians now set their sights for their future overseas—in Europe or North America if they or their kin can get there—if not as a home (and many migrants seem to want to return to The Gambia), then at least as a source of waged jobs and trading opportunities more lucrative than any available domestically. Women and elders who know they will never get there, nonetheless count on able-bodied male kin to make good in this way. How to get there, legally or illegally, and then what to do are under discussion by the men of the younger age grades (up to about forty years) much of the time in the fields and during their leisure hours on the *crinting* of the village *bantaba* platforms. Importantly, a trip overseas is seldom just an individual venture, but usually is a family and even a village affair. Compound heads occasionally sell large parts of their compounds' herds to finance promising young men to travel for schooling or work; and these are about the only purposes short of an emergency or major ceremony for which they will willingly do so.

Savings from within the village unfortunately are seldom enough to launch a hopeful youth on the all-important sojourn overseas. International remittances have therefore been institutionalized in some villages, into patterns to supplement the savings. Villagers who have reached Europe or the Americas send money back (usually with travelers, sometimes through bank wiring), and their kin back home know who is "on deck" to take off next when the money comes—for this, like most things in rural Gambia, follows a fairly strict order of age and seniority. In some villages, for instance one remote Fula and Serakuli village in Fulladu East District, the young men have followed a staged itinerary. In this village, in 1992, the prevailing pattern was to go to Spain and farther north by the geographically indirect routes of Nigeria and the Canary Islands. Those who had reached Spain, France, or Germany sent money to others waiting at the Lagos waystation, and other young men following along behind from back home knew not to depart until hearing that those ahead of them had left Lagos for Europe.

In a country where over 90 percent call themselves Muslim, a further major reason why rural people save for travel is the *hajj*. This holy pilgrimage to Mecca not only elevates one's status and prestige for life but is also perceived, as one of the five pillars of the faith, to help secure salvation after death. Only a small minority of men, and even fewer women, ever make it there. Like labor migration, *hajj* travel is frequently aided from outside the country, in this case by Islamic charities based in Saudi Arabia and other Arab countries.

Other reasons why Gambians save are many, though none is as important as labor migration or the *hajj*. Animals, hard goods of all kinds, consumables, and bus seats are all bought and sold now with cash, though most of these are sometimes bartered too and probably always will be.[39]

Illiquidity Preference and the "Squawk Factor"

Cash in The Gambia is an odd commodity surrounded by ambivalent attitudes (Shipton 1989). As in some other parts of Africa south of the Sahara, nothing is more sought after than money, but nothing is more quickly disposed of than money. Indeed, money is even seen as something to get rid of, something to convert into longer-lasting forms. Several features beside those already noted make money into an unstable form of wealth in The Gambia: its nearly universal fungibility, divisibility, and portability. These features make money contestable. Everyone needs it for something, particularly in the lean season from June to August; and one with money will usually have an almost infinite number of relatives or neighbors with pressing needs. Though few farmers have the means to measure inflation, nearly all are aware of the process. Rural Gambian saving strategies are mainly concerned, then, with *removing wealth from the form of readily accessible cash, without appearing antisocial.* In communities in which one has many relatives, as is usual, this is a delicate balancing act, and besides any ethical issues involved, the "squawk factor,"[40] the potential for complaints and accusations, must enter every individual savings decision.

Nonetheless, individuals do keep some cash reserves (in Mandinka, *fangkanto*; in Fula and Wolof, *fangkanta*). Much of the cash that rural Gambians keep, they keep at home; and when asked how they preferred to save money, nearly half said they preferred to keep it for themselves.[41] About 25 percent said they preferred to use banks—far more than had actually used them, suggesting problems of access. Other ways of saving mentioned included entrusting money to another individual; post-office savings; burial; and other means, including savings clubs (Table 11-1).

TABLE 11-1   Preferred Means of Saving Money as Expreessed in Interviews, 1988

	Men	Women	Both
Keeping for self	47%	46%	47%
Banks*	31%	19%	25%
Money-keepers	16%	21%	18%
P.O. Saving	2%	0%	1%
Burial	2%	0%	1%
Other**	2%	14%	8%
TOTALS	100%	100%	100%
n =	51	52	103

* "Preferred" means stated can differ from means actually practiced. Far fewer than the percentages indicated actually used banks.
** Includes rotating saving and credit associations.

We review below some of the various ways of saving cash. Perhaps the oldest way of removing money from the public eye in The Gambia, as in some other parts of Africa, is literally to bury it in an earthen pot, bottle, or box.[42] This old practice seems to be disappearing, and no one is proud to use the method—only 2 percent of the men and none of the women named burial as their preferred way to save. Secrecy is the essence of this way of saving, of course, and probably more still practice it than the figure suggests. But metal locks, now available in every Gambian market town, have made burial seem less necessary. The main advantage left in burying one's wealth is the safeguard against house-burning. In those villages in which farmers have gradually replaced thatch with metal roofing, this function too is being obviated.

Most cash savings in the farming communities today are kept well concealed, usually together with clothes, jewelry, or other valued possessions, in a locked box or trunk, under or beside the owner's bed or sleeping platform. Locking customs deserve some attention; they differ from what foreign visitors sometimes expect. Most Gambian houses constructed as permanent dwellings now have lockable fixtures on their exterior doors, but just about anyone who can afford to do so keeps a lockable box within. When asked about why they lock the boxes inside their houses too, Gambians often speak of their spouses. Where cash is concerned, many marriages include very little free and easy sharing, nor is it usually expected that spouses will share knowledge of how much cash they possess. Bluffing and negotiation are routine and well understood. Rural Gambians are sometimes surprised to hear how, in the United States (until lately, at least, such a 'world beacon' of individualism through radio broadcasts), spouses often leave cash in bedroom drawers or handbags hung in pantries, known and accessible to each other, and how many indeed lock nothing away from each other within their houses.[43] To rural Gambians, these Americans seem an unnatural sort of marital communists.

But owners must protect their cash from themselves as well as from their kin and neighbors. Hence the custom of the box called *kondem* (from the English "condemn") or *kondaneh* (from the French, *condamnée*) in local languages, resembling a western "piggy bank" in function (though this term is seldom heard in a Muslim country). The farmer engages a carpenter to build a box (usually costing about 5 to 10 dalasis) that must be broken to be opened, with a small slot for inserting money. Both younger and older adults of both sexes do this. (*Kondem* boxes are common not just in the countryside but also in the cities, where they are likely to be made with plywood boards.) Village saving clubs occasionally have group *kondem* boxes. Like old burial pots, the boxes are evidence of something contrary to the "liquidity preference" that foreign economists sometimes assume. Just as important, or more, is an *illiquidity preference*—if complex and socially embedded decisions must be reduced to "preferences." By buying their boxes, Gambians show they are willing to *pay* money to remove their cash from their own temptations.

Rural Deposit-Takers

Another widely used strategy is the money-keeper or money-guard.[44] Some rural Gambians give money to others in their villages to hold for them. They may choose any trusted person—there are no specialized deposit-takers—but often the depositor will choose a relative or other person who is likely to have other cash available for his or her own urgent needs.

In our 1988 survey, 46 percent of the female and 20 percent of the male respondents had entrusted money to other individuals in 1987 and 1988.[45] More had given deposits than taken them: in the same period, 16 percent of male and 15 percent of the female respondents had received deposits from others. An individual may hold money for several persons simultaneously, as these figures suggest; and more occasionally, an individual deposits with more than one keeper at a time. The great majority of depositors of both sexes had made their deposits in January and February, in the season of groundnut harvesting and marketing, and more than half said that they had made only one deposit in a year. Sixty three percent had withdrawn their deposits in May and June, reflecting the importance of land preparation and planting expenses as a purpose of saving. Otherwise the withdrawals were spread about evenly through the year. Only rarely does an individual leave money in deposit for more than a year.

Who were the money-keepers? Mostly they were people from families like those of their depositors, but often rather better off. Seventy three percent of the depositors identified as their money-keepers people who were mainly farmers by occupation. Thirteen percent named shopkeepers or traders, 4 percent named government employees, and 10 percent named others. Seventy one percent of the depositors (80 percent of the depositing men and 64 percent of the depositing women) left money with men. So, while roughly equal proportions of men and women appear to take deposits, more people entrust their money to men than to women. A village headman (*alkalo*) or other local notable sometimes holds several deposits simultaneously.

Why the bias toward men? Interviews suggested several possible reasons, none a clearly consistent favorite. Some suggested it is because men tend to be more respected and feared and are considered more likely to pursue or punish a thief. This

is not a watertight answer, though, because some women seem to have magical powers exceeding most men's. Savers may sense that men's higher prestige gives them
more to lose if they should fail to refund the savings. (These are also reasons why
some depositors choose village headmen.) Men are likely to have had more formal
schooling than women, and to be more comfortable doing arithmetic with large
numbers. Having more cash on average than women, men are sometimes deemed
less likely to dip into the cash, though this idea may be illusory. Perhaps men, who
commonly have more consanguineal kin in their respective villages than women, are
expected to have more alternate cash sources for their own emergencies (though
they also have greater cash obligations). Perhaps, too, for reasons of pride, men simply did not wish to admit saving with women as much as women did with men.

  Money keeping is very local. Seventy nine percent of the 48 depositors we interviewed named as their money-keepers other members of their respective villages,
reflecting the importance of both residential nearness and kinship—because these
often coincide—in determining trust or confidence. To isolate the role of kinship, 69
percent specified known relatives as their money-keepers, and 45 percent named
their parents, spouses, full siblings, or offspring (see Table 11-2).

TABLE 11-2 Relationships of Informal Money-Keepers to Depositors, 1988

Money-keepers	Depositors Interviewed		
Kin	Male	Female	Both
Spouse	1	10	11
Parent	4	5	9
Sibling (full)	0	2	2
Offspring	0	0	0
Other kin	6	5	11
Subtotal, kin	11 (55%)	22 (79%)	33 (69%)
Non-kin	9 (45%)	6 (21%)	15 (31%)
Totals	20 (100%)	28 (100%)	48 (100%)

Seventy-nine percent of female depositors used kin as their safe-keepers, as against
only fifty-five percent of men depositors. Among the women depositors, thirty-six
percent named husbands as the money-keepers, whereas among the men depositors,
only five percent named their wives, raising interesting questions about who trusts
whom with money in marriages. There is much variability here, as open-ended interviews revealed; some women interviewed seemed to feel much safer than others in
entrusting cash to their husbands. Only twenty-four percent of the male and female
depositors identified their respective money-keepers to be unrelated friends.

  Gambians prefer to entrust their money to their elders. Thus, they use their parents but not their offspring as money-keepers. That women entrust their money to
their husbands more than men to their wives (Table 11-3) fits the age pattern too,
because most husbands are older than their wives, some by many years.

  The asymmetries between the genders, and between younger and older adults,
in cash entrustments reflects important local concerns about knowledge and power

TABLE 11-3   Genders of Depositors and Money-Keepers, 1988

Depositors	Money-Keepers		
	Male	Female	Total
Male	16 (80%)	4 (20%)	20 (100%)
Female	18 (64%)	10 (36%)	28 (100%)
Total	34 (71%)	14 (29%)	48 (100%)

within family compounds. Husbands prefer to keep wives from knowing just how much cash they have partly because the latter will then know the limits of what they can demand or extract (for instance, by borrowing in a husband's absence and letting the creditor eventually press the husband for repayment when this man returns). Wives, for their part, prefer not to let their husbands know just how much they have because the latter may simply demand it, although Islamic custom, as interpreted locally, discourages men from taking away the money that their wives have earned.

Likewise, sons who still live in their fathers' compounds know that their fathers may simply demand cash that the sons have earned. For a father to appropriate a son's cash without eventually using it to the benefit of the earner or of other family members would be considered improper but not beyond the father's power. It is not uncommon for a father simply to demand the totality and take it, but some fathers do use this for those sons' eventual marriage payments. In this way, the intrafamilial extractions can serve as a forced saving mechanism and fuel the marriage-payment system in a culturally conservative way. Sons who wish not to yield their fathers this control, like wives who wish to avoid husbands' confiscations, can under-represent their earnings and quietly ask others to safeguard their cash for them. That women more often deposit their cash with men than men with women, and that juniors deposit their cash with elders but not vice versa, reflects not just a perception that women or juniors are less likely to use it well—something that depends on personalities—but perhaps more importantly, recognizes women's and juniors' susceptibility to husbands' or fathers' demands.[46]

How big are the amounts involved in money-keeping? In the 1987 survey, they varied from 20 dalasis ($2.90 U.S.)—the lowest reported, at any rate—to over 2,000 ($290), the median deposit being about 251 dalasis ($37). Though women are more likely to deposit with money-keepers than men, the men deposit bigger sums. In their last visits with money-keepers before being interviewed in 1988, depositing men had left a median sum of 530 dalasis ($77) for safe keeping, as compared with the depositing women's median of 150 dalasis ($22). And 26 percent of the male depositors, as against only 10 percent of the female, reported having entrusted amounts of 1,000 dalasis ($145) or more.

Terms, Risks, and Incentives in Informal Money-Keeping

Interest payments or service charges are unheard of in village money-keeping, and the depositor often expects to receive back the same notes or coins lent. It is generally agreed that the money-keeper should not use the money deposited, but it is not so clear who holds the legal right to the money during the period of the deposit. A Basse court record describes a civil case in which a shepherd entrusted 80 dalasis ($11.60 U.S.) to a shopkeeper for safe keeping, and the shop's cash was later stolen by thieves. The shepherd sought the full 80 dalasis. The court ruled that the shopkeeper owed the shepherd 40 dalasis, half the amount deposited. Villagers interviewed disagreed among themselves about the correctness of the decision.

If money-keeping can entail some financial risk to the money-keeper, why does he or she agree to perform the service? The obvious and ostensible reasons include helping the saver, cementing a social bond, and demonstrating trustworthiness to the community by eventual word of mouth. Another possible reason is that the cash, though normally expected not to be used, nonetheless gives the money-keeper a reserve available for family emergencies: for instance, if the need arose to taxi a snakebitten child to the hospital or to pay a son's court bail at short notice, cash would be on hand. Because the money belongs to someone else, this emergency reserve is easier to defend from the daily requests of spouses, other kin, or neighbors than money of one's own.

A bigger question is why the *depositor* chooses the money-keeper system, rather than one that might pay interest, as with a bank. Islamic prohibitions against interest, discussed elsewhere (Shipton 1991), are only part of an answer, because local loans with interest are countenanced in practice. When asked what they liked most about the money-keeper system, farmers tended to talk more of trustworthiness and safety than of proximity or convenience.[47] Because most deposit-taking goes on within villages and among kin, those who save this way are displaying trust *not just in the individuals* to whom they are confiding their savings, *but also in the networks and groups* to which both they and the keepers belong: the mechanisms to which they would turn for support as a last resort if keepers refused to return the money.

Banks in the western Sahel are unlikely to attract more customers without more and better public relations in the more honorable sense of the term—not just better interest rates or accessibility, although these would probably interest customers in their services. It may help to recruit some elders, where literacy or other qualifications permit, because local practice suggests they are more trusted than juniors.[48] But banks and other formal institutions should expect only to supplement rather than supplant the local money-keeping system, because the latter has devoted practitioners. In the 1988 survey, for instance, informants who used the services of "informal" money-keepers were asked whether they were content with this system of saving. Ninety four percent replied yes. Conversely, when asked if there were any problems with it, 98 percent replied no.[49] A bank might envy such user confidence.

Deferred Wages

Wage-earners have a related way of saving, which is to ask employers to withhold wages over short times to let them accumulate. Some agricultural wage laborers prefer to be paid only quarterly, and a study of Gambian share contracting in farming found that most workers prefer arrangements in which they receive their main compensation seasonally rather than at shorter intervals (Robertson 1987:221). As in the village money-keeping customs described above, individuals entrust their money to others who they know are more solvent than they are, and who have reputations to lose in the case of failure to repay.

The wage-deferment system is incidentally familiar to researchers who hire local research aid. While some assistants in the city or countryside constantly request advances, others just as constantly request delays. Acquisitive spouses are the main concern, but not the only one.[50] A young Gambian assistant deeply in his elder brother's debt once insisted I withhold his own pay for four consecutive months, whereupon, his job over, he would quickly buy himself an expensive travel ticket for overseas. Once employed abroad, he hoped, he could return his brother's favors and still have something left for himself. Four years later, still in the country when I visited and rehired him, he asked again for the same arrangement.

Indigenous Financial Groups

The practice of saving cash in groups has a long if poorly recorded history in The Gambia, and it is a history in which immigrant and local populations have shared many ideas. The practice seems always to have been more common and routinized in the cities than in the countryside. A common urban form is the "friendly society" or "provident society," a kind of local welfare organization or contribution club more commonly known by the borrowed French term *vous* (from *rendez-vous*). By 1906, the Treasurer for the Colony recorded that "Bathurst (now Banjul) is well supplied with friendly societies [or provident societies], there being no less than thirty-one," and others may have gone unregistered with the government (Archer [1906] 1967:123).[51] Often organized for the ostensible purpose of collecting a kind of community chest as insurance for members' personal or familial emergencies, they tended to be constituted by ethnic or religious identity, by provenance, or by a mix of these factors. Hence, by 1945, the Gambia Colony's annual report listed, among others, the Ijebu Descendants Friendly Society of Nigeria, the Gambia Portuguese Mutual Aid Society, the Sierra Leone Descendants Provident Society, the McCarthy Island Descendants Society, and the Mandingo Mohammedan Society (Ijebu are a subgroup of Yoruba from Nigeria) (Great Britain, Colonial Office 1945:362).[52] Some were political as well as economic, social, and religious forces. The last mentioned fed indirectly into the leadership of the People's Progressive Party, during which evolution the nation's first President, Dawda K. Jawara, still in office in 1993, rose to power. Like their counterparts in other countries south of the Sahara, friendly societies in The Gambia showed that African institutions do not always exist for a single purpose alone, and that financial institutions, like churches or soccer stadiums in many countries, can in some cases be used as arenas to test or voice political sentiments that are riskier to express in other contexts.

Rotating and nonrotating groups for monetary savings and credit within villages are now an important part of rural as well as urban financial life, particularly for women (see Shipton 1992a). Particularly noteworthy are the rotating saving and credit associations. These are variously known in local languages as *osusu* or *esusu* groups (a term probably Yoruba in origin and heard up and down the coast)—or as merry-go-rounds to anglophones or *tontines* to francophones. Formed by local initiative, these groups meet at regular intervals, and members contribute mutually agreed amounts of cash for one member to take away from each meeting, until all have had a turn. The groups usually form on the basis of common gender, age-grade membership, class, or occupation; and these factors may be combined. Being of comparable socioeconomic circumstances helps keep some members from exploiting others, and being connected in nonfinancial ways gives members many possible sanctions to impose on one who does not cooperate.

Saving with a group, like converting money to large livestock or gold earrings, helps an individual shelter her or his wealth from the daily demands of spouses, other kin, and neighbors, because a member of one of these financial groups can always invoke some responsibility to the group to avoid seeming selfish when refusing to give or share. Saving in a group thus controls the squawk factor. These and other principles embodied may merit emulation in exogenous financial projects to serve rural Gambians. These are powerful devices, however, and, to turn the issue around, group saving can obviously involve at least temporary privations for family dependents.

Amounts Commonly Saved

It is nearly impossible to determine the amounts of farmers' total personal cash savings. Indirect questioning in the villages in 1987 and 1988 suggested that most farmers' liquid cash savings could be counted in the hundreds of dalasis (sometimes held partly in francs CFA) at any given point during the "trade season" from December to March, a few farmers' rising into the thousands; but that most had cash savings of less than 100 dalasis ($14 U.S.) at any given time during the rest of the year. Men appear generally to have larger sums at their disposal than women have during the trade season, but women seem usually to save more than men, as a proportion of their wealth and perhaps also in absolute sums, in the lean season. Thus, men's cash savings seem to fluctuate more than women's. One reason for this may be women's considerable involvement in nonfarming economic activities outside the crop season, when many men are idle. A second may be that because men usually do their land preparation before women do, and may preempt the use of animal-drawn tools for their own fields, women often expect to have to hire labor in preparing their own. There are indications that elders tend to save more in cash than juniors.

Interviews indicated that most cash savings over about 100 dalasis for periods longer than a few weeks are made for specific target expenditures.[53] People with thousands of dalasis in savings are usually those with ceremonies upcoming such as weddings to finance, or young men planning to travel to find work. Savings in these cases will usually include earmarked contributions from kin.

Rural Gambians vary somewhat by ethnic group in saving habits. Fula, descendants of pastoralists, appear still to hold stronger preferences for livestock than most other Gambians (Mills, Kabay, and Boughton 1988:19–20). Serahuli, heirs to an ancient and constantly recreated tradition of long-distance, cross-border trade, are widely believed to keep larger stocks of cash and other valuables in their houses than other indigenous rural Gambians, and my observations suggest there is some truth in this idea (although stereotypes may exaggerate these tendencies). They may use heavier boxes or even chained or cement-anchored safes. Mauritanian and other merchants tend to do the same. Many merchants, however, appear to reinvest cash quickly in merchandise rather than saving large amounts. Small shopkeepers commonly deposit cash savings with larger traders in their villages or in larger towns.

While urban savings are beyond the scope of this chapter, it is worth noting that most saving methods described above, including the *kondaneh* boxes, the money-keepers, and rotating savings and credit associations (*osusu* groups), are also common in the cities of Banjul and Serrekunda. *Osusus* are common, for instance, among salaried secretaries and messengers of government ministries, and not just among people without access to banks or other "formal" financial institutions.[54]

Banking

The history of rural savings banking in rural Gambia is a lackluster one. Institutional banking in The Gambia dates officially from 1884, when by Ordinance no. 11, the British colonial government established the Treasury Savings Bank, founded on January 1, 1886. Whatever may have been the barriers to prospective savers, they did not at first include stiff requirements of minimum deposits: the Bank received amounts of as little as 1 shilling, with a maximum of £500 sterling including interest deposited.[55]

The start was modest, though early customers included expatriates. By 1899, 203 depositors had accumulated £2,456 in bank savings; by 1903 the figures had grown to 349 depositors with a total of £2,290, or an average of about £6.6 sterling per depositor.[56] By the end of the Second World War, the then Government Sav ings Bank had 5,753 depositors (including expatriates) with a total of £101,492 (Gambia 1945:361).[57]

A second, private bank, the Bank of British West Africa Ltd., headquartered in Liverpool and London, set up a branch at Bathurst (now Banjul) in 1902, at first primarily for government banking business. It evolved into the Bank of West Africa, later the Standard Bank of West Africa, later the Gambian branch of the Standard Chartered Bank Gambia Ltd., a subsidiary of the multinational Standard Chartered Bank.[58] The GambiaCommercial and Development Bank (GCDB), founded in 1972 as a mainly state-owned corporation but officially unprofitable in the end, was sold to the international Meridian Bank in 1991–92.[59] This latter bank and the Standard Chartered Bank conducted nearly all of the country's commercial banking as of 1992. Interest rates on savings have not been consistently positive in real terms (i.e., with inflation taken into account), and bank lending rates too have remained artificially low even though lately officially decontrolled.[60]

The commercial banking system remains almost useless for rural people, at least as direct customers. Gambian farmers perceive banks as remote, intimidating, and not fully trustworthy, and by and large they do not go to them.[61] The senior officers of the banks in The Gambia, on the other hand, imagine smallholding farmers to be too poor and financially inactive to be of interest, and not particularly trustworthy as borrowers.[62] There were only two up-river branches in The Gambia in the late 1980s: outside Banjul and nearby Serrekunda and Bakao, commercial banks were found only in Farafeni and Basse.[63]

The numbers of rural bank depositors clearly reflect distances, both social and geographic. A 1975–6 survey of rural Gambian villages found that only two (2 percent) of 94 informants had bank savings (Dunsmore et al. 1976:307). In our 1987 survey, 4 (3 percent) of 138 male and female informants stated they had deposits in commercial banks; 4 others (again 3 percent) said they had money in post office savings. Only 1 of 69 women interviewed in our survey had a savings account in either a bank or post-office savings.

Branch bank information confirmed that most farmer depositors held amounts below about 250 dalasis ($36), amounts smaller than they or their neighbors tended to entrust to village moneykeepers. Very few of the depositors were women, and almost no farmers, male or female, borrowed from banks. In May 1987, the Basse branch of the GCDB (one of only two branches of the bank outside the greater Banjul area) reported that 49 percent of its 858 savings depositors had less than 250 dalasis in their accounts (i.e., less than the value of one sheep). Interviews with bank staff suggested that most of the roughly 100 farmers (people whose primary source of income is farming) saving at the bank were among those with less than 250 dalasis. Only an estimated 10 to 15 percent of the 858 depositors were women. Only about 5 farmers were currently borrowing from the branch.

Because saving at home or with money-keepers, instead of with financial institutions, costs farmers the opportunity to earn interest (about 12 percent offered by the banks by 1992), the problems with banking appear serious. When asked in a neutral fashion why they preferred other means of saving to banks, villagers pointed out several drawbacks to banks: the distance and prohibitive travel costs, inconvenient opening schedules, requirements of minimum deposits, difficult paperwork, and their personal distrust of bank clerks. Some rued their experience with the Agricultural Development Bank, which had taken deposits from its inception in 1981 to 1983 and ceased operating without refunding them. While Islam, strictly speaking, forbids interest charges, the fact that many rural Gambians do charge interest in informal lending (and do so with a variety of legal devices—in Arabic, *ḥiyal* [singular, *ḥíla*]—to dodge the prohibitions) suggests that the interest-collecting aspect of savings banking is unlikely by itself to stop many savers who would otherwise be interested in banking.[64]

Rural Gambians are generally *more concerned about security* of savings, and about availability for emergencies, *than about interest* earned or forgone.[65] But many have remained unaware that banks pay interest on savings. And most have not had access to the kind of information or schooling that would let them calculate inflationary losses and interest opportunity costs. Many are unable to assess how quickly they lose purchasing power by hoarding money or depositing it with keepers who pay no interest. Others, however, are merely being prudent in refusing to place their deposits in banks that have not provided consistently positive real rates of interest.

Although few farmers use banks to date, most interviewed seemed to like very much the idea of mobile banks, saying they would like to see these tried, or tried again, in their areas.[66] Many said they would prefer to see small branch banks set up near them, since they would have doubts about putting their money into something that would roll away. But clearly, inaccessibility had discouraged potential savers.

Agricultural Seasonality and the Future of Rural Savings Banking

Seasonality puts banks to a stern test, whether their branches are stationary or mobile. The predominance of rain-fed agriculture in the economy and the covariance of incomes make financial intermediation hard. Most farmers are likely to deposit at the same time (the trade season, December–February) and to withdraw at the same time (June–September). This has been so since at least the first decades of the twentieth century. Moreover, most farmers who borrow are likely to do so at the same time of year when everyone is making withdrawals, and not to repay until the following trade season, when they have the cash again or are more willing to part with it. A bank has stronger financial incentives to make the rounds (if using mobile branches) or stay open (if using stationary ones) in the "trade season," when farmers have significant sums of money to deposit, than during the rest of the year, when farmers are more interested in withdrawals.[67]

The commercial banks are the existing organizations with the most managerial competence to handle a system of rural branch banks. Unfortunately they have tended to be the organizations least interested in serving the needs of the poorer rural people. A broad-reaching system of rural savings banking would probably require added safeguards provided by large international development organizations.

If banks are to serve Gambian farmers, and particularly women, it is likely to be largely by group access through *kafo* groups and other village-based associations. Nongovermental aid organizations can usefully help make banks more familiar and accessible to women's groups. Serving to explain the pros and cons of banking, they can also function as screening mechanisms for the banks on one hand, and bureaucracy-cutters for the farmers on the other. Brokering the two-way flow of information is a role the NGOs can more easily serve than banking itself, because most lack the funds to keep trained money managers on their staffs. The large agencies, for their part, can back up new bank experiments with guarantees, and they can help coordinate the activities of a large and heterogenous set of NGOs that compete for agency funds and whose leaders have trouble communicating among themselves.

An innovative recent experiment in rural banking, the Village Saving and Credit Associations (VISACAs), has suggested the potential of NGOs in mobilizing rural savings. Slowly and carefully begun in 1988 as a pilot project in the Jahally–Pachar irrigation project area of McCarthy Island South Division, and supported by French and German aid organizations, it has given over the managerial initiative to local people with evenly mixed-gender management committees.[68] Serving more women than men, and *kafo* groups as well as individual clients, it has used members' own savings as a basis for short-term lending. It has maintained real positive interest rates for both deposits and loans, and kept up excellent repayment rates on the loans.[69] Whether the program is replicable over a broader area, particularly without irrigated rice present to help stabilize cash incomes, remains to be seen.

Public expressions of interest in the possibilities of mobile banking (and small rural branch banking) suggest other practical paths for public or private agencies to follow. Untried linkages between banks and other agencies with more public outreach and good will, and untried adjustments in interest policies, suggest much room remains for experimentation. The aim should not be to "capture" local savings—something neither ethical nor practicable—but by offering more options, to augment and supplement them.

Conclusions

To conclude, rural Gambians save in many ways, some subtle. The diversity and complexity of rural savings have their own rationales, and currency instabilities make it sensible to put savings into forms other than money. Saving, like borrowing and lending, is part and parcel of social life; and any institution that becomes involved in Sahelian rural finance is also involved with individuals' networks of kin, neighbors, and age-mates.

It is untrue, as sometimes said, that rural Gambians do not carry over wealth from year to year. But most of what they do save over periods of years is in nonmonetary forms. They choose these methods for many reasons: to avoid inflation or political and regulatory control over their assets; gain the benefits of milk, manure, and traction that animals provide, or gain increases through livestock breeding; consolidate their savings into indivisible forms or forms their relatives may help keep them from spending rashly; avoid guilt associated with overt interest earnings; and cut their losses to unscrupulous bank clerks or collapsing banks. Diversifying savings into many forms means reducing risks. It also means keeping the total wealth less conspicuous, both to other local people and to tax collectors. There is obviously sense in these strategies, even though some of the means of saving that farmers choose provide them suboptimal earnings in monetary terms. Planners in institutions really wishing to assist Gambians to save resources might do well to consider interventions in crop storage—incidentally an approach low in recurring expenses—or animal health.

It is also untrue that Gambian farmers are uninterested in monetary savings. The *kondaneh* boxes, the rural deposit-takers, and the requests for infrequent wage payments all testify that many rural people want ways of saving cash. So too does rural people's liking to convert small notes to large ones when they can (as, similarly, men try to convert small livestock to large stock). While some economists assume farming people to have a "liquidity preference," these patterns indicate the opposite, an "illiquidity preference." More precisely, rural Gambians show that while they want to keep their wealth in forms accessible in emergencies, they also want to keep it in forms that they or their many claimants cannot just fritter away.

Part of the reason why rural Gambians, like people in many other parts of West Africa, seem to save only a limited amount of their wealth in liquid form is the squawk factor: a social pressure against personal hoarding. This is why group saving approaches appear often to hold at least as much promise as others based merely on individuals: group saving makes it possible to save without appearing selfish. The principle, at the very root of the *osusu*, might usefully guide experimentation in "institutional" financial systems as well.

Most of the saving strategies described in this chapter are not unique to The Gambia, nor are the principles behind them. Instead, this small country, long a focal point for trade and an ethnic microcosm of the western end of Africa, is likely to afford a fair cross-section of saving habits and rationales found well beyond its narrow borders. The same kinds of questions will be worth asking, and what Gambian rural people, in their deeds as well as their words, suggest to those who would intervene in their economic futures may well turn out to be similar elsewhere when the right questions are asked. They seem to be saying that they need balance between savings in cash and kind, between liquidity and illiquidity, and between individualism and group responsibility.

Notes

1. The occasion was a visit of the Governor to the eastern Gambian town now spelled Fatoto. Elsewhere in her account Lady Southorn noted similar jewelry among women of "the tribes" of The Gambia generally (1952:41).
2. He described a Mandinko-occupied region near the headwaters of the Gambia River, east of present-day Gambia.

3. In the report by the United Nations Development Program (UNDP) (1991), The Gambia ranked second to last among 160 countries, ahead only of Sierra Leone, in the "human development index," combining measures of life expectancy at birth, adult literacy, mean years of schooling, educational attainment, real GDP per capita, and adjusted real GDP (see Table 1 of the Report:121). By the time of the 1993 report, based mainly on 1990 data, The Gambia was listed as 167th out of 173 (Ibid.: 137). The factor weightings are rather arbitrary. The World Bank's *World Development Report* (1993), another standard reference source, does not list The Gambia in its statistical tables except in a residual summary of thirty three small countries. Among these, The Gambia appears as the third poorest, with a per capita GNP of U.S. $360.

4. A recent survey listed 108 nongovernmental aid organizations (NGOs) in The Gambia, of which 53 were international (Graham, Meyers, and Cuevas 1993:45). A number of Islamic institutions not listed could be added. Six international, seven national, and one unclassified NGO were listed as directly involved in financial services.

5. The 1983 official population was 687,817 (The Gambia 1986:8). Barrett (1988) traces the history of food-marketing on the Gambia River since 1400, and Haswell (1975) and Snyder (1981:Ch. 4) trace, from different theoretical perspectives, the more recent history of commodity relations in lower Casamance and central Gambia, respectively.

6. This chapter is part of a larger continuing study of rural Gambian financial thought and practice. Its findings tie in closely in with Shipton (1991 and 1992a).

7. Shipton (1992a) analyzes Gambian village-based saving and credit organizations, rotating and nonrotating, in more detail.

8. Here are the words of one colonial traveling commissioner, for instance, who missed the point in commenting on the South Bank in 1918–9 (quoted in Gamble n.d. [b]:14) "If they were not so hopelessly improvident . . . they would now be in absolute affluence . . . our people have hardly the remotest idea of saving. If they have money they will spend it if what they happen to want, from a wife to a kola nut, is put before them at the moment . . ."

9. For the structured surveys in 1987 and 1988, five villages were randomly chosen in Upper River Division, MacCarthy Island Division, and Western Division (on both sides of the river). While I lived and interviewed mainly in two villages in Foni Berefit District and Fulladu East District, together with locally known and trained assistants, other such assistants surveyed three further villages, occasionally visited briefly by me. 138 farmers were visited in 1987; and in 1988, these were revisited with others added, for a total of 167 (counted after information discards). In four of the five villages, 95 to 100 percent of the compounds were visited in the second, larger survey. (The fifth village, being too large to cover, required a more limited but systematic sample of one side.) One man and one woman were interviewed in each compound, each several times.

10. Our informants in the 1988 survey, by first language, were Mandinko (36 percent), Fula (28 percent), Wolof (21 percent), Jola or Diola (8 percent), Serahuli (4 percent), and others (3 percent). In the 1983 national census, not a wholly reliable source but the best available, the largest ethnic groups in The Gambia were listed as follows: Mandinko (40.4 percent), Fula (18.8 percent), Wolof (14.6 percent), Jola (10.3 percent), Serahuli (8.2 percent), and others (7.7 percent), including Arabic-speaking Mauritanians (Gambia 1986:8). International seasonal labor migrations, among other things, make census-taking difficult. Some have also questioned whether the national census may have under-enumerated Fula for political reasons.

11. I hope to discuss in more detail elsewhere some of the interethnic similarities and differences in Gambian economic life.

12. A patrilineage is a group of kin related, or putatively related, through males. By conventional anthropological definitions it is rather smaller or more localized than clan, and it differs from a clan in that its members can normally trace the genealogical links that connect them with the founder or apical ancestor. In The Gambia as elsewhere in Africa, however,

anglophones commonly speak of a *clan* to refer to a lineage.

13. Many Jola subgroups have tended to resist caste as an unwanted Mandinka influence. Some scholars dispute the use of the term "caste" on the grounds of differences perceived between West African and Indian forms of classification. In my view the term can accommodate both. See Tamari (1991) on the comparative history of castes in West Africa; Diop (1981) and Dupire (1970:427–49) on Senegambian Fula/Peul castes; and Diop (1981) on Wolof castes and their economic importance. Pélissier's grand sweep over Senegalese ethnic groups (1966), which include nearly all Gambian ethnic groups, is as comprehensive as any.

14. European, Islamic, and endogenous African ways of conceiving of interest and usury—and mixtures of these interpretations in The Gambia—are discussed by Shipton 1991.

15. For livestock counts see Derman and coworkers (1985:112), Mills, Kabay and Boughton (1988), Sumberg (1988), and Sumberg and Gilbert (1988). As elsewhere in Africa south of the Sahara, livestock loans and (among some groups) secrecy about numbers owned make livestock tallies difficult.

16. Marriage payments among Gambian peoples are paid mainly in cash and manufactured goods, however, not in cattle as among many eastern African groups.

17. A versatile term, *fangkanta* seems sometimes to be used as what Jane Guyer, in this volume, has called a cognitive "receptor category," an old idea that accommodates new ideas or practices.

18. This applies to other permanent, heritable lineage property such as home compounds. For other African comparisons see Shipton 1989.

19. West African literature refers often to earrings as wealth. See, for instance, Camara Laye's autobiographical novel, *The Dark Child* (1955), in which the father is a goldsmith, and Sembene Ousmane's novelette and film, *The Money Order* ([1972] 1987), in which earrings are pawned to a usurious Mauritanian merchant in Dakar as a desperation measure, and lost.

20. In 1795–7, Park ([1799] 1971:305) observed of "Manding" near the source of the Gambia River, "When a lady of consequence is in full dress, her gold ornaments may be worth altogether, from fifty to eighty pounds sterling." As a point of reference, a healthy young male slave downriver sold, Park generalized, for 18 to 20 pounds sterling (Ibid.:26).

21. Only one such transaction was reported in interviews.

22. See also Chambers and Leach (1989) on the importance of trees as a form of saving in poor countries.

23. In a preliminary count of data from the two villages studied in Western Division, women who grew groundnuts harvested an average of 73 percent as much as men who grew them. On average, the men sold 73 percent of their crop, stored 20 percent as seed, and stored 3 percent as food. The women sold 65 percent of their crop, stored 13 percent as seed, and stored 23 percent as food. While only 27 percent of the men who grew groundnuts kept any after harvest for use as food, 92 percent of the female groundnut growers kept some for food. All the male growers and 91 percent of the female growers kept some for seed. Of course, some groundnuts originally intended as seed get consumed before planting time.

24. Comments like this one, recorded at the Commissioners' Conference in 1925, are fairly common in the colonial record:

> His Excellency [the Governor] said that the Protectorate natives were singularly improvident. As soon as they had reaped their crops they sold quantities of cereals at a low price to Bathurst traders . . . It was a fact that foodstuffs so sold immediately after the harvesting for a mere song were repurchased later when the pinch of hunger arrived at usurious prices. The Protectorate natives had to be protected from themselves (Quoted in Gamble n.d.[b]:116).

> Note the mixture of arrogant ethnocentrism and well-meaning paternalism that interthreaded in British Gambian government throughout the colonial period. Haswell's better

considered longitudinal study (1975) focuses on poverty ratchets, including economically coerced crop sales to creditors.

25. A similar mixture of group and individual responsibility appears in village dry-season vegetable gardens, one of the most popular kinds of projects sponsored by foreign private voluntary organizations. Wells, fencing, and seed nurseries usually belong to village collectivities; but the small garden patches within them and crops from these belong to individuals.

26. Because the volume of a storehouse increases faster than the surface as its size increases, by simple geometric principle, there is an economic advantage in larger storehouses. But, as seen later, there are social disadvantages in stores that are used by more than one village.

27. Seed and crop stores, once constructed, take relatively little monitoring and followup. From the perspective of development planners, this is a great advantage of this kind of "savings" scheme over financial credit programs. Where development projects provide sacks, some or even most sacks are likely to be used for other purposes, such as bedding. This is one of those "intersectoral leakages," infuriating to project managers but perfectly natural to farmers.

28. Park ([1799]1971:28) did not discuss cattle sales, however, leaving open the question of whether they were sold for the currencies that he observed. He did note that slaves were given values in iron bars.

29. There is a long history of European and North American visitors' expressions of discomfort with market price fluctuations in African countries, but much of the impetus for the Gambian and other governments to float their currencies in the 1980s and 1990s has come from economists from those countries. With advice funded by the U.S. Agency for International Development, The Gambia floated the dalasi in January 1986.

30. Pick and Sédillot (1971) give a thumbnail sketch of currency histories in African and other countries worldwide.

31. Like the West African pound that it replaced, the Gambian pound divided into 20 shillings and 240 pence.

32. At the beginning, and still at the time of writing, the dalasi has come in denominations of 25-, 10-, 5-, and 1-dalasi notes, and 1-, 5-, 10-, 25-, and 50-butut coins and 1 dalasi (100 butut) coins.

33. McPherson and Radelet (1991) describe the government's economic program, which is regarded so far as having reversed a sharp decline in the country's economic performance as a whole.

34. Fula cattle do change hands, often in long-term entrustments that are a sign of strong friendship between members of different villages. The practice is paralleled among other West African Fulani groups.

35. The page cited here is according to Gamble's pagination. The McCallum source is unnamed.

36. At a minimum of 4 shillings per year for a compound of up to four houses, with extra charges for extra houses, the tax was effectively also a tax on *people*, because more women in a polygynous family meant more houses. An extra shilling per house was charged for houses of family members and two for houses occupied by strangers.

37. The rates collected in 1992 were 30 dalasis per compound of one to four houses, (and 7 dalasis per additional house) plus 5 dalasis insurance per house. Other taxes were by then levied on shops, animals (2 dalasis per cow), and lodgers including seasonal migrant farmers (25 dalasis each).

38. Haswell (1975) documents the increase of foreign trade goods in The Gambia, and particularly in Genieri village, from the 1940s to the 1970s. She emphasizes the increasing dependence on credit from foreign and ethnic minority traders, which she considers to be a general symptom of poverty.

39. Cash does not, that is, necessarily supplant barter in an inexorable or irreversible way.

40. The phrase comes from David Leonard (1977) in a very different application.
41. Survey response percentages in this chapter refer to the 1988 survey unless otherwise indicated. Figures given are "valid percentages," i.e., they refer to totals excluding "no answer" or "unintelligible" responses and those discovered in cross-checks to be inaccurate. Figures are rounded to the nearest percentage point.
42. Saving by burial has long occurred elsewhere in Africa. The late President Jomo Kenyatta of Kenya once reported on the Kikuyu, "they say it is better to buy a sheep or goat instead of shillings which, if buried in the ground (the only form of saving money the majority of the people know), would rot and lose their value" (Kenyatta [1938] 1965:66).
43. This is not, of course, to say all Gambian marriages are suspicious or hostile. They vary as anywhere. But ties between spouses often seem more distant than some "blood" kin ties, particularly those between fathers and sons or mothers and daughters; and cash is more likely than other commodities to be stashed privately. As discussed below, spouses sometimes do specifically entrust money to each other for safe keeping. See Field (1940), Moock (1986), and Shipton (1989), among a quickly growing number of other sources, for other discussions of the separation of resources between spouses elsewhere in Africa south of the Sahara.
44. For comparisons from Senegal and Niger, respectively, see Tuck (1983:66) and Graham, Curevas, and Negash (1987:Ch. 4, 18–21).
45. The difference between the figures is more than might be accounted for by men's superior access to banks. It suggests that men have greater confidence in their own saving methods, perhaps, or that women are more readily accepted as depositors.
46. Given the commonly felt tension between the genders over control of cash, the cases of women who *choose* to deposit their money with their husbands are interesting. Some seem simply to trust them. But another possible explanation, hard for me to prove now, is that wives who turn to husbands to safeguard cash can, in doing so, make it widely known that the money is really theirs to begin with, and in this way enlist potential witnesses who would be able to help make it a scandal for the husband not to refund the money. I thank one of the volume's anonymous referees for pointing out this possibility.
47. In the 1988 survey, farmers who used money-keepers were asked what they liked about this system of saving. Sixty-two percent cited safety or trustworthiness. eighteen percent said they liked being able to withdraw whenever they chose, 7 percent cited proximity of the moneylender, and 13 percent had other answers. Of course, the reasons mentioned are not mutually exclusive.
48. Whether men should be recruited in preference to women, to reflect local financial practice, or the reverse, to pursue political ideals, is an important related, ethical question. As so often, foreign agents have here the awkward choice of being sexists or cultural imperialists.
49. One informant mentioned the problem of risk. Opinion polling of this sort is of limited use in most African contexts because informants' finely developed etiquette can produce much second-guessing. Also, of course, this subsample was self-selected as people who liked money-keepers.
50. As a Luo houseman in Kenya once said to his employer, within my hearing, "Don't pay me now for this past month; you know my wife will just eat it!" Of course, husbands can likewise "eat" women's pay.
51. He noted these "friendly societies" in passing "to show that the various interests of the Banjolian receive due attention." If all such interests received attention from government, these usually independent organizations would probably not have needed to form in the first place. By the late 1940s, civil servants themselves paid a small part of their salaries into a Government Thrift Fund for mutual assistance in emergencies.
52. The Hastinian Friendly Society, begun in 1908, had 8 members and reported £18 invested; the Mandingo Mohammedan society, begun in 1935, had 285 members and £36 invested;

and the McCarthy Island Descendants Society, established in 1941, had 33 members with a reported total of £56 invested.

53. Little research has been done on attitudes toward the money notes and coins themselves and their denominations. Gambian coins in the smallest Gambian denominations (in multiples of bututs, hundredths of a dalasi) are sometimes used alone, especially by women and children, but men and others who save large amounts like to convert their money into the largest notes possible, to help protect themselves against temptation. Printing more notes in denominations of larger than 25 dalasis might not just serve the convenience of bank clerks and the rich (who queue up in urban banks to count out many hundreds of notes for deposits or withdrawals) but also help and encourage cash saving among poorer people, for better or worse. There would be dangers, however, in problems of innumeracy.

54. In 1988, lower-ranking Gambian workers in several ministries and a major foreign-aid mission in Banjul had *osusu* groups, which did not involve their supervisors. Why salaried workers with access to banks use *osusu* groups too (or instead) is an interesting question that should also be asked the other way around. Convenience and diversification, both to hedge risks and to keep one's total assets secret, are likely reasons.

55. Paying 2.5 percent annual interest, the Bank invested its money in England through the Crown Agents at rates of 3 percent or better when it could.

56. According to the Bank's (and Colony's) Treasurer from 1903 (Archer [1906] 1967:272).

57. At this time, it still paid only 2.5 percent interest on deposits.

58. As the only bank operating in the country by 1960-1, as the colonial era drew to a close, the Bank of West Africa, as it was then called, held £293,000 in depositors' savings (Colonial Office 1961:15) and had only one branch at Bathurst.

59. Graham, Meyer and Cuevas (1993) extensively review Gambian banking and other institutional finance in the 1980s and early 1990s.

60. Between 1986 and 1991, nominal interest rates on bank savings deposits varied between 12.5 and 18 percent, and lending rates for agriculture between 15.5 and 25 percent, while inflation as measured by a consumer price index fluctuated between 5 and 38 but generally fell from the 30s to below 15 percent (Graham, Meyer, and Cuevas 1993:84-5).

61. In 1986, 48 percent of the money supply of The Gambia was reported to be outside of the banking system (Ramamurthy 1986:25).

62. Recent experience of the Village Saving and Credit Associations in The Gambia gives the lie to the stereotype about farmer trustworthiness: repayment rates have averaged over 95 percent since the program began in 1988.

63. The postal savings system is marginally more accessible but still hard to withdraw from, and useless as a source of credit.

64. Shipton (1991) discusses Gambian variants of *ḥiyal* further. A few informants, including Mauritanian shopkeepers, have said that they did not bank because to do so would be to charge interest, an act discouraged in Islam. However, because some of these merchants do charge interest in informal lending, and because Mauritanians in Senegal have in recent years been victim to persecutions requiring temporary flight, the stated reason is probably not to be taken at face value.

65. They sometimes also save money with institutions or clubs (where they do) in order to gain access to credit when needed.

66. In the 1987 survey, when farmers were asked whether or not they like the idea of mobile banks, 60 percent replied yes, 11 percent replied no, and 29 percent were uncommitted, some of these lacking familiarity with the idea. The Agricultural Development Bank had tried mobile banks from 1981 to 1983 before folding.

67. A bank able to use Gambian capital domestically or overseas during the period of savings, and to import capital during the period of withdrawing and borrowing, might be most able to keep its system afloat. So banks with international links would be best placed to accommodate Gambian seasonality.

68. The VISACA project, supported by the French *Centre International de Développement et de Recherche* (CIDR) and the German *Kreditanstalt für Wiederaufbau* (KFW), has maintained a low-profile expatriate adviser in Sapu.

69. The VISACA depositors numbered some 1,384 people in six villages by March 1992; deposits cumulatively mobilized by December 1991 totaled about 400,000 dalasis (about $49,000U.S. at an average exchange rate of 8 dalasis = $1). Loan repayment rates between 1989 and 1991 averaged 94 to 95 percent, nearly a third of the borrowers having repaid ahead of schedule. The program was found to have attained an average internal rate of return of about 26 percent per year (Ouattara, Graham, and Cuevas 1993:6, 12–13).

Sources

Archer, Francis Bisset. [1906] 1967. *The Gambia Colony and Protectorate: An Official Handbook.* London: Frank Cass.

Ba, Cheikh. 1986. *Les Peul du Sénégal.* Dakar, Abidjan, Lomé: Les Nouvelles Editions Africaines.

Barrett, Hazel R. 1988. *The Marketing of Foodstuffs in The Gambia, 1400–1980.* Aldershot, U.K.. and Brookfield, VT: Avebury.

Berry, Sara. 1985. *Fathers Work for their Sons.* Berkeley, CA: University of California Press.

Chambers, Robert, and Melissa Leach. 1989. "Trees as Savings and Security for the Rural Poor." *World Development* 17: 329–42.

Derman, William, Frank Casey, Sarah Lynch, Cynthia Moore, and Charles Steedman. 1985. *Rural Development in the Gambia River Basin.* Ann Arbor, MI: Center for Research on Economic Development, University of Michigan.

Diop, Abdoulaye-Bara. 1981. *La Société Wolof: Tradition et Changement.* Paris: Karthala.

Dunsmore, J. R., A. Blair Rains, G. D. N. Lowe, D. J. Moffatt, I. P. Anderson, and J. B. Williams. 1976. *The Agricultural Development of The Gambia: An Agricultural, Environmental, and Socio-Economic Analysis.* Land Resource Study 22. Surbiton, England: Land Resources Division, Ministry of Overseas Development.

Dupire, Marguerite. 1970. *Organization Sociale des Peul: Etude d'Ethnographie Comparée.* Paris: Librairie Plon.

Field, M.J. 1940. *The Social Organisation of the Ga People.* London: Crown Agents for the Colonies.

The Gambia. *Blue Books of Statistics.* Annual. London: His (Her) Majesty's Stationery Office.

——— . 1945. *Annual Report.* London: His (Her) Majesty's Stationery Office, for the Colonial Office.

——— . 1961. *Annual Report.* London: His (Her) Majesty's Stationery Office, for the Colonial Office.

The Gambia. 1986. Population and Housing Census, 1983. Provisional Report. Central Statistics Department, Ministry of Economic Planning and Industrial Development.

Gamble, David. n. d.[a]. "Gambian Fula," marked 1/16; Gambian National Archives Report 76/31.

——— . n.d.[b]. "Trade and Agriculture—Cattle." Gambian National Archives Report 76/13.

Gastellu, Jean-Marc. 1981. L'Egalitarique Economique des Serer du Sénégal. Paris: ORSTOM.

Graham, Douglas H., Carlos E. Cuevas, and Kifle Negash. 1987. *Rural Finance in Niger*. Report to the U.S. Agency for International Development.

———. Richard L. Meyer, and Carlos E. Cuevas, eds. 1993. *Financial Markets in The Gambia, 1981–91. Report to the USAID Mission in Banjul, The Gambia*. Columbus, OH : Dept. of Agricultural Economics and Rural Sociology, Ohio State University.

Guyer, Jane, and Pauline Peters, eds. 1987. *Conceptualizing the Household*. Special Issue of *Development and Change*, 18:197–213.

Haswell, Margaret R. 1975. *The Nature of Poverty: A Case-History of the First Quarter-Century After World War II*. New York: St. Martin's Press.

Kenyatta, Jomo. [1938] 1965. *Facing Mount Kenya*. London: Heinemann.

Laye, Camara. 1955. *The Dark Child*. London: Collins.

Leonard, David. 1977. *Reaching the Peasant Farmer*. Chicago, IL: University of Chicago Press.

Linares, Olga. 1992. *Power, Prayer and Production: The Jola of Casamance, Senegal*. Cambridge: Cambridge University Press.

McPherson, Malcolm F., and Steven C. Radelet. 1991. "Economic Reform in The Gambia: Policies, Politics, Foreign Aid, and Luck." In *Reforming Economic Systems in Developing Countries*, ed. Dwight H. Perkins and Michael Roemer, 115–136. Cambridge, MA: Harvard University Press.

Mills, Bradford F., Mohamed B. Kabay, and Duncan Boughton. 1988. "Soil Fertility Management Strategies in Three Villages of Eastern Gambia." Unpublished report, Gambia Agricultural Research and Diversification Project, Banjul.

Moock, Joyce Lewinger, ed. 1986. *Understanding Africa's Rural Households and Farming Systems*. Boulder, CO: Westview.

Ouattara, Korotoumou, D. H. Graham, and C. E. Cuevas. 1993. "Alternative Financial Networks: The Village Savings and Credit Associations (VISACA) in The Gambia." In *Financial Markets in The Gambia*. ed., Douglas Graham, R.L. Meyers, and C.E. Cuevas, Report to the USAID Mission, Banjul.

Ousmane, Sembene. [1972] 1987. *The Money Order*. London: Heinemann Educational Books.

Park, Mungo. [1799] 1971. *Travels in the Interior of Africa*. New York: Arno Press.

Péissier, Paul. 1966. *Les Paysans du Sénégal*. Paris: Centre National de Recherche Scientifique.

Pick, Franz, and René Sédillot. 1971. *All the Monies of the World*. New York: Pick Publishing.

Ramamurthy, G. V. 1986. "Agricultural Credit Policy and Structure: The Gambia." Report to the United Nations Food and Agriculture Organization, Technical Cooperation Program.

Robertson, A.F. 1987. *The Dynamics of Productive Relationships: African Share Contracts in Comparative Perspective*. Cambridge: Cambridge University Press.

Shipton, Parker. 1989. *Bitter Money: Cultural Economy and Some African Meanings of Forbidden Commodities*. American Ethnological Society Monograph No. 1. Washington, D.C.: American Anthropological Association.

Shipton, Parker. 1990. "African Famines and Food Security." *Annual Review of Anthropology*, 19:353–94. Palo Alto, CA: Annual Reviews.

Shipton, Parker. 1991. "Time and Money in the Western Sahel: A Clash of Cultures in Gambian Local Rural Finance." In *Markets in Developing Countries: Parallel, Fragmented and Black*, eds. Michael Roemer and Christine Jones, 113–139; 235–44. Washington D.C. and San Francisco: ICS Press.

Shipton, Parker. 1992a. "The Rope and the Box: Group Savings in the Gambia." In *Informal Financial Markets in Developing Countries*, eds. Dale W. Adams and Delbert A. Fitchett, 25–41. Boulder, CO: Westview.

Shipton, Parker. 1992b. "Debts and Trespasses: Land, Mortgages, and the Ancestors in Western Kenya." In *Rights over Land: Categories and Controversies*, eds. M. Goheen and P. Shipton. Special issue of *Africa*, (62) 357–88.

Snyder, Francis G. 1981. *Capitalism and Legal Change: An African Transformation*. New York: Academic Press.

Southorn, Lady Bella. 1952. *The Gambia: The Story of the Groundnut Colony*. London: George Allen and Unwin.

Sumberg, J. 1988. "Notes on Cattle, Sheep and Goats." Report, Department of Animal Health and Production, Ministry of Agriculture, The Gambia.

Sumberg, J. and E. Gilbert. 1988. "Draft Animals and Crop Production in The Gambia." Report, Department of Animal Health and Production, Ministry of Agriculture, The Gambia.

Tamari, Tal. 1991. "The Development of Caste Systems in West Africa." *Journal of African History*, 32:221–50.

Tuck, Laura. 1983. "Formal and Informal Financial Markets in Rural Senegal." Report to the U.S. Agency for International Development.

United Nations Development Program. 1991. *Human Development Report*. Annual. New York: Oxford University Press.

World Bank. 1991. *World Development Report*. Washington, D.C.: The World Bank.

12

The Capitalization of Money and Credit in the Development Process: The Case of Community Banking in Nigeria

Akin L. Mabogunje

At the very onset, it is imperative to state the fundamental hypothesis of this paper. Put simply, it is that if the value attached to money and credit in a given society is not transformed in line with the operations of the prevailing mode of production, to that extent the development process will be impaired and circumscribed. Development in this context is conceptualized as a profound, society-wide wealth-creating process whereby the resources of the given society—land, labor and money—are being transformed into economic assets, "capitalized," so that they can generate still more wealth in an ever-deepening and sustained spiral of growth. In human history, the most dramatic transformation in societal capacity for such mass-oriented wealth creation occurred with the adoption of capitalism as a mode of production by one nation after another around the world. The willingness of these nations to assiduously subject their resources of land, labor, and money to new rules that would enhance their wealth-creating capabilities has been the critical factor in this transformation.

In Nigeria, it is generally assumed that capitalism is the prevailing mode of production. It is, however, also realized that large areas of economic life still operate outside of this mode. Indeed, large proportions of the nation's resources and factors of production, especially land and to some extent labor, are still deeply enmeshed in pre-capitalist social relations. And, although there is an almost full-blown money and credit market in the country, the vast majority of the population has been excluded from the market until recently, with the establishment of community banks in the country.

In the context of the present volume on instability, values, and social payments, the objective of this paper is to assess or evaluate what is entailed in the almost revolutionary development of community banking in Nigeria. It also attempts to offer reasons for the remarkable success of this initiative within the short time period of less than three years. The paper is divided into six parts. The first reviews the pre-colonial and pre-capitalist situation of money and credit in Nigeria. The second examines the incomplete transition to capitalism in the Nigerian development process and its effect on the nation's socio-economic transformation. The third part elaborates on this phenomenon, especially as it has affected credit provision for rural development in the country. The fourth then considers the rise and development of community banks, and the fifth evaluates the prospect of these banks for the capitalization of money and credit in the country. A concluding section assesses the impact of these changes for the overall economic development of the country.

Money and Credit in Pre-colonial Nigeria

In his travel in the mid-nineteenth century across most of what is now northern Nigeria, Heinrich Barth, the German explorer, had occasions to comment on the state of money and credit in the pre-capitalist societies through which he was passing. Arriving in Kukawa, the capital of the Kanembu Empire of Bornu in April, 1851, Barth described what he found in regard to money. It is necessary to quote from him *in extenso* in order to illustrate the general position of money at this time:

> The fatigue which people have to undergo in purchasing their week's necessaries in the market is all the more harassing as there is not at present any standard money for buying and selling; for the ancient standard of the country viz the pound of copper, has long since fallen into disuse, though the name "rotl" still remains. The "gabaga" or cotton strips, which then became usual, have lately begun to be supplanted by the cowries or "kungona" which have been introduced, as it seems, rather by a speculation of the ruling people than by a natural want of the inhabitants, though nobody can deny that they are very useful for buying small articles, and infinitely more convenient than cotton strips. (I shall have occasion to mention what an influence the introduction of cowries into Bornu, by draining the Hausa country of this article, has had upon the demand for cowries in Yoruba and on the coast in the years following 1849). Eight cowries or kungona are reckoned equal to one gabaga, and four gabaga or two-and-thirty kungona, to one rotl. Then, for buying larger objects, there are shirts of all kinds and sizes, from the "dora", the coarsest and smallest one, quite unfit for use, and worth six rotls, up to the large ones, worth 50 or 60 rotls. But while this is a standard value, the relation of the rotl and the Austrian dollar, which is pretty well current in Bornu is subject to extreme fluctuation due, I confess, at least partly, to the speculations of the ruling men, and principally to that

of my friend the Jadj Bashir. Indeed, I cannot defend him against the reproach of having speculated to the great detriment of the public; so that when he had collected a great amount of kungona, and wished to give it currency, the dollar would suddenly fall as low as to five and forty or fifty rotls, while at other times it would fetch as much as one hundred rotls or three thousand, two hundred shells, that is, seven hundred shells more than in Kano. The great advantage of the market in Kano is that there is one standard coin which, if a too large amount of dollars be not on a sudden set in circulation, will always preserve the same value (1965 vol. 2:55).

Four points of interest are indicated clearly in this description of the monetary situation in pre-colonial Nigeria. The first is high instability due to the short life of particular currencies. The pound of copper (the *rotl*) had been supplanted by the cotton strips (the *gabaga*), which, in turn, is in the process of being supplanted by cowries (the *kungona*). Secondly, there is the instability arising from the unwieldy and unstandardized nature of the currencies, which makes them more useful for buying small articles. Thirdly, there is the instability arising from the high susceptibility of the currencies to personal manipulation through speculations by members of the ruling elite. Fourthly, there is the instability arising from external sources of supply for particular currencies as evidenced by the draining of cowries from Hausaland on its introduction to Bornu. It is, however, noteworthy that where the market is relatively large, and cannot be easily influenced by the speculative activities of a few individuals, there is noticeably a certain degree of stability in the value of money.

The same instability was recognized with respect to credit provision. In the typical case, credit is provided through some form of rotating credit associations known variously as *esusu*, *bam*, or *adashi* in different parts of the country. Fadipe describes the *"esusu"* in Yorubaland as a society that:

> has for its purpose the saving of money by members for a fixed period of time—sixteen days to one year. There is usually a given unit of contribution, and a person who is rich enough could double or treble or multiply that unit for his own sixteen-day contribution. The most prevalent form of esusu differs from the slate club in England in that every week there is a share-out day for one or another member. . . . At every week's contribution into the pool by members, someone collects his total for the whole period (1970:256).

Apart from gifts from family members or inheritance, such rotating credit based on the individual's prospective contributions over a given period provided the majority of Nigerians in precolonial days with all the credit they required. Indeed, it was credit secured in the course of social interaction through savings activities. Certain deductions—usually about 4 percent—are always retained by the president and treasurer of the societies both for their services, as well as for providing a feast for members at the end of the life of the *esusu*, that is, at the end of each year. For enhancing the growth of economic activities, this type of credit ran the risk of falling due at the time when other exigent needs may occur and it is the only source of fresh income available. Thus, a person who lost his father or mother would come to depend on his *esusu* to meet the usually substantial funeral expenses. If this event happened at a time when it was not yet his turn to collect, he approaches the President and asks to be allowed to be the next to take his share from the pool. However, as Fadipe again noted, where his request had already been anticipated by one whose claim is equally or even more urgent, he is forced by necessity to "pawn" himself or some other near relative.

"Pawning" or "pledging" is thus the other method by which credit is raised in pre-colonial Nigeria. It involves a relationship with a money-lender. In a pawning transaction, what is pawned is pledged as security for a loan received and, accordingly, has to be kept and used by the lender until the loan is repaid. Such productive or profit-making use of the pawn or the pledged land has the character of interest taking but it is always usurious and often bears no relation to the actual value of the loan. Indeed, Bolnick (1992) suggests that such "interest" charge was strictly a moral obligation associated with proper cultural behaviour. Credit secured under this situation is often for the purpose of paying off debts already contracted or meeting some projected expenditure. The principal causes of debt, according to Fadipe (1970), are personal improvidence and extravagance, performance of funeral rites in one's family, fines imposed by the authorities for real or alleged offences, or obligations to help one's parents out of financial embarrassment occasioned by any of the above causes.

Clearly, the role of money and credit in pre-capitalist Nigerian society was highly circumscribed. In such a society, according to Polanyi (1963:67), the economic system was submerged in general social relations; markets and money were merely accessory features of an institutional setting controlled and regulated more than ever by social authority. Money in this context was no more than a medium of exchange, facilitating in particular the transaction involved in long distance trade. And credit, as is evident from the description above, was seldom for the economic reason of enhancing productive capacity.

The Incomplete Capitalist Transformation In Nigeria

All this was to change with the colonial subjugation of Nigeria from 1861 to 1960. The mission of colonialism in Nigeria as elsewhere in the developing world has been described as one of integrating pre-capitalist economies into the global capitalist system. The pre-capitalist, pre-colonial economies all over the country had been characterized as operating a mode of production based largely on kinship relations. It was kinship that determined access to all factors of production notably land, labor, capital, and entrepreneurship. Kinship relations determined the individual's access to farmland and residential accommodation. It underpinned his access to the labor of himself and his family members. It influenced his associational relations even in the *esusu* society and certainly determined who could be "pawned" or what could be "pledged" in the attempt to secure some credit. More than this, it affected what occupation an individual could engage in and what craft guild he could belong to. In none of these relations could money *qua* money have an effect in determining their availability or use.

Access to factors of production by means of kinship relations came to be posed during the colonial period against access by means of the market and the money nexus. To create this situation effectively entailed the introduction of the process of capitalist transformation. This requires that all factors of production be conceived of as commodities, each with a price tag that allows them to be exchangeable in a market economy that is controlled, regulated, and directed only by the market for them. In such a self-regulating market economy, all production is for sale and all incomes derive from such sales. Accordingly, there are markets not only for goods and services, the output of the production process, but also for land, labor, capital (money), and entrepreneurship, the factors of production. The prices for the latter are usually referred to respectively as rent, wage, interest, and profit.

The act of transforming these factors of production from their web of kinship relations to mere commodities exchangeable in a market is not casual. It requires determined effort by the State. To transform or commoditize land, for instance, requires that it be individualized, allocated into plots, surveyed, and provided with a title, whose deed is then registered by and with the State. This was what happened in Britain during the Enclosure Movement of the late eighteenth and early nineteenth century, which presaged the capitalist transformation of that country. In the same manner, to commoditize labor requires pushing human beings out of their farms and cottages in order to sell their labor for a wage. In colonial Nigeria, this process was precipitated through the establishment of a taxation system that could be paid only in the currency introduced by the colonial State. Individuals thus had the option of either selling the produce of their farms or their own labor through migrating to urban centres where wage employment was to be found. However, to completely commoditize human labor and therefore turn the individuals concerned to a proper proletariat, it is necessary that people have nothing to sell but their labor. In Nigeria, because land has not been fully commoditized, most people still have rights to family lands even when they've moved to the city. As such, their class responses in any conflict with capital are often muted because of the escape from total penury provided by such safety nets.

The commoditization or capitalization of money and credit was, of course, a similar process that required the intervention of the State. This required the creation of a nationally based banking system and a centrally managed currency. The existence of a nationally based banking system enables money to come to perform other functions outside of serving as a medium of exchange associated with its existence in the economy. Money thus becomes a unit of account, a standard of deferred payments and a store of value. Even as a medium of exchange, money becomes a vital factor for two different sets of exchanges taking place in a transformed capitalist economy. These two sets are the exchange of factors of production for rewards (rents, wages, interest, and profits), and the exchange of those money incomes for goods and services (Hoyle and Whitehead 1987:14).

Unlike land and labor, however, money is a factor involved in exchanges not only between individuals within a country but also between countries. As such, it is necessary that nations must not only manage their currencies within their territorial borders through a Central Bank so as to guarantee its stability but must also agree amongst themselves as to how to stabilize the relational values of their currencies, thereby integrating all national economies globally. And as Polanyi (1963:202) observed, the gold standard was introduced in order to remove national currencies from politics and to link domestic trade with that of the world. Although the growth of global economic relations in the first half of the twentieth century forced countries to go off the gold standard and to begin the process of using reserved currencies, the process of commoditizing and capitalizing money had been initiated. Henceforth, national currencies would have exchange value and would be bought and sold as mere commodities in the market. Thus, the existence of a nationally based banking system with a centrally managed currency enables the creation and capitalization of credit on a large scale.

These developments arising from the capitalist transformation of the economies of most European countries were introduced to Nigeria in the course of its colonial subjugation. The British, at the beginning of their colonial adventure in Nigeria, were confronted with a wide variety of currencies. These included the cowry, the brass rod, and the *umumu* (a minute iron arrow) in the Nsukka area of eastern Nigeria, and the manilla, which could not be withdrawn from circulation until 1949. The first known application of legal tender to provide Nigeria with a single currency seems to have been an Order-in-Council and Proclamation of 10th June, 1843, which applied to Her Majesty's Colonies and Possessions in Sierra Leone, the River Gambia, Cape Coast, or elsewhere on the Western Coast of the continent of Africa, and their dependencies (Great Britain 1953:69) A local ordinance of the Colony of Lagos in 1862 made the Dutch 2.5 guilder piece legal tender at 4 shillings, but the Ordinance was found to be invalid owing to constitutional defects, which must have been a constant source of anxiety in those days of the ever changing status of Lagos. A Gold Coast Proclamation of 1875, which applied to Lagos re-enacted the Order-in-Council of 1843 and provided Lagos with varieties of currency at fixed prices. Bronze coins were at a discount and whereas three pennies exchanged for 22.5 "strings" of cowries, a silver 3-penny bit was worth 25 "strings"; cowries were in general use at sixpence a "head" of 2,000 cowries. The total estimated circulation in the colony in 1892 was £120,000 with about one tenth in gold; there was no paper money.

A year later in 1893, at the initiative of the Lagos Office of the shipping Company of Elder Dempster Co. Ltd. and with the support of the colonial government, the Bank of British West Africa (BBWA) was floated (Asabia 1992). This was the first bank in the country and for over thirty years it enjoyed the monopoly of government patronage. In 1899, another bank—the Anglo-Africa Bank, later to be known as Bank of Nigeria from 1905—was set up by a strong group of traders and soon opened branches in Calabar, Burutu, Lokoja, and Jebba. The rivalry between these two banks came to an end in 1911, when the latter was taken over by the former. By then, the whole geographic area had been proclaimed the Colony and Protectorates of Nigeria on 1st January, 1900.

The question of an official currency for the territory was not settled until November, 1912, when the West African Currency Board was established. Its function was "to provide for and control the supply of currency to the British West African Colonies and Protectorates, to ensure that the currency is maintained in satisfactory condition, and generally to watch over the interests of the dependencies in question so far as currency is concerned" (Great Britain 1953:71). The members of the Board were appointed by the Secretary of State for the Colonies. Its headquarters was in London and the Accountant-General of Nigeria was the local Currency Officer. Notes and alloy coins became legal tender for any amount. The currency was interchangeable with sterling at par, subject to remittance charges.

This development of a colonial, territory-wide currency operating in the context of a fledgling banking system, whose stability was guaranteed by the Bank of England began the process of integrating the pre-colonial economy of Nigeria firmly into the global capitalist economy. In the years ahead, more banks were opened, such that by 1992 there were 66 commercial banks in the country with 2,275 branches; 54 merchant banks with 116 branches and 4 other special-purpose and development banks

(Central Bank of Nigeria 1993:154). Up until 1959, the BBWA continued to perform some of the functions customarily reserved for a Central Bank. But in that year, on the eve of Nigeria becoming an independent country, the Central Bank of Nigeria (CBN) was established.

Nonetheless, the mission of the International Bank for Reconstruction and Development (IBRD) (the World Bank), which was invited in 1953 to report on the development prospects of the country described the money situation as follows:

> Since Nigeria's economy is at an early stage of development, with most production in the hands of small peasant farmers, deposit banking plays a very much smaller role that it does in developed economies. Demand deposits are less than half the size of the currency issue. This may be contrasted with the situation in the United Kingdom where demand deposits are nearly three times the size of the note issue. Further, this comparison of deposits with currency overstates the use of banking facilities by the private sector, as nearly half the deposits are made by government or by semi-government organizations. For the private sector, currency outweighs deposits more than three to one, compared to a ratio in India, for example, of less than two to one. Finally, it should be noted that banking is even less significant for the African sector. An overwhelming part of the demand deposits is held by Europeans and European firms. Nigerian commercial interests and individuals, on the other hand, use currency probably 10 times as much as demand deposits (IBRD 1955:152).

The continuation of the practice of treating money simply as exchange goods to be stored in houses as in the nineteenth century ensured that it was not capitalized and used to create credit. It is, of course, a well known fact that the funds put by customers in the banks in the form of current and savings accounts are the real resources that banks have to create credit. The facilities granted by banks to their customers in the form of overdrafts and loans are derived resources and differ from the original deposited deposits. Both types of deposits—initial and created—command the confidence of the public and the banks and are honored any time clients present their claims. Experience in the advanced industrialized countries with well developed banking habits shows that banks can go down to as low as an actual deposit base (cash ratio) of 8 percent for the loans and advances that they give (Aboyade 1983:254). Thus, deposit of money in a bank allows the creation of credit of as much as ten times the original deposit. These possibilities arising from a nationwide system of banking money are what is entailed in the concept of the "capitalization" of money.

Moreover, money put in a bank, whether in savings or current account, is able to earn interest. This is because in a capitalist system, just like transformed land and labor, money is being put out as credit to work for reward in a money market. It has thus been capitalized as have the credit facilities that it then makes abundantly possible. This is why in developed countries, demand deposits are often more than twice the size of the currency in circulation outside the banking system. By contrast, in Nigeria in 1953, demand deposits in commercial banks were only £24.5 million compared to £51.4 million of currency in circulation (IBRD 1955).

Table 12-1 provides some detailed illustration of what is entailed when money and credit become capitalized.

TABLE 12-1   Money Supply (M₁) Situation in Selected Countries

	1960	1970	1980	1985	1990*
NIGERIA	£ (Millions)	£ (Millions)	N (Millions)	N (Millions)	N (Millions)
Currency Outside Banks	79.2	342.3	3,186	4,910	14,941
Private Sector Demand Deposit	39.3	289.0	4,422	6,396	22,293
Domestic Credit to Private Sector	55.4	475.5	6,744	12,844	36,631
SIERRA LEONE	Leone (Millions)	Leone (Millions)	Leone (Millions)	Leone (Mililions)	
Currency Outside Banks	12.5	18.9	86.1	442.1	—
Private Sector Demand Deposit	5.8	9.7	64.7	453.8	—
Domestic Credit to Private Sector	5.5	19.3	90.9	1113.0	—
SOUTH AFRICA	Rand (Millions)	Rand (Millions)	Rand (Millions)	Rand (Millions)	
Currency Outside Banks	217	512	1,861	3,552	—
Private Sector Demand Deposit	656	1,735	6,472	17,689	—
Domestic Credit to Private Sector	989	3,578	16,115	47,217	—
UNITED KINGDOM	£ (Millions)	£ (Millions)	£ (Billion)	£ (Billion)	
Currency Outside Banks	2,081	3,320	10.24	12.73	—
Private Sector Demand Deposit	7,743	6,315	20.81	48.89	—
Domestic Credit to Private Sector	4,535	10,089	56.58	121.44	—
UNITED STATES	$ (Billion)	$ (Billion)	$ (Billion)	$ (Billion)	
Currency Outside Banks	29.5	50.0	118.8	172.1	—
Private Sector Demand Deposit	114.5	175.5	295.7	407.0	—
Domestic Credit to Private Sector	120.2	306.7	1,745.1	3,3481.8	—

Sources: International Monetary Fund, *International Financial Statistics,* Washington D.C. (1965–1988)
* Central Bank of Nigeria, *Annual Report and Statement of Accounts,* 1992, Lagos, 1993:23

It shows the pattern between developing countries (represented by Nigeria and Sierra Leone) and developed countries (South Africa, United Kingdom, and the United States) in the relation between the three variables of currency outside the banking sector, private sector demand deposits in banks, and domestic credit by banks to the private sector. The pattern in Nigeria between 1960 and 1990 shows that until the 1970s (specifically after the oil boom of 1973), currency in circulation was still, as in 1953, greater than demand deposits in the banks. The situation changed around 1975, but even in 1990 it still represented as much as 40 percent (Sierra Leone 49 percent in 1985) of money supply. Compare this with South Africa (17 percent), the United Kingdom (21 percent), and the United States (30 percent). The situation is even more revealing in respect of the relation between the ratio of currency in circulation to demand deposit and the size of domestic credit to the private sector. The trend illustrated in the table is that the lower this ratio (i.e., more money is in demand deposits in banks) the greater the amount of credit provided to the private sector.

One result then of the high ratio in Nigeria (that is, a relatively high proportion of money still being kept as currency in circulation outside of the banks) is that most economic actors continue to depend for their credit needs on some form of rotating credit society or the other. The unregenerated nature of this system and its pre-capitalist orientation are perhaps best underscored by the fact that in most cases no interest rate concept is entertained. Thus, in a twelve-month cycle, the first person who collects from the pool in January takes home the same amount as the last person who collects in December. The fact that if the former was clever and immediately saved his money in a bank for a year, he would come away in December with an amount greater than that of his compeer collecting that month hardly ever enters the calculation. In some of the societies, the contributors have to pay to the coordinator a certain percentage of their total contribution, thereby earning in effect a negative interest.

Inadequate Credit Provision and Rural Underdevelopment

The persistence of the traditional methods of credit provision for most producers in Nigeria even after the introduction of a national currency and the banking system was not unconnected with the mode of operations of the banks once they had been established. Indeed, as the IBRD report (1955) indicated, the business of the European banks for most of the period of their dominance had been to provide services rather than to extend credit. The greater part of their income derived from service charges in connection with the international trade of European trading companies as well as their relations with the government. Most of the banks played virtually no part in developing local African entrepreneurship on the grounds that the business experience and sense of responsibility of the Nigerian community at large were not of an acceptable level. Consequently, the task of providing credit to African enterprises and of educating African businessmen to attain higher standards of experience and responsibility fell on African banks and governmental lending institutions.

The first of these African banks—the National Bank of Nigeria—was established in 1933. Its success soon led to the establishment of another Nigerian bank—the African Continental Bank in 1947. The Co-operative Bank of Western Nigeria was established in 1953. By Independence in 1960, the number of commercial banks in the country had increased to 7. By 1970, the number had doubled to 14 with 297 branches throughout the country (Asabia 1992:5). The number had again doubled by 1986, when the country had 29 banks with 1,313 branches. This remarkable growth in the number of bank branches was largely the result of the "Rural Banking Programme" instituted by the CBN in 1977. Nonetheless as Asabia (1992:6) rightly observed, "mere increases in the number of bank branches is not a conclusive measure of the success or otherwise of the rural Banking scheme." Thus, even with this remarkable growth in branch banking, only 389 of the 1,313 branches were to be found in the rural areas. At any rate, by 1992, the number of banks in the country (excluding community banks) had risen to 120, of which 66 were commercial and 54 merchant banks (CBN 1993:153). Between them, the number of their branches rose to 2,391.

Despite these remarkable developments in the number of banking institutions, the CBN could still emphasize that its ability to manage the excess liquidity in the economy was impaired because "the non-bank sector still controlled a big chunk of the economy's liquidity" (1993:148). This persistence of a significant proportion of the nation's money and credit outside of the banking system is due in no small measure to the fact that although most of the banks are now wholly or partially owned by Nigerians, they operate on the basis of a capitalist mode of production, which the Nigerian economy was still far from being.

This incompleteness in transformation is perhaps best appreciated in the context of the provision of bank credit to farmers. Here, as Oluwasanmi and Alao (1965) rightly observed, "commercial systems of tenure in which right of ownership are shared between the individual and the community present commercial banks in tropical Africa with formidable difficulties in accepting land as security for loans." The fact that land is a non-negotiable property in most tropical African countries precludes the development of mortgage financing of long-term farm investment either by banks and other lending institutions or by state-supported credit agencies. The 1951 study of 370 cocoa families to which reference has already been made showed that only 5.3% of the outstanding loans were secured by mortgages or pledges of land as compared with 78.6% of the loans being made on personal security (Galletti, Baldwin, and Dina 1956:535).

The failure to engage in land reform that would enable farmers to capitalize their land thus has implications for their ability to "capitalize" the money in their possession. If the banks and similar financial institutions will not assist them with their credit needs because of their inability to provide a negotiable collateral, the necessity to put their money in such institutions hardly exists. They can continue to keep their money out of the banking system as long as they depend for their credit needs on traditional and informal systems of funds mobilization.

Over the years, therefore, government has tried various means of facing up to this challenge. The Post Office Savings Banks Scheme begun in 1908 was one of the earliest. By 1953, the scheme could boast of 197,656 accounts at 162 Post Offices and a savings mobilization of some £4.06 million. This amount, it must be noted, was considerably in excess of the savings deposits held by commercial banks at this time. However, as the World Bank Mission observed, "the present arrangements for the investment of funds fail to achieve one of the most important aims of savings institutions in underdeveloped countries: the mobilization of capital for domestic use. At the moment the savings are entirely invested outside Nigeria" (IBRD 1955:162). The Post Office Savings Bank Scheme continued until 1972, when it was reconstituted into the Federal Savings Bank. The latter was transformed into the FSB International Bank Limited in 1988. Throughout its existence, however, the Post Office Savings Scheme had, at best, only a marginal effect on the provision of credit in rural areas.

Five other schemes of government were initiated to address these problems of credit provision to the rural populace and small-scale producers in the country. These are: the formation of cooperative societies and the establishment of Co-operative Banks, the Nigeria Local Development Board and its regional successors, the Nigerian Agricultural and Co-operative Bank (NACB) and the obligatory rural banking scheme. Co-operative societies as well as thrift and loan societies began to be formed in the country in the wake of the expansion of export crop production in the 1930s. By 1939, there were 130 such societies in the country, a figure that had jumped to 1,336 by 1953 (IBRD 1955:291). In the later year, the co-operative movement in Western Nigeria felt strong enough to start the Co-operative Bank of Western Nigeria, financed by a grant of £1 million from the reserve of the Cocoa Marketing Board. Later a Co-operative and Commerce Bank of Eastern Nigeria was set up in 1962. In the 1970s, Kaduna, Kano and Sokoto States created their own Co-operative Banks.

The Nigeria Local Development Board was set up in 1946 to provide special credit facilities for small-scale farmers and businessmen on a nationwide basis. The Board was abolished in 1949 and three Regional Development Boards were created in its place. In 1955, the Regional Development Boards were in turn dissolved. In Northern and Eastern Nigeria, their functions were merged with those of the respective Regional Development Corporation, whilst in Western Nigeria a new organization—the Western Region Finance Corporation—was set up to provide agricultural and industrial loans. In spite of their much-heralded establishment, these various institutions responded only marginally to the credit needs of small-scale producers in the country. In the case of the Western Region Finance Corporation, for instance, it was estimated that up to the excision of the Mid-Western Region in 1963 only 4 percent of farmers in Western Nigeria benefited from its loan facilities (Oluwasanmi and Alao 1965:42).

The creation of a new Federal structure of twelve states in 1967 undermined the continued viability of these various regional institutions. It led the Federal Government to establish the NACB in 1973. The functions of the bank, among others, are to grant direct loans to individual farmers, co-operative societies, and other bodies. Although this bank has shown some creditable results with regard to credit provision to co-operative societies and medium to large-scale individual farmers, its performance with respect to small-scale producers has not been remarkable. Consequently, in order to further expand the access to credit for such producers throughout the country, the government initiated the mandatory rural bank branching scheme for commercial banks in 1977. As of 1991, the number of such rural bank branches stood at 774 (CBN 1993:151).

Despite this expansion in the number of rural banking facilities, the access of the small-scale producers to credit remained constrained because of the problem with collateral. To confront this problem head on, the federal government through the CBN introduced in 1978 the Agricultural Credit Guarantee Scheme. This was to reassure commercial banks of the determination of government to underwrite as much as 75 percent of defaulted loans made to farmers and small producers who borrowed no more than N5,000.00. As of 1992, the cumulative number and value of loans guaranteed under this scheme, stood at N165,446 and N935.6 million, respectively. It was noted, however, that the volume of loans under the scheme peaked in 1989 and has continued to decline since then (CBN 1993:156). The decline was attributed to the increasing reluctance of banks to give any more of such guaranteed credit due to the high rate of default. Some banks abstained from extending any more credit to areas where less than 75% of previous loans had been settled. Others slowed down their activities because of the credit squeeze on banks by the monetary authorities, the high rates and the lack of collateral that prevented farmers from requesting large sums of money to justify the transaction costs of lending.

The Rise And Growth Of Community Banking In Nigeria

This then was the situation in 1986 when Nigeria had to confront various distortions in its economic operations that required the drastic adoption of a structural adjustment program. One major area of distortion has been the neglect of the rural areas, resulting in a sharp decline in agricultural production and a heavy dependence on food imports. To correct these distortions, the federal government not only banned the continued importation of various food items that the country could produce itself, notably maize, rice, wheat, and cooking oil, but also set up a Directorate of Food, Roads, and Rural Infrastructures in the Presidency to begin the long-term program of rural rehabilitation and development. The Directorate had three broad mandates. These were: first, to mobilize rural communities for their own development; secondly, to provide them with necessary infrastructure of roads, water, and electricity; and thirdly, to promote their productive activities.

It was relatively easy for the Directorate to record significant achievements in respect of the first two of its mandates. When, however, it came to the task of promoting the productive activities of rural dwellers, things floundered on the ground that it was not easy to secure credit for the thousands of small-scale farmers on whom the whole program depended. It was in this circumstance that it became necessary to return as it were to the drawing board. The critical question was twofold: first, how can funds be mobilized to provide credit for a large number of small producers? Second, how can, in the context of a largely pre-capitalist social relations of production, it be ensured that the credit provided will be repaid promptly so as to make the process sustainable over time?

Three facts were clearly patent. The first was that most communities in Nigeria had a long tradition of helping themselves through community development associations (CDA) called by such names as Town Unions, Improvement League, Progressive Associations, and so on. Over the years, these CDA have built up a track record of mobilizing funds to provide their communities with schools, health centers, post offices, roads, water supply systems, electricity systems, churches, mosques, and so on. These CDA also exercised a veritable power of sanction to ensure that their members played their part individually in contributing to the fund and ensuring accountability on the part of those who had to see to the execution of community projects (Little 1965). The common denominator of these community projects, however, was that they were all essentially infrastructural in character. Communities have not designed any institution in the modern context to help effectively with their productive activities. The second fact was the widespread tradition of savings and the use of rotating savings and credit institutions called by such names as *esusu, bam,* and *adashi* in different parts of the country. Most communities in Nigeria do applaud thriftiness and putting away of some money against the rainy days.

The third fact was that, given the inability of conventional commercial banks to provide needed credit to the rural majority, a sizeable proportion of money supply remained outside of the banking sector. It is common knowledge that most rural Nigerians keep their money and their savings in such places as under their pillows, under their mattresses, in gourds kept in the ceiling, and sometimes buried in the ground. Such money kept out of the banking system is money not capitalized and allowed to yield as much credit as possible. And as already pointed out in Table 12-1, inadequate use of the banking system by a vast majority of Nigerians had meant a serious limitation in the relative size of demand deposits and in the capacity of the banking system to create credit.

To transform the situation dramatically, a proposal to establish community banks was presented to and accepted by the Federal Government of Nigeria in October, 1989. In his budget speech on January 1, 1990, President Babangida announced that the country was to embark on a novel system of community banking. A community bank is defined as "a self-sustaining financial institution, owned and managed by a community, for the purpose of providing credit, banking and other financial services to its members, largely on the basis of their self-recognition and credit-worthiness" (National Board of Communitay Banks [NBCB] 1992:11). The bank is meant to be a "unit" bank, having no branches and serving only a community, whether in the rural or urban area. Its primary promoter is the community development association, but other shareholders include local trade associations, social clubs, age classes, and corporate bodies, as well as sons and daughters of the community at home and abroad and long-term residents. The latter group of shareholders, however, cannot own individually more than 5 percent of the share capital of each community bank. Shareholding is to be broad-based, with no fewer than fifty individual shareholders. They must represent a wide cross-section of the community and recognize the paramount role of the CDA. The chairman of the association is expected to be one of the seven directors of the bank. The emphasis on community ownership is to ensure that the power of sanction of the community can be invoked to deal with defaulting members who fail to pay back loans and to keep board members in line.

Government itself, apart from designing the new institution, keeps patently out of being seen as owning any share in the bank. It, however, reduced the minimum share capital for a community bank drastically to as low as N250,000.00, compared to N50 million for conventional commercial banks. This figure is net of the banking infrastructure (safes, ultra-violet lights, deed boxes, office furniture, building and banking hall equipment), which the community is expected to find ways of acquiring through donations from their members. The minimum capital of N250,000.00 is in truth only the start-off working capital for the bank. Hence, when the accounts of community banks are audited at the end of each year, their asset value invariably jumps to over N1 million. Consequently, in recent times, most community banks are applying to raise their share capital to at least N5 million.

Government supports the community bank initiative in at least three ways. First, it offers each bank a matching loan of up to a maximum of N500,000.00, after such a bank has demonstrated its capacity to operate effectively for at least three months on its own. This matching loan is offered at a concessionary interest rate. The loan must be paid back within a five-year period and until this is done, no dividend can be declared by the bank. Secondly, government provides training for community bank staff on a continuing basis and at little or no costs to the banks. Thirdly, government seeks to enhance the activities of the banks through helping communities to promote local economic development. The agency of government that sees to all of this is the NBCB. This Board not only promotes and appraises prospective community banks, but also grants them provisional licenses to begin operation. It monitors and generally supervises their activities to ensure that they operate strictly within the law that sets them up.

In respect to the issues of the capitalization of money and credit, the primary function of a community bank is to increasingly mobilize savings and deposits from that large section of the population that, until now, had tended to operate outside of the banking sector. Its other function is to mobilize all economic actors within its catchment area into occupational associations in order to provide a reference group for determining who could be given loans at minimum risks. Consequently, the saying goes that "in community banking, mobilization is the name of the game."

The first community bank was commissioned on 31st December, 1990. Six months later in June, 1991, only 9 other community banks had been opened. By December 1991, the number had jumped to 98. By June of the following year it was 156; by December, 1992 the number had risen to 402 and by June, 1993, it was 645. Community banks are now to be found in all states of the Federation, including the Federal Capital Territory. Some 70 percent of them are located in the rural areas. Most metropolitan centers have a sizeable number, ministering to the needs of the informal sector operators, who have no access to the conventional commercial banks.

The Capitalization of Money and Credit

The rapidly expanding spread of community banks to all parts of the country has been a most potent factor in the increasing capitalization of money and credit in the Nigerian economy. Table 12-2 shows the remarkable speed with which these banks have drawn money into the banking sector from the traditionally non-banking rural areas and a large segment of the urban informal sector.

TABLE 12-2   Mobilization of Deposits by Community Banks, 1991–93 (Millions of *Naira*)

	DEC 1991	MAR 1992	JUNE 1992	SEPT 1992	DEC 1992	MARCH 1993
Number of Community Banks	98	129	156	203	402	510
Number Reporting	87	101	146	180	334	376
Total Assets	140.4	204.4	398.0	616.0	981.2	1,404.1
Loans and Advances	25.6	30.6	60.2	117.7	149.8	266.6
Demand Deposits	31.5	43.7	82.9	114.3	208.0	257.6
Savings Deposits	41.5	66.6	118.4	203.0	304.2	475.7
Time Deposits	17.5	27.0	57.2	89.0	127.5	196.6
Total Deposits	90.5	137.3	258.5	406.3	639.7	929.9

Source: NBCB Quarterly Reports

By December, 1991, some N90 million had been mobilized by 87 reporting community banks, with demand deposits accounting for 35 percent of the total. A year later, the total deposits mobilized by 334 reporting community banks had jumped to N640 million, that is, more than a 700 percent increase. Of this amount, demand deposits accounted for a declining 33 percent. Three months later, total deposits had again jumped to N930 million for 376 reporting banks, whilst the proportion of demand deposits had dropped further to 28 percent.

It is, of course, unclear as yet what proportion of these deposits represents mere transfer of funds from existing banking institutions. There is no doubt that in the present euphoria of communities feeling a strong proprietary interest in owning their own banks, a good number of the enlightened sons and daughters of the community who already have accounts with commercial banks did transfer some money to their community banks. But, by far, a substantial part of the deposits of these banks are those of first-time depositors—farmers, market women, traders, artisans of all types, small industrialists, and so on. At any rate, the NBCB has recently commissioned a study to help establish, among other things, what proportion of the deposits of community banks is made of new deposits and what proportion is simply transfers.

Not unexpectedly, the existence of this growing volume of deposits in community banks, which can operate on the basis of character lending, has made dramatic difference to the access of small producers to credit. Again, Table 12-2 shows that in the period from December, 1991, to March, 1993, the amount of loans and advances given by community banks rose from N26 million to N267 million. In the latter month, agricultural pursuits accounted for N45.3 million (or 17 percent), food processing for N43.3 million (or 16.2 percent) whilst commerce accounted for N86.6 million (or 32.4 percent). This should be compared with the total sanctions for the small holder loan scheme by the NACB, which in 1990 stood at N84.5 million and involved 26,395 beneficiaries. These figures represent 16.4 percent and 85.9 percent of the total value and number of loans, respectively, disbursed by the bank in that year (NACB 1991). By the same token, the total number of loans to small-scale farmers in 1992 guaranteed under the Agricultural Credit Guarantee Scheme was 20,185 and amounted only to N62.2 million (CBN 1993:156). In short, within the very limited period of its existence, community banks are already making a significant difference in credit provision to a large number of small-scale producers whether in farming, trading, transportation, or craft activities.

One of the important features of credit provision in this context is, of course, the fact that a price (interest rate) is paid for the use of money. The interest rates charged by Community Banks are in the same range as those by commercial banks. Because of the present inflationary situation, these vary from 26 to 36 percent. What has indeed become clear is that for most small-scale producers, access or timeliness rather than the rate of interest charged is of greater consequence. As the chairman of the butchers' association who is a board member of one of the community banks noted, a 3 percent per month interest on a loan to buy an additional cow to slaughter is nothing compared with twice the price that they often had to pay to cow-dealers when they buy on credit. On the other hand, interests paid by community banks on savings and time deposits are lower, but are sufficiently attractive to entice operators of rotating credit associations to start depositing with community banks. Some community banks in turn have devised schemes to directly involve small savers, especially market women, in a revised form of self-imposed, small unit compulsory savings.

Community banks, by the law setting them up, cannot engage in any foreign-exchange transactions. They do, however, operate checking accounts and to that extent need correspondent banks, from among the list of conventional banks, for the purpose of clearing these checks. Considerable difficulties have arisen in the relations between community banks and their correspondent banks especially, on the issue of check clearance and commission on turnover. These difficulties are, no doubt, partly a result of the competitive pressure being felt by commercial banks. Consequently, a proposal to have a second-tier community bank that can perform such services as check clearance, syndicated loans, and so on for community banks is now before the Central Bank. Such a bank would not be open to the public, but would serve only community banks and will certainly reduce their dependency status, making them a more vigorous agency for economic development.

Community banks are already finding themselves cast in the role of promotional agencies for local economic development. In most rural and semi-urban areas, while there is a strong tradition of savings, which is not being channelled into bank deposits, there is equally a lingering tendency or attitude that regards borrowing, even for business purposes, in a somewhat negative light. The fact that credit is the oil that keeps the wheel of production turning smoothly on a sustained basis is barely recognized in such traditional setting. One of the tasks of community banks, working with and through the CDA, thus has been that of public enlightenment as to the use of credit. A good number of them often have had to hold sessions with their people to distinguish between credit provision for enterprise development and borrowing for consumption, immediate gratification, or social nonincome-yielding purposes. Other community banks invite members of different trade or occupational associations in the community to what are called "customers' forums," during which questions are allowed to be asked and answered and new depositors enrolled.

The situation with regard to deposit mobilisation has matured sufficiently for the Nigeria Deposit Insurance Corporation (NDIC) to indicate its willingness to insure deposits in community banks. The high rate of repayment of loans, which in most banks is well over 90 percent has reassured the NDIC as to the relatively lower than anticipated riskiness of deposits in community banks. Equally important has been the growing appreciation of the effectiveness of community sanctions on the behavior of both the borrowers and the management of the banks. The emphasis thus is increasingly to improve the professional training of the management and staff of community banks. The NDIC has offered to insure the funds of depositors in community banks at an annual premium of 0.568 of 1 percent of total deposits, although it will be willing to pay back depositors only up to a maximum of N30,000.00 (thirty thousand naira only) in case of bank failure, compared to N50,000.00 (fifty thousand naira only) for conventional commercial banks.

Conclusion

Clearly, as more and more money enters into the banking sector with the rise of community banking in Nigeria, there can be no doubt that increasingly money and credit are being capitalized. Money is serving not just as a medium of exchange, a unit of account and a store of value, but also as an asset critical for the creation of credit in the economy. In the same manner, credit provision is now increasingly seen in the economy as a way of making money work such that it can earn an income or interest. This is strikingly different from the strategy of credit provision in traditional systems such as *esusu* or *adaski* or other forms of rotating credit, which derive from the essentially pre-capitalist base of much of the present-day Nigerian economy.

The transformation of this pre-capitalist base and the completion of the transition to a full and mature capitalist economy remains the fundamental challenge of economic reform and policy development in Nigeria. It has already been emphasized that the colonial era succeeded mainly in achieving the capitalization of human labor. The process turned an increasingly large proportion of the population from self-employed, subsistence farmers, artisans, craftsmen and traders into wage and salaried earners who were willing to sell their labor on the labor market, as well as entrepreneurs anxious to earn profit from taking risks in starting new enterprises. In all of this, the point was made that it was the determined intervention of the state through, among other things, the institution of a general system of taxation and public education that made this transformation possible. In the same manner, it was such determined intervention of the State through, among other things, the institution of a nationwide system of community banking at the grassroots level that is bringing an increasing proportion of money supply into the banking system and thereby increasing the capital value of money and credit in the economy.

This process of capitalization is, however, going to be efficacious only as long as community sentiments remain strong enough both to provide the incentive for behaving in an appropriate manner and to ensure effective sanctions against financial misdemeanor and improprieties. The experience throughout the world, however, shows that the deepening of capitalist relations of production in any society tends to weaken the efficacy of communal or kinship relations. In its stead, emphasis shifts to those social relations based on property rights, contractual obligations, and the money nexus.

It is thus clear that the sanction base of community banking would need to shift progressively from peer pressure to more concrete penalty involving the forfeiture of collateral security provided at the point of consummating a loan agreement. Collateral security for the vast majority of Nigerians, particularly in the rural areas, remains unattainable as long as their land resources remain uncapitalized and embedded in the thrall of pre-capitalist kinship relations. Again, although the idea of land individualization and land sales is not unknown to people in rural areas, unless the State engages in a determined land reform, with emphasis on the provision and registration of individual titles to land, the capitalization of land will not take place. This would mean that even community banks would not be able to follow up on their present success and lend larger tranches of loan to customers. Community sanctions can be depended on to encourage repayment when the amount borrowed is relatively small. As the amount increases in size, it would be unrealistic for the banks not to insist on more concrete security, which they can dispose of to recoup part or all of the amount outstanding in the case of default.

The capitalization of money and credit must thus be seen as a process of further undermining the pre-capitalist foundation of the present Nigerian economy and making the Nigerian society better disposed to completing the transition to a full-fledged capitalist economy. The individualization of land with proper title duly registered by the State as well as the emergence of an efficient land market is thus a *sine qua non* for raising the level of loans community banks can offer their customers. Such a development would have the additional consequence of further deepening the process of capitalizing money and credit in the economy.

Over the next few years, the prognosis is that the number of community banks in Nigeria will increase even more rapidly and the majority of communities throughout the country would have come to own and manage their own community banks. A vastly increased proportion of money supply would have been attracted into the banking sector. More and more, money and credit would have been capitalized and monetary policies in the country would have become more robust in their efficacy. The safety and soundness of the banking sector of the economy, however, would have become a problem of really serious dimension. Improved management capability can minimize the intensity and catastrophic proportions of this problem. Only a determined effort by government to complete the transition of the economy to full capitalist status can avert the crisis and put the Nigerian economy firmly on the path to a sound and self-sustaining growth. The expectation then is that the present process of increasingly capitalizing money and credit will be seen clearly for what it is. This is that the Nigerian economy is at the threshold of a more dramatic transformation, which involves nothing less than the total and final transition to a full-blown and mature capitalist economy.

Sources

Aboyade, O. 1983. *Integrated Economics: A Study of Developing Economies.* London and Reading, Mass.: Addison-Wesley.

Asabia, S. O. 1992. *Essay in Money and Banking.* Ibadan: Fountain Publications.

Barth, Heinrich 1965. *Travels and Discoveries in North and Central Africa , Being a Journal of an Expedition Undertaken under the Auspices of H. B. M.'s Government in the Years 1849-1855,* 3 vols. London: Frank Cass and Co.

Bolnick, B. R. 1992. "Moneylenders and Informal Financial Markets in Malawi." *World Development,* 201:57–68.

Central Bank of Nigeria. 1993. *Annual Report and Statement of Accounts for the Year Ended 31st December, 1992.* Lagos: Author.

Great Britain. 1953. *The Nigeria Handbook.* Lagos: Government Printer.

Fadipe, N. A. 1970. *The Sociology of the Yoruba,* ed. F. O. Okediji and O. O. Okediji. Ibadan: Ibadan University Press.

Galletti, R., Baldwin, K. D. S. and I. O. Dina. 1956. *Nigerian Cocoa Farmers.* London: Oxford University Press.

Hoyle, Julia and Geoffrey Whitehead. 1987. *Elements of Banking.* London: Heinemann.

International Bank for Reconstruction and Development. 1955. *The Economic Development of Nigeria.* Baltimore, MD: Johns Hopkins Press.

Little, Kenneth 1965. *West African Urbanization: A Study of Voluntary Associations in Social Change.* Cambridge and New York: Cambridge University Press.

National Board for Community Banks. 1992. *The Community Banking System in Nigeria: An Introduction.* Abuja: NBCB.

———. 1992–1993. *Quarterly Report.* Abuja: Author.

Nigerian Agricultural and Cooperative Bank Ltd. 1991. *Annual Report and Accounts 1990.* Lagos: NACB.

Oluwasanmi, H. A. and J. A. Alao. 1965. "The Role of Credit in the Transformation of Traditional Agriculture: The Nigerian Experience." *The Nigerian Journal of Economic and Social Studies,* 71:31–50.

Polanyi, Karl. 1963. *The Great Transformation: The Political and Economic Origins of Our Time.* Boston, MA: Beacon Press.

EPILOGUE

13

Stable Prices, Unstable Values: Some Thoughts on Monetization and the Meaning of Transactions in West African Economies

SARA S. BERRY

The chapters in this volume provide a wealth of evidence on changing forms of currency, patterns of circulation, and strategies of monetary control in West Africa which raise intriguing questions about the role played by monetization in the economic and social history of the region. As several of the authors remind us, West Africans have used money for a very long time.[1] Nonetheless, the monetization of West African economies accelerated and intensified in the nineteenth and twentieth centuries, both as a result of increased commercial activity (G. Dupré, Ch. 3; Law, Ch. 2) and as colonial governments sought to establish single, specialized currencies in place of the multiple and multi-purpose currencies that circulated in pre-colonial times (Arhin, Ch. 4; Ekejiuba, Ch. 6).

In the introduction to this volume, Guyer poses a number of questions about the ways in which changing patterns of monetary circulation and control affected processes of valuation in West African economies and societies, particularly in the colonial and post-colonial periods. She points out that both currencies and the political and economic conditions underlying their use not only have undergone long-term transformations, but also have been subject to persistent short-term instability. Fluctuations in prices, incomes, patterns of trade and production, and the social and political conditions in which they occur are as important a part of regional history as the spread of commercialization and the creation of colonial/national states, and must be taken into account in any analysis of the long-term consequences of monetization.

Monetary and economic instability has arisen from multiple sources, as Guyer explains. The progressive incorporation of West African economies into global markets has meant that both states and ordinary people have become increasingly vulnerable to fluctuations in global market conditions. It has also subjected West African economies to the interests of powerful outsiders, whose pursuit of profit and/or market control has sometimes helped to destabilize the conditions under which West Africans work, trade, and invest. But economic instability has not only been imposed on Africa by global markets and powerful foreign interests, but has also arisen as an often "unintended consequence" of multifaceted struggles over wealth and influence "at the interface" of local interactions among Africans as well as between them and outsiders.

In this essay I would like to explore a bit further some of the sources of instability that have arisen through the encounters of local economies and societies in West Africa with global markets, colonial rule, and post-colonial states, and consider their implications for processes of valuation. After briefly reviewing some of the basic ideas about monetization and economic development embedded in neoclassical and marxist theories, I will suggest that West African economic history in the twentieth century bears out these arguments only in part. Drawing on the papers in this volume and my own recent work on aspects of African agrarian history, I will argue that during the twentieth century, West Africa has experienced not only accelerated commercialization and accompanying instabilities in prices and money supplies, but also a destabilization of the social and institutional processes through which claims on goods and services are defined and legitimated. In other words, at the same time that money was changing hands with increasing frequency and in an expanding range of transactions, the question of what was being transacted was becoming increasingly contentious and ambiguous. In the following pages, I will elaborate the historical basis of this argument and consider what it might mean for understanding the relationship between instability and values in West African economic history.

Theories of Monetization: Some Unresolved Questions

In both neoclassical and marxist theory, monetization is assumed to act as a catalyst to economic growth and structural change. By permitting (or compelling) people to participate in supra-local circuits of exchange, monetization promotes specialization and exchange and, hence, economic growth. At the same time, the depersonalization of exchange made possible by the use of money also opens the door to the sale of land and labor, giving rise to new forms of dispossession and exploitation. Marxists argue that commoditization and the alienation of labor lead to class conflict and social upheaval as well as to capitalist accumulation. Neoclassical theorists are less concerned with the disruptive consequences of monetization, stressing its positive effects on the efficiency of resource allocation and possibilities of economic growth over the potentially negative ones of rising inequality and potential instability. Nonetheless, in both theoretical traditions, monetization is portrayed as both progressive, in the sense that it promotes specialization, exchange, and accumulation, and also potentially disruptive.

In both theoretical traditions, arguments about the effects of monetization on economic growth and stability rest on somewhat contradictory assumptions about the implications of monetization for the determination of value. In marxist theory, money is viewed as both transformative and epiphenomenal. On the one hand, money is essential for commoditization and, hence, for capitalist accumulation. But marxists also insist that exchange is superficial: the laws of motion of capitalist development spring from material processes of production, not from exchange. This contradiction underlies a central debate in marxist economics over the determination of value. If value springs only from labor, then the form of circulation is irrelevant. But if commoditization is a necessary condition for capitalist accumulation, then capitalist values are determined, in part, by circulation.[2]

Similarly, neoclassical analysis of the historical effects of commercialization in economic development rests on a contradictory view of the social foundations of market-based economic growth. Monetization widens the market, by facilitating exchange between people who do not meet face to face, thereby enabling processes of specialization and exchange to transcend cultural and social boundaries. But money functions—as a medium of exchange, store of value, or unit of account—only insofar as it is accepted by potential transactors. Thus, in neoclassical theory, monetization both creates new spheres of social interaction, and pre-supposes them. Neoclassical economists recognize that values are determined, in part, by cultural factors but, by treating culture as exogenous to the central "economic" processes of resource allocation and distribution of output and wealth, they remain deliberately agnostic about how culture and economy interact over time.

Monetization and the Development of Capitalism in West Africa: An Unfinished Story

As several of the papers in this volume remind us, currencies, such as iron rods, gold dust, cowries, and cloth circulated in West Africa long before the nineteenth century, although their use was often restricted to certain types of transactions or specific groups of people. Control over currency supplies and rates of exchange served as an important mechanism for exercising control over people (Guyer, Introduction). Before the commercial revolution of the late nineteenth century, Teke chiefs, priests, and elders controlled the production and circulation of raffia cloth, which served both as a key item in payments of bridewealth and other prestations, and as a medium of exchange (M.-C. Dupré, Ch. 1). In Asante, the state prohibited exchanges of cowries for gold, not only to protect internal markets and regulate the money supply, but also to retain control over the ultimate symbol of state power (Arhin, Ch. 4). Throughout the region, the dynamic complexities of pre-colonial political history were manifested in, inter alia, the "apparent profound propensity for currencies to proliferate." (Guyer, Introduction: 22).

The existence of multiple currencies also provided opportunities for foreign merchants, as well as local traders and chiefs, to profit from arbitrage and manipulation of exchange rates. Law (Ch. 2) notes that rulers' inability to control the import of cowries was a source of weakness in the monetary systems of Yorubaland and Dahomey, and argues that cowry "inflation may have contributed to the impoverishment of the Dahomian monarchy" in the late nineteenth century. In southern

Nigeria, European trading firms actually resisted the introduction of standardized currencies during the early years of colonial rule (Ofonagoro 1979; Niger Company papers) and African traders, such as the Aro, who adopted British currency at an early date, derived substantial profits from arbitrage (Ekejiuba, Ch. 6). Guyer (Introduction) also suggests that the multiplicity of currencies may have exerted a stabilizing influence on stores of wealth and conditions of exchange. The possibility of diversifying their monetary portfolios doubtless enabled many West Africans to cushion the impact of sudden changes in supplies of currencies or rates of exchange—-though it did not shield them from fundamental shifts in patterns of trade, such as the dramatic intensification of commercial activity in the latter half of the nineteenth century (M.-C. Dupré, Ch. 1; Law, Ch. 2; Arhin, Ch. 4).

Beginning in the nineteenth century, the pace and intensity of commercial activity increased throughout the region, and money was used by more people, more often, in a wider range of transactions. Taxes, labor, and other services, as well as agricultural and manufactured products increasingly were paid for in money—in transactions among Africans as well as between Africans and Europeans. The monetization of everyday life operated at all socio-economic levels. In Asante, for example, the growth of money payments for access to land and labor was paralleled by the monetization of a wide range of social transactions, from marriage payments and funeral ceremonies to service obligations to the Asantehene's court (Arhin, Ch. 4) Guyer, Ekejiuba and Falola also describe the increasing monetization of social payments in Cameroon and Nigeria, and Mikell traces "the transformation of uxorial duties of women from a domestic obligation to a good possesing monetary value" in Brong-Ahafo (Ch. 10:225).

As Europeans imposed colonial rule throughout the region, they sought to encourage commerce, mobilize resources (revenues, provisions and labor) for their own use, and also took steps to promote (or enforce) the use of single, standardized currencies within the territories under their control (Hopkins 1973; Falola, Ch.7; Arhin, Ch. 4). Colonial regimes also promoted the use of specialized currencies—-i.e., those which have no alternative uses in the economies in which they circulate as money—-in place of such pre-colonial currencies as cloth or metal rods, which were objects as well as instruments of exchange (M.-C. Dupré, Ch. 1; Guyer, Ch. 5; Ekejiuba, Ch. 6). Their efforts met with varying degrees of success. In Cameroon, European currencies replaced pre-colonial *bikie* in marriage payments quite quickly whereas, in eastern Nigeria, manillas were still in circulation in the late 1940s. By the time of independence, pre-colonial currencies had largely disappeared, but the official currencies that replaced them were not necessarily more stable. African governments introduced new national currencies, as symbols of their liberation from colonial rule as well as instruments of monetary control, and both the designs and the names of some national currencies have changed more than once since independence (Ekejiuba, Ch. 6).

Standard economic theories lead us to expect that monetization will promote economic growth, and this was undoubtedly the case in West Africa. Both the standardization of currencies and their spread facilitated specialization and exchange, thereby helping to widen markets for goods and services within the region, as well as stimulating the growth of agricultural and extractive production for export (Hopkins 1973; Hogendorn 1975). Monetization also helped to multiply channels of access to investable surplus. In western Nigeria, the pre-colonial practice of pawning children or other dependents in exchange for loans was first supplemented, then replaced by the use of farms or other goods as collateral, with interest paid in produce or in cash (Falola, Ch. 7; Ekejiuba, Ch. 6; see also Konings 1986). Moneylending at high rates of interest was frowned upon, but practiced with increasing frequency, as people's needs for cash outran their incomes (Falola, Ch. 7; Shipton, Ch. 11). As Mabogunje (Ch. 12) reminds us, monetization of rural credit markets remains a cornerstone of rural development policy in the 1990s.

The growth and diversification of commercial activity also brought new sources of instability to West African economies. In both French and British colonies, the supply of official currencies was determined by the balance of payments: export surpluses gave rise to net increases in the money supply, while deficits were offset by exports of specie (Hopkins 1973). Prices of colonial exports and imported commodities fluctuated with changing world market prices, and the growing importance of agricultural and mineral exports linked people's incomes more closely to changes in world market conditions. During the depression of the 1930s, export earnings plummeted, driving down local income and employment, and the money supply shrank accordingly (Guyer, Introduction). Since the late 1960s, West African economies have been subjected to a series of debilitating shocks, ranging from drought to oil price shocks and the growing instability of global commodity prices and capital flows.

Instability in prices, exchange rates, and incomes has arisen from local as well as international sources. Prices and incomes are affected by fluctuations in weather, local and regional movements of labor, shifts in economic policies and variations in local conditions of production and exchange (Guyer, Introduction). Colonial regimes were well aware of such fluctuations and anxious to minimize their effects on trade and market conditions within West Africa. In addition to tying colonial money supplies directly to the balance of trade, both French and British officials made periodic attempts to regulate prices and supplies of goods. In the early decades of colonial rule, officials resorted to requisitioning foodstuffs or labor for their own use when market supplies seemed unreliable, though the French did so more consistently than the British (Guyer 1978; Thomas 1973; Freund 1981 ; Oyemakinde 1974). In 1939, British authorities took direct control of the marketing of key agricultural exports, in order to forestall any repetition of the cocoa hold-ups provoked by precipitous declines in trade and export prices during the depression of the 1930s. Similarly, after independence, most West African governments maintained the export marketing boards, extended price controls to domestic crops and other commodities, and attempted to control exchange rates and import spending as well (Hopkins 1973; Austen 1987; United States Department of Agriculture 1981).

Governments' efforts to protect their currencies against the effects of inflation or long-term shifts in the structure of trade were never completely successful, and have sometimes exacerbated instability rather than alleviating it. As Law's and Arhin's chapters (Ch. 2; Ch. 4) show, pre-colonial states found it difficult to protect their revenues from the inflationary effects of rising cowry imports. Ekejiuba, Arhin, and Falola (Ch. 6; Ch. 4; Ch. 7) suggest that colonial and post-colonial governments were not much better at controling prices and regulating money supplies, despite the greater material resources and increasingly sophisticated financial institutions at their disposal. Throughout the twentieth century, prices fluctuated widely, and currencies sometimes depreciated or disappeared despite government efforts to stabilize them. Widespread smuggling of currencies as well as goods and other illegal transactions have persistently undermined African governments' ability to manage either foreign trade and capital flows, or domestic prices and expenditures. In eastern Nigeria, new currencies were introduced seven times between 1900 and 1984—a history which helps to explain why pre-colonial currencies remained in circulation until the late 1940s; why hoarding and mutilation of currency remain widespread today; and why in spite of the near complete monetization of many aspects of social life, commodity production and exchange, social payments continue to be made mainly in kind. (Ekejiuba, Ch. 6). In general, African economies have become more, not less, vulnerable to the vicissitudes of world markets and to fluctuations in domestic production and exchange, since the end of colonial rule.

In the early 1980s, many scholars and international agencies argued that West Africa's persistent economic problems were due primarily to their own governments' mismanagement of economic policy and public revenues, and proposed widespread deregulation of production and exchange as a basis for economic reform.[3] By the early 1990s, however, it was clear that "structural adjustment policies" had not been very successful either in alleviating poverty or in stabilizing economic conditions (Food and Agriculture Organization of the United Nations 1991; Weissman 1990). This suggests, in turn, that West African governments' limited success in controlling prices, production, and money supplies cannot be attributed entirely to international forces or to their own inexperience or ineptitude. Rather, as I will argue in more detail below, both colonial and post-colonial regimes have pursued multiple, sometimes contradictory agendas of social restructuring and social control, with significant—if often unintended—consequences for patterns of resource allocation and processes of valuation.

Commercialization, Governance and Access to Wealth

Although they differ profoundly on the social and political merits of commercialization, both marxist and neoclassical economists agree that monetization tends to detach exchange from the personalities and social positions of the exchangers. If goods are exchanged for money, buyers and sellers need not be known to each other; even if they are, their acquaintance is not likely to have much effect on either the possibility or the terms of commercial transactions between them. As monetization spreads, it is argued, social distance ceases to act as a barrier to trade or an important determinant of value.

In pre-colonial African societies, access to both goods and productive resources was often linked to social identity and status. Rights to use land, for various purposes—- cultivation, pasture, hunting, residence, and so forth—-were often predicated on membership or status in kingroups or communities (Arhin, Ch. 4; Berry 1989; Bassett 1992; Kopytoff 1986). Similarly, access to labor was mediated through relations of social dependence or subordination, including kinship, marriage, clientage and slavery (Berry, 1993). As Guyer (Introduction:23) points out, many scholars have taken the position that in pre-colonial Africa "the ultimate purpose of material wealth [for ordinary people as well as rulers] was to transform it into allegiances." While "spheres of exchange" were probably not as sharply delineated or mutually exclusive as suggested by Bohannan and others, there is extensive ethnographic evidence that access to particular goods was linked to specific social relationships. In this volume, for example, M-C. Dupré (Ch. 1) shows that among the Teke and neighboring peoples, social rank and identity were closely linked with rights to produce or consume particular kinds of goods, including cloth, and Arhin (Ch. 4) describes the efforts of the Asante state to restrict the use of gold to political office holders and state-sanctioned forms of trade.

Under colonial rule, the increasing monetization of everyday life did act to weaken previous links between people's social position and their access to particular goods and productive resources. Thus, Arhin argues that monetization undermined the collective control of wealth in Asante, thereby weakening the state's ability to regulate social relations, and individualized access to wealth and power. Similarly, Guyer, Mikell, and Ekejiuba (Ch. 5; Ch. 10; Ch. 6) all suggest that the monetization of marriage payments may have acted to dilute patriarchal control over marriage arrangements.

As these authors also make clear, however, monetization did not necessarily work to reduce levels of expenditure on social payments or to diminish their importance in legitimating and defining social relationships. On the contrary, Guyer shows that while the composition and distribution of Beti marriage payments changed in the 1940s and 1950s to reflect changing patterns of access to wealth and control over marriage arrangements, the level of bridewealth payments increased, and they remained central to the negotiation of marriage alliances. Similarly, Ekejiuba (Ch. 6) shows that in Igbo society, the "real" market cost of a whole range of social payments (associated with marriage, funerals, title-taking, and other forms of homage) has risen over time. In short, wealth continues to be used to gain control over people, as well as vice versa, and exchange remains closely tied to the definition of social identities.

I have argued elsewhere[4] that colonial rule redefined the way in which Africans acquired rights to land and labor, not by detaching access to productive resources from social identity and status, but by reshaping the way in which social identities and relationships were negotiated. By imposing themselves as rulers over African peoples, colonial regimes assumed responsibility for maintaining order as well as facilitating the commercial exploitation of African resources. The task of governing extensive territories, inhabited by scattered and diverse peoples, was not an easy one, and it was made more difficult, in practice, by the fact that colonial administrations were expected to pay their own way. Since overly zealous efforts to raise revenue could undermine the very social order they were trying to maintain, colonial officals were continually obliged to find ways to keep down the costs of governing their subject peoples, as well as to extract resources from them.

One way to cut costs was to employ Africans, both as laborers and as agents of colonial rule. African functionaries were cheaper than European personnel and many were employed by colonial adminstrations, as clerks, soldiers, policemen, and artisans, as well as unskilled laborers. In addition, colonial officials frequently attempted to use African rulers and systems of governance as agents of colonial administration. By preserving established structures of authority, adhering to "customary" rules and practices, and using African chiefs as local administrators, colonial officials hoped to minimize the disruptive effects of conquest and commercialization, as well as to save money. Thus, whatever their opinion of the inherent abilities of African employees or the merits of African customs and structures of authority, most colonial regimes sought to incorporate them into the lower echelons of the colonial state, rather than simply to replace them with European personnel and practices.

The idea of constructing the edifice of colonial administration on indigenous foundations was ingenious but far from problematic. Motivated, perhaps, by wishful thinking as well as ethnocentrism, most European officials assumed that traditional African societies consisted of clearly bounded social units—tribes, lineages, villages—which had not changed very much over time. In reality, this was very wide of the mark: pre-colonial communities were neither static nor internally cohesive. By attempting to integrate them into the apparatus of colonial rule officials were, in effect, building their administrations on a foundation of conflict and change. The basic strategy of "indirect rule" tended to perpetuate conflict and change, rather than stability.

Moreover, the tensions generated by colonial conquest and the logic of indirect rule were exacerbated by the way in which it was implemented. To build colonial administration on a foundation of "native law and custom," European officials had to find out what those laws and customs were. In practice, this meant consulting local informants—informally, at first, and later more systematically, through commissions of inquiry and the employment of professional anthropologists. But collecting of information about customary systems of law, government and social organization was not a one-sided process. Africans quickly realized that the influence they might hope to wield under the aegis of European rule depended, in part, the way they described "traditional" rules and structures of authority to their European interlocutors. Accordingly, far from evoking consensus as to existing social boundaries and obligations, colonial administrators elicited multiple, often conflicting interpretations. These were usually sorted out on an ad hoc basis, as officials carried out their daily routine, and subject to periodic reinterpretation. Over time, then, indirect rule had the effect of generating multiple debates over the legitimacy of competing interpretations of "native law and custom" rather than either preserving traditional systems intact or replacing them with European inventions.

Such debates pervaded a wide range of social arrangements, including the negotiation and adjudication of property rights and economic contracts. For example, the growth of agricultural production for export or sale in local markets led not only to increased demand for land, but also to the monetization of transactions in rights to land. But monetary transactions did not necessarily serve to extinguish multiple or competing rights to land, either temporarily or permanently. "Sales" of land, by individuals or by persons claiming to act as representatives of lineages or communities, could be challenged—both on the grounds that people (whose relationship to the seller gave them rights to his/her property) had not been consulted about the sale, or on the grounds that the seller's own claims to jurisdiction over the land were invalid. As one study of land rights in Adansi concluded, in 1947, because customary court judgments "turned on questions of historical fact . . . rather than Court decisions on legal principles . . . it has not proved possible to abstract . . . any general principles of Akan land tenure" from court records (Kyerematen 1971:36). Such debates have, if anything, intensified in the post-colonial period, as African leaders worked to mobilize political support through "traditional" as well as recently constructed social networks and allegiances.

Similarly, commercialization did not simplify or eliminate debates over the division of labor or the distribution of output based on customary social obligations. In Ghana, for example, the monetization of agricultural labor has generated intense debates over women's rights to remuneration for labor performed within the frame-work of a conjugal relationship. Akan women have argued, for example, that by work-ing on their husbands' farms (or other enterprises), they acquire claims on the resulting conjugal property. Such claims have been vigorously contested, on the grounds that they both contravene the inheritance rights of a man's matrilineal kin, and threaten the whole basis of corporate lineage responsibility (Mikell, Ch. 10). The resulting debates over property rights and the division of labor within Akan families have not been resolved or eliminated either by decades of adjudication in customary courts, or by legislative intervention. Even the new marriage and inheritance laws, enacted in 1985 to guarantee women a fair share of their own contributions to the resources of the conjugal family, have so far proved to be "a case of good intentions with ambiguous results" (Mikell Ch. 10:238).

Because the legal status of claims on goods and services was subject to ongoing, unresolved debate, people's ability to exercise such claims depended not only on their command over monetary or material wealth, but also on their ability to partici-pate effectively in these debates. Debates over property rights and contracts were carried on in multiple social arenas—-superior and customary courts, government offices, chiefly councils, family meetings, and other venues of ajudication and social negotiation. In most of these arenas, people's ability to negotiate successfully over disputed claims to goods and services depended on their ability to mobilize support-ers, who would testify on their behalf and to whom others would listen. This was true not only in "informal" settings, such as family or village councils, but also in offi-cially sanctioned ones, such as courts and administrative agencies.

Customary courts, for example, dealt primarily with issues of divorce, debt and land disputes, all of which involved competing claims to various forms of property. For the most part, cases turned on the testimony of witnesses, whose reliability was likely to be judged in direct proportion to their influence in local or regional social and political circles. Thus, one study of rural litigation in western Nigeria in the 1970s concluded that even if judges adhered to statutory law, "the processes by which facts-in-law were produced before the courts did not change . . . Thus the necessity of recruiting support in litigation survived the march of legal rationality" (Francis 1981:221). Allegiances, especially with influential people, remained crucial to the exercise and defense of claims on goods and services, even when these claims were established through monetary transactions. Creating allegiances may no longer have been the primary purpose of holding material wealth, but remained a necessary con-dition for acquiring and controling it. Accordingly, wealth continued to be invested in building allegiances and maintaining the social relationships and the institutions that sustain them.

In short, indirect rule had the major "unintended consequence" of linking the definition and enforcement of claims to goods and productive resources to ongoing debates over social identities and structures of authority. Struggles for power in the postcolonial period have acted, more often than not, to prolong these debates (Berry, 1993), and the associated ambiguities of claims on goods and services. Thus, at the same time that colonial and post-colonial regimes adopted policies designed to stabi-lize prices and standardize media of exchange, the practices of colonial and postcolo-nial governance have tended to destabilize the meaning of commercial transactions.

Monetization, Instability, and the Negotiation of Value

So far, I have argued that far from streamlining and depersonalizing processes of exchange, colonial and postcolonial governments' efforts to promote orderly commercialization contributed to the ambiguity of many transactions involving claims on material goods and personal or productive services. Because access was linked to social identity and social identities were often subject to ongoing debate, the valuation of goods and services was inextricably bound up with the negotiation of social identities and allegiances. Values were shaped by struggles over precedence and jurisdiction, as well as by calibrations of supply and demand. In the long run, monetization tended to redefine links between exchange and social identity, rather than simply attenuate them, and posed new questions about the meaning of commercial transactions rather than give clearer answers to old ones. Even if prices remained stable, values were rendered unstable because property rights and contracts were subject to prolonged and inconclusive debate. In other words, instability has arisen not only from changes in prices and the purchasing power of money, but also from the legal, judicial, and political processes through which "contracts" were defined and enforced.

If money payments do not give rise to precise or definitive transactions, it follows that money prices are not unambiguous indicators of value. Neoclassical economics distinguishes between "real" and "money" values, with the former referring to prices that have been "corrected" for variations in the general level of prices (i.e., the purchasing power of money) across space or over time.[5] Variations in the purchasing power of money can, of course, be profoundly disruptive to people's wealth and livelihoods and, for that matter, to social order. As Keynes (1920:236) wrote, predicting the consequences of reparations for the German Economy after World War I, "Lenin was certainly right. There is no subtler, surer means of overturning the existing basis of society than to debauch the currency."

Prolonged or rapid inflation, indeed, has been an important source of economic and political instability in various periods of West African history (Law, Ch. 2; Ekejiuba, Ch. 6; Guyer, Ch. 5). But some of the ways in which monetary values are expressed or interpreted in African economies are not easily explained in terms of inflation. For example, a number of observers have noted that in local West African markets, prices often remain nominally stable, even in rapidly changing circumstances. Shifts in scarcity and demand are reflected in shifts in the quantity or quality of items bought and sold at a given price, rather than in changes in prices charged for the same items. In western Nigeria, for example, the price of an enamel bowl of cassava flour or the cost of plowing an acre may remain constant for a long period of time, while the amount of flour in a bowl or land in an "acre" varies (Guyer, Introduction). I would suggest that this apparently idiosyncratic feature of local marketing practices may be, in part, a manifestation of the underlying ambiguity of commercial transactions. Falola (Ch. 7) notes that, for Yoruba buyers and sellers, colonial currencies resembled cowries in that their origins were exotic and, ultimately, mysterious. The origins of monetary wealth were also a mystery: money could "'travel" in mysterious ways to certain people and also . . . abandon them without notice. Thus, someone with ritual powers could 'manufacture' money through magic by 'inviting' it to visit (Falola, Ch. 7). By the same token, allowing money prices to fluctuate in response to external, uncontrollable forces may appear riskier than holding them constant, while "coping" with short-run vagaries in supply and demand by adjusting more mundane and manageable entities, such as cassava flour or plowed land.

Studies of Yoruba ideas about wealth have also pointed out that money and monetary wealth are often represented as having a dialectical and potentially dangerous relationship to power. The wealthy person who converts cash to power (*oloro*), by taking titles or accumulating clients, is considered superior to one with cash alone (*olówó*) (Falola, Ch. 7). But power can be also dangerous, depending on how it is used, and power based on wealth of mysterious origins is especially so (Barber 1982). Such ideas are not peculiar to the Yoruba. In many rural (and urban) African communities, attitudes towards cash are ambivalent. Noting that "nothing in the Gambia is more sought after than money, but nothing is more quickly disposed of," Shipton (Ch. 11:257) argues that anxiety about money helps to account for the varied forms in which money is saved. People may hoard cash, convert it to fixed assets,[6] or entrust it to other people, not only to prevent their savings from disappearing— through inflation or the demands of relatives an d friends—but also to avoid being suspected of anti-social activities. The popularity of "money-keepers" and rotating credit societies—who neither invest nor pay interest on deposits—reflects the fear of witchcraft as well as inflation (See Shipton 1989; Crehan 1991; Cohen and Atieno-Odhiambo 1989).

If the meanings of monetary transactions are ambiguous or unstable, it might be expected that people would avoid them, preferring to rely on barter or even autoconsumption. In practice, the extent of monetization has made this impossible for most West Africans; instead, they try to maintain or create allegiances to enable them to negotiate successfully over rights to goods and services. But the ambiguity of social relations not only makes it imperative for people to invest time and money in maintaining them, as a condition for negotiating rights to wealth and resources; it also renders the returns to such investments uncertain. In Ghana, Akan women who have invested labor in their husbands' farms or businesses find that their claims to a share of the resulting conjugal property remain uncertain, even when their husbands support them (Mikell Ch. 10; Okali 1983). Similarly, Yoruba parents who invested in their descendants' careers have sometimes found their own seniority eclipsed by their children's access to superior forms of wealth and influence (Berry 1985). And, in southern Niger, the monetization and rising cost of marriage payments has been accompanied by an increasing imbalance in the social and emotional significance of marriage to men and to women, leaving many Hausa women increasingly dependent on marriage at the same time that conjugal alliances are becoming less secure (Cooper 1991).

Economic instability plays into such tensions by inducing people to diversify their social as well as their economic portfolios. Just as many Africans have responded to unstable prices and markets by diversifying their income earning activities and channels of access to income and wealth, so the uncertainty of "returns" to investments in kin groups or community ties often leads people to try to maintain a multiplicity of social ties. As Falola and Shipton's chapters (Ch. 7; Ch. 11) show, for example, monetization has often been accompanied by the preservation or even multiplication of local institutions for obtaining credit or managing savings. Similarly, people join social clubs, churches or Muslim brotherhoods, cooperatives and political parties, *and* concurrently maintain ties to kin, affines or members of their ancestral communities (Berry 1989, 1993) In short, instability contributes to the proliferation of institutions and social memberships, as well as their continued salience for access to goods and opportunities.

Multiple networks, like multiple enterprises, can be difficult to manage. Studies of working people's and local leaders' daily schedules suggest that many Africans devote astonishing amounts of time to maintaining networks, cultivating patrons, or assisting their followers (Barnes 1986; Guyer 1991; Pottier 1988). But even leaders' energies are finite and most people's time is fully taken up in coping with daily struggles for livelihood or modest advance. Hence, as enterprises and social memberships proliferate, people inevitably shift their time and attention from one activity to another, as circumstances demand. Intermittent participation is well known to undermine the effectiveness of managerial performance, in small enterprises as well as large (Berry 1985). By the same token, intermittent participation in a variety of social institutions is likely to weaken the consistency with which people are able to organize collectively, in any one institutional framework, around the consistent pursuit of long-term objectives. As is also well known, local organizations, from cooperative societies to political groups, have often proved short-lived in Africa, undercutting their effectiveness as potential bases for grassroots political mobilization (see, e.g., Ihonvbere 1991; Berry 1985). And "corporate" institutions, such as lineages or traditional communities, often turn out on closer examination to have looser structures, more varied histories, and more permeable boundaries than scholars used to assume (Moore 1986; Vail 1987; Peel 1983; Berry, 1993).

Finally, my line of argument prompts a couple of comments on the relevance of recent debates among economists over the role of markets in economic development to West African experience, and vice versa. Economists have argued that both underdevelopment and institutional anomalies (such as the persistence of "informal" institutional arrangements for gaining access to commodities and productive services) are manifestations of incomplete markets or information asymmetries, which inhibit the full employment of available resources and their optimal allocation among alternative uses (Bardhan 1989). Such generalizations sound a bit odd when juxtaposed with empirical descriptions of monetary and commercial activity in West Africa offered by the papers in this volume and elsewhere. Information on the availability of productive resources or the results of employing them is often readily available, especially in communities or neighborhoods where people have interacted on a daily basis for some time (Udry 1990). In other words, information may be plentiful, even excessive, but at the same time, there is no consensus on what that information means. In such cases, people are not likely to allocate resources to unproductive uses out of ignorance; they are, however, likely to invest them in the means of negotiation, in order to enhance or protect their access to income or the means of production.

*****

At a recent conference, a discussion of the African debt crisis led one economist to remark that international firms are reluctant to invest there because "in Africa, everything is negotiable."[7] Scholars may have been reluctant, or frustrated, in their attempts to understand contemporary African crises for much the same reason. Certainly, if values are determined, in part, by multiple, interacting, and inconclusive negotiations over the meanings of transactions as well as their prices, contemporary

West African economic history poses a challenge to established ways of conceptual-izing as well as documenting economic and social change. Perhaps we may begin by studying the processes of negotiation through which values are debated, resources allocated, and wealth created and circulated—-as well as their outcomes.

Notes

1. Money consists of currency—objects that serve as media of exchange and/or stores of value—and claims on goods and services that are denominated in monetary terms.
2. These debates are closely related to the issue, also long debated in marxist economic the-ory, over whether capital is productive, independently of the labor embodied in it.
3. For influential statements of this p osition see, inter alia, World Bank (1981), Bates (1981), and Berg and Whitaker (1986).
4. I have developed this argument at greater length in Berry (1992) and (1993).
5. For example, if a basket of millet sells in Kano for 5 shillings one week, 10 shillings the next *and* the general price level doubles in the same period of time, the "real" value of millet has not changed. The "real" value of the shilling has, of course, fallen by half.
6. Like people in other commercial economies, West Africans seek to cope with unstable prices and economic conditions by holding liquid assets and/or diversifying their portfo-lios of assets and sources of income. Both "strategies" reinforce people's tendency to invest in social relations. For one thing, if the purchasing power of money is unstable because of volatile or disorganized conditions of exchange, holding cash—especially domestic currency--is not necessarily an effective way to achieve liquidity. Better to hold commod-ities or internationally convertible currency, which are in chronic undersupply (partly because people are so anxious to hold them for speculative purposes or as a hedge against inflation) and therefore more immediately convertible into other forms of wealth than a weak domestic currency.
7. This statement was made by Carol Lancaster at a conference on "African Governance and Democracy," Carter Center, Emory University, Atlanta, GA, 1990.

Sources

Austen, R. W. 1987. *African Economic History.* London and Portsmouth, NH: James Currey & Heinemann.

Barber, K. 1982. "Popular Reactions to the Petro-naira." *Journal of Modern African Studies,* 20:431–50.

Bardhan, P. K., ed. 1989. *The Economic Theory of Agrarian Institutions.* Oxford: Claren-don Press.

B arnes, S. 1986. *Patrons and Power: Creating a Political Community in Metropolitan Lagos.* Bloomington, IN: Indiana University Press.

Bassett, T. J.1992. "Introduction." In *Land in African Agrarian Systems,* ed. T. J. Bassett and D. E. Crummey, 3–31. Madison, WI: University of Wisconsin Press.

Bates, R. W. 1981. *Markets and States in Tropical Africa.* Berkeley and Los Angeles: Uni-versity of California Press.

Berg, R., and J. Whitaker, eds. 1986. *Strategies for African Development.* Berkeley and Los Angeles: University of California Press.

Berry, S. S. 1985. *Fathers Work for Their Sons: Accumulation, Mobility and Class Formation in an Extended Yoruba Community.* Berkeley and Los Angeles: University of California Press.

————. 989. "Social Institutions and Access to Resources." *Africa*, 59:41–55.

————. 1992. "Hegemony on a Shoestring." *Africa*, 62:327–355.

————. 1993. *No Condition is Permanent: The Social Dynamics of Agrarian Change in Sub-Saharan Africa.* Madison, WI: University of Wisconsin Press.

Cohen, D. W. and E. S. Atieno-Odhiam bo. 1989. *Siaya: The Historical Anthropology of an African Landscape.* London, Nairobi and Athens, OH: James Currey, Heinemann and Ohio University Press.

Cooper, B. 1991. "The Women of Maradi: A History of the Maradi region of Niger from the 'Time of Cowries' to the 'Time of Searching for Money,' 1900–1989." Ph.D. dissertation, Boston University, Boston, MA.

Crehan, K. 1991. "Consuming Kin: Bulozhi and Its Images in Northwestern Zambia." Paper presented to the Seminar in Atlantic Culture and History, Johns Hopkins Univer sity, Baltimore, MD.

Food and Agriculture Organization of the United Nations. 1991. *The State of Food and Agriculture, 1990.* Rome: Author.

Francis, P. 1981. "Power and Order: A Study of Litigation in a Yoruba Community." Ph.D. dissertation, University of Liverpool, England.

Freund, B. 1981. *Capital and Labor in the Nigerian Tin Mines.* Atlantic Highlands, NJ: Humanities Press.

Guyer, J. I. 1978. The Food Economy and French Colonial Rule in Central Cameroon. *Journal of African History*, 19:577–98.

————. 1991. *Representation Without Taxation: An Essay on Democracy in Rural Nigeria, 1952–1990.* Working Papers in African Studies no. 152. Boston, MA: Boston University African Studies Center.

Hogendorn, J. S. 1975. "Economic Initiative and African Cash Farming." In *Colonialism in Africa*, ed. P. Duignan and L. Gann, 283–328, vol. 4. Cambridge: Cambridge University Press.

Hopkins, A. G. 1973. *An Economic History of West Africa.* London: Longman.

Ihonvbere, J. 1991. "Community Awareness of and Responses to Environmental Degradation in Koko, Nigeria." Paper presented to a Workshop on Resource Conservation and Ecological Vulnerability, sponsored by the Social Science Research Council's Project on African Agriculture, Dakar, Senegal.

Keynes, John Maynard. 1920. *The Economic Consequences of the Peace.* New York: Harcourt, Brace and Howe.

Konigs, Piet. 1986. *The State and Rural Class Formation in Ghana: A Comparative Analysis.* London and Boston: Routledge and Kegan Paul.

Kopytoff, I. 1986. *The African Frontier: The Reproduction of Traditional African Societies.* Bloomington, IN: Indiana University Press.

Kyerematen, A. A. Y. 1971. *Inter-state Boundary Litigation in Ashanti.* African Social Research Documents no. 4. Cambridge: Cambridge University Press.

Moore, S. F. 1986. *Social Facts and Fabrications.* Cambridge: Cambridge University Press.

Niger Company. *Papers.* Oxford: Rhodes House.

Ofonagoro, W. I. 1979. *Trade and Imperialism in Southern Nigeria: 1881–1929.* New York: Nok.

Okali, C. 1983 *Cocoa and Kinship in Ghana: The Matrilineal Akan of Ghana.* London and

Boston: Kegan Paul International, for the International African Institute.

Oyemakinde, W. 1974. "Railway Construction and Operation in Nigeria, 1895-1911: Labour Problems and Socio-Economic Impact." *Journal of the Historical Society of Nigeria,* 7:303-324.

Peel, J. D. Y. 1983. *Ijeshas and Nigerians.* New York and Cambridge: Cambridge University Press.

Pottier, J. 1988. *Migrants No More: Settlement and Survival in Mambwe Villages, Zambia.* Bloomington, IN: Indiana University Press.

Shipton, P. 1989. *Bitter Money: Cultural Economy and Some African Meanings of Forbidden Commodities.* American Ethnological Society Monograph Series, no. 1. Washington, D.C.: American Anthropological Association.

Thomas, R. G. 1973. "Forced Labour in British West Africa: The Case of the Northern Territories of the Gold Coast." *Journal of African History,* 14:79-103.

Udry, C. 1990. "Credit Markets in North ern Nigeria: Credit as Insurance in a Rural Economy." *World Bank Economic Review* 4:251-69.

USDA. 1981. *Food Problems and Prospects in Sub-Saharan Africa.* Washington, D.C.: United States Department of Agriculture.

Vail, L., ed. 1987. *The Creation of Tribalism in Southern Africa.* Berkeley and Los Angeles: University of California Press.

Weissman, S. R. 1990. "Structural Adjustment in Africa: Insights from the Experiences of Ghana and Senegal." *World Development* 18:1621-34.

World Bank. 1981. *Towards Accelerated Development in Sub-Saharan Africa .* Washington, D.C.: World Bank.

INDEX

cash
  conversion to assets in Nigeria, 165
  converting commodities to, 147
  Gambian preference for illiquidity, 257–259, 268
  as Gambian savings, 253–265
  personal stores, 16
  shortage in Zaire, 3
  vs. assets, 166
cash crops, 125
  in Nigeria, 143
  as pledge for credit, 171–172
cash purchases, 19
castes, in Gambia, 248, 270n.13
Catholic Church, 122
  and bridewealth payments, 114
  sixas, 125
cattle, lending to relatives, 250
cattle in Gambia, 255
Central Bank of Nigeria, 283
cereal banks, 252
Chaillu Mountains, 39, 40
changeability, 3
Chaudouin, E., 66
chiefs
  as local administrators, 305
  policy initiatives, 76
children, 213
  Akan responsibility for, 228–229
  husband's maintenance for, 233
  legal claim to, 130n.12
  man's right to, 129n.10
  of marriage, 69n.4
  pawning of, 175–176, 302
  payment for education, 103
  status of, 125
Chilver, Elizabeth, 25
Cholet, 89
Christianity, 106, 124, 237
  and Ghana funeral practices, 197
  and women's rights to property, 238, 239
chronic instability, 5
Clapperton, H., 62
Clarke, W.H., 61
class conflict, Marxist view, 300
cloth, 2, 8, 15, 214. *See also* raphia cloth
  as Biafran currency, 147
  as Nigerian currency, 136, 146
Co-operative Bank of Western Nigeria, 285, 287
co-residence by spouses, 232
cocoa, 103

labor needs of, 189
  and monetization of women's labor, 232
  price rise and marriage costs, 118–119, 194–195
Cohen, Abner, 15
collateral, 168
  agricultural products as, 182n.39
  assets as, 179
  jewelry as, 251
  problems in Nigeria, 293
  property as, 173
collective assets, 20
collective funds, 12–13
colonial cash, 111
colonial currency
  Aro switch to, 143
  impact, 1
  introduction of, 80
  supply, 303
  terminology for, 117
colonial rule, 305
  anchor as symbol, 91
  in Asante, 102
  change in asset definition during, 167–168
  currencies at beginning, 15
  financial infrastructure, 10
  informal credit options, 168–170
  monetization during, 305
color, of raphia cloth, 42
Comaroff, J., 189
commerce, marriage currencies and, 92
commercial banking, in Gambia, 265
commercial relations, of the Teke, 48
commercialization, 306–307
  and instability, 308
  and social capital, 134
commodities
  converting to cash, 147
  production factors transformed to, 281
  to store wealth, 146
commoditization, 222n.16, 281
commodity currencies, 90
  development of, 91
Communaute Financière Africaine, 4
community banks in Nigeria, 288–292
  and correspondent banks, 292
  deposits, 290
  insuring deposits in, 292
community development associations, 288
community gatekeepers, 21
Company Act of 1906 (Ghana), 12
Company for Colonial Explorations, 90